The Holocaust Kingdom

The Holocaust Kingdom

a memoir by

Alexander Donat

HOLOCAUST LIBRARY

An imprint of the
UNITED STATES HOLOCAUST MEMORIAL MUSEUM
WASHINGTON, D.C.

A portion of this book appeared under the title "Our Last Days in the Warsaw Ghetto," in the May 1963 issue of *Commentary*. *The Holocaust Kingdom* was published in 1965 by Holt, Rinehart and Winston. It was republished in 1978 by Holocaust Library, an imprint of Holocaust Publications, New York, with a grant from Benjamin and Stefa Wald. This printing is published by the United States Holocaust Memorial Museum, 100 Raoul Wallenberg Place, SW, Washington, D.C. 20024-2126.

This work was translated from the Polish in conjunction with its first American book publication. To enhance clarity and restore Alexander Donat's original precision, a small number of nonsubstantive punctuation, grammar, usage, and syntactical corrections have been incorporated into this printing with the participation of his son, William (Wlodek) Donat, and Alexander's wife, Lena, who also actively participated in the preparation of the original manuscript. A few self-explanatory footnotes have been added by the editor and by William Donat (W. D.), and W. D.–footnoted corrections of three of the most consequential individuals' names are addressed in the afterword. Additionally, the table of contents has been minimally recast to reflect those portions of the work that are in the voice of Alexander Donat and those that are in the voices of other participants.

Library of Congress Cataloging-in-Publication Data
Donat, Alexander.
   The Holocaust kingdom : a memoir / Alexander Donat.
   p. cm.
   Previously published: New York : Holocaust Library, c1978.
   Includes index.
   ISBN 0-89604-160-3
   1. Donat, Alexander. 2. Jews—Poland—Warsaw Biography. 3. Holocaust, Jewish (1939–1945)—Poland—Warsaw Personal narratives.
   4. Warsaw (Poland)—History—Warsaw Ghetto Uprising, 1943.
   5. Warsaw (Poland) Biography. I. Title.
D810.J4D68   1999
940.53'18'092—dc21   99-22131
CIP

Printed in the United States of America.

CONTENTS

And I looked, and behold a pale horse: and his name

that sat on him was Death, and Hell followed with him.

And Power was given unto them over the fourth part

of the earth, to kill with sword, and with hunger,

and with death, and with the beasts of the earth.

REVELATION 6:8

PART I

VOICE OF
ALEXANDER DONAT

CHAPTER 1

BEHIND THE WALLS

THE ORDEAL BEGAN on the sixth day of the war. On the evening of September 6, 1939, the government radio made an urgent appeal: German panzers had broken through Polish defenses and were headed for Warsaw; all able-bodied men were ordered to leave the capital immediately and assemble to the east, across the Bug River. A new army would be formed there to stand against the invaders.

My name was Michal Berg.[1] My family had lived in Poland for generations and my father had settled down in Warsaw around the turn of the century. I was thirty-four years old then, publisher of the morning daily newspaper *Ostatnie Wiadomosci* (Latest News), a Warsaw tabloid. Hasty preparations, hurried farewells. With the paper's entire staff I joined the exodus, leaving behind my wife, Lena,[2] and our twenty-one-month-old son, Wlodek.

Hundreds of thousands left Warsaw that night. In the pale twilight dawn, a torrent of people with knapsacks headed eastward on foot, bicycles, motorcycles, carts, carriages, automobiles, trucks, and buses. Through the golden shine of the Polish autumn the stream flowed east, or rather crawled. It was our first meeting with war's disorganization: burning towns, outbreaks of spy and paratroop manias, the despair of unbelievably swift defeat, and the incessant dive-bombing by Nazi Stukas.

Who can describe that fateful Polish September of 1939? In vain all Poland prayed for the miracle of rain, rain which would turn the notoriously bad Polish roads into swamps impassable to German tanks. But the sun shone with merciless brightness in a flawless sky. The army was on the run, the government was on the run, we were all on the run. In Lutsk, in southeastern Poland, we watched Soviet tanks rolling in. Allies, we thought at first.

The war ended for Poland on September 27. After a bitter battle Warsaw surrendered, and there seemed no further point in staying in Lutsk. Jews had to face the decision: to return to Nazi-occupied Warsaw to join

---

1. The actual name was Aleksander Grynberg. Although named Mojzesz at birth, as a very young child he became Saszek and then, Aleksander (of which Saszek is a diminutive). Grynberg itself had been changed from Prurzanski a generation earlier. See afterword—W. D.
2. Actually Lonia, a transmutation from her given name of Leah, which became Leona when we came to America. See afterword—W. D.

their families, or to remain under Soviet rule. The new Nazi-Soviet border was not too difficult or too dangerous to cross. Wave after wave of refugees from Nazi-held Poland brought terrifying reports of what was happening there. From that side thousands fled Nazi persecution; from the other, thousands returned, overwhelmed by family attachments or possessions. How many lives might have been saved then, at the very beginning of the war, when the Soviet Union opened its gates to refugees from Nazism.

At the beginning of November, I returned to Warsaw to take my wife and child to the security of the Soviet Union. But Lena refused to go. She took me on a tour of our beautiful seven-room apartment and talked about how miserable life was in Russia. It was November, already turning cold, and how could we expect to sneak across the frontier with a baby not yet two years old? And what about the seventy-two-year-old aunt who lived with us? And the rest of our family? Lena was sure the Germans would be vicious, but what could happen to women and children? She was a licensed pharmacist, and war or no war they would need her. She could support herself and our son. But I was in danger. Hadn't I published the *Brown Book* and other exposés of the Nazis? The sensible thing was for me to return to the Soviet-held sector of Poland. The war wouldn't last long and we'd be reunited then. In the meantime, they'd make out somehow.

She persuaded me and I went back via the well-known escape route Malkinia-Bialystok. But not for long. Rumors grew more persistent that the borders were going to be closed and all contact with the Nazi-held area cut off, that refugees would be registered and have to opt for Soviet citizenship. This meant separation from my family, perhaps for a lifetime. I knew it was a fateful decision and I made it. At the end of December 1939, I set out for Warsaw once more, but now it wasn't easy. The frontier was well guarded, and the trip in temperatures of forty below was not uneventful. Finally, on January 2, 1940, I did succeed in rejoining my family in Warsaw, to share with them whatever fate had in store for all of us. I was there to stand and fall with them, to shield and protect. We knew we faced dreadful anguish, but never in our wildest dreams did we anticipate the ultimate holocaust. On this road to calvary I entered in love and humility, even with a drop of pride.

One of the results of the September exodus and the subsequent migrations to the East was that Warsaw Jewry was a body without a head. Leaders in every walk of life had left. We needed heroes and were left with mediocrities. To these the Nazis handed the tragic scepter of a spurious "Jewish autonomy," and these men were to lead us along the tortuous road to disaster. An early decree (October 4, 1939) appointed a Jewish Council, the *Judenrat,* as the supreme authority of the Jewish community of Warsaw. Its head was to be titled *Obmann,* or "Elder of the Jews," and an engineer named Adam Czerniakow was appointed to the job. He in turn co-opted twenty-four councilors to serve with him. So was born the monstrous organization which came to be so bitterly hated by Jews. Czerniakow and the Council members—many of whom I knew personally—were in the main decent men who honestly hoped to serve the Jewish community. The theory was that it was desirable to have a buffer between the Jewish population at large and the Nazi occupation authorities, and the Judenrat would be that buffer.

Warsaw Jews had never paid much attention or given much respect to their community leaders and therefore the appointment of the Judenrat made little stir. No one was eager to serve on it. Because Jews had been excluded from civil service in prewar Poland, the Judenrat's aides and staff workers were men without skill or experience, inefficient and timeserving, prone to nepotism and corruption.

After I returned from Lutsk our apartment on Orla Street was jam-packed, sufficiently crowded to suit even the taste of the Judenrat's housing authority. In addition to my wife and my son, there was our elderly Aunt Sarah Eisner, who kept house for us; Stefa, a Gentile governess, indispensable since my wife was now the breadwinner of the family; Miriam Orleska, a well-known Jewish actress; Rudolf Langer, a lawyer, and his wife; Ignacy Moskowicz, a former Lodz textile manufacturer, and his wife; and Slawka Szenwic, an office girl whose mother later joined her after being deported from Plock.

The Jewish intelligentsia was the first target in the Nazi process of pauperizing the Jews. Lawyers were no longer permitted to appear in court; doctors were forbidden to have non-Jewish patients; journalists, writers, artists, musicians, and teachers were now all superfluous because practicing their professions had been declared illegal. Their very existence was an anachronism. Without practical skills or experience, such people were ill adapted to survive in the jungle Warsaw was swiftly becoming.

It is not easy to declass oneself, even if one is willing, but the most energetic intellectuals got into trade in the early stages of the German occupation. They became dealers in foreign currencies, gold, dry goods, wristwatches, flour, anything they could lay their hands on that could be sold or traded. Unfortunately many discovered that trade is no occupation for normal people in abnormal times; I was one of those.

Nothing had prepared me for such a life. After a very few attempts, it was clear I would never be a success as a businessman. A cousin of mine phrased it succinctly: "As a businessman, you're a good carpenter." When I bought anything, prices instantly sank; when I sold, prices doubled the next day. I still knew how to operate a Linotype, a skill learned in my student days, but such skill was as much in demand as the ability to teach classical philology.

Not only intellectuals suffered under the Nazis; all Jews were fair game for persecution. Beginning in December 1939, every Jew over twelve was required to wear the Jewish armband. Quite an industry sprang up to produce these armbands; some were made of finest linen, with or without embroidery, but there were paper and celluloid ones, too. For the first few weeks armband peddlers loudly hawked their wares and, except for a few rare rebels, Jews accepted the armbands and wore them with dignity, feeling that to do so disgraced not us but those who imposed them on us.

No Jew was permitted to have more than 2,000 zlotys in cash either on his person or in his home. The remainder of his money had to be deposited in a bank from which he was permitted to withdraw no more than 500 zlotys a month. When currency-control measures were invoked, everyone had to have his paper money validated at a bank. Long queues lined up at bank windows, but Jews were forcibly thrown out and subjected to other indignities. Jews also had to file special returns detailing all their wealth. Synagogues were closed down and Jews prohibited from assembling for religious services as an antityphus measure. Jews who wanted to travel needed special passes, presumably a precaution against "the spreading of typhus by Jewish black marketeers." In sections of the city where many Jews lived posters in the streets warned passersby: "This is a quarantined zone."

Nazi commissars *(Treuhänder)* were put in charge of every branch of Jewish business and property. These so-called trustees had orders never to pay bills owed to Jewish firms or individuals, but to collect all debts Jews owed. No Jewish creditor was permitted to collect a debt, but every Jewish debtor had to pay up all his own debts and, in some cases, the debts of others as well. Tax officials began to force payments of every conceivable kind of tax, legitimately owed or not. The moment a German trustee took charge, all Jewish employees were dismissed from their jobs and all contracts with Jewish suppliers were canceled. In this manner the very roots of Jewish economic life were sapped.

The most unmistakable indication of Nazi intentions concerning the

Jews was the food ration. Germans in Warsaw were allotted 2,500 calories a day and could obtain a wide variety of goods at fixed prices in special stores. The Jewish ration came to less than 200 calories a day for which Jews paid twenty times the price Germans did.

Jews resisted as best they could. They tried to arrange for trustees over their affairs who came from among their Polish or *Volksdeutsch* (ethnic German) friends. They could then continue business on a "partnership" basis by sharing the profits with the trustee. Others managed to make deals with the trustees who were imposed on them. When the Postal Savings Bank (PKO) blocked all Jewish accounts, German acquaintances could be persuaded to make false claims against the accounts of Jews alleged to owe them money. The German acquaintances would then share the money received with the owners of the accounts.

There was a stubborn, unending, continuous battle to survive. In view of the unequal forces, it was a labor of Sisyphus. Jewish resistance was the resistance of a fish caught in a net, a mouse in a trap, an animal at bay. It is pure myth that the Jews were merely "passive," that they did not put up resistance to the Nazis who had decreed their destruction. The Jews fought back against their enemies to a degree no other community anywhere in the world would have been capable of were it to find itself similarly beleaguered. They fought against hunger and starvation, against disease, against a deadly Nazi economic blockade. They fought against murderers and against traitors within their own ranks, and they were utterly alone in their fight. They were forsaken by God and by man, surrounded by hatred or indifference. Ours was not a romantic war. Although there was much heroism, there was little beauty—much toil and suffering, but no glamour. We fought back on every front where the enemy attacked— the biological front, the economic front, the propaganda front, the cultural front—with every weapon we possessed.

In the end, it was ruse, deception, cunning beyond anything the world had ever before seen, which accomplished what hunger and disease, terror and treachery could not achieve. What defeated us, was Jewry's unconquerable optimism, our eternal faith in the goodness of man, our faith that even a German, even a Nazi, could never have so far renounced his own humanity as to murder women and children coldly and systematically. And when, finally, we saw how we had been deceived, and resorted to the weapon which we were least well prepared to use—historically, ideologically, and psychologically—that is, when we finally took up arms, we inscribed in the book of history the unforgettable epic of the Ghetto Uprising.

One of the most powerful instruments of Jewish self-defense sprang up spontaneously during the first weeks of the war. Tenants' committees (so-called House Committees) were organized in every apartment house. Where the Judenrat was an institution created by the Nazi occupiers to transmit their decrees to the Jewish population, the tenants' committees were created by the Jews themselves to defend their own interests. The man who promoted them in Warsaw was generally believed to be the eminent historian, Emanuel Ringelblum. Eventually the individual House Committees were grouped into a federation, the ZTOS *(Zydowskie Towarzystwo Opieki Spolecznej)*, the Jewish Society of Social Welfare, and what remained of active social and intellectual leadership in Warsaw gravitated toward this organization. As the Judenrat became increasingly remote from the people, the ZTOS became more closely identified with them. These committees resisted all efforts by the Judenrat to make them its tools and they also served as the core of opposition to it. Small wonder, then, that the ZTOS was unpopular with the Judenrat and later also with the Jewish police.

The tenants' committees were democratically elected and served as the real authority in each apartment house. At first they confined themselves to helping poor tenants, especially poor children. Gradually their activities were extended to health and hygiene, education and entertainment. In some buildings they organized communal kitchens and coordinated fuel and food purchases. At one stage a certificate issued by any tenants' committee was a document respected and honored by all Jewish authorities. The first big campaign the committees organized was a clothing collection for Jewish prisoners of war who came back to Warsaw in large numbers in March 1940. Forbidden to wear their uniforms and without any civilian clothes, these men were helped by the tenants' committees.

But even the tenants' committees were helpless against the mounting plague of looting. Any German, in uniform or not, could rob a Jewish house or individual with impunity. Many highly placed occupation authorities, including all ranks in the *Wehrmacht* and *Schutzstaffel* (SS) as well as German and *Volksdeutsch* civilians, were officially and unofficially involved in looting. So were some Jewish criminals who tipped Germans off about the best places to plunder, or threatened Jews that they would do so in order to blackmail them. The Germans stole goods off the shelves of stores; furniture from private homes; bed linen, silver, glassware, rugs, paintings, china, cameras. They even stole food—coffee, tea, and cocoa being most popular.

To carry off what they wanted, the Germans would stop Jews in the streets and force them to help move the heavier things. Victims of the robbery themselves were also "persuaded" to help. Such situations gave rise to all kinds of abuse. But in time the German thieves lost confidence in the reliability of these Jewish "assistants," because pieces of furniture that came down one flight of stairs mysteriously mounted another flight, and somehow found their way back to where they had been in the first place.

In the early days of the occupation, many Jews, especially those who lived in predominantly non-Jewish neighborhoods, were simply dispossessed by Germans who took their apartments and everything in them. Victims were permitted to take no more than a small valise at the time of eviction and were frequently beaten up as well if they did not seem sufficiently delighted with what was being done to them. I know of one elderly couple who, in anticipation of being robbed, had carefully buried their valuables in the walls or under the floors of their apartment. When they were suddenly evicted, they lost not only their home and furniture, but also all their buried treasure.

Persecution of Jews was not at first well organized. A German would simply attack a Jew in the street, and there were many who obviously enjoyed that kind of thing. A speeding car might swerve to the curb, Germans jump out of it and set on the first Jew they met. Anything might serve as a pretext. Some Jews were beaten for not having taken off their hats, others for having done so—"You don't know me. I'm no friend of yours."—and some for politely stepping off the sidewalk when they saw Germans coming. Still others for having failed to do so. Armband etiquette might also serve as an excuse: armbands were being worn too high or too low, were dirty or torn, or were too elegant and expensive looking.

Assaults in the street became more and more frequent. A few Germans would stop some decently dressed Jews and order them to sweep the street, abusing them for the amusement of passersby. Later such incidents became more serious. One lady, walking in the street, wearing a Persian lamb coat was dragged to Gestapo headquarters. There she was ordered to take off her underwear and scrub the floor with it. Then, made to put the dirty, wet underwear back on, she was thrown into the street without her coat. It was a very cold day and she caught pneumonia and died.

The main centers of Nazi terror were in three places: Gestapo headquarters in Szuch Avenue; a building on Wiejska Street where the Polish parliament had formerly been housed; and Blank's Palace in Senatorska Street. All three became notorious as torture chambers in the first months of the occupation.

Hunger, filth, and disease increased by leaps and bounds because the Germans were herding thousands of Jews into Warsaw daily. Most were penniless and only a handful could look after themselves; the bulk succumbed to the dreadful conditions of the refugee reception centers. The threat of typhus was everywhere. It was a feat to move through the crowded streets without coming into contact with lice-infested individuals. I knew people who stayed in their apartments for months to avoid contacts of that kind and yet, in the end, found that they too had lice. Lice were so ubiquitous that people began to tell each other quite seriously that typhus was not only a lice-borne disease but also airborne.

On the floor above our Orla Street apartment there lived Dr. Izrael Milejkowski, the Judenrat member in charge of public health. In the evenings after curfew he often dropped by for a cup of tea and we either played cards or talked politics late into the night. Small, with a Mephistophelian smile, he was an ardent Zionist, had a fine sense of humor, and always knew the latest jokes. Milejkowski took his work very seriously and often discussed it with us. For hours on end he described the unequal struggle against hunger and typhus, which was decimating the Jewish population. Worst of all were the conditions in the reception centers for recent Jewish refugees from other parts of Poland. The mortality rate was climbing appallingly swiftly and in his judgment our survival depended on checking the typhus epidemic.

Though Milejkowski was a dedicated physician, he could do almost nothing in the face of the conditions decreed by the authorities of the Third Reich. And his German counterpart and superior, Dr. Wilhelm Hagen, treated him and his efforts with contempt, and gave him no cooperation. Milejkowski and his aide Dr. Antoni Wortman, honest men with the best of intentions, could not even control their own employees. The Judenrat disinfection squads were composed of hungry people concerned with the fate of their own families. A few zlotys were enough to bribe them. The rich therefore bribed their way out of the fumigation proceedings, which they thought would damage their properties, and only the poor people were induced to follow the prescribed delousing procedure. This made the entire elaborate public-health program a farce. No matter how rigorous the rules, doctors could be persuaded not to report cases of typhus so that the patient might remain in an overcrowded apartment where he would certainly infect others. Besides, there never was enough room in the hospitals. In addition, fumigation equipment was of the poorest quality and the "soul snatchers," as those fumigation squads were called, never sealed the rooms as hermetically as they should have; nor was there ever enough coal to provide hot water and steam in the delousing baths.

One day Dr. Milejkowski came home visibly shaken. His face was ashen and he seemed to have aged immeasurably. At one of the refugee reception centers an eight-year-old child had gone out of his mind with hunger, and begun to scream, "I want to rob and steal. I want to eat. I want to be a German!" Milejkowski also told us that at the funeral of some children who had died of hunger, the children in the orphans' home in Wolska Street had sent a wreath inscribed, "From children who are starving to children who have died of starvation." Milejkowski wept as he told me this, and we cried with him. We felt powerless. The same thing would be happening tomorrow and the day after that and the day after that.

Destitute former musicians wandered the streets and in the courtyards all day long, turning Warsaw into a city of song. It was enough to drive one mad. They were, of course, trying to earn a living and, after a month or two of this, they would be forced to sell their instruments and be standing at the street corners with outstretched palms. A little later their bodies and those of their families would be found in the streets one morning covered with newspapers—a common enough sight—which no one got used to.

Polish-Jewish relations deteriorated. Just prior to the war and at the opening of hostilities, anti-Semitism had slackened. The threat of a common enemy and the wartime sharing of experience had brought Poles and Jews closer together. But the idyl was short-lived. Poisonous Nazi propaganda soon reawakened native anti-Semitism: "It was the Jews who started the war that destroyed Poland." "On the far side of the Bug River the Jews are living like kings and helping the Soviets to persecute Poles." "Jews are typhus carriers." Most important, Jews were outlaws deprived of the protection of the law and hence fair game for any malicious Pole or German. The lowest elements of the population were quickest to grasp the spirit of the new order. The word *Jude* became the first and not the least firm of the new ties between Polish hooligans and Nazi gangsters. Assaults on Jews in the streets, beatings, and robberies were most often committed by juvenile delinquents. And they became ever more frequent. There were also more and more instances of Poles denouncing fellow citizens as Jews to the German authorities. On Easter Sunday 1940, gangs of Polish youths, led by malicious agitators, tried to start a real pogrom in Franciszkanska and Elektoralna Streets, but Jewish self-defense groups broke up the attempt and scattered the gangs.

Slogans about Jewish "exploiters," "parasites," and "Shylocks" were appealing to the Polish populace, which had been exposed to anti-Semitic propaganda from early childhood. Jewish forced laborers, recruited from among the poorest Jews, were taunted when they were marched through the Polish quarters of the city with a brand-new insult:

Hitler's wonderful, Hitler's grand:
He put the Jews to work.

Another version went like this:

Marshal Smigly-Rydz
Didn't teach the Jews a thing.
But Hitler's pulled it off:
He taught the Jews to work!

Only occasionally would a Jew respond in similar vein: "Well, you Poles wanted a Poland without Jews. Now you have the Jews without Poland!"

A real witch of an old woman roamed the streets of Warsaw with a heavy stick and used it on every Jew who crossed her path. One day when I was coming back from a visit to my former offices, she set upon me as I was crossing the Saski Square (formerly Pilsudski Square, later Adolf Hitler Square and out of bounds to Jews). Not a single person came to my aid and I had a hard time escaping her. Fortunately no Germans were around.

Despite such humiliation and discomfort all that winter of 1940, everyone's hopes were concentrated on one idea: if only we can hold out until spring. However battered and bruised, Warsaw Jewry remained optimistic and confident of its own strength. People said to each other, "God forbid that the war should last as long as we can hold out!" Even the brief, ill-fated Norwegian campaign, which Warsaw followed with bated breath, did not shake our faith in the future. Armchair strategists believed that Britain had tricked the Germans into attacking Norway in order to pin down the Nazis' meager fleet.

In 1939, before the Nazi invasion of Poland, anti-Semitic pressure had forced me to make changes in the organization of my newspaper. The competition was saying that good Polish readers should not read a paper published by Jews. Since my readers were largely Poles, I had had to incorporate and take several Poles into the management to give the firm an "Aryan" complexion. These included a member of the Polish national senate and a member of the Warsaw city council, who became president and vice president respectively. I myself remained discreetly behind the scenes with power of attorney, but with my name carefully kept off the newspaper's masthead and out of the papers of incorporation. The vice president, Stanislaw Kapko, was a man in his late thirties or early forties, with blue eyes and a small mustache, blond and imposing looking, a natural leader. Not only was he my business associate, but we became friendly as well.

Now at our old newspaper offices Kapko had opened a business for importing food from the Lublin area and he was showing unusual acumen. Whenever I called, he was always happy to see me and assured me he wanted to help. Handing me 1,000 zlotys he would tell me that I didn't have to worry about repaying it until after the war. Due to him, back wages owed the paper's employees were paid up and in addition he managed to give each of them 100 pounds of flour. Had the September exodus from Warsaw happened a day later my own financial position might have been less precarious because the news agency which distributed my paper would have made its biweekly payment for copies sold, a considerable sum of money. When I left Warsaw there had been enough newsprint for several weeks of publication, but to make matters worse, when I returned from Lutsk, not a scrap of it was left. Those employees who stayed in Warsaw had "taken care of it," and it was gone. My printing plant, only recently equipped with two rotary presses—one of them brand-new—was now, of course, in the hands of a "trustee."

The trustee in charge of Warsaw's graphic-arts industries was a certain Anton Hergl. He had been sent from Germany to Warsaw as a machinist to help install several new German presses which Warsaw's biggest newspaper publisher, the Press House, had purchased from a German firm in 1939. After the surrender, he came forward as a German agent to take charge of the expropriated Jewish printing shops. Hergl permitted some few such shops to continue work in order to guarantee himself a considerable and steady income in graft for that permission. At the same time he was ruthless with the other confiscated plants. Though he paid none of their suppliers' outstanding bills, he was assiduous in collecting every debt owed them by Jewish firms. Early in 1940, I had a letter from Hergl informing me that he had a promissory note which I had been given by a firm in payment for advertising in my paper, and which I in turn had endorsed over to one of my creditors. Though the original firm which had given me the note was out of business, having been expropriated by Hergl, I was now held personally responsible and told to pay the entire sum by a given date—or else. There was nothing I could do, no appeal or recourse: we had to pay Hergl.

As an investment for my son, Wlodek, I had built an apartment house only a short time before. Like all other Jewish property, it was taken over by a "trustee." Not only did I never receive a cent for it, but the trustee frequently reminded me how considerate he was not to ask any payments from me. At the same time, the trustee of the apartment house in which I lived constantly dunned me for the back rent I had owed since September, though none of the genuine landlords expected or asked for payment during that extremely disturbed period. One day I received a summons from the tax office ordering me to pay immediately nearly 20,000 zlotys, a fantastic sum, in settlement of a tax claim for 1937. My taxes for that year had been paid, but the Germans had retroactively canceled a Polish law under which money invested in new apartment houses was exempt from taxation. It was impossible for me to get the money, but I knew the consequences if I didn't. I therefore went to see my former lawyer, Henryk Lande, who, as a Jew, was now forbidden to practice, but who kept his office running by using a Polish lawyer as a "front." After much negotiation and many glasses of vodka, the tax claim was finally settled by a 1,000-zloty bribe; my perfectly legal tax exemption was "restored" and the claim annulled.

With things going that way I was faced with the immediate problem of somehow making a living. One day in early spring I made an appointment to talk to a man about a job. I was to meet him in front of a bombed-out building in the business district and as I stood there waiting—for he was late—a German truck suddenly pulled up. A soldier called out, *"Komm, komm. . . ."* I was taken with the sickening fear, but I had to obey. I walked briskly to the truck, keeping a military bearing. "Your papers!" the German demanded sharply. He took them and put them in his pocket and a moment later I was on the truck being driven through the sunny streets of Warsaw in the direction of Nowy Swiat.

A few minutes later we turned into Obozna Street and went straight into Dynasy. This had once been an amusement park, but now the Germans had set up a motor pool and repair shops there. It was a place for which Jewish labor was recruited off the streets as I had been, and it differed from other such labor-impressment places in that people were usually held as long as a week rather than for a single day's work. It was a place notorious for torture and people were killed there daily by the head sadists and executioners, Schultz and Krüger. These two were especially fond of personally torturing Jews who still wore the old-fashioned caftan or those who were well-dressed and prosperous looking. A number of Jewish prisoners were already there when we arrived. One of the Germans asked, "Who speaks German?" A principle I adopted then and adhered to throughout the war was never to volunteer for anything. One Jew did raise his hand and the German said, "All right, Moses, you're in charge." Schultz called every Jew Moses and every Jewish woman Sarah. Why bother to memorize new names every week?

Schultz looked over the assembled prisoners, and then began the inevitable calisthenics: twenty deep knee bends. Fortunately the weather was good, for on rainy days the orders were to fall flat on the ground and to do twenty push-ups in the mud. Schultz singled out two prisoners who looked most Orthodox and most puny and ordered them to have a fistfight. The loser was the one who was knocked down or had his face bloodied. The winner could then take a stick and beat the loser's rear. If he selected too thin a stick or didn't hit hard enough, the winner also was beaten up.

After these preliminaries we were put to work pushing trucks and cleaning spare parts. We were beaten frequently and on trivial pretexts: for not pushing fast enough, for not cleaning something quickly or thoroughly enough, for failing to stand at attention when spoken to, and so on. Why I was punched in the jaw I do not know to this day. When I got back home that evening, everyone who saw me rushed up, concerned about my face.

The next day I left the house at seven in the morning. At noon Krüger lined us up. "Get going," he ordered. "In one hour, I want a suitcase because I'm going on furlough to the *Vaterland*." I was selected for the job and my neighbors were startled as I went from door to door trying to find among them a suitcase for Krüger. I was lucky and within the hour had returned with one, but on the way back I prayed that no other German would catch sight of me with that beautiful suitcase as I carried it through the streets, or still worse, would recruit me for some other job. When I got back, the expressions on the faces of the others told me something had happened. Against the wall of the garage, an elderly Jew was lying motionless, blood from his head making a puddle on the concrete floor. He was left there until work ended at five o'clock and then two of us carried him away.

To celebrate Krüger's departure an extra treat had been organized. The Germans made a pious Jew work all day wearing his phylacteries, and at the end of the day Schultz played William Tell with him, using the phylactery headpiece as the apple. He took careful aim and was delighted whenever his pistol shot hit the bull's eye; whenever he missed, the Jew was beaten. There were other such games as well. One crew of Jews was set to pushing a heavily loaded truck and another crew a light passenger car. Both crews had to move their vehicles at exactly the same rate of speed and were beaten when they failed to do so.

Every day that week someone was ordered to bring some valuable object the following day: a pair of shoes, a suit, a shirt, an overcoat, a wrist-watch, silk stockings for Frau Krüger. I had really been lucky to have to "find" only a suitcase. Finally Krüger left and the last day of my forced labor passed without any special violence—nothing more than the calisthenics and an occasional kick. Our papers were returned to us with a Dynasy stamp on them and marked with the number of days work we had put in. When, subsequently, I presented my papers at the Judenrat labor office, the clerks were so impressed that they exempted me from all work for three months.

Every male in the Jewish quarter was obliged to work. At the request of the German authorities, the Judenrat had to supply work parties for various jobs at different sites, including the special labor camps. The younger people were at first quite willing to go because sometimes there was a chance to earn money and to buy food. However, when conscripted for such labor, it was possible to get a "replacement" by paying a sum of money to the Judenrat. In that fashion a group of professional replacements grew up, but lasted only until it was discovered that the labor camps were actually places of torture and young men came back from such assignments more dead than alive. Working conditions there were almost unbearable, meals were a farce, and workers were brutally treated. It became increasingly difficult for the Judenrat to round up men for those work parties and then the manhunts began. The blow, as usual, fell hardest on the poor, since anyone who could possibly do so paid the Judenrat a fee to escape conscription. Tenants' committees were charged with the task of outfitting men for the labor camps and of caring for their families while they were gone, a difficult if not impossible task.

Still without a job, I was myself reduced to selling off what belongings we still had, for, aside from my wife's earnings as a pharmacist, we had no other income. From time to time Kapko continued to give me money—"We'll settle accounts after the war."—and I was able to get a few things from my old newspaper office: a typewriter, for instance, which could be converted into cash.

Late in May 1940, I was standing on the back platform of a streetcar, when there was a commotion in the street. The Germans were staging a colossal manhunt; Poles were being impressed to be sent to Germany for forced labor. To my astonishment a man standing next to me suddenly took a Jewish armband out of his pocket and put it on his sleeve, giving me a wink as he did so. A few moments later the streetcar was stopped and several young Poles were seized, but people with armbands were not molested and my neighbor, secure in his adopted Jewish status, looked on his Polish compatriots' plight with studied indifference. The Germans later caught on to such tricks and in subsequent manhunts made their potential victims show identification papers.

When I got to Kapko's office (or mine) that day, I had to wait before he saw me. When I finally got to see him, I could tell something had happened because his face was so pale. "It's dreadful," he said, very agitated, "dreadful. I can't believe it."

"What's the matter?" I asked.

"The matter! Belgium has surrendered!" Hysterically, he repeated in a louder voice, *"Belgium has surrendered!"*

I could hardly believe my ears. Brave little Belgium! At that moment Kapko was suddenly realizing that the war was not going to end anything like so soon as he had thought. Never again was I to hear from his lips those generous words, "Pay me back after the war." Without a word, I took a few of my things and left.

The defeat of Belgium and Holland were terrible blows to us in Poland and undermined our confidence that spring would bring some relief. Instead spring brought only news of successive defeats: first Norway, then Holland, Belgium, and finally France. The day Paris fell was one of black despair, for Poles had a long and special affection for France. Now there seemed no hope at all. Hitler was moving from one triumph to the next. Bells rang all over the Reich for three days continuously. Then came the terrible thought: Suppose Hitler actually *did* win the war!

It was hot in Poland that summer of 1940, and there was no hope within her borders. At bottom we never really doubted that Hitler must one day be defeated, but now it seemed to us that it would take so long that it would rule out any hope for us. The possibility of our destruction became very real. Could we hold out if the war went on and on? Those bodies in the street covered with newspapers suddenly became ourselves in the near future. Far away Churchill and de Gaulle made speeches full of promises, but they sounded as faint and remote as God in His heaven seemed to us. We were alone and death was staring us in the face.

I had become superfluous as a human being. I got up early every morning, but only because the Germans began their daily manhunts for labor battalions early; if you were in bed when they arrived, you were caught. I lived in instant readiness to depart by the back door should there be a strange knock on the front door. It is characteristic of superfluous men to keep diaries, and so I, too, began to jot things down. Everything that had happened since September was still clear in my memory.

I was not very cheerful at this point because I had no job to keep me busy and to help me support my household. Everyone I knew seemed to have some sort of occupation. Even my small son had his day filled, hour by hour, on a strict schedule. I seemed to be the only person who had nothing to do. I kept looking for a paying job, but my efforts came to nothing. All my acquaintances seemed somehow to be managing and my own failures in this regard made me very unhappy.

Every able-bodied man knows how humiliating it is for a husband and father to ask his wife for money for cigarettes, how little such a situation is conducive to domestic harmony. My wife, however, was very tactful and understanding, never impatient, never addressing a single reproach to me, although she might well have done so, and with good reason, for my disposition was by no means sunny. She was aware that I was suffering and did everything possible to bolster my morale. "In time of war," she said, "the scum gets to the top. Decent people can only suffer." Her argument did not really persuade me, but I was grateful for her sympathy.

On paper I was employed by the Society for the Protection of the Health of Jews, the TOZ *(Towarzystwo Ochrony Zdrowia)*, whose head was Nehemia Finkelstein, an old friend of mine and prewar publisher of the Yiddish daily, *Haint* (Today). When he became director of TOZ, he put my name on the rolls. I now received a pink *Arbeitskarte* (work card) which had to be stamped once a month at the *Arbeitsamt* (Employment Office). The card protected me from being impressed into forced-labor details and from a number of other unpleasant possibilities. However, I never actually worked for TOZ; ours was a purely fictitious association.

To keep busy I devoted myself to the tenants' committee in my house and eventually became its chairman. My duties brought me into frequent contact with the ZTOS offices where I met many of the leaders of the Jewish community, including the Jewish historian, Emanuel Ringelblum. As a spokesman of the Poale Zionist organization, he had lectured widely and I had met him when I was a high school student. Later I ran into him from time to time when he was teaching history at a girls' high school. Ringelblum was a walking encyclopedia, full of news and gossip and avid to know everything that was going on. It was a tonic to talk to him, though he was scarcely optimistic.

Everywhere people were dying of starvation. Daily the newspaper-covered corpses lay in the street. On leaving the house in the morning, it was not unusual to be accosted by the weak voice of a starving man leaning against the wall of a building faintly asking for bread; nor was it unusual on coming home that evening to see the same man lying full length, his breath stilled forever. In the reception centers for refugees, now openly called death centers, the death toll still mounted. In the hospitals, typhus patients rose from their beds and fled from the appalling conditions, ravenous with hunger and eaten by disease. In private homes the story was the same, especially in the crowded, dingy flats of the poor where the relatives of the deceased would hastily drag their bodies into the streets at night and leave them there to be discovered in the morning. The purpose was to avoid paying 20 zlotys to the undertaker and to avoid reporting the death so that they could keep the dead man's ration card.

While hunger and typhus decimated the Jews who remained in Warsaw, the younger men were being systematically destroyed in the labor camps. Letters from those camps were tales of horror. Backbreaking labor, long hours, the cruelty of the guards, mainly Ukrainians, showed visibly in the men who returned, weak, sick, mutilated, their feet wrapped in rags, often dressed in nothing more than their underwear after having walked several hundred kilometers, begging food from the peasants as they made their way back to Warsaw. Mothers would bring the tenants' committees letters from their sons, beseeching us to do something, but even when we could take up such cases with the Judenrat, it rarely could do anything to help. Although young people had initially joined the forced-labor battalions voluntarily in the hope of being fed and earning a little money, as well as to avoid being a burden to their families, now able-bodied young men hid to avoid the roundups, which more and more resembled the impressment of Jews into the tsarist armies under Nicholas I. At first employees of the Judenrat's labor office carried out these "requisitions" of manpower; later that dirty job was handled by the ghetto police. Only those who could bribe their way out were spared.

In those desperate days my son was the only ray of sunshine. With his blond ringlets, blue eyes, and flawless complexion, he looked like some little prince out of a fairy tale and when he was taken out for his daily walk, people often stopped to stare at him and ask whose little boy he was. Every morning at seven the boy's grandfather came to visit him and it was hard to tell who enjoyed the visits more. Everyone in the family doted on Wlodek and he had not yet been permitted to lack anything, but before he reached his third birthday he was to experience what it meant to be an enemy of the Third Reich.

We lived on the second floor, facing the front, and consequently we were the first victims of German looting. In the spring of 1940, two German noncoms made off with all our household linen. Because we had been married only a few years we had a great deal of virtually new linens. As the two Germans were making off with all they could carry, one of them noticed and added to the pile a very attractive plaid blanket with which we used to cover Wlodek's feet when we took him out in a sleigh. Wlodek burst out sobbing, begging the German please not to take his blanket. Nothing, of course, could persuade the German to leave it behind, but he did relent enough to say gruffly, "We're just borrowing it. You'll have it back in a month." When Wlodek's grandfather arrived the next morning, the child dissolved into tears all over again, and as he told the old man the story, his grandfather began to cry. The following day to everyone's horror at the extravagance, Grandpa showed up with an enormous rocking horse, far larger than Wlodek himself. The next time Germans on the prowl paid us a visit Wlodek clutched his hobbyhorse by the neck, fear in his eyes, and cried, "This is *my* horse and you can't have him!"

What was so painful about the looting was the fact that increasingly we depended on the sale of our belongings as a source of income. After the second German visit, we took our most valuable Oriental rugs down to the cellar to hide them, resolved to sell them at the first opportunity. We didn't have to wait long. A Gentile friend agreed to come and look at them and an hour before he was due we started to haul the rugs back upstairs, but we were intercepted by two Germans who appeared out of nowhere and carried the rugs off. On another such visit I almost lost my life. One day my sister-in-law, with my wife's knowledge and consent, left some groceries in our apartment. We stored her tea, coffee, and other things on top of an armoire in our bedroom, in plain sight. But my wife forgot to tell me about it and when, next day, a marauding German came by demanding coffee, or tea, or chocolate, I replied with confidence that nothing of the kind was in the house.

"*Und was ist das?*" the German asked, pointing at the groceries atop the armoire. When I looked up, I nearly passed out. Stammering an awkward explanation, I began to lift down the bags of groceries. The German said nothing for a moment, then drew his gun and began to shout at the top of his voice, "Why are you Jews all such liars?" Though I was sure that my end had come, I escaped with only a crack on the skull from a gun butt, and even while staring into the muzzle of that gun I realized how ludicrous that German's sense of outrage was. Here was an honest, straightforward German who had forced his way into my apartment to steal, who had asked me an honest, straightforward German question about where he could find the loot, and I had lied to him!

It was early fall when we began to lose our furniture to the looters. We did our best to make everything look as unattractive as possible—taking drawers out of desks and bureaus, staining fabrics, and the rest—but it was no use. Our things were all relatively new and of good quality and there were plenty of people in the market for exactly what we had. One German showed up with his Gretchen and they selected our fine Bechstein piano and two large armoires we had. He pasted stickers on each piece and handed me an order requisitioning them. He said he would be back next day to move them out. This time, I resolved not to be had so easily. Through the friend of a friend of a friend I learned that there was a Jewish woman who specialized in "handling" such cases. She granted me an audience in a tiny bar at the corner of Gesia and Smocza Streets. Over the bar was an inscription, which attested both to the artistic nature and stern realism of the proprietor:

Credit went out with the bustle,
And will only come back with it.

In smaller letters, perhaps for the benefit of those who did not know what a bustle was, was inscribed: "To give credit is to lose a customer."

To describe the negotiations that followed would try the pen of a Gogol or a Sholom Aleichem and would require twenty pages, but when I left, I was lighter by 200 zlotys and the requisition was countermanded. We lost no time in selling the piano and the armoires.

As the looting did not let up and more and more marauding gangs roamed the streets, people actually began to hope that the rumors about establishing a ghetto, which would seal off the Jews from the rest of Warsaw, were true. "Let them go ahead and close us in," people said. "Things couldn't possibly get worse than they are right now."

It was clear that the German military governor of Warsaw was carrying out the program he had enunciated: "Hunger and poverty will take care of the Jews. The Jewish problem will be solved in the cemetery." But the Jews were not dying off quite as quickly as the Nazi schedule called for. The rumor raced around that the Jewish "problem" was now going to be settled: "The old ones will be killed; the middle-aged will be sent to concentration camps; and the children will be baptized and given to Christian families." All things now seemed possible to us. We could feel the ground slipping out from under our feet. So the second round in Germany's planned extinction of the Jewish people began; the Jews were sealed up behind ghetto walls where the process of killing them off by starvation and typhus could be intensified.

For a year walls had been under construction in various places, but it was still impossible to be sure just where the boundaries of the putative ghetto would fall. Everyone was kept guessing, on edge, and everyone had a different version of which streets would be included in the ghetto, which excluded. Then, finally, there was general apathy on the subject. Characteristically, the Nazi tactics began with a careful alternation of solemn promises which inspired hope and terror, which provoked despair. Their agents constantly planted contradictory rumors. There would be, there would not be, a ghetto. A definite date has been set; but no, by enormous bribes the project has been postponed indefinitely. The Nazis want a ghetto, but the Wehrmacht and the health authorities are opposed. This demoralizing uncertainty was kept up right down to the last minute before the ghetto was actually established.

Rosh Hashanah of 1940 fell on October 3. On that date the Germans proclaimed the establishment of a ghetto in which all Jews would in the future be quartered. The same day, as if they had not already desecrated the Jewish New Year enough, the Nazis appeared in large numbers in various Jewish neighborhoods to recruit forced labor. Prayers were being said in many private homes and some Jews had put up Yiddish signs reading "House of Prayer." Those houses were raided and the worshipers, many still in prayer shawls, were driven into the streets, abused, and then loaded onto trucks to be taken away for forced labor. Older, bearded men were particularly singled out.

By the terms of the Nazi decree all Jews in predominantly Gentile neighborhoods were to move to the ghetto, all non-Jews living in the quarter where the ghetto was to be located had to leave. The transfer was to be accomplished within four weeks, by October 31, and though it was what had been anticipated for months, the panic was indescribable. More than 100,000 Jews and even more non-Jews were affected. Jewish property "outside" included many stores, workshops, and factories: all these had to be abandoned. Jews moving to the ghetto were permitted only their bedding and what was called a refugee bundle *(Flüchtlingsgepäck)*. Jews who lived in Aryan sections and who attempted to circumvent the decree about what could be taken with them were frequently caught by the police, by janitors of the buildings where they lived, and often by "friendly neighbors." Moving vans were stopped in broad daylight and hijacked as soon as the hoodlums involved ascertained that the property belonged to Jews. Many Jews forced to move to the ghetto left their finest possessions to Gentile acquaintances either to be returned to them later, or not at all.

Those who lived on the border of the future ghetto suffered most. They were left guessing to the last minute about whether they would be inside or outside the walls. People who lived on Walicow, Ceglana, Zlota, and Sienna Streets especially literally sat on their suitcases waiting to learn their fate. Cousins of mine who lived on Sienna Street moved seven times, an extremely unnerving experience. For all, the transfer confirmed the old Jewish saying that to move twice was almost like having one's house burn down once. Of the half-million people who eventually were penned inside the ghetto walls, half had come either from the Aryan sections of Warsaw or from the provinces. The moves involved the loss of the bulk of their belongings and a severe comedown in the world. And with the shifting of domiciles, men also lost most of their means of making a living.

The streets of Warsaw looked as if the genius of chaos ruled. Wagons, carts, wheelbarrows, baby carriages, frequently pushed by women and children while the men toted the heavy bundles, jammed the streets. The two-way shift of populations, Poles and Jews, was macabre and explosive with panic and hatred. Thousands, half-crazed because they no longer had roofs over their heads, stormed the housing bureaus of the Judenrat and the Warsaw municipal authorities. As in the days of the bombing of Warsaw, signs blossomed on the fronts of houses advertising "exchanges." The Judenrat sent inspectors out to list empty living quarters and apartments that could hold more people. Some families willingly invited others to share their apartments to avoid having to accept unknown tenants later on. Unscrupulous individuals, some of whom worked in the housing bureaus, did a lively business in bribes. So confused and difficult was the entire operation that the Germans, at the very last moment, extended the date for sealing the ghetto to November 15, 1940.

When, on that date, the ghetto was finally closed off, thousands of new problems were created. Some 1,700 dwellings of all types made up the ghetto, 27,000 apartments in an area of 750 acres, with six or seven persons to a room. Because Jews had not previously been permitted to exercise the exalted profession of janitor, some 1,700 Polish janitors and their families had to be moved out and 1,700 Jewish janitors chosen to replace them. Similar replacements were required in business, industry, and municipal administration. A Jewish police force (the ghetto police) of about 2,000 was created. There was a wild scramble for these new jobs and an obscure Judenrat councilman named Kupczykier suddenly became the most prominent man in the ghetto because he made appointments to the Jewish police. The Judenrat took over management of all ghetto real estate. It also was empowered to appoint janitors, superintendents, and managers for the larger buildings. Bribery flourished. People paid as much as 3,000 zlotys to get a manager's job. Jews in the pay of the Gestapo, of whom Abraham Ganzweich was the most notorious, could also be bribed to obtain jobs. He founded the infamous organization subsequently known as "The Thirteen," because it was housed at 13 Leszno Street, which early took over managing a large number of the ghetto apartment houses. The tenants' committees fought stubbornly to have their own men appointed to the now-important position of janitor. Often, two or three candidates for a job—all of whom had bribed some Judenrat employee—discovered that two or three other candidates—all of whom had bribed members of The Thirteen—had simultaneously been "appointed" to the position.

As though by concerted agreement, members of the Jewish intelligentsia, with lawyers predominating, made a mass assault on the new police jobs. The war had ravaged the ranks of lawyers perhaps more than any other single group. All justified themselves in the same way—"Better us than the Germans!"—but once it became known that the police would not be paid salaries, the rest of us realized something of what we might expect from their ministrations.

A special problem was created by the Jewish converts to Christianity. The Germans treated them as Jews and the Jews looked on them as renegades. They were by no means a negligible number altogether and some had been baptized as long as fifty years. In the case of mixed marriages, where there were children born as Catholics, the establishment of the ghetto broke up many families. Some converts, deep inside, still thought of themselves as Jews and Prodigal Sons; others had become completely estranged and hated their origins. For these last, confinement in the ghetto was torment. Still other converts continued even in the ghetto to think of themselves as Gentiles and remained aloof.

Rudolf Langer, the elderly lawyer who lived with us on Orla Street, had years before converted to Christianity. For some reason he lived in terror of blackmailers and informers. Gray-haired, highly cultured, and distinguished-looking, he did his best to calm his wife, also a convert, when she loudly lamented that the Nazis had forced her to share the fate of the Jews. "They haven't got the right," she repeated over and over again, "I'm not a Jew." As fate would have it their only child, a daughter they worshiped, had fallen in love with a deeply committed Jew. Not only had she gone back to the Judaism her parents had renounced; she had become an ardent Zionist to boot.

To the Jewish community's credit it must be said that, throughout this period, these converts were never discriminated against, though it must also be admitted that they were never very popular. Several Christian churches with priests remained in the ghetto. Among the converts were a number of prominent scientists and people from the stage. For a while the Catholic organization *Caritas* took care of them and they had the illusion of being in a privileged position in the ghetto. So potent an illusion was it that after the ghetto was established several hundred Jews converted to Christianity. Dr. Milejkowski, with whom I often discussed these matters, used to refer to the converts as *Zwangsjuden* (compulsory Jews).

Just before the ghetto was sealed off there was a wave of visits to Jews there by their Gentile friends. They brought food parcels and what we needed even more: expressions of sympathy. Among those who came to visit us were the Maginskis.[3] Stefan Maginski had been one of our editors. His wife Maria had been active on the Cracow stage and though no longer young was still very good-looking. Both were now having a hard time of it. Stefan was a night watchman in a factory and he told me that Kapko sometimes helped him out. We talked politics and discussed the probable future of the Jews, and Stefan told me the latest Aryan political jokes.

One concerned the German Reich's being divided into two parts: *General-Gouvernement* (the official German designation for the territory of Poland under occupation), and *General-Bombardement* (the first British bombings of Germany had just taken place). A second told how Hitler was willing to give the Jews back their freedom and dignity, but only if they gave him the rod Moses used to divide the Red Sea. (Hitler was at the English Channel and was faced with the problem of crossing it if he was to invade Britain.)

---

3. The actual name of this Polish family, possibly of ethnic German derivation, was Magenheim. See afterword—W. D.

Though both we and the Maginskis did not doubt that Hitler would eventually be brought to his knees, on that cold evening in 1940 victory seemed far away indeed. Our chances of living to see it seemed still more remote.

Wlodek supplied the only note of gaiety on that visit. He was only one month from his third birthday and though his face was thinner than it had been, it remained radiant. We regaled the Maginskis with his bright sayings and verbal inventions, and Wlodek, aware that we were talking about him, outdid himself in being charming. He recited a poem by Tuwim, which he had memorized, and generally won their hearts. Our good-bys were sad—both women had tears in their eyes—and we silently asked, "Shall we ever see each other again?" We never suspected how crucial a role in our lives the Maginskis would one day play.

When the ghetto was officially sealed off, a sociological "experiment" without parallel began. Half a million people, locked behind walls in the heart of a great city, were increasingly isolated from that city and from the rest of the world. Had the ghetto been only one phase of Nazi "Jewish policy," intended to segregate Jew from Gentile because of the "noxious cultural and economic influences of Jews," or had it been intended only as a prelude to eventual "resettlement" in Madagascar or elsewhere, it still would have caused enormous damage and suffering. But the real purpose of the Warsaw ghetto was to exterminate its inhabitants after robbing them of all their worldly goods.

This anomalous city within a city had its own internal government, which included a police force, postal service, public-health administration, and many types of commerce and industry. But ghetto self-government turned rapidly into a cruel mockery, and even the well-meant efforts of the Judenrat served only to hasten our inevitable doom. What most Jews thought of the Judenrat at that time is suggested by a joke then current. Hitler summons the Nazi governor of Poland, Hans Frank, and asks, "What have you done with the Jews?" Frank replies, "I appointed a Judenrat and turned the Jews over to them." "Oh, fine," Hitler replies, "in that case they'll really be taken care of."

At each gate of the ghetto three guards were posted: one German, one Polish, and one Jewish—a member of the newly created ghetto police force. These last had no uniforms but wore blue caps with *Jüdische Ordnungsdienst* inscribed on them, and either stars or metal insignia. Belts and jackboots enhanced their authority; later they were issued rubber truncheons.

Crowds of Poles and Jews gathered on both sides of the gates, trying to get in or out. At first, passes were easy to get; the price was 5 zlotys at the Judenrat office. Or you could bribe the guards.

A number of Aryan factories remained open in the ghetto and their owners received special police passes. The plan was gradually to replace Polish workers with Jews. The big Czyste Street Jewish hospital was outside the ghetto walls and nearly a thousand doctors, nurses, and other hospital personnel daily had to get to work there. The Germans gave no more than a few dozen individual passes a day, and every morning at seven the rest had to line up at one gate to be marched in columns to the hospital. Polish pharmacies stayed open, too, and special police passes were issued for managers and clerks. Every day the people in the pharmacy where Lena worked brought in food at the low prices which existed outside the walls.

Once the gates were closed, looting fell off rapidly, and manhunts and beatings in the streets seemed to be over. But as I soon discovered, that was an illusion. Walking in Leszno Street one day, I stopped to talk to an acquaintance. Suddenly people around us began to run in all directions. Before we could grasp what was happening, three men in SS uniforms—with the skulls on their caps that gave them, in ghetto slang, the name of "corpses"—fell upon us. As German regulations required, we bared our heads at once, came to attention, and stood rooted to the spot. They ran past us, brandishing their clubs, in pursuit of the Jews who had fled at the sight of them. In a few moments bloodcurdling screams and the sound of falling bodies told us that the SS men had found those they were chasing.

The ghetto as a whole was thought of as composed of three sections: an "aristocratic" part, which included Leszno, Orla, Elektoralna, and Chlodna Streets; the "renegades" quarter centered in Sienna Street, where many converts lived; and the remainder where the "rabble" was housed.

A patrol car manned by "corpses" cruised along Leszno and Karmelicka Streets every afternoon between one and four o'clock on its way to Pawiak Prison. Never did it make a trip without pausing to shed its ration of Jewish blood.

Karmelicka Street seemed to be the SS favorite. Narrow as it was, it was for all practical purposes the only street connecting the populous Zamenhof-Nalewki quarter with Leszno and Chlodna Streets adjoining the so-called Little Ghetto. In the pungent slang of the area, Karmelicka Street was called the Dardanelles, and the boundary of the ghetto, Malkinia.

All day long Karmelicka Street was full of people, crowded together from wall to wall across its entire width. The "corpses" enjoyed driving down the street full speed, without warning. Not content with running down their victims, they would get out of their cars wielding their clubs at random, felling men, women, and children indiscriminately, or singling out one victim, stopping a few paces from him and beckoning, *"Komm, komm. . . ."* Once you were caught in Karmelicka Street, there was no dodging or evading. A more perfect arena for the Nazi sadists could scarcely have been devised. Their favorite targets were the "rickshas," two-seat, man-propelled tricycles which were the ghetto's primary means of transportation. They collided with them head-on and full speed, turning them over together with the passengers and the driver. One of the ghetto poets, Leonid Fokszanski, celebrated the thoroughfare at about this time in a poem ironically titled, "There's Room for All."

To cross Chlodna Street, commonly called Gibraltar, was almost as bad as crossing the Dardanelles. Many lives were lost attempting to "run the Straits." In addition to the normal Nazi beatings and commands to do arduous calisthenics or to lie in the mud, selected victims were ordered to pick up a heavy brick in one hand and a hollow one in the other. When they'd done so, they were ordered to bend forward and because of the imbalance of weights, they invariably fell down, which provided another pretext for beating them. Chlodna Street was haunted by the notoriously brutal guard, "Frankenstein," who required at least one sacrificial victim daily.

To handle all ghetto exports and imports a special organization called *Transferstelle* was set up in Krolewska Street; it charged exorbitant fees. Goods shipped in by train were unloaded at a siding on the corner of Dzika and Stawki Streets at the so-called *Umschlagplatz*[4] (reloading point), later to become a tragic landmark. By controlling the flow of goods going out and coming in the Germans hoped to starve the ghetto to death. But a city of half a million takes a lot of plugging up.

Never was so unique or elaborate a smuggling system put into operation as that devised by the ghetto Jews in their struggle to survive. The official food ration barely sustained life for two or three days a month, and smugglers consequently became the ghetto's most important citizens, its heroes, for though there were a thousand ruses, a smuggler risked his life in employing any one of them.

Tycoons among the smugglers organized huge rings, which employed dozens and even hundreds of people on both sides of the wall. One of the

---

4. Although earlier printings of this book have referred to "the Umschlagplatz" in accordance with usual American usage, the definite article has been omitted in this printing. See afterword—W. D.

THE WARSAW GHETTO
before the "Resettlement" of Summer 1942

■■■■■ Ghetto walls   ◯ Ghetto gates   ■■▭■■▭■■ Railroad

■ ● ■ ● ■ The cauldron, site of the final resettlement tragedy

Inset: In an area of about 750 acres a ghetto was established for 450,000 people. Thus in an area equalling 4.6 percent of Greater Warsaw, 37 percent of the population lived.

1. Author's residence (Orla 5); 2. Pharmacy (corner of Wolynska and Zamenhof Streets); 3. Printing plant (Leszno 24); 4. Judenrat (Grzybowska 26); 5. The Thirteen (Leszno 13); 6. AHAGE (Mila 41); 7. *Befehlstelle* (Zelazna 103); 8. The Great Synagogue (Tlomackie), converted into a warehouse for looted Jewish property; 9. The Pawiak prison.

biggest rings was located at 7 Kozla Street. That house abutted on an Aryan one fronting on Freta Street and where the two houses joined, passages connecting Jewish and Gentile apartments were cut through on every floor. These passages were artfully concealed by cupboards, stoves, bookcases, armoires, and so on. During the day goods were collected in the Gentile flats and at night transferred to the Jewish flats and immediately distributed. Men who carried the merchandise away and parceled it out also shared in the profits and both Polish and Jewish "teams" were kept busy twenty-four hours a day. Even milk got through—piped. The tenants in both buildings, the janitors, and on the Jewish side the members of the ghetto police who served as lookouts were all in on the smuggling.

Such smuggling lasted only until the Germans eliminated all adjacent buildings. Once that was done, the ghetto was enclosed by walls that ran through the middle of the street and the nature of smuggling changed. Goods either had to be thrown over the walls or passed through openings in the walls made for that purpose. Smuggling became riskier and daily more people lost their lives attempting it. But the Biblical saying in Lamentations, "They that be slain with the sword are better than they that be slain with hunger," remained appropriate and executing smugglers never stopped their trade.

The thousands of Jewish workers who marched out of the ghetto every morning for forced labor also were constantly engaged in bringing back food, paid for by money or valuables they smuggled out with them. The Jewish police at the gates played an important role in this activity; it was one of the few ways they could help alleviate conditions in the ghetto. They bribed German and Polish guards so that whole cartloads of goods could be brought in at one time. Wagons entered the ghetto drawn by a team of horses, and left empty and drawn by a single horse. The other horse was slaughtered for food. The "fiddlers," as such Jewish policemen were called, earned enormous sums of money, which were pooled and later divided equally in their respective precincts.

Gentile members of smuggling rings tossed parcels to their Jewish confederates from streetcars, which crossed portions of the ghetto without stopping. Hearses served to transport foodstuffs. Garbage collectors and Poles employed by the public utilities—such as gas, light, water—also played important roles in smuggling. And last, the Jewish servants of the Gestapo took advantage of their position to line their pockets.

Perhaps the most dramatic part in keeping the ghetto supplied with contraband was played by hundreds of poor children between the ages of four and fourteen, who would cluster at the gates looking for a chance to slip out. Many of them wore loose-fitting windbreakers, which they kept tightly belted so that they could slip contraband under their jackets and keep their hands free. Sometimes the lining of their clothes served the same purpose. On their small legs, and with their bulging middles, they looked like sparrows. Occasionally a guard would look the other way when a covey of those sparrows slipped out of the ghetto in search of food. Often, however, they opened fire on them; children, too, were enemies of the Third Reich. Henryka Lazowert wrote a touching little song called "The Little Smuggler," which was popular for some time. Its refrain was:

> Around walls, through holes, past guards,
> Over the rubble, fences, and barbed wire,
> Hungry, determined, and bold, I sneak . . .

For almost a year and a half the battle of the ghetto was fought daily along the walls, a running battle involving great heroism and many casualties. Every crust of bread that went to sustain life was dearly bought with Jewish blood. Leon Berenson, the famous lawyer, used to say that when the war was over a monument should be erected to The Unknown Smuggler.

Smuggling was a two-way business; the ghetto imported food and exported manufactured goods and every kind of personal possession. An amazing variety of things were made inside the ghetto, including chemicals, pharmaceuticals, soap, rubber goods, and electrical appliances; Jewish resourcefulness surpassed itself in "converting" various and unpromising raw materials into finished goods.

Almost every ghetto activity was illegal and involved bribing the Jewish police, informers, blackmailers, or other parasites on the ghetto's will to live. The Jewish police had a cynical wisecrack which summed up the situation: "If you want to hear the music, you have to put a coin in the slot." Rarely in human history can there have been a more musically inclined police force. Daily it grew more brutal and arrogant, and beating and torture became common. The gulf between the police and the people widened; the policemen were contemptuously dubbed *Dachshunds* and heartily detested. But there were, of course, exceptions. Not all policemen were completely corrupted and many refused to enter this distinguished profession. My cousin, Michal Machlis, for instance, who lived across from us on Orla Street, was an attorney. He had made a living of sorts by peddling various goods and services, and by playing chess for money. After the ghetto was

closed, he had no way of making a living and he slowly began to starve. He
visited us daily and I can still see his emaciated face and lusterless eyes.
Nevertheless, he steadfastly refused to join the ghetto police despite the
urgings of his friends, and he likewise turned down tempting offers from
The Thirteen.

The Thirteen was the Gestapo's special agency of informers and
stooges, set up in spite of the fact that both the Judenrat and the Jewish
police scrupulously followed Nazi orders and were infiltrated with Gestapo
spies. The leader of this so-called Anti-Usury and Anti-Speculation Bureau,
the notorious Abraham Ganzweich, was no mere spy, but a provocateur
and diversionist on such a grand scale that people called him the Azef[5] of
the Warsaw ghetto. His job was to demoralize the ghetto by persuading it
that Hitler's victory was inevitable and resistance therefore useless. Of
medium height, slender, dark-haired, with sharp features and piercing
magnetic eyes behind thick glasses, Ganzweich was an unusually capable
man, highly intelligent and very persuasive. A born demagogue, he spoke
four languages fluently—German, Polish, Yiddish, and Hebrew—and
before the war had taught Hebrew and written for newspapers. He had
frequented Labor Zionist circles and had, apparently, been in the employ
of the Nazis even then. He was reputed to have been an espionage agent
for the Nazis against the Russians in Bialystok, Vilna, and Lvov. To the
ghetto he presented himself not as a Gestapo agent, but as a benefactor
who would be able to serve the Jews in their hour of need, thanks to his
close relations with the Germans.

Ganzweich cast his nets wide and into every area of ghetto life. Among
his many roles, he posed as champion of the poor against the "plutocratic
exploiters" of the Judenrat, a patron of Jewish arts and letters—he particularly wooed Jewish intellectuals—and wished to be considered a great
ghetto leader, a kind of Messiah. Elaborating the view that German victory
was unquestionable, he spread lies to the effect that Jews would eventually
be resettled in conquered territory, and that the ghetto was a desirable institution because it preserved Jewish national and cultural autonomy. Thus,
he recommended that Jews not only obey the Germans, but collaborate
with them. Lawyers, doctors, writers, journalists, and other "intelligentsia"
were invited to lectures, conferences, discussions, and lavish dinners where
these ideas were pressed on them. At one of these Ganzweich was asked
bluntly, "Where do you come from? Who are you, really? In whose name

---

5. Jevno Azef (1869–1918) was an infamous and audacious double agent who betrayed both
the tsarist government and the revolutionaries.—Editor's note

do you speak?" And Ganzweich replied, "The Devil himself sent me here, but it is my intention to do good."

Nor were his endeavors wholly ineffective. Many were taken in, and some of them were prominent individuals. Even Dr. Ringelblum, who had no dealings with Ganzweich, went so far as to seek him out for "a little talk" to satisfy his curiosity. By a few grandstand gestures Ganzweich made it clear that he could pull important strings. His intervention caused the release from prison of Dr. Janusz Korczak, the famous writer and educator. In addition, Ganzweich boasted that, because of his influence, Sienna Street and Grzybowski Square were left inside the ghetto walls.

Though familiarly known as The Thirteen, the title of his organization—Anti-Usury, Anti-Speculation—appealed to the hungry masses to whom it seemed that merchants were profiting at their expense. The only practical result was that merchants were held up from still another quarter. One of Ganzweich's agents would discover that kasha was being sold above the legal ceiling price in a particular store. The merchant would work out a bribe satisfactory to the bureau, hide 90 percent of his kasha, and then offer the remaining 10 percent to the public at the legal price—with maximum fanfare. All this for less than three ounces of kasha per customer!

Ganzweich made enormous amounts of money. He received the income from nearly a hundred houses in Leszno Street. The Germans allowed him thirty passes to the Aryan side, which he sold for exorbitant sums. He organized an emergency ambulance service, whose employees were exempt from forced labor and had other privileges. To become a member of that service, with its special card and hat bearing red piping, people paid small fortunes.

At Passover, Ganzweich contributed a few thousand zlotys to help impoverished Jewish writers. When he celebrated his son's bar mitzvah with an elaborate reception at the Nay-Azazel Theater, the poor were treated to bread and coffee, which was reported to have cost him tens of thousands of zlotys. When his father died, eulogies appeared in the semi-official Jewish newspaper, *Gazeta Zydowska,* signed by "A Group of Doctors, Lawyers, Journalists and Writers," though without individual signatures.

At the same time as he played on popular distrust and dislike of the Judenrat, Ganzweich used every stratagem to gain control of it. Once, his Gestapo sponsors even arrested Adam Czerniakow, Obmann of the Judenrat. Rumors of a merger between The Thirteen and the Judenrat, in which Ganzweich would become vice president of the new organization, were rife, but it never took place. Probably this was because of behind-the-scenes struggles for power between the German civilian commissioner of the ghetto, Dr. Heinz Auerswald, Czerniakow's superior, and the high-ranking Gestapo officers who sponsored Ganzweich. What Ganzweich wanted was a mandate from the Jews to speak in their name. "Then," he promised, "I can get you anything you want from the Germans." The ghetto would immediately go to work for the Wehrmacht, manhunts and beatings would cease, and sufficient food rations would be made available.

Subsequently, two of Ganzweich's assistants, Moritz Kon and Zelig Heller, set up their own shop across the street from The Thirteen at 14 Leszno Street. They specialized in smuggling vegetables and acquired some very profitable concessions, including the public market in Leszno Street, the fish trade, and the horse-drawn streetcar line inside the ghetto. (Those cars were called *konhellers* as tribute to the concessionaires, but they were also known as "lousy cars" in honor of their insect-bearing qualities.) Kon and Heller also earned tremendous sums by smuggling friends and relatives from the Lodz and Bialystok ghettos to the Warsaw ghetto, by getting prisoners released, civil actions dismissed, and having orders confiscating property annulled—all of course as "services" obtained from German officialdom. Though neither Kon nor Heller had as grandiose notions of social leadership as Ganzweich, they did contribute to rabbis and pious Jews, and to Jewish religious schools, and were not averse to an occasional rabble-rousing gesture. Thus, from time to time, a little drama would occur: A policeman seizes a boy for stealing bread. A crowd gathers around and suddenly a man steps forward and punches the policeman in the nose. He gives the boy 10 zlotys. When the policeman has recovered sufficiently to ask for his assailant's papers, the man is revealed as Moritz Kon and while the crowd applauds, the policeman sheepishly departs.

I was still trying to get a job and make some money. One of the ghetto's greatest problems was the scarcity of coal, which commanded fantastic prices. I remembered that the little briquettes known as cannel coal in England had been much in demand during the First World War and I got together with a friend to try to manufacture similar pellets of processed coal.

I had studied chemistry and my knowledge now came in handy. After some experimenting we managed to turn out an acceptable little "coal brick." Our best customers were the communal kitchens, but we were forced to abandon the project after a short while because of the shortage of coal dust and the poor quality of the chemical binder. Although Kapko had promised us coal dust and his friend Abraham Stolcman of the Judenrat had assured him it could be delivered to the ghetto, the Warsaw municipal gas factory did not make the coal dust available. So ended my first attempt at business enterprise inside the ghetto.

The premises we had rented for our coal-brick business were at 41 Grzybowska Street, by coincidence next door to the building where my newspaper printing plant had been located. By making a hole in the wall I managed to get into the printing plant and survey the almost new presses standing there silent and dust-covered. The Germans had requisitioned the plant and sealed it up, so I was risking my life simply by being there. One day that winter a large truck pulled up outside and while I watched from the sidewalk opposite, mechanics dismantled the expensive rotary presses, the Linotypes, and the other equipment, loaded them onto trucks and drove away. At a time when every crust of bread was precious a sizable fortune was disappearing before my eyes. I made an appointment with Kapko at the Leszno Street courthouse, which had entrances from both Jewish and Aryan sides. He subsequently spoke to Hergl, who warned him not to intervene "if he knew what was good for him."

For some time I manufactured sulphur candles for fumigation purposes, melting down the sulphur on an ordinary kitchen stove. Since I couldn't control the temperature, the premises were often flooded with poison gas. I had no gas mask and although I was more than eager to make some money, I had to drop that project, too. My next effort was in the "import business." I had relatives in two provincial cities where food was more plentiful than in Warsaw, and they mailed me large parcels of food, which I then sold in the ghetto. For a while all went well. The Jewish post office operated efficiently. Then, abruptly, the parcels stopped coming through. The post-office employees maintained that the Germans were confiscating them; but Jews said that the post-office people themselves were stealing them. Like the others, that business venture failed also.

In despair I asked Dr. Milejkowski to find me a job on the Judenrat. Through him I had met Czerniakow several times and had had some interesting talks with him. I admired the frankness of his approach to ghetto problems, and finally, at his suggestion, I drew up several projects "to increase the resources of the Judenrat." After several weeks I was informed that the Germans had refused permission for them because, as Czerniakow told me with a sad smile, my projects "were evidently not harmful to the Jews."

Finally I joined a tailor shop in association with several other people, but we had only one real tailor in the group. After brief negotiations with the Judenrat production office, we were assigned premises in a building

on Prosta Street formerly occupied by a business college. We bought a
number of sewing machines and had no trouble finding tailors to work
for us. An experienced engineer was hired as manager, and his presence
made us feel secure. I took charge of the bookkeeping and other associates
of the production and stock room. The arrangement was that the German
contractor Toebbens would supply us with fabric and trimming and pay
us on a piecework basis. Workers, also paid by the piece, would receive
extra rations and hot soup as well. We calculated our costs so that, if things
worked well, we might show a profit by selling some of the trimmings on
the side.

All went well until we made our first delivery of uniforms, which were
rejected. Our manager talked to Toebbens' deputy, an "ethnic German"
giant named Jahn, and we learned that on receipt of a certain sum, the
uniforms would be accepted. The amount of Jahn's bribe was exactly equal
to our total profit. When the second lot of uniforms was ready for delivery,
Toebbens himself appeared at the shop carrying a riding crop and began
to lay about him, accusing us all of sabotage. A few days later we were evicted
from the premises, Toebbens appropriated our machines and equipment,
and put our manager in charge of the works. He warned us that if any one
of us so much as set foot in the plant, he would deal with him personally.
The whole episode took eight weeks. To add to the calamity, the stockroom
supervisor sold the remaining trimmings, pocketed the proceeds, and told
us that the trimmings had disappeared. If we didn't accept his explanation,
we were perfectly free to lodge a complaint with the Germans. Except as
a valuable lesson for the future, that business venture was a total loss.

In March 1941, the Polish pharmacists who, until then, had been
granted passes to enter and leave the ghetto daily were informed that their
businesses would be taken over by the Judenrat on April 1. For the purpose of running these pharmacies an office was set up, which involved the
assistance of a group of financiers. Jewish employees had to contribute a
sum, in return for which they would share in whatever profits might be
made; in that way the necessary capital, some 300,000 zlotys, was collected.
This turned out to be one of the most efficiently run and managed ghetto
agencies. A licensed pharmacist was to be in charge of each drugstore, and
my wife was duly appointed manager of the one at the corner of Wolynska
and Zamenhof Streets. The Polish proprietors had left only the bare walls
when they departed, and everything had to be rebuilt from scratch, but so
well was it done that the pharmacies were a striking contrast to the filth
and shabbiness of the ghetto around them. Drugs came into the ghetto

through the regular *Transferstelle* channels, and wholesale storage of pharmaceutical articles was organized and maintained.

While hundreds of thousands grew steadily poorer, a handful of men were making enormous fortunes: the leading smugglers, bakers, a few contractors working for the German army, some Judenrat big shots, the ghetto police, and The Thirteen. The money so easily, if dangerously, gained was also easily spent. While the ghetto was dying of hunger, champagne toasts were being quaffed, and drunken orgies and banquets held in the night clubs which had recently mushroomed. One of the best-known of these was The Casanova, in the cellar of the Hotel Britannia at 18 Nowolipie Street, where smugglers split their take and Jewish Gestapo agents treated their German protectors to drinks.

Also in operation were some decent cafés where poets and chansonniers of the ghetto were to be heard, and five theaters continued performances in Yiddish and in Polish. Vera Gran, Pola Braun, and Marysia Ajzensztat, "the nightingale of the ghetto," sang; poets Wladyslaw Szlengel, Leonid Fokszanski, and Henryka Lazowert recited their works; Diana Blumenfeld and other actors presented skits.

Our tenants' committee organized an entertainment to provide for the increasing number of destitute. Most of the skits ridiculed local bigwigs; children danced the hora, and I recited some of my own satirical verses on the ghetto police—"The Juke Box"—and on the Judenrat, entitled "Four Letters" because the Polish word for council is *rada*. Four-letter words, incidentally, have the same connotation in Polish as in English.

Our show was not all jokes and satire, however; we could not forget where we were. When a young girl sang the famous Yiddish lament, "Eli, Eli," at the words "Save me, save me from danger," a wail went up throughout the hall, and when she came to, "My God, my God, Why hast Thou forsaken us?" the cry seemed to give voice to the feelings of all those whose husbands and fathers had been exiled, whose families had been broken up and scattered, who struggled against poverty and hunger, misery and degradation, sickness and death.

One of the most celebrated ghetto sights was the famous Rubinstein, half-madman, half-clown. Small and dark, he roamed the streets with his peculiar hopping gait, uttering wild yells or singing, *"Alle glaych, urym yn raych!"* (Everyone's equal, rich and poor!). It was never clear just how mad he really was, but in that mad time and place Rubinstein certainly made out better than many normal people. When he was hungry, he would stand in front of the best-stocked food store in the ghetto, screaming at the top of his lungs, "Down with Hitler! Down with the German murderers!" which was quite enough to bring the proprietor running out to load Rubinstein with food and get him to stop that bullet-inviting blackmail. The nouveaux riches of the ghetto often invited Rubinstein to dinner in restaurants to amuse them and he never disappointed his hosts. "How many of us are going to survive?" he would inquire, and then answer his own question, "Fifty-five." Asked to explain, he would do the following arithmetic: Add 26 Grzybowska (the Judenrat address) to 13 Leszno Street (the address of The Thirteen) and 14 Leszno Street (Kon and Heller) and you got 53. By adding the chief undertaker of the ghetto, Pinkiert, and himself, Rubinstein got 55.

To the question, "Who should drop dead?" Rubinstein would reply, "Forty." Adding the Judenrat's 26 to Ganzweich's 13, you got 39; then add Hitler to get 40.

Only those who were madmen did not fear the Germans and dared to behave aggressively, and perhaps in that situation they were normal in being able to comprehend the nature of the Nazis.

Normal people walked past the food-store windows on Karmelicka Street and looked at them, admiring the lavish displays of delicacies, pastries, cold meats. Those luxuries came from abroad, from relatives sending food parcels to ghetto residents via Portugal and other neutral countries, and for many families such parcels were their sole source of income. The Judenrat tried repeatedly to cut down the lavishness of the displays in order to avoid provoking both the Germans and the starving people of the ghetto. It was not unusual for people dying of starvation to be found right beside those shop windows, and the sight of their bodies covered with newspapers lying next to such lush displays of food was doubly unbearable. Yet, not once in the history of the ghetto did starving mobs ever attempt to break into those stores. Parcels were snatched in the streets; food stalls and vendors' baskets were pilfered; and sometimes a starving youth would snatch a passerby's bundle, tear off the wrapping, and sink his teeth into whatever it contained. The victim might scream or strike the thief, or the ghetto police might even intervene, but the practice continued, though the victims were often as badly off as the thieves. The loaf of bread, or the single roll, might be a whole day's income.

Hunger and typhus went right on taking their toll in increasing numbers and Dr. Milejkowski called my attention to the fact that twice as many men as women were dying in the ghetto. The begging in the streets had become more than one could bear. Even late at night, after curfew, when the streets were almost silent as the tomb, the appalling voices of the starving, begging for bread, still assailed our ears with the same lament they had cried all day long: *"Yiddische kinder, git a shtikl broit"* (Jews, give us a piece of bread).

On May 13, 1941, newsboys appeared on the streets crying, "Kurier Warszawski" and "Hitler's Lies for Twenty Groszen," and so we learned of Rudolf Hess's flight to England. People went wild. The war would now soon be over. Our suffering had not been in vain after all, and liberation was just around the corner. Conjectures and wisecracks temporarily took our minds off our situation:

Hess iz geworen a mes (Hess has become a corpse),
Mit Hess iz geshen a nes (Hess has wrought a miracle).

From sources outside the ghetto we learned that, day and night, trains were moving troops and enormous quantities of material eastward. In the ghetto, orders for mattresses, carpentry products, and other military items steadily mounted. Finally, on June 22, when Hitler invaded the Soviet Union, the enthusiasm of the ghetto was indescribable. Spirits soared. Our prayers were answered. With Russia on our side victory was certain and the end for Hitler was near; with the Russian invasion the meaning of Hess's flight became clear to the ghetto's armchair strategists. It was all quite simple. Hitler had sent Hess to England to strike a bargain. He would attack Russia and destroy communism if England would make peace with the Third Reich and give him material support. Perfidious Albion had replied "All right. But how can we trust you after all your broken promises? Attack Russia first and then you have our gentlemen's word of honor that you can count on us." Now, the English had Hitler over a barrel: he had attacked the Soviet Union and Churchill had instantly offered the USSR every assistance.

Unfortunately, the campaign in the East did not go as we had hoped. The lightning advance of the German panzers; the occupation of enormous areas; the encirclement, dismemberment, and surrender of entire Soviet armies were death blows to our morale. We pored over the communiqués, trying to read something hopeful between the lines, but the BBC broadcasts to which a few people listened secretly, confirmed the German boasts. Our conviction of catastrophe grew; even the most optimistic of us now feared the worst. Suppose we had been wrong all the time? Might not the future belong to the murderers after all? Perhaps Hitler really would win the war?

We tried not to lose all hope. We recalled Napoleon's fate in the boundless wastes of Russia and reminded ourselves of "General Winter." As in September 1939, we had prayed for rain, so now we hoped for a Russian winter to end all Russian winters. At the same time we could no longer tell ourselves that the war would soon be over. Our suffering had a long way to go. "What good will it do me when I am dead," one ghetto dweller said to another, "If they come to my grave and say *mazel tov* (congratulations), you won the war?" Our world was collapsing around us and we began genuinely to despair.

At the end of 1941, the ghetto was shaken by the public hanging of eight Jews who had been caught outside the ghetto without official permission. Hitherto such offenses had been punished by sentences of varying length in the Gesia Street jail, but now it was decreed that leaving the ghetto was an offense punishable by death. Anyone, women and children included, caught outside the ghetto would be shot. The eight had been arrested by the Polish police, six of them women, one a mother and another very pregnant. One of the women had tried to bribe the policeman, but he had insisted on 100 zlotys and she had only had 50 with her. The hanging took place early in the morning at the prison and there were present, in addition to German and Polish authorities, high-ranking Jewish police officers. The executions were doubly threatening because similar charges were pending against almost a thousand ghetto residents. According to Dr. Milejkowski, his superior, Dr. Wilhelm Hagen, was directly responsible for the execution. It was the only way, Dr. Hagen claimed, to stop Jews from spreading typhus outside the ghetto.

Despite the executions, smuggling went on as before. The long cold spell of winter combined with the lack of coal, gas, and electricity for heating made people feel that they would as soon die from a bullet as freeze to death. Small children roamed the streets in rags, sobbing and screaming, and many actually froze to death. Though posters everywhere proclaimed "Children's Month" and carried slogans like "Our Children Must Not Die!" and "Children Are Sacred!" often the same posters were used to cover the bodies of children who had died during the night.

People who had fled to the Soviet zone in 1939 were now returning en masse, undeterred by the increasingly deteriorating conditions in Warsaw. Refugees in the Soviet zone who had opted for Soviet citizenship had been allowed to stay in eastern Poland and most of them perished when the Germans invaded. Ironically, those who had refused Soviet citizenship had been deported to special camps and villages in the Far North, in Siberia, and in Kazakhstan, where they suffered a good deal, but for the most part survived the war.

In December 1941, two events served to lift our spirits. One was America's entry into the war, which Jews greeted with a batch of jokes. It was said that there were now three powers involved in the war: *Rasse* (race), the Germans; *Masse* (masses), the Russians; and *Kasse* (cash), the Americans. Another joke said, "The Germans are waging four types of war: total war in Poland, lightning war in France, installment war against England, and catastrophic war in Russia." A third joke referred to the fact that Hitler's war machine had come to a standstill in the Russian winter, and described Hitler in front of a statue of Frederick the Great appealing to him:

> *Komm herunter* (Come down)
> *Grosser Reiter* (Great rider).
> *Dein Gefreiter* (Your corporal)
> *Kann nicht weiter* (Can go no farther).

The second was the German request for civilian fur coats for their troops on the Russian front. The universal ghetto reaction was, "If Hitler needs *our* fur coats to win the war, things can't be going very well for him." There was a rush to hide fur coats in cellars, attics, or houses of Aryan friends. Fur coats were smuggled out of the ghetto virtually en masse and sold. Only a few impractical fur pieces were actually turned in at the collection point in order to get a receipt; such receipts could also be bought for a small sum. Those who couldn't sell or hide their fur coats burned them. It took me most of one night after curfew to dispose of our fur coats that way. As a result of the German request, we calculated that almost overnight the ghetto had become poorer by several million zlotys. A new industry, the manufacture of fur substitutes, now sprang up, as did a fertile new field for blackmailers, since it was a capital offense to conceal a fur coat—the same penalty as for possessing a radio. There was a squirrel collar on Wlodek's winter coat and it took him a long time to understand why the Third Reich needed his coat collar to win the war.

I was still searching for a way to make a living and for a while I manufactured soda water in a tiny factory in Wolynska Street, supplying Ems, Vichy, and seltzer to pharmacies and grocery stores. Then, finally, my fortunes took a turn for the better. Izak Rubin, my wife's cousin, a lithographer by trade, had lately been using his skill to produce printed babushkas. As many Jews were obliged to sell their bed linen, contractors bought it up, laundered and dyed it, then printed it in various colors and designs. The kerchiefs were smuggled out of the ghetto to be sold eventually in villages all over Poland.

There were ten lithographic shops in the ghetto and competition was driving them to price themselves out of existence, a situation exploited with profit by the purchasers of printed cloth. Under the leadership of the Warsaw printer, Jona Rachman, an effort was being made to overcome mutual distrust and to cooperate in stabilizing prices. In this effort, Izak Rubin asked me to take a hand. A printers' "trust" was set up in which I was named controller. My office was in the largest litho shop, Biederman's, at 6 Gesia Street. Prices were soon stabilized and business boomed to everyone's satisfaction. Though mine was only a tiny share in the business, with my earnings added to my wife's, we were able to live better than we had since the outbreak of the war. Once more I was head of the family. I threw myself into my work, getting up at seven and coming home just before curfew; and since the job had nothing to do with either the Germans or the Judenrat, I enjoyed it. We all felt we were contributing to the economic survival of the ghetto.

But if some events lifted our morale, Hitler's rabble-rousing speeches depressed our spirits and Goebbels' repeated warnings, "the Jews won't be laughing much longer," gave us little cause for rejoicing. Still there were a few of us who managed to shrug and pretend not to be intimidated by the threats. Then came the news of a wave of massacres wiping out whole Jewish villages all over Poland. In April, Lena's cousin Helka Dorfman told us that her brother, Izak, had called from Lublin to tell of the terrible occurrences there. Fantastic rumors circulated that enormous barracks-cities were being built in Lublin province and that Jews from all over Europe were to be shipped there. No one knew why, or how they would live once they got there. There were no less disquieting rumors from other regions. It was said that in Zamosc all the Jewish children had been taken away from their parents. The centuries-old Jewish community of Poland was in mortal agony, jarred to its roots.

On the night of Friday, April 17, 1942, the Germans unleashed on the Warsaw ghetto a wave of terror which did not let up until the great "Resettlement Operation" began. Gestapo men went from flat to flat with lists of names, ordering people into streets. They were told to walk straight ahead and were shot through the back of the head. Fifty-two corpses were left lying in their own blood that night. Among the victims were a baker, an engineer, a lawyer, some social and cultural leaders, typesetters, and even some well-known Jewish agents of the Gestapo and colleagues of Ganzweich, such a diverse group that it was hard to understand what the principle of selection had been. Only later did we realize that the Germans had been after the ghetto's illegal press. Papers had appeared almost openly and the Gestapo had tried to get all those involved, paying off a few personal scores at the same time. Every few days another such swoop left people murdered in the streets in front of their houses; and there were more and more shootings along the walls. At the Gesia Street prison, executions were daily occurrences and in our neighborhood, cars would pull up in front of 12 Orla Street, victims would be forced out of them and made to enter the building. Though some of them put up desperate resistance, the pistols or submachine guns soon sounded and when the murderers left, they would tell the Jewish policeman at the corner to remove the corpses. The victims were usually people caught outside the ghetto and the Gestapo typically chose our quiet street for the executions so that they could be plainly seen and heard.

During this period a former schoolmate of mine, a psychiatrist, had an unusual experience. He visited outside the ghetto quite often and one day, having completed his errands, was taking a streetcar back toward the ghetto. A stranger spoke to him and said, "I know you. Don't you remember me?" My friend protested indignantly that he was a doctor, and that he had a perfect right to be where he was, but the stranger said, "You're just the kind we're looking for," and indicated that my friend would have to accompany him to Gestapo headquarters on Szuch Avenue. He took his papers away, and made him stand on the front platform reserved for the German military.

At the next stop three German officers boarded the streetcar and hearing two Polish civilians quarreling wanted to know what was going on in their section of the tram. My friend told them in German that the other man was holding him on the false charge of being Jewish and had forced him to stand on their platform. As they argued the streetcar passed the ghetto. It was getting late and the gate my friend had to enter was soon to be closed for the night. One of the officers mentioned that they were leaving for the Russian front the following day, that this was their last night in Warsaw. My friend had a brainstorm and invited them to have a drink. "After all," he said, "the Gestapo won't run away. We'll have a drink and wish you a pleasant journey." The officers accepted the invitation eagerly and the five of them got off the streetcar and went into a well-known bar on Widok Street. After the third round one of the officers told the Gestapo man to give my friend his papers since no one was allowed to go around without papers. After the fifth round the Gestapo man went to the telephone and one of the officers then said to my friend, "Now, get out quick, hurry!" He got up at the same time and escorted my friend back to the ghetto, taking him right to his own house in Mila Street because it was after curfew. Was this one of the advantages of being a psychiatrist, or was my friend just lucky? Or were there, after all, some decent Germans?

On May 29 a colossal manhunt swept through the ghetto and I had a narrow escape. I was coming back from the TOZ where I had left my working card to be stamped. A young policeman at the corner of Gesia and Zamenhof Streets stopped me and asked to see my work card. Instead of handing him the usual 10 or 20 zlotys, I naively told him the truth. He took me to the precinct station and there again, instead of handing over the usual 50 or 100 zlotys, I repeated my story. After several hours I was finally released due to the personal intervention of the precinct officer whose sister was a schoolmate of my wife's.

That same day more than 900 people were rounded up and held at 19 Zamenhof Street, allegedly for medical inspection. At the same time their families were told to pack a knapsack with their clothes and some food. Later we were told they'd all been sent to the Todt Organization in Bobruisk where all of them perished. Another version of the story said these people were used in an experimental run to test the efficiency of the newly built gas chambers at Treblinka.

One day at the beginning of June, I stopped after work to see my friend Rachman at his printing shop. I was told he had gone to the Judenrat, but would be back shortly. When he came back, he was trembling and white as a sheet. He wouldn't tell me what the matter was because he'd been sworn to secrecy, but he advised me not to spend the night at home. Next day I learned that the Judenrat had given him the text of a poster to print announcing the execution of 110 Jews (including 10 women and 10 Jewish policemen) for "disobedience to the authorities." The execution took place at Babice, near Warsaw on June 3, 1942.

In mid-May the ghetto had been shocked by another Nazi act which, though it cost no victims, was hardly reassuring. Large trucks with motion-picture equipment moved through every street of the ghetto, their cameras grinding. Little scenes were staged to show Jews in the worst possible light. For instance, a crowd was gathered and Jewish policemen ordered to disperse them by wielding their clubs. A child was told to slip out of the ghetto by one gate and to buy potatoes in a store across the street. As the child returned, a Polish policeman caught him and was about to beat him when a German guard interfered and said, "Children must never be beaten!" Young girls were stripped and forced to enact obscene brothel behavior. Well-dressed young ladies were taken to restaurants and photographed eating elaborate meals and as they left the restaurants, were made to walk past starving children begging at the door. Shots of luxurious apartments were juxtaposed with shots of the crowded reception centers for refugees. In every way the effort was made to suggest that Jews were insensitive to the sufferings of other Jews. "What use was to be made of such propaganda?" we asked ourselves.

To cap our misgivings on the score, an enthusiastic article appeared in the official German *Warschauer Zeitung* describing how 100,000 Jews in Warsaw were now productively employed in working for the Germans, where previously they had been social parasites engaged only in buying and selling in order to cheat Christians.

In the ghetto "Wanted by the Police" posters were put up in doorways and other public places; these posters bore the names and photos of Ganzweich and some of his henchmen, but rumor had it that those individuals had made their escape. Presumably a new SS group was to take over the ghetto and was liquidating those who had collaborated with its predecessors.

In the middle of June the curfew was extended from nine to ten o'clock at night and several blocks along Bonifraterska and Muranowska Streets were excluded from the ghetto. For a short time this bolstered Jewish belief that the ghetto would not be liquidated. If the Germans intended to destroy the ghetto, surely they wouldn't extend the curfew or go to the pains of "taking back" a few insignificant blocks? On Saturday, July 18, Czerniakow made an official statement to the Judenrat and the Jewish police, declaring that the Germans had given him assurances that they had no intention of resettling the population of the ghetto, and that any persons found spreading such rumors would be severely punished. At the very same moment, however, eyewitnesses reported that a train composed of several dozen freight cars was being made up at Umschlagplatz.

Profound gloom seized us and ghetto morale sank to the depths. So far 100,000 of us had died of starvation, disease, and exposure. One hundred a day. But a mere hundred a day was too slow a pace to satisfy the Nazi beast. We felt we faced something different from ordinary ordeals, something monstrous. What was impending was not simply cutting down ghetto space, or more manhunts for forced labor, more random executions. The sense of impending doom was palpable; the end of time had arrived. There was to be a third stage in the Nazi plan for the Jews: total extermination. The final martyrdom. *Kiddush HaShem.*[6]

"*Es wird schon was kommen!*" said the Gestapo's man, Kon, darkly and without explaining himself further. Those terrible incomprehensible words soon passed from mouth to mouth. *Es wird schon was kommen. . . .* He was right: something *was* going to happen.

---

6. The sanctification of the Name [of God].—Editor's note

CHAPTER 2

ELI, ELI

VAGUE RUMORS, DARK HINTS, were the preliminary stage. Several members of the Judenrat had been arrested and were being held hostage; it was whispered that they had been executed. On Wednesday, July 22, 1942, the day before Tisha b'Av (the anniversary of the destruction of the ancient Temple in Jerusalem), the storm broke. It was a dark day to match our foreboding, with heavy clouds over a silent city. Shopkeepers closed their stores; streets were empty; even the beggars had disappeared. In the unnatural silence those who found themselves outdoors looked nervously over their shoulders.

Early in the afternoon, black and white posters appeared all over the ghetto:

1. By order of the German authorities all Jewish persons living in Warsaw, regardless of age or sex, are to be resettled in the East.
2. The following are exempt from resettlement:
   a. All Jewish persons employed by the German authorities or German government agencies, who can produce adequate proof of their employment;
   b. All Jewish persons who are members and employees of the Jewish Council (Judenrat) on the day this order is published;
   c. All Jewish persons employed by German firms, who can produce adequate proof of their employment;
   d. *All Jews capable of work* who so far have not been included in the work process; these are to be barracked in the Jewish living quarter; [italics mine]
   e. All Jewish persons belonging to the staff of Jewish hospitals or disinfection squads;
   f. All Jewish persons belonging to the Jewish police;
   g. All Jewish persons who belong to the immediate family of persons covered in a. through f. Only *wives and children* are considered members of the immediate family. [italics mine]
   h. All Jewish persons who on the first day of resettlement are bedridden in one of the Jewish hospitals and not qualified for discharge. Such inability to leave the hospital must be attested to by a doctor appointed by the Judenrat.

3. Each Jewish resettler may take 15 kilograms (33 pounds) of personal belongings as baggage. All baggage exceeding 15 kilograms will be confiscated. All valuables such as gold, jewelry, money, etc., may be taken along. Enough food for three days should be brought.
4. Resettlement begins on July 22, 1942, at 11 A.M.

It was announced, too, that all administrative authorities in the ghetto were now suspended and their powers assumed by a new resettlement agency.

The decree's final paragraph specified:

Failure to comply with the above decree will be punished by death. The Judenrat will be responsible for carrying out the above provisions and if they are not carried out to the letter, the hostages already under arrest will be shot. In carrying out its tasks, the Judenrat will choose a special committee whose head will be the Chairman of the Judenrat and his aide—the Commandant of the Jewish Police. Delivery of 6,000 Jews daily to assembly point at the Jewish Hospital in Stawki Street adjoining Umschlagplatz is mandatory. For this purpose the hospital must be vacated immediately. All Jews presently employed must remain at their jobs. The Judenrat is responsible for the prompt burial of Jews who die in the course of the Resettlement Operation. Burial must be done on the day death occurs.

That document had reached the Judenrat in the morning. SS *Sturmbannführer* (Major) Hermann Höfle appeared at the Judenrat offices with several high-ranking SS officers, declaring that he had been directed to initiate a resettlement operation by Odilo Globocnik, SS and police chief of the Lublin District. Globocnik was chief of resettlement for all German-occupied Poland and supervised all camps in Lublin province. The code name for this resettlement was "Operation Reinhard" in honor of former Security Police and SS Chief Reinhard Heydrich, the Nazi proconsul in Czechoslovakia who had just been assassinated by Czech patriots. Headquarters of the Resettlement Operation, the so-called *Befehlstelle* (command post), was at 101–103 Zelazna Street. In addition to Höfle, the officers in charge were *Hauptsturmführer* (Captain) Michalsen, *Sturmführer* (Second Lieutenant) Mundt and the special SS unit *Treblinka*. The headquarters staff also included members transferred from the Warsaw Gestapo and other commissioned and noncommissioned officers of the SS.

To carry out the operation, detachments of Ukrainians, Latvians, and

Lithuanians were brought in. The Jewish police also got a new chief, Jozef Szerynski, a convert to Christianity, whose name had been Szenkman. A virulent anti-Semite, Szerynski had been an inspector in the Polish police force before the war. After the ghetto was established, he was appointed commander of the Jewish police force. Subsequently, however, he was arrested by the Germans for complicity in the disappearance of a batch of the fur coats collected for the Wehrmacht on the Russian front, and his aide, Jakob Lejkin, took his place. At the inception of the Resettlement Operation, Szerynski was released from jail by the Germans and was to prove more zealous than ever in executing their orders, hoping thereby to regain some of his lost influence with the Nazis.

Once the posters were up, the strangely deserted streets were suddenly filled. Thousands gathered around them, studying them in silence, scrutinizing every word and letter. After the weeks of rumor and anxiety, the first feeling was relief. Whether this was the instinct of self-preservation, or the egotism of the strong, I don't know. One thing the posters made clear was that only those who were unable to work, who were a burden to society, were subject to resettlement. That was about 20 percent of the ghetto population. The remainder were evidently to be used in German businesses or military projects; that is, drafted for something much like forced labor. The intention of Operation Reinhard was painful and unmistakably cruel; it selected for resettlement those who were weakest and least able to look after themselves: the old, the sick, the crippled, the orphans. From the beginning of the war, however, resettlements and relocations of one sort or another had been everyday occurrences, so that no one thought that this one would be any different. True, Nazi brutality spoke in every line of the decree: there would be shootings, victimization of the weak, and beatings, but still everyone reassured himself, it *was* a resettlement.

Through their agents the Nazis did everything to maintain this illusion. Every few days the Judenrat was given official German reassurances on that score. The whole operation had been planned with military precision down to the last detail. There was, first, the element of surprise, to effect "psychological preparation" of the victims. The people were then divided against themselves in new ways and along new lines. New "privileged" groups were created. In fact, there seemed to be a logic in it: productive Jews would be put to work for the Germans, and the unproductive ones— well, weren't they the inevitable victims of war?

The first trainloads were to leave that day, July 22, and there were no difficulties in filling the quota. Prisoners from the Gesia Street prison and people from the refugee reception centers were loaded into horse-drawn carts and escorted by Jewish policemen to Umschlagplatz. At the beginning no Germans participated in the actual details of the Resettlement Operation.

Everyone in the ghetto frantically set about getting papers to prove employment. An *Ausweis* (work certificate) was a permit to live. As people rushed in search of them, streets were busier than usual. Instead of saying "Hello," or "How are you?" people now greeted each other with "Are you covered?" Unmarried girls were marrying members of the Jewish police with unusual haste and eagerness until scarcely a bachelor remained among them. German-owned and operated businesses were besieged.

In addition to the workshops already in existence, such as those of Toebbens or Schultz, a number of new German firms mushroomed in every branch of commerce. Some of these businesses were already in production when the decree appeared, but most were only in the planning stage. The *Befehlstelle* authorized each such business to employ a certain number of Jews, but the quotas were constantly fluctuating. Apartment houses adjacent to factories were vacated to provide living quarters for the factories' employees. Within a few days the face of the ghetto was transformed beyond recognition. Wooden fences were erected around each of the German factories and shops, thus splitting the ghetto into a number of isolated, fenced-off smaller ghettos. The Jewish managers of those workshops, in partnerships with the German owners, did a thriving business in selling work certificates to half-crazed Jews who had as yet found no employment. Often people used their last penny to buy an *Ausweis*. Firms were jammed with lines of applicants overflowing down stairways into the courtyards, weeping, swearing, screaming. Managers and their clerks worked until they dropped from weariness, taking money from the job applicants, answering questions, making out lists. The situation was a gold mine for every speculator and swindler. Not only were work certificates made up and sold to prove employment in nonexistent businesses, but bona fide work certificates were sold and resold several times over.

Within a few days everyone in the printing shops—owners and employees—received beautiful German work certificates made out by the office of the "trustee" for the industry. The approximately 300 people so affected exhibited their new documents proudly and for some time kept working happily. As with so many others in different fields, it seemed that so far as we were concerned the resettlement problem had been solved.

Lena, in her capacity as manager of a pharmacy, was in an even more secure position and she traveled to and from work daily without a qualm. Since our little Wlodek had two working parents, "obviously" he was also perfectly safe. Only our elderly Aunt Sarah and Wlodek's governess had as yet no "legal" basis for remaining in Warsaw. We hid them as long as we could, but they eventually perished anyway.

It rained all day July 23, Tisha b'Av, but the operation continued according to plan. Jewish policemen reinforced by Judenrat officials wearing white armbands—the so-called soul-snatchers—continued their work of the preceding day, methodically emptying the refugee reception centers and the "death houses," buildings where there had been a very high mortality rate from hunger and typhus.

On this second day of Operation Reinhard the first of many blood-chilling roundups of street waifs began. These orphans resisted vigorously, biting and kicking ghetto policemen, screaming at the top of their lungs when caught and carried away, but the well-fed police were bigger and stronger. In tribute to the homeless children of Warsaw it must be said that they were the first to *resist,* to put up a fight against the Jewish agents of the Nazis.

That second day, the large orphanage at 3 Dzika Street and the center for homeless children at 6 Gesia Street were evacuated. My kerchief-printing plant was located in the same building and the spectacle of Jewish police loading the children into wagons to be deported was enough to make the paving stones cry out.

Early on the morning of July 24, we heard the incredible news that Adam Czerniakow, Obmann of the Judenrat, had committed suicide. At 9:30 the previous night some Gestapo officers had called on him and shortly thereafter he took cyanide. On his desk lay a slip of paper containing only three words: "Till the last . . ." Although the Judenrat was unpopular, Czerniakow had always been liked personally and respected as an honest man. His suicide shattered us. No one knew what his conversation with the Gestapo men had been about, and Czerniakow went to his grave with his secret. Had it been a demand to step up deportations to 10,000 a day? Had he learned the terrible truth about what the Resettlement Operation was? Was he so outraged by what had already occurred that he wished his death to serve as a protest? Or, having already delivered up the most defenseless people in the community for which he was responsible, did he choose death rather than sanction any further murder of his people? Whatever his motives or intention, his death did not help us. We felt it was desertion, not leadership. Czerniakow failed to sound the alarm and summon his people to resistance. If he had been given a glimpse of the bottomless abyss to which we were consigned, he did not pass his knowledge on to us. His suicide only intensified our despair and our panic. If it bore witness to his personal integrity, it did not attest to his greatness.

Marek Lichtenbaum was appointed to replace Czerniakow. An engineer by profession, he and his sons had made a fortune constructing the ghetto walls. His reputation was that of a coarse, brutal man. Actual power was now in the hands of the Jewish ghetto police who roamed the streets like wild beasts, seizing men, women, and children with increasing brutality.

The day after Czerniakow's suicide a group of SS officers called on the Judenrat to express their condolences and to give their word as officers that resettled Jews were in fact being resettled and not being mistreated in any way. That same day, July 24, the Judenrat announced that "the rumors circulating in the ghetto about the Resettlement Operation" were false. Simultaneously, Gestapo agents spread a report—"based on reliable sources"—that only the poorest, least productive elements of the population would be resettled, that the entire operation would continue for no more than a few days, and certainly would be over by July 31. Letters supposedly written by people already deported were circulated; they were said to have been brought back by Polish policemen and railway workers who had accompanied the resettlement trains and reported that those resettled were doing well.

The following two days, a Saturday and Sunday, brought no letup. If anything, the operation gained momentum and the noose was drawn tighter around our necks. There was no time to think calmly and plan some kind of escape. The ghetto was increasingly disorganized: stores closed down, bakeries stopped baking, smuggling ceased, and food became unobtainable. Famine stalked the city.

The roundup procedure began with cordoning off an apartment house. Ghetto police blocked all exits, and then fifteen or twenty of them, with an officer in charge, ordered all occupants into the courtyard. Here papers were checked; those who failed to pass muster were immediately loaded into a wagon. While this was going on, other policemen went through every apartment to make certain no one was hiding. At first, persons hiding had been able to escape when discovered by paying a small bribe, but the police were growing more brutal and callous.

Eventually whole streets were sealed off at one time and everyone on the street had to have his papers checked. In the early stages of the deportations every valid *Ausweis* was scrupulously respected; this was another German ruse to give Jews false confidence in documents, an illusion which led thousands to their deaths.

In our apartment house, roundups were under the command of my former lawyer, Henryk Lande, now a captain of the ghetto police. On one roundup when I was stopped and produced my documents for him, Lande looked it over and said softly, "If I were you, I wouldn't feel so sure that this is enough. I'd get something better." I then learned that almost from the beginning there had been a special *Ausweis,* stamped *Einsatz Reinhard,* which bore the Nazi eagle and a swastika with the inscription, "Not subject to resettlement." At that stage such an *Ausweis* was a guarantee of security.

I saw a young mother run downstairs into the street to get milk for her baby. Her husband, who worked at the *Ostbahn,* had as usual left earlier that morning. She had not bothered to dress, but was in bathrobe and slippers. An empty milk bottle in hand she was headed for a shop where, she knew, they sold milk under the counter. She walked into Operation Reinhard. The executioners demanded her *Ausweis.* "Upstairs . . . Ostbahn . . . work certificate. I'll bring it right away."

"We've heard that one before. Have you got an *Ausweis* with you, or haven't you?"

She was dragged protesting to the wagon, scarcely able to realize what was happening. "But my baby is all alone. Milk . . ." she protested. "My *Ausweis* is upstairs." Then, for the first time, she really looked at the men who were holding her and she saw where she was being dragged: to the gaping entrance at the back of a high-boarded wagon with victims already jammed into it. With all her young mother's strength she wrenched herself free, and then two, and four policemen fell on her, hitting her, smashing her to the ground, picking her up again, and tossing her into the wagon like a sack. I can still hear her screaming in a half-crazed voice somewhere between a sob of utter human despair and the howl of an animal.

Another young woman I knew after much trouble finally persuaded a friend of her husband's, a man who managed a shop, to register her with his firm so that she could have an *Ausweis.* "I'm doing it for you because you're Leon's wife," the man told her, but it cost her every penny of what remained of the possessions she and her husband had owned when he had left in September 1939. "You know I'm not taking this for myself. You understand, don't you? It's because of the others. . . ." Then he explained to her how the very next day she must move to the shop area and bring her eight-year-old boy with her. There she would be safe. She needn't worry about having no money or about leaving her apartment; she must bring only the absolute necessities with her, no more than the apartment house janitor's wheelbarrow could carry in one trip; but everything would be all right.

And, indeed, she was reassured. Calmly she went about doing what she had to do, fighting for the life of her child. Her husband, she knew, would be proud of how well she had managed. Holding her little boy's hand, she told him, "Now, you mustn't be afraid. Mother is looking out for you." As she was turning the corner into the street where they lived, the little boy ran ahead as children do. He skipped around the corner before she got to it. Why had she let him do it? How could she have let her sense of danger relax even for an instant? The street seemed so calm. When she heard him scream, "Mama! Mama!" she sped around the corner and had just time enough to see a little body with a familiar striped sweater disappearing among the mass of other bodies in the wagon surrounded by police. She thanked God that she was in time to explain, that she had an *Ausweis*.

"But, Madam," the police said, "how can we be sure that this is *your* child?"

She had not, it seems, quite understood. No more than any of us did at first. And when she finally did understand, she was beaten brutally "for resisting the authorities," but not a sound, not a sob, escaped her. The policemen showed that they were not, after all, completely heartless. By surrendering her *Ausweis* to them—a commodity more valuable than gold at that point—she was permitted to get into the wagon, too, to accompany her son to Umschlagplatz and what lay beyond.

As the wagon began to move away, anyone within earshot could hear the voice of an old woman coming from beyond the boards of the van, repeating monotonously, "Tell Zalme Katz his mother was taken away. . . . Tell Zalme Katz his mother was taken away. . . . Tell Zalme Katz . . ." And those who listened very carefully could also hear among the other sounds coming from the van the voice of an eight-year-old boy in a striped sweater crying, "O Daddy, why did you go away and leave us?"

All the wagons went to Umschlagplatz near Stawki Street. Those selected for resettlement waited in the hospital in indescribable crowding and confusion. After a sufficient number of victims had been rounded up, usually by four or five in the afternoon, the hospital was emptied and the cattle cars filled. Gun butts and clubs drove the people into the square where two SS officers made the "final selection." The overwhelming majority, some with bundles over their shoulders and leading children by the hand, passed through the gate into the railhead proper and were then jammed into the railroad cars (capacity: 40 men or 8 horses) more than 100 people to a car; then the doors were shut and bolted from the outside.

Most able-bodied males were "rejected" by the SS officers and sent to the *Dulag* (transit camp) in Leszno Street where, if shop managers or supervisors intervened on their behalf, they were released. The very old and crippled were "rejected" too, but in another way; they were part of the German category of *Transportunfähig*, "unfit for transport," and were taken to the cemetery and shot. The entire procedure was run in a manner intended to reinforce the impression that the Resettlement Operation was genuine.

Because loading usually didn't begin before late afternoon, efforts were made to obtain the release of persons who had been rounded up during the day. Intervention by shop managers or the Judenrat officially, or unofficially by bribing Jewish policemen, were the methods, and a well-organized network of corruption quickly grew up involving the Jewish police, Ukrainian and German guards. It was an enormously profitable business and one of the low points of ghetto depravity, yet some individuals rounded up and taken to Umschlagplatz were thus able to obtain their release as many as three or four times.

Many individuals carrying large amounts of money made no effort to buy their release when caught in the roundups. They firmly believed in the resettlement myth and felt they would need the money where they were going. I knew one man who had a contact with the police. Although penniless himself, he arranged to be released with his brother-in-law who had also been picked up and who was rich enough to pay for both of them. But the brother-in-law refused. "At a time like this," he said, "you don't spend your money on other people. I might need this money soon to save my own life." Later, I learned from a few men who managed to escape from the cattle cars, all of which went directly to Treblinka, that just before making their escape those without money were refused small sums by men who had money, but who themselves had no intention of attempting to escape.

Much later, when I was in the concentration camp at Majdanek, Dr. Isaac Schipper, the historian, told me that at the beginning of Operation Reinhard a number of Jewish social and political leaders met secretly in order to discuss resistance, but the majority voted against active resistance in any form on the grounds that the operation would be concluded by July

31, and that resistance would merely give the Nazis a pretext for bloody reprisals.

Though the operation had been under way for a week, it did not stop; instead, it took on ever greater proportions. On my way home from work one day, I stopped at 24 Leszno Street to give Rachman my daily report. One of Biederman's lithographers rushed in, frantic. The Germans were conducting a terrible roundup in Gesia Street. All escape routes had been blocked off, everyone found in the street was being lined up and marched off to Umschlagplatz whether or not he had an *Ausweis*. Because it was the time of day when people left work, the street had been very crowded and the roundup enormous. Up to that point roundups had taken place earlier in the day, the early morning and late afternoon hours being relatively safe. This was the first late-afternoon roundup and also the first operation *in which Ukrainian guards and German troops took part personally*. The Germans tore up work certificates and clubbed their owners with rifle butts and riding crops. Quickly the roundup became a street massacre. The screams of the wounded and the moans of the dying could be heard for blocks, and after the column of thousands was marched off to Umschlagplatz, Gesia Street looked like a battlefield, bodies everywhere—dead, dying, wounded—lying in puddles of blood.

The next Sunday another bloody roundup took place, Ukrainians and Germans again participating. With the gunfire we heard shouts that we were to keep on hearing and remembering for a long time to come: *"Alles runter! Alle Juden runter!"* "Everything downstairs! All Jews downstairs!" The tone was bad enough, but the humiliating impersonality of that "Everything downstairs!" where normal speech called for "Everyone" was even more shocking.

The roundups taught us that our work certificates were a very precarious form of security after all. A number of printers and lithographers who had such documents, including the Biedermans, had been caught and "resettled." After long deliberation we decided that, all things considered, the "shops" offered the greatest security. The German businesses were still expanding. Toebbens, for example, had taken over chemical, electrical, metallurgical, and woodworking factories, as well as bakeries, pharmacies, barbershops, and medical clinics, all part of a systematic looting of Jewish business. The most likely shop seemed to be the *Allgemeine Handelsgesellschaft Zimmermann*, colloquially known as the AHAGE, a Berlin firm which manufactured paper products. Before the Resettlement Operation, Dawid Krynski, a close friend of mine, had had frequent business

dealings with the AHAGE and he was now put in charge of its hastily organized new ghetto branch. AHAGE was a logical place for printers and
lithographers, and Krynski and Fenigstein, the two managers, agreed to
accept a limited number of printers for a fixed sum per person, presumably to be paid to the Polish managers outside of the ghetto branch. Fortunately, I was one of the limited number accepted.

The food situation had grown worse as a result of the increased tempo
of violence, large-scale roundups, and the reorganization of the ghetto on
a "shop basis." Food prices soared. Bakers and shopkeepers, unprotected
by working papers, went into hiding. Smuggling was only sporadic, so that
hunger gripped the ghetto, and the Nazis were quick to exploit it. On July
29, 1942, a public announcement signed by ghetto police chief Lejkin said
that all who volunteered for resettlement would be given three kilos of
bread and a kilo of jam. The promise was later repeated with the added
incentive that entire families who volunteered would not be separated. For
days there was a bitter spectacle in the ghetto streets. Thousands of Jews,
in families and sometimes larger groups, marched toward Umschlagplatz
of their own free will, having sold their lives for three kilos of bread and
one kilo of jam. Children from families whose parents already had been
"resettled," and parents who had lost their children the same way, came
forward voluntarily in the hope of joining their families. Some days there
were so many volunteers that people had to be turned away to wait for the
next day's shipment.

Despite the volunteers, forced roundups continued unabated and a
pattern began to emerge as the Great Pogrom rolled on. Roundups began at eight in the morning and stopped at around six, after a morning
and afternoon manhunt. Operations were directed by SS officers from the
Vernichtungskommando who controlled several hundred Ukrainians, Latvians,
and Lithuanians, as well as hundreds of ghetto policemen. The procedure
had been modified by now and made more ruthless. A house or street was
surrounded. The deafening *"Alles runter! Alle Juden runter!"* resounded,
echoed by the Jewish police's "Everything comes down!" in Polish. Doors
were smashed in by boots or gun butts, and apartments searched. Anyone
found hiding was killed on the spot—old, sick, or crippled included. Everything of value was stolen. Pillows and feather beds were slashed with bayonets in search of "hidden Jewish wealth." When the raiders had finished,
it looked as if an earthquake had struck.

After several thousand people had been rounded up in the cordoned-
off streets, they were marched under guard to Umschlagplatz. The horse-

drawn wagons used in the early stages were soon abandoned and the victims driven on foot. For the slightest wavering in the ranks, the faintest suggestion of an effort to escape, shots rang out, and the route to Umschlagplatz was consequently lined with corpses. Some hundred people a day lost their lives that way. Sometimes there was no pause at Umschlagplatz and the victims were loaded directly onto the cattle cars. No more document checking, no more *Ausweis* inspection: those who were not actually inside a shop, in the new ghetto meaning of "shop," were doomed.

We made up our minds to spend nights from then on in the AHAGE area on Mila Street. We were assigned part of one room there, temporarily, and moved into it with only the absolute necessities. Nobody was left in our old Orla Street apartment, though occasionally I dropped in to see how things were going. My days were spent inside the printing shop at 24 Leszno Street, while Lena and Wlodek spent theirs at the pharmacy, which was only a block away from the AHAGE, and still considered a safe place. But Lena's life was complicated by having Wlodek constantly with her, and the responsibility began to prove too much for her. The pharmacy was on the corner of Zamenhof and Wolynska Streets, where all the traffic to Umschlagplatz had to pass. Through the windows, day after day, Lena witnessed the tragic procession of the doomed, the endless line of young and old, weak and strong, with and without bundles, with extinguished eyes and faces setting out on their journey to an unknown destination almost certain to bring them further suffering. The shouts of the SS men, the noise of gunfire, the thud of clubs on human flesh, the groans of the wounded and beaten, and the last *Sh'ma Yisroel* (Hear, O Israel) of the dying punctuated the monotonous shuffling of weary feet on the pavement. To be forced to watch and listen to this day after day was enough to drive anyone out of her mind. The sight of children, who accounted for a large percentage of each "shipment to the East," was especially unnerving. Alone, or with their mothers, or in groups shepherded by teachers, they were ragged and unhappy, in short pants and skirts, barefoot or in sandals, most without knapsacks, food, or water, and with shaven heads.

Ukrainian guards, often very drunk, kept dropping into the pharmacy to ask for alcohol or some remedy or other. Wlodek was kept in a small room that served as an office, and it was sternly impressed on him that he must never come out into the store. When things looked especially dangerous, he was locked in a medicine cabinet. It was impossible for the child not to be affected by the nervousness around him. He was only four and a half and had been accustomed to constant care and attention; this new life frightened and bored him. He kept running out into the store, tormenting his mother with constant questions and requests. Lena's already frayed nerves had the added strain of not having a moment away from Wlodek. More and more often she spent the night at the pharmacy with him because it seemed the safest thing to do.

One day a Jewish policeman noticed Wlodek and asked whose child he was.

"Mine," Lena replied.

"Hide him in the closet!" the policeman yelled in an unnatural voice. "Haven't you got any brains? Put him in a closet!"

It was an easy thing to say, but how could a small, restless child be kept in a closet all day?

One morning, Lena's cousin, Izak Rubin, rushed into the pharmacy. Earlier in the day he had been caught in a roundup and was on his way to Umschlagplatz. He had cast imploring glances at the pharmacy, hoping that Lena would notice him among the marchers. Even if she could do nothing, he would have liked a farewell look, a wave of the hand. Near Muranowska Street, just two blocks from Umschlagplatz, he had been spotted among the victims by my brother-in-law, Mietek Haus, a policeman, who was on duty there at the time. Instantly, Mietek fell upon Izak and began to beat him with his rubber truncheon and kick him, at the same time carefully edging him toward the sidewalk. When the surprised escort asked what the matter was, Mietek pretended to be furiously angry and explained that this insolent fellow, Izak, had been trying to sneak into the ranks to join his wife. The Ukrainian guard smashed his rifle butt down on Izak, but Mietek had saved his life by that ruse. Unfortunately there were all too few such cases.

The Great Pogrom continued and more people were thrown to the Moloch. Until then policemen's parents had been exempt from resettlement and many a Jewish policeman had justified his ruthlessness toward other Jews by maintaining that he was, at least, protecting his own family. Now, however, even policemen's parents were to be deported. I knew policemen who gave their mothers overdoses of luminal or potassium cyanide rather than let them be deported. Others, weeping bitter tears, loaded their mothers onto the cattle cars themselves, then turned back to their task of fulfilling their daily quota of "five heads."

There was talk of policemen who committed suicide, and of some who "handed in their caps"—that is, resigned—but every man had to fulfill his daily quota of five victims, for failure meant death to those nearest and dearest to him. Those Jewish police who tried to avoid participating actively in the roundups were coerced; their colleagues saw that no one kept his hands clean. "What are you," they asked, "a virgin or something?" Policemen even beat up some of their more sensitive coworkers to emphasize the point. Those police whose parents were "resettled" grew more brutal and barbaric. "If *my* mother had to go, do you think I'm going to spare you?" was their refrain.

But it was the deportation of Janusz Korczak and the children in his care which made an enormous impression on the ghetto and was a clear indication of the purpose and brutality of the resettlement program. Korczak was an unusual man. Not just an ordinary educator or writer, he had always been a symbol. Trained as a physician, he had devoted his entire life to children, and had been given the title "Father of Orphaned Children." He had replaced the humiliating name of *orphanage* with the more dignified "Child's Home."

It was Wednesday, August 5, 1942, when the Nazis came for the children in Korczak's charge. It was not clear whether Korczak told the children what they might expect or exactly where they were going, but his staff of teachers and nurses had the two hundred orphans ready for the Nazis when they raided the orphanage at 16 Sienna Street. The children had been bathed, given clean clothing, and provided with bread and water to take with them. The Nazis burst in, but the children, though frightened, did not cry out or run and hide. They clung to Korczak who stood between them and the Germans.

Bareheaded, he led the way, holding a child by each hand. Behind him were the rest of the two hundred children and a group of nurses clad in white aprons. They were surrounded by German and Ukrainian guards, and the ghetto police. One could see how weak and undernourished the children were. But they marched to their deaths in exemplary order, without a single tear, in such a terrifying silence that it thundered with indictment and defiance.

When the Judenrat heard of what was happening in the orphanage, everyone there tried desperately to telephone, to do something, but they tried only to save Janusz Korczak, not the two hundred children. Korczak was told of their efforts in his behalf, but refused aid; instead, he chose to go with the children to Umschlagplatz.

Other orphanages besides Korczak's, some of them larger, were liquidated by the Nazis in the very same manner, and there were many other nurses and teachers who refused to leave their charges but heroically went with them to their deaths. Korczak became a model of heroism and humanity in the night of barbarism.

Long before the time of murder, Korczak had written, "There is no greater mishap than to be born a man." He died, as he had lived, simply and with dignity. "Oh, how difficult is life, how easy death!" he wrote in his ghetto diary, and in his death he became a monument to the 100,000 murdered Jewish children of Warsaw.

Their deaths also gave the ghetto its first insight into the true significance of "resettlement." Why had the Judenrat tried to save Korczak? If the two hundred children were really going to be resettled somewhere in the East, wasn't it perfectly natural for their teacher and shepherd to go along with them? What we had suspected all along—but could not or did not want to believe—was now confirmed. What we had dismissed as the hysterical outpourings of morbid imaginations was now reality. This was not resettlement; this was deportation to death. Moreover, the Judenrat knew, the heads of the Jewish police knew, and they had not told us.

Hardly had the footsteps of the victims on their way to Umschlagplatz stopped echoing in the streets where they had lived, when the looting began. First, there was the "official" looting by the Germans. While the roundups were still in progress, an organization called the *Werterfassung* (literally the Seizure of Assets organization, but more formally the Property Control Office) was set up, its purpose the confiscation, sale, and utilization of the various properties left behind by the resettled. Its headquarters were at 20 Niska Street and it was commanded by Hauptsturmführer Geipel. Geipel made up work parties of roundup victims to do the heavy work, each party led by an SS man, assisted by several ghetto policemen.

These work parties systematically went through apartments, stores, and workshops, moving furniture, clothing, machines, and raw materials to SS warehouses. The employees of the *Werterfassung*, of course, did their own private looting, often in cahoots with the SS men. In addition to these official looters, there were neighbors of those whose apartments had been left vacant, janitors of apartment houses, individuals moving to new living quarters inside the "shop areas," all of whom took part in the wholesale pillage. Why, they rationalized, should the Germans get all the property? Gentile Poles were also among the looters, and last, but not least, was the looting done by the employees of the ghetto undertaker, Pinkiert, who robbed the corpses of the slain. Since more than 10,000 people were killed or died in the ghetto during the Resettlement Operation, the undertakers' haul was considerable.

In ghetto slang this looting was at first called *fasunek* (more or less equivalent to the German *organisieren*). Later the word *szaber* became popular, the term deriving from a popular and colloquial word in the vocabulary of locksmiths meaning "to smooth or polish." Women's apparel obtained in this fashion was described as "manufactured by Maison Chabrée," and textile products were known as *ciuchy*, from a Jewish word, *tsikhen*, meaning pillowcases.

Roundup followed roundup without respite, the daily quota having risen from 6,000 to 10,000 "heads" a day. As the roundups continued and mounted in frenzy, more and more people who had escaped from the trains en route to Treblinka, or even from the death camp itself, came back to the ghetto. From them we heard terrible stories about the victims of the resettlement program.

Treblinka was on a railroad spur off the regular line to Malkinia and the trip from Umschlagplatz took about four hours. Nearly every cattle car had a dozen human dead by the time the trains arrived at Treblinka, where they were met by SS men and unloaded with fantastic brutality. Those still able to stand were driven into a large square, ordered to strip, and leave all their things on the ground. The purpose, they were told, was for all of them to have a shower. The naked people were then lined up in columns, and sadistically driven to a barracks-type building on which a sign read: "Showers." Screams, shooting, and blows created an atmosphere of panic, so that the victims would call out to one another, "Come on! Hurry up! Or a tragedy may happen!"

The crowd would literally race into the building to "prevent a tragedy," and once they were inside, guards sealed the doors hermetically. A quarter of an hour later all the people inside were dead of poison gas. A special Jewish team, working on the double, with its own reasons for panic—equally to "prevent a tragedy" to themselves—dug large pits and buried the bodies in them. Every few days the teams of gravediggers were themselves gassed and replaced.

Clothing and personal possessions were loaded onto freight cars for shipment to SS warehouses; the few who had escaped and brought us the news had secreted themselves in those freight cars. And yet even those eyewitness reports were hard for us to believe. Surely the Germans, even the Nazis, were not capable of such utter inhumanity?

True or false, the machine was much stronger than we were. We were atomized, blown to bits, scattered to the winds, helpless beyond hope. Some of our own people were helping our mortal enemies to exterminate us. All we could do was find a hole and cower in it, keep as quiet as mice, and wait. Maybe, somehow, on an individual basis, survival was still just barely possible.

Then a new blow fell. Between August 10 and 15, 1942, four German decrees were published in what was termed an "internal resettlement," ordering the ghetto reduced in size. By 6 P.M. on August 10 the entire so-called Little Ghetto, the streets south of Chlodna, were to be evacuated. Anyone found there afterward would be shot on sight. Tens of thousands of people had one day to move to the Big Ghetto where few buildings remained which had not already been assigned to workshops. The move was carried out under what might well be called enemy fire because roundups were going on in the streets at the same time. Consequently, the great majority left everything behind and came to the Big Ghetto with no more than they could carry on their backs.

A few days later all streets south of Leszno had to be similarly evacuated. Our apartment on Orla Street was affected and I spent the night there hurriedly packing our most important things. At 6 A.M. on August 15, I pushed a handcart to the AHAGE on Mila Street, but since we had not yet been assigned permanent quarters there, I had to leave everything in the courtyard. On August 20 the boundaries of the ghetto were still further reduced to run along Franciszkanska and Gesia Streets. Some families had to move three times in ten days and all while resettlement manhunters were scourging the streets. My family and I were not only penniless now, but homeless. How satanic this particular German move was can be appreciated only by those who experienced its effects. When a man—particularly a city dweller—loses his home, he loses his roots, the ground under his feet, the base for resistance.

Whenever I tried to induce the AHAGE to assign a definite apartment to me, or pushed them on the question of when we were going into active production, I saw how extremely disorganized the outfit was. Although its Polish managers displayed much bustle and zeal, AHAGE was curiously inert. Something was very wrong there. When I confided my feelings to Rachman, he agreed and suggested that there might be a chance to incorporate our printing shop into the *Werterfassung* organization, which would make us an "SS printing plant" and give us a better chance of survival than staying with AHAGE. Rachman immediately drew up a list of thirty-eight printers and went to negotiate the transfer; next day the list was accepted, and the printing plant taken over by the SS *Werterfassung*. We were assigned the task of processing raw materials found in the ghetto to fulfill military and civilian demands; in addition we were to set up a bindery and manufacture stationery products. However, we were careful not to burn all our bridges to AHAGE.

The lithography shop at 6 Gesia Street was also taken over by the *Werterfassung* for processing the enormous quantities of bed linen abandoned in the ghetto and making kerchiefs to be sold in Polish villages. A few days later Geipel came to the Gesia Street plant early one morning and ordered us to be in full production by noon that day. When I pointed out that we had no raw materials, that they still had to be collected, laundered and dyed, all of which would take time and trained workers, he merely glanced at his wristwatch and repeated, *"Bis zwölf."*

I rushed to Leszno Street to tell Rachman what had happened, but in the meantime Nowolipki and Dzielna Streets were cordoned off and there was no way to return to Gesia Street until 4 P.M. When I finally did get back, the doors of the lithography shop were sealed with the inscription: *Sichergestellt* (Secured) *SS Werterfassung.* Workmen began to emerge from their hiding places to tell me that Geipel had come at noon and closed the place up. Three workmen who had come forward when Geipel arrived had been sent to Umschlagplatz, and the rest had hidden in the basement. Of the three taken, two had escaped en route and the third was sent to the Dulag.

When the SS took over the printshop, I gained some security personally, but new problems were created as well. At this stage, only people actively employed in workshops legally endorsed by the SS had a chance to escape deportation. Those so employed lived in quarters adjacent to their workplace. Such combined working-and-living quarters were surrounded by high fences, either of wood or barbed wire, and each such compound was guarded by its own group of German civilians and ghetto police, who kept out strangers and prevented workers from leaving.

Nights when I stayed in the printing plant at 24 Leszno Street, I was comparatively safe. It was a large building from which all former tenants had been evacuated; our plant was on the ground floor with its entrance on one of the two apartment house courtyards. The building served to house not only the legally employed workmen, but also their families, many of whom spent the nights there because it seemed safer. A small shop belonging to Ulrich Wentland was also in the building, but fronted on the street.

Anyone who lived in a shop area had to stay inside it. If he was caught either in the street or in a so-called wild house, he was fair game. He could be beaten, robbed, rounded up for resettlement, or simply murdered. Outside the shop area one was on one's own: papers, passes, and work certificates were no longer of the slightest use, and no excuses were accepted. The most dangerous times to be out were during the day between 8 A.M. and 5 P.M., and the most dangerous places were the recently evacuated ghetto areas, out of bounds to Jews on pain of death. One such no-man's-land separated the Leszno Street printing plant (now outside the reduced ghetto) from the ghetto proper, which began on Gesia Street. Thus, all day long, I was cut off from my wife and son, who spent their days in the area north of Gesia Street. During the early morning hours, before roundups began, and in the late evening, after they were over, groups of workers moved back and forth across no-man's-land, but it could cost one one's life to attempt it during the day while the Nazi murderers roamed the streets.

With the Great Pogrom in high gear, I lived in perpetual dread. Every morning when I said good-by to my wife and child at the AHAGE and set out for the printing plant, I was consumed with anxiety about what might happen to them during the day while I was away. Whenever news came of a roundup on Zamenhof, Wolynska, or Mila Streets, I was struck with terror. Nor was I the only one. Everyone queued up at the telephones and often it was hours before I could get through to the pharmacy. Sometimes I grew so frantic with worry that I ran into the street in broad daylight and headed for the pharmacy, wildly, imprudently rushing into the jaws of death, putting myself at the mercy of those very forces from which I wanted to protect my family.

Izak Rubin, with whom I became very close in those days, courageously accompanied me on these expeditions. Tall, broad-shouldered, fair-haired and blue-eyed, he was the very image of the Aryan. We walked at a brisk military clip, making no effort to keep our heels from resounding on the pavement. We never looked back, but went straight ahead with that air Germans like to call *dienstlich,* as if we were men on a serious mission. We never stopped or glanced at any Germans we met, but simply accentuated our military bearing. Never in my whole life have I been so devoured by fear as on those trips through the barren streets of the ghetto, echoing with the shots and cries of a resettlement roundup on some nearby street.

Only once during those trips did we come face to face with a German. He beckoned and we marched up to him, stood at attention, and barked: "Workers of the SS *Druckerei* reporting obediently. Directed to go to the storehouse in Niska Street to pick up paper." Whether it was Izak's physical appearance, the insolence of our manner, or the uniqueness of our announcement, he let us go. We often went by places the Great Pogrom had just passed. Sometimes, only half a block ahead, we could see the tail end of a column being driven to Umschlagplatz, and we would slow down until it had passed the pharmacy.

The noose grew still tighter. Pharmacies were being closed and their personnel sent to Umschlagplatz for deportation, though some, which happened to fall within new shop areas, were occasionally absorbed by those shops and so survived. It was some small comfort to note that only pharmacies outside the truncated ghetto had so far been sealed up, and Lena's pharmacy was squarely in the middle of the ghetto. We told ourselves that surely the Germans would leave one pharmacy untouched to serve the remaining Jewish population.

Increasing numbers of workshops were being affected by the resettlement, too. The *Befehlstelle* subjected their licenses to constant revisions, concessions were suddenly withdrawn, and then a shop would be liquidated, its employees sent to Umschlagplatz. As the roundups came closer to the shop areas, hideous scenes drew nearer as well. Ulrich Wentland's shop, in the same building as our printing plant, was one of those whose concession was canceled. The SS men appeared one morning, lined up all the employees in the courtyard—Wentland himself, of course, was not present—and marched them off to Umschlagplatz. There were also roundups at the AHAGE. We deluded ourselves that for the time being our plant would be left alone. One morning, however, Geipel appeared with his orderly, lined all of us up in the courtyard, and picked out an old Jew with beard and caftan. Without thinking, the old man began to run, and Geipel gave an almost imperceptible flick of his riding crop, and said to his orderly, "Hans . . ." He did not use the usual vulgar terms such as *umlegen* (lay him out) or *kaltmachen* (literally make him cold, or make a corpse of him); he just said "Hans"—and the orderly knew what he meant. Quickly Hans lowered his submachine gun and fired, but the old man, no fool, was running in zigzags. Still, one of the bullets had found its mark; there was a trail of blood, though the old man had escaped death . . . for the moment.

One afternoon, making my way to Zamenhof Street, holding my breath, I came to the doors of Lena's pharmacy and found them closed, and the windows shuttered. A curt notice on the door spoke louder than the Book of Job: *Sichergestellt. SS Werterfassung.* The light of the sun had gone out; my wife and son had been in that pharmacy. Like a madman I raced for the AHAGE in Mila Street, but no one there knew anything; no one had seen anything. When I finally found my sister, Roza, she told me she had seen Lena and Wlodek being led through the street to Umschlag-platz. Her husband, Mietek the policeman, had been keeping an eye on them. Immediately, I got in touch with Fein, a policeman I knew to be one of the most adroit wirepullers at Umschlagplatz and a close relative of one of the other pharmacy employees who had also been caught in the roundup. Fein went to Umschlagplatz and I waited for him in the Krynskis' apartment at 41 Mila Street where we sometimes spent the night.

The next two hours were the longest of my life. While I waited for Fein's return, Izak bombarded me with questions I was in no condition to answer. As the hands of the clock moved inexorably toward 4 P.M., when the cattle-car loadings began, my anxiety and terror skyrocketed. I alter-nated wildly, hysterically, between despair and belief in miracles. When the clock struck four, I was drenched with cold sweat and around me the desk and floor were littered with cigarette stubs. Then the door opened and Fein came in holding one of Wlodek's hands while the child clutched a loaf of bread in the other. Wlodek was unaccountably talkative, bright, with an almost springtime radiance.

Fein told me what had happened. Geipel had come into the phar-macy about 1 P.M. and ordered the entire staff to line up in the courtyard. He had their Arbeitskarten taken away from them, then summoned ghetto policemen to take all seven of them to Umschlagplatz, where they were to be "kept at his own personal disposition." He wrote down the number of the policeman in charge and warned that he would hold him responsible for the whole group. Then Geipel took all their papers. He kept asking Lena whether Wlodek was her child and where her husband worked, and she had the impression that he was somehow sympathetic. He seemed to be trying to save her, but she was afraid to tell him the truth, so she gave vague replies instead, saying that her husband worked for the Judenrat.

All seven were held in a room guarded by two policemen. It was the first such case the policemen had encountered and they were scared stiff. Fein was unable to do anything with them because they were afraid that at any moment Geipel would return and ask for the pharmacy staff they were supposed to be "holding for his personal disposition." Fein had man-aged to get Wlodek out only by pretending that the boy was his son—and, of course, bribing a guard. At the last instant, Wlodek refused to leave, in-sisting that no one left Umschlagplatz without a loaf of bread. Fearing that "his sentry" would be relieved at any moment, Fein ran out to get a loaf of bread and returned, and only then did Wlodek agree to go with him. Where Wlodek had picked up the notion, I do not know. Perhaps he had seen a shift of nurses leaving Umschlagplatz hospital, each of them carrying her daily bread ration.

Fein also brought a farewell letter from Lena which read:

My dear:
    Now that our child has escaped, I am
completely calm and ready for anything. Roza
loves him and will be a good mother to him.
Thank you for everything. Remember me.
I love you.

Lena

That day, for once, no shipment was made up because the executioners had gone to the nearby town of Otwock to wreak their havoc there. At sundown, two women employees of the pharmacy, Halina Jankelewicz and Pola Z., both natives of Lodz, escaped. They had managed to get out of the room in which they were held by asking to go to the toilet when they saw the hospital workers of Umschlagplatz assembling for departure.

Dressed in white like the medical staff, they had walked right out of Umschlagplatz, holding up pink Arbeitskarten at the checkpoint—they had given Geipel false papers and kept their own. Their escape was not discovered until the guards were relieved, and the reaction at ghetto police headquarters was a paroxysm of fury. Strict orders were issued to find the two women and the child "at all costs," and next morning two thousand police set out on the manhunt.

I was in the Krynskis' flat with Wlodek when the door opened and a Jewish policeman, almost albino in coloring and with bulging eyes, came in. At once he went for Wlodek, who was standing there clutching my trousers. "I've come for the child. My orders are to take him back to Umschlagplatz."

I was flabbergasted. How had he found us? "How did you happen to come here?" I asked.

The policeman laughed smugly. "I got your address from Izak Rubin by telling him that I had a letter from your wife."

I made an enormous effort at self-control and said, "Well, my bad luck. I guess it's your lucky day. How much do you want?"

"I'm not taking anything. You don't understand the situation. The big shots are foaming at the mouth. The whole force is on emergency duty. We have to get back those who escaped."

"How can you ask a father to hand over his own child? Aren't you human?"

"What makes you think I'm human? Maybe I'm a wild beast. I have a wife and three children. If I don't deliver my five heads by 5 P.M., they'll take my children. Don't you see, I'm fighting for the life of my own kids, so don't give me that human being stuff. Hand over the kid or I'll call for reinforcements and we'll take both of you . . . for resisting the authorities, you know."

"You'll call nobody," I said, "and you won't get out of here alive either." I grabbed a chair and started for him. I wanted to squash him like a bug, like a snake. He dodged and began to yell at the top of his lungs. We grappled, and a crowd rushed into the room to separate us. Among them were Dawid Krynski, Izak Rubin, and the head of AHAGE guard, a ghetto police officer. While Dawid and the AHAGE guard grabbed the policeman, I sent Wlodek out with Izak, enjoining him not to let the child out of his sight for a second. Then I turned back to the roomful of quarreling people. The AHAGE police officer finally proposed a compromise: if I told them where the two women who had escaped were, they'd let Wlodek go free.

I knew perfectly well where the two women were hiding—one of them was at that moment on another floor of the very same building—but I had no intention of betraying them. I said I didn't know where they were.

"All right, we'll give you a chance to find out. Now come along with us. We've got to see Szmerling and make a report."

Escorted by two policemen, I was taken to Szmerling, the police officer in charge of Umschlagplatz operations, who had the power of life and death over the thousands who daily passed through there. A six-footer with a goatee, Mieczyslaw Szmerling was said to be impressed by no pleas or arguments except hard cash. Bloodcurdling stories about his sadism to deportees and his zeal in carrying out German orders had earned him the nickname "the hangman with the whip." Before I could open my mouth he began to shout at me, "Do you realize what those two women have done to me?"

I said that I hadn't come to apologize for them. They were merely trying to save their lives. And I was there to ask him to release the other five members of the group.

"You bring back the women and the child and then we'll talk. Not before."

I told him to forget about the child. The boy wasn't registered any-where and Geipel had no documents for him. As for the women, I didn't know where they were. I could look, of course, but I couldn't ask them to go to their deaths just to please Mr. Szmerling. If he gave me his solemn promise to release them all, I might be able to persuade them to turn them-selves in.

"The two women *and* the child," Szmerling reiterated.

"No. Only the two women," I replied.

"Bring them in. I'll do what I can, but I *don't promise anything.*"

That was the way our conversation ended. When I left the building, I noticed that I was being followed. I went to the Judenrat building and by tracking through its labyrinthine rooms and corridors, I got rid of my shadow. But I had an impossible task. How could I ask anyone to give her-self up to the Germans, to risk her life, on Szmerling's word?

As I was leaving the Judenrat building, I ran into Halina Jankelewicz and her husband. I told her in detail what had happened and she did not hesitate for a moment. Brushing away her husband's protests, she said she would go to Umschlagplatz and give herself up. Next I went to where Pola Z. was staying and asked her to come out on the landing, where again I re-counted the whole story. Without a word, she turned back into the flat and I heard her saying to her old mother: "Mother, I won't be back tonight. I'm going to stay at the Feins' place." Amid all the selfishness, cowardice, and degradation, the courage of these two young women in walking back into the jaws of death on the outside chance of saving the lives of their five coworkers was a moving testament of faith. Even as I witnessed it, I was ap-palled at having encouraged it.

The next few days were a nightmare of waiting and wondering. Nothing happened because the German execution squads were still in Ot-wock, doing their bloody work there. On the evening of the fourth day, however, the executioners returned and the Jews collected in the interval were finally loaded onto the cattle cars. As the sun sank that night, so my hopes and heart sank, too. Szmerling had not kept his bargain. Two inno-cent women . . . and Lena!

Izak and I stood outside the Umschlagplatz gate, waiting. The Jew-ish police had already left for the day, and the white-garbed hospital staff was beginning to file out. As the nurses in their trim white aprons marched by, I scanned their faces desperately, but there was no face I knew. The last of the hospital column was passing through the gate and I had looked at every face right down to the very last row of marching women, and then I fainted: the last row was ours! The old son-of-a-bitch had set all seven free, as well as four members of another pharmacy who had been caught in a roundup that same day. It was the only instance I ever heard of Szmerling's saving anyone from deportation without hard cash. For fear of Geipel he had not been able to release the women until the "shipment" left. Now, if worst came to worst, he could always pretend he had shipped them off with the others.

For the women, the time had been a Golgotha; for four days they had lived under a death sentence and until the very last moment even the policemen guarding them had no inkling of Szmerling's intentions. In fact, because the women were a "special" case, they had been isolated all the time; their only contact with the outside world a window looking out on the sea of human misery which was Umschlagplatz. The last two hours, during which time the cattle cars were being loaded and the buildings on the square emptied, had been the worst of all: the noise hellish, the square echoing with the sound of hobnailed boots, the cries of victims to one another, the cursing of Ukrainian guards, the pistol and rifle shots, and the wails and screaming of the wretched. As their building's turn to be evacuated arrived, a Jewish policeman told them to lie flat on the floor and not to make a sound. He locked all the doors. But his last words were: "If the Ukrainians don't find you, you're saved."

As they lay there, they heard the Ukrainians go through the building room by room, floor by floor, ferreting out those who were hidden, killing the sick and the crippled, beating and robbing all who came into their hands. Then, at last, the building grew still. The locomotive at the railhead was getting up steam, the brakes hissed as they were released, and there was the slow chugging of the train as it began to move, carrying a four-day harvest of thousands to their death. The women who were saved were unable to suppress their relief: life is sweet even on the graves of one's fellow men.

But one escape from Umschlagplatz was no guarantee of any security. Roundups were now more ferocious than ever and the pharmacy was no longer a refuge for Lena and Wlodek. I entrusted the child to my sister Roza, who lived in an apartment house, inhabited only by policemen and their families, where I hoped he would be safe. But she brought him back a few days later because her neighbors did not approve of the presence of a strange child who, they said, exposed their own children to danger.

All my energies were caught up in the endless roulette of guessing where the next roundup would be, and in finding a place of safety for Lena and Wlodek. I took them to the printing shop with me, but the next day a delegation of workmen came to see me, asking me to take them away on the ground that they were endangering their wives and children who were hidden in the plant. I combed the ghetto, but could find no hiding place for them.

Toward the end of August the full fury of the roundups was directed at the shop areas. Families were broken up, murders and looting were the order of the day, and scenes of vicious cruelty marked the selection of victims. Selection was absolutely random: some were ordered to stand on the right, some on the left, and no one knew which side was the side of life, which of death. The official quota of workers for each shop was counted off and the rest sent to Umschlagplatz. In some few cases, instead of spot selection, the manager of the shop had to supply the set number of victims, a terrible choice for Jewish managers who knew their colleagues and workers intimately—and their families as well. Caught between the imploring eyes of their friends and fellow workers and the implacable stare of the SS, they were confronted with an appalling choice, but they either made the selection or they and their own families were sent to Umschlagplatz.

At this lowest depth a shot rang out which marked a turning point in the history of the Warsaw ghetto, and perhaps a turning point in the history of the Jewish people. On August 25, Israel Kanal, a Jewish militant, attempted to assassinate the chief of Jewish police, Jozef Szerynski. Though the shot only wounded Szerynski, an attack had finally been made. Moreover, before this, little posters had appeared in the ghetto titled "Death to a Dog" and proclaiming that Szerynski had been "condemned to death." It was an omen of things to come.

We were spending our nights at the Mila Street AHAGE, but rumors of the imminent liquidation of AHAGE were becoming more insistent and I was frantically searching for a safer place. On the night of September 1, 1942, I was lying wakefully in the dark in a room on the second floor. It was the anniversary of the outbreak of World War II and I lay there thinking over what had happened to us in the three bitter years since the war had begun. Even in that dark hour we believed Nazism would be defeated. But our own particular war was lost. Nothing could repair the ravages in our ranks. We were going to our deaths daily, alone and forgotten, forsaken by God and man alike. We did not even leave behind graves to which someone, someday, might come to mourn us. They killed young and old alike, leaving us neither past nor future, depriving us of the eternity of cradles and of graves.

Suddenly the night was filled with the roar of motors overhead. From the distant world we had all but ceased to believe still existed came a reminder that we were not altogether forgotten. As the bombs began to explode and the houses of Warsaw collapsed or went up in flames, we realized that we still had friends and allies. No one ran to the shelters; instead, we listened spellbound to the symphony of destruction where we were, and we blessed the Soviet pilots above. The air raid brought new hope to the ghetto, and hundreds of prisoners took advantage of it to make good their escape from Umschlagplatz. It reminded us that we were only one small sector of the great war between the forces of light and the forces of darkness.

The very next day, with some obscure but certain instinct, we moved from the AHAGE to 33 Gesia Street, a building which housed Judenrat clerical workers. The following day AHAGE was subjected to a terrible roundup which took hundreds of victims, and so great was the panic it caused that Dawid Krynski could not even rescue his sister Ewa: she was marched off in a column that was loaded directly onto the cattle cars. A few days later Dawid himself was shot trying to escape from the ghetto.

The final episode of the Resettlement Operation we called "the cauldron," and it was no less than an enlarged Umschlagplatz. Instead of dragging the victims there, the Germans turned the entire ghetto into one huge Umschlagplatz of greater scale and cruelty. On Saturday night, September 5, 1942, we were awakened by shouting and a loud knocking on the door. A Jewish policeman stood there and he told us the *Befehlstelle* had just issued an order that the next morning at 10 A.M. all Jews were to report to an area formed by Smocza, Gesia, Zamenhof, and Szczesliwa Streets, and Parysowski Square. Everyone was to be "registered" here, and was to bring along two days' food and something to drink from. All apartments were to be left unlocked, their doors open. Curfew was canceled that night so people could go about making their preparations, but anyone found outside the prescribed area after ten o'clock on Sunday morning would be shot on the spot.

At dawn on September 6, the ghetto swarmed with men, women, and children, dressed for a journey and carrying in bundles and knapsacks what little they had left after three years of being systematically robbed.

After so much running and hiding, so many moves, not much of importance was left, and by that time we were resigned to losing our possessions. We made up two or three bundles and went out into the streets. The registration was to be on a group basis; that is, a Jew had the right to live only insofar as he belonged to a group the Germans considered useful: the others were doomed. We therefore had to join our work groups. At the corner of Zamenhof Street, Lena and Wlodek turned left toward the Judenrat offices and I turned right toward Leszno Street. The moment we separated I was terrified. What had I done? At first I hadn't realized that this was the final selection, but when I saw the reinforced guards, I knew this was something more than a mere registration. There had been no plan in my mind, but here a child was a death sentence. I had abandoned my wife and child. I must have been insane. I ran after them, but they had already disappeared into the surging crowd.

When I got to Leszno Street, I was numb. Mechanically I did what the others did. About 10 A.M. an SS man appeared and called thirty-eight names from a list. He formed us into ranks and marched us back toward the ghetto. The entrance at the corner of Gesia Street was guarded by heavily armed SS men, Ukrainian and Latvian guards, and Jewish police. We marched all the way across the cauldron along Zamenhof Street, from Gesia to Niska, and I did not see a single face I knew. On Niska Street we were lined up alongside other groups, each in the charge of an SS man, and I realized that all the groups were composed of people attached to the *Werterfassung*, and that some sort of selection was going to be made. While we were waiting, word spread that we were going to be searched and people began to try to hide their valuables, under loose paving stones, in cracks in the walls of the buildings behind them, anywhere they could find. Panic-stricken, they tried to get rid of what money, gold, diamonds, wristwatches, they had been able to salvage. My entire fortune, three ten-dollar gold pieces, remained in my pocket: I made no attempt to hide them.

The selection soon began and, as far as printing-shop personnel were concerned, took only a few minutes. People were counted off and there was no search. We were marched back through the cauldron and again I failed to find a single familiar face. We came to the exit gate of the cauldron and went through it; via Zamenhof, Nowolipki, and Karmelicka Streets, we came back to 24 Leszno. We were legal; we had a right to live.

But it was a bitter victory for me. My mind was in turmoil, my thoughts filled only with self-reproach for having left Wlodek with Lena instead of taking him with me. I had committed the unpardonable sin, and I felt suicidal. While others tried to sleep in the deserted apartments in the rest of the building, I lay on the cold floors behind the printing presses, tossing and turning and trying to figure out a scheme for rescuing my family. I did not sleep that night and at dawn I was on my feet. Most of the others in the printing plant, including some who had left their most valuable possessions in Niska Street, had also spent sleepless nights. Rachman said we had to go back to the cauldron at all costs. He told the SS man in charge that we needed to go to the *Werterfassung* warehouse to get a load of paper for an urgent official job, and then eight of us, escorted by the SS man, set out, pushing a two-wheeled cart in front of us.

When we reached the guards at Gesia Street, our SS man produced some sort of pass and they let us by. Once through the gate, we went to the warehouse and while we loaded the handcart my colleagues collected their hidden treasure; then we started back toward Zamenhof Street. We moved slowly through the throngs of the cauldron desperately searching for faces we knew. I went up to the first Jewish policeman I saw and reeled off the names of policemen I knew, asking if he had seen any of them, but he kept shaking his head until I mentioned my brother-in-law, Mietek.

Then he nodded and pointed. "He's over there." A moment later I saw him, but he had no news of Lena. However, he had seen my cousin, my cousin had seen Lena's brother, and so on. I followed every clue and the miracle occurred: in that maelstrom of 100,000 maddened people I found my wife and child in a hall in the Judenrat building. There Lena stood in one corner, pale but calm, with dark circles under her eyes. She said nothing, only clutched my hand to verify that it was indeed I. Tears filled her eyes. Wlodek was tugging at her skirt, repeating, "Mommy, I'm hungry. Please give me a piece of bread. . . ."

I ran back down into the courtyard like a man possessed and told Rachman of my incredible luck: I'd found them but what, I asked him, could I do to save them. Rachman took one look at my face and disappeared.

Lena regained her composure sufficiently to tell me what had happened. She had taken Wlodek to the Judenrat building as soon as we separated, trying to find someone she knew in the pharmacy department, but everything was in total confusion. Crazed people jammed the narrow streets, surging back and forth all day long, shoving and stepping on one another, shouting and swearing. There was nowhere to sit, nothing to lean against, nowhere to lie down, and many of the older people simply dropped where they stood and were trampled to death by the restless throngs. Rifle and submachine-gun fire echoed on every side as the Germans shot down those they found outside the cauldron.

When the first selections were made in Mila Street, the shop workers were forced to form ranks and pass by an SS officer flanked by Latvian and Ukrainian guards. The German owner or manager of each shop was also present. As each man came by, the SS officer gestured *rechts* or *links* with his riding crop: right meant Umschlagplatz; left, return to the shop. Neither technical skill, family relations, nor anything else was taken into consideration: life depended on a sadistic whim. Real experts were sentenced to death despite the entreaties of the German managers. To be accompanied by a child was a sentence of death. The slightest show of resistance brought a hail of bullets, and dozens were shot down. Finally, the SS officer stopped the process of individual selection and with a broad gesture of his riding crop indicated that all *that*—human beings who waited to be reviewed— was to go to the right, to Umschlagplatz. Those who were left were to return to the shop area under SS escort. The unfortunate victims were immediately marched to Umschlagplatz and loaded onto the cattle cars. The selection process was adjourned at sunset and tens of thousands of people settled down on sidewalks and streets, in the hallways and on staircases of buildings.

All that day Lena had held on to Wlodek, pushed by the crowds, hungry, despondent, feeling helpless. Wlodek was miserable with fear and fatigue. That night they slept on a dirty floor somewhere and at dawn began to make their way back to the Judenrat. On the way Lena met her brothers, Adek and Marek; their wives; and a schoolmate, Samek, with his wife and two-year-old daughter, Miriam. They were all young and healthy, worked for the German metalworking firm Army Supply II in the ghetto, and their chances for survival would have been good—except for the presence of the child. Samek did not speak a word but looked like an animal at bay.

At the Judenrat Lena went to see Dr. Gliksberg, the councillor in charge of pharmacies and he offered her a single one of the orange-colored cards that was a life ticket. "Doctor," she protested, "I have a child!"

"What do you want me to do?" he asked. "What would you do? Should I give a little child the chance to live, or an adult?" Gliksberg said simply there was nothing more he could do to help her.

Lena refused his offer, certain that the end had come. Miracles don't happen twice. Holding Wlodek by the hand, she stood quietly in a corner of the great hall. Wlodek kept squirming, tugging at her; he was hungry. She had deliberately withheld the bread she was carrying so that if she had to give him the dose of cyanide she had with her, he would not vomit on a full stomach and suffer unnecessarily. From moment to moment she wondered when to give him the cyanide. It was such a lovely autumn day and it didn't seem right to die just then. She looked at his beautifully sculptured face and tousled blond hair and thought how bitter it was to take the life of this her only child. But potassium cyanide was our last weapon. Lena was feeling calm and resigned, almost detached from the whole wretchedness around her when I appeared in the doorway. Now I would not leave them. I was ready to give my life to make up for my dereliction of the day before.

When Rachman returned, he asked to speak to me alone. He told me that his partner's wife had a life ticket from the Judenrat printing shop, but that she didn't believe in German papers. She was hiding in a cellar and my wife could have her number. "When they call for the printing shop," Rachman said, "she can join the group with my partner's wife's number." I grabbed the orange-colored card and explained the plan to Lena. Rachman, embarrassed, said, "You understand, of course, this doesn't belong to me and it's worth a fortune. . . . " Without a word I took the three ten-dollar gold pieces from my pocket and gave them to him. It was all I had but little enough in any case to pay for Lena's life.

I was lifting Wlodek into the handcart on top of the rolls of paper when Rachman's face suddenly blanched. Right behind me was the brutal *Obersturmführer* (First Lieutenant) Karl Brand, head of the Jewish section of the Warsaw Gestapo, watching what I was doing. Rachman seemed certain my last moment had come, but I read the Nazi's absolute indifference. It never occurred to him that the cart and the child in it were going to get out of the cauldron. Had he known, he would likely have shot Wlodek and me on the spot. "It's your funeral," was all Rachman managed to say as we pushed the cart carefully toward the exit. Our SS man was there and went with us, but he asked no questions.

That was Monday, September 7, 1942.

The "cauldron" phase of the Great Pogrom continued for an entire week after that. Every day columns marched to and fro, their numbers gradually depleted by the captious and methodical executions of the Nazis. Husbands were separated from wives, parents from children, brothers from sisters. Parents suddenly seized by panic deserted their children in the streets.

When it came to the turn of Army Supply II to march past the SS officer, Lena's brother Adek and his wife were in one row. With them was Samek and his wife, and they had given their two-year-old Miriam a sedative and put her into a knapsack slung over Samek's shoulder. The column advanced slowly while up ahead the SS officer grandly dispensed life and death, *left* and *right, links und rechts.* In the tense silence the wails of a baby suddenly rose. The SS officer froze and a thousand men and women held their breaths. A Ukrainian guard ran out, plunged his bayonet several times into the knapsack from which the criminal sounds had come. In seconds the knapsack was a blood-soaked rag. *"Du dreckiger Schweinehund!"* the SS officer shouted indignantly, bringing his riding crop down on the ashen face of the father who had dared to try smuggling his child past. Mercifully, the Ukrainian's bullet put an end to the father's ordeal then and there. Thereafter it became routine for guards to probe every bundle and knapsack with their bayonets.

Adek, Samek, and their wives were only three ranks away from the SS man at that point. All the blood drained from Samek's face, but his wife was stronger at that moment—or was it weaker?—or did she merely have presence of mind? "Take off the knapsack!" she hissed. As if in a trance, he did so and without losing his place in the ranks, he edged over to the end of the row of marchers and carefully deposited the knapsack on the curb. It took no more than a fraction of a minute. Then be went back to his original place, eyes vacant.

Nearby, a young woman was sitting on the steps in front of a store. With her was a little girl of about five. Both had been selected for deportation and were waiting to be marched away. The little girl was hungry and pulled at her mother's dress. The mother produced a portion of half-eaten roll from somewhere and broke off a bit. She drew the child in front of her, drank in her every feature, then handed her a bit of the poisoned bread. When the child began to eat it, the woman turned her own head away and stuffed the rest of the roll into her mouth, swallowing rapidly. The little girl ate greedily, but began to cough, then vomit. Screaming, she yanked at her mother's dress, but the woman was already dead. Terrified, the girl struck her mother's body with her fists, yelling over and over again, "Mommy, answer me! Answer me!"

The noise was not unnoticed by the SS officer and he cast an angry glance in the child's direction and saw her hitting her mother's body. "Look at that, Franz!" he said to one of his fellow officers, his voice loud and disgusted. "A child beating its mother. Can you imagine a German child doing that!" A young man standing among the group of lucky ones who had been selected to live raised his coat collar and turned his back on the scene on the opposite sidewalk. The little girl did not see her father as he turned away, but he did not have to hide his face for long. The SS man took careful aim and put an end to the irritating source of noise.

There were many anonymous heroes who did not break down, who neither deserted their families nor tried to save their own skins at any cost. One ten-year-old boy called out hysterically but determinedly, "Mama, Mama, keep right on going. Don't look back at me." And then he ran out of the ranks, hoping thereby to save his mother's life. But his mother, unable to accept his sacrifice, ran after him. Clinging together they rejoined the column and walked on, released from all fear, possessed of a new peace.

After the selection of shop personnel was over, the Germans conducted a methodical manhunt through the rest of the ghetto to find those who had tried to avoid the cauldron by hiding. Since all apartments had, in compliance with German instructions, been left unlocked, the manhunt was also accompanied by looting on an unprecedented scale. The search turned up groups of ragged, filthy, hungry people and many abandoned children. All were driven with rifle butts and riding crops to Umschlagplatz, including all the patients and the entire medical staff of the Stawki Street hospital.

The cauldron was systematically emptied and not a single square of that terrible area was free of Jewish blood. At least 3,000 people were murdered there, more than 400 a day, and that did not include those who died of hunger or exhaustion in their hiding places, and the more than 50,000 who were deported in the week from the sixth to the thirteenth of September 1942. We were now at the next-to-the-last scene of the last act.

Once again Warsaw, the martyred city, had a golden Polish autumn, but in the glaring sunshine the ghetto was almost a ghost town. Most of its people were resettled; its houses still stood, but their glass-shattered windows stared like blind eyes. Streets were covered with blood and excrement, bodies had not yet been removed, and scattered everywhere were bundles and suitcases, open and in disarray, pots and pans, little wagons, isolated pieces of clothing, chamber pots, prayer books. Over everything, streets and debris, suspended in the air like motes or glittering on the ground like snowflakes, were tiny feathers, the incongruous white down from the feather beds of Jewish homes. Bonfires blazed in broad daylight to burn the wreckage of lifetimes and they gave off an acrid stench which settled over the ghetto, offending the nostrils and making the eyes smart. Smoke, flame, and that peculiar snow of tiny white feathers are always my vision of the last days of the Jewish community of Warsaw.

Down one of the sun-drenched, deserted streets a column of Jewish slaves marches. Dead men on furlough from death, condemned men reprieved briefly to work for the greater glory of the Third Reich, the thirty-eight of them in this column keep perfect step. They are singing a brisk, cheerful, military song because the SS man in charge is keen on military bearing; he likes to feel himself at the head of an army. The faces of the singing men are emaciated. There are no tears in their eyes though every one has lost a wife, a mother, a child, a brother, a sister, and some their whole families. What keeps them alive? What keeps them marching and singing? Is it despair, memory, intoxication at still being able to walk the earth?

A new kind of life began to take shape over the mass grave of the past. We spent several nights in the printing shop and there, for the first time in weeks, we were given bread and hot food. We slept anywhere, on the floor, on piles of boards, on any surface. Now pale and frightened all the time, Wlodek slept beside me and even in his sleep kept a tight hold on my hand or my clothes. The lively child whose nature had been movement and playfulness now sat for hours at a time without moving. Whenever I seemed to be leaving him, his only reaction was to tighten his grip on me, uttering only the single word: *"Daddy."*

After the cauldron had been completely evacuated, we were quartered at Niska Street in the *Werterfassung,* one room to a family. Every morning at eight we assembled downstairs, formed ranks and were marched to work by "our" SS man. The route took us across the entire ghetto to the gate in Gesia Street, then across no-man's-land to Leszno. At six every evening we retraced our steps along the same route. The new boundaries of the ghetto ran along Stawki and Dzika Streets, the northern limit; Gesia, Franciszkanska, and Swietojerska Streets, the southern; Smocza Street the western; and Bonifraterska and Nowiniarska Streets, the eastern. New walls were promptly erected to contain that area.

The offices of the Judenrat were at 19 Zamenhof Street and its printing shop temporarily located at 15 Zamenhof Street. Every night Lena stood at a second-story window there to watch us go by. Wlodek never looked squarely at his mother, only sideways. He was afraid some German might notice; he had learned his first lesson in conspiratorial existence.

On the last day of the cauldron all Jewish policemen and their families had been assembled on Ostrowska Street and hundreds of them and their families were sent to Umschlagplatz. So did the Germans reward their faithful service. A crowd of thousands looked on in stony silence as the policemen with heads bowed walked to the loading platforms to share the fate they had so zealously handed out to others. Of the nearly

2,000 policemen on the force before the deportations began, only 240 were left. Most of the remaining ones were given jobs as factory guards at various shops; those who were deported were for the most part men of little influence.

There were three exits from the central ghetto now, all heavily guarded, and the ghetto itself was broken up into various "islands" separated by no-man's-lands. Each island was a prison shut off by walls or wooden fences and between 8 A.M. and 5 P.M. no one was permitted to be on the streets under penalty of death. Those caught in the no-man's lands between the islands were shot on the spot. Even moving about within any given shop area required a special permit, and going from one shop area to another was forbidden. That ruling caused a new kind of suffering, since many families had been broken up and different members worked in different shops. Sometimes, members of a family did not see each other for weeks on end.

Life in the factories was difficult and wearisome. German owners and managers sweated every ounce of energy out of their Jewish slave labor. Food was wretched and the factory guards were either ethnic Germans, who treated workers with sadistic brutality, or former ghetto policemen. "Legally," the Jewish laborers were "the property" of the SS and each enterprise paid 5 zlotys per day for their services to the SS treasury.

The Resettlement Operation ended on Rosh Hashanah of 1942, but the Germans gave the Jews "a little surprise" ten days later. On Yom Kippur, another special selection was made in which hundreds of "illegals," chiefly women and children, were rounded up, dragged out of workshops and hiding places to the usual accompaniment of brutality and murder. Once more the streets of the deserted city echoed to the footsteps of another procession of the doomed.

In a period of eight weeks, more than 300,000 people had been deported in cattle cars to the extermination chambers and mass graves of Treblinka. There was now no further doubt about the destination or its purpose: the incredible was a matter of fact. One of those who had miraculously escaped from the death factory at Treblinka was a man who had formerly been the janitor of the building we lived in on Orla Street, and we had the story from his own lips. The nation of Kant and Goethe was deliberately and systematically murdering defenseless men, women, and children in its gas chambers.

There were now 30,000 "legal" inhabitants in the ghetto, legality meaning that they possessed German documents giving them the right to live. Nearly as many "wild ones" were hidden. Now, slowly, a few at a time, the "illegals" began to emerge from their hideouts. Izak Rubin was one of them. During the cauldron action he had hidden himself among a group of lithographers at 43 Nalewki Street. Goldsobel's printshop was located there in the courtyard and somehow Geipel had overlooked it when he was sealing up all the printing establishments. Jozef Goldsobel, the owner's son, and some other young people, had hidden there in a camouflaged attic under the roof. They came out only at night for food and water; nearly caught several times, they escaped over the rooftops to adjacent buildings. Only when the Resettlement Operation was finished did they emerge, dirty, unshaven, emaciated, terror in their eyes. After a short while they went back to their old trade. A few kerchief makers began once more to collect rags, the presses were put back into service, and the bed linen of murdered families was once more processed into kerchiefs.

Lena, too, was "illegal." The number I had bought from Rachman had provided her with an escape from the cauldron, but when the legitimate owner came out of hiding, it belonged to her. The surviving pharmacy division, when Lena reported there, received her with open arms, though a few days before the same people had condemned her child to death. The small number of permits to live had been appropriated by the administrative higher-ups and their families and now there weren't enough professional pharmacists to get a commercial operation going again.

One pharmacy did open for business at the corner of Gesia and Zamenhof Streets, just opposite the ghetto gate. Its employees were assigned quarters at 44 Muranowska Street, at the corner of Zamenhof, where Lena and Wlodek occupied one room of an apartment. I moved there shortly after they were installed. The other room was occupied by the Zandbergs, pharmacists originally from Lodz. The kitchen was occupied by a Mrs. Uger, widow of a well-known newspaperman from Lodz. On the same floor, the fourth, the apartment opposite was occupied by the Kacenelenbogens and their fifteen-year-old daughter, Ada. These plus two elderly people from Lodz, who also lived in the building, were all that remained of the professional pharmacists in the ghetto. Some weeks later the pharmacy itself was moved from Gesia Street to the building in which we lived.

Our daily schedule was as follows: We got up at seven. At eight I joined the printers' group in Niska Street, just around the corner, and Lena left to open the pharmacy where, on alternate days, she worked until three in the afternoon. On the other days she worked from three to nine in the evening, and Jozef Zandberg worked the morning shift. Wlodek spent most of his day with Lena, or was left with one of the Zandbergs, to whom we became very attached.

All factories observed approximately the same working hours, and only Judenrat employees were permitted to go to their jobs individually. From 8 A.M. to 6 P.M. the ghetto was empty and two notorious Nazi murderers, Klostermeyer and Blöscher,[7] rode bicycles through the empty streets shooting every Jew they found out-of-doors. Some days their scores were as high as twenty "wrecked" Jews and no day passed without some undertaking business for Pinkiert.

The printing shop at 24 Leszno Street was one of the only two permitted to exist after 1939 when Hergl, the German "trustee," closed down all private Jewish firms. He had licensed these two printers; many of the others, by bribing Hergl for permission, "combined" their plants with them. When the SS took over all Jewish businesses after the resettlement started, Hergl disappeared from the scene and the two printshops were joined into one. It was owned by Abram Keisman and Jona Rachman, who, officially, became its managers within the framework of the *Werterfassung*. Rachman, an intelligent and energetic man, soon became the leading voice in the enterprise. I was the only Linotype operator in the shop and since the Linotype was in a separate room, I had the luxury of being alone with my thoughts for hours at a time.

The eight-hour day was interrupted only once, at noon, when we got a bowl of soup and a piece of bread. We did everything possible to look busy all the time, but our first and greatest concern was to "tame"—or as we sometimes said, "poison"—the SS man assigned to supervise us. One of our weapons was to see that this bully was served an enormous well-cooked lunch prepared and served by one of our own women. Such meals were not familiar to that particular German and copious quantities of vodka accompanied it. Through our daily contacts with this man and others like him, we eventually managed to make a number of "deals." For many SS men ghetto duty was an easy and safe assignment, which provided them with a source of considerable income.

By 6 P.M. we were back at our living quarters. At that hour columns of workers were returning from jobs all over the city, and the section of Zamenhof Street between Mila and Niska Streets became a central meeting place. There people could chat for a few minutes, exchange the latest news

---

7. SS-*Oberscharführer* (SS Sergeant) Heinrich Klostermeyer and SS-*Sturmmann* (SS Private) Josef Blöscher served in the ghetto branch office of the Gestapo headquarters in Warsaw.—Editor's note

and gossip, and make business deals. Those who had been working on the Aryan side passed on copies of illegal newspapers they had picked up there and brought news of the fate and whereabouts of friends and relatives.

When we had dispersed to our separate quarters, the sense of our tragic predicament made itself most intensely felt. At night the whole of the ghetto was plunged into darkness; there were no lights in apartments, on staircases, or in the streets. Empty buildings were sinister and we lived among the ghosts of their murdered inhabitants. Our isolation was almost unbearable and drove the most unlikely people to cling together. Our wounds were still open, and when we remembered the thousands who would never return, we were ashamed of having survived. Young people began to form irregular liaisons—the expression was "to be cousins"—out of the need for companionship as much as the prompting of desire. Youngsters of twelve and thirteen, feeling the loss of their parents, ruthlessly went their own ways, a pseudo-tough veneer covering their gnawing hunger for love and security. There were orgies of gluttony and all-night drinking parties. Vodka was the great comforter, though the surcease it gave from pain was short-lived and the intolerable memories that wracked us soon returned until we felt we were one great abscess. We had all lost someone close to us in the Resettlement Operation, and nobody lacked occasion for private grief and mourning. Our first reaction was tearful self-pity. We counted our dead; licked our wounds; and we bemoaned our fate.

We behaved like automatons, living on our reflexes. The population was now overwhelmingly young, with nearly two men to every woman. A child was a rarity, to be guarded jealously from even as much as a stranger's glance in the street.

When we left our Orla Street apartment, we had been forced to abandon, among other things, a library of more than 2,000 books, and in our room at 44 Muranowska, there was only one book to read. It was Chaim Nachman Bialik's *In the City of Slaughter.* In the Warsaw ghetto, recovering from our Great Pogrom, we read what he said about another time, another place, another pogrom:

> Only a lost people can lament so:
> Smoke and ashes—this is its soul,
> And its heart a desert wilderness,
> Without an ounce of anger or revenge. . . .
>
> Where is the fist that shall smite?
> Where the thunderbolt to avenge?

To shake the world and rend the sky?
To overthrow My seat, My throne?

After the first sorrow came the soul-searching. How had it all come
to pass? How could 300,000 people have let themselves be led to slaughter
without putting up a fight? How could young healthy parents hand over
their children without bashing in the criminal skulls of guards and executioners alike? Was it not a father's first, most elemental duty to save his child's
life even at the cost of his own? Or for a son to die defending his mother?
Why had we not lain in wait, axes in our hands, for the assassins? There is
a time to live and a time to die, and when the time to die comes, we must
stand up and accept death with dignity. Over and over, the ghetto Jere-
miahs asked each other aloud, "Why didn't we go out into the streets with
whatever we could lay our hands on—axes, sticks, kitchen knives, stones?
Why hadn't we poured boiling water on the murderers or thrown sulphuric
acid? Why hadn't we broken out of the ghetto walls and scattered all over
Warsaw, all over Poland? Perhaps 20,000, even 50,000 of us would have
been slain, but not 300,000! What a disgrace, what an unspeakable shame!"

It was an agonizing self-appraisal. We were bitter to the point of
self-flagellation, profoundly ashamed of ourselves, and of the misfortunes
we had endured. And those feelings intensified our sense of being abandoned alike by God and man. Above all we kept asking ourselves the age-
old question: *why, why?* What was all that suffering for? What had we done
to deserve this hurricane of evil, this avalanche of cruelty? Why had all the
gates of Hell opened and spewed forth on us the furies of human vileness?
What crimes had we committed for which this might have been calami-
tous punishment? Where, in what code of morals, human or divine, is there
a crime so appalling that innocent women and children must expiate it
with their lives in martyrdoms no Torquemada ever dreamed of?

In vain we looked at that cloudless September sky for some sign of
God's wrath. The heavens were silent. In vain we waited to hear from the
lips of the great ones of the world—the champions of light and justice,
the Roosevelts, the Churchills, the Stalins—the words of thunder, the threat
of massive retaliation that might have halted the executioner's axe. In vain
we implored help from our Polish brothers with whom we had shared good
and bad fortune alike for seven centuries, but they were utterly unmoved
in our hour of anguish. They did not show even normal human compassion
at our ordeal, let alone demonstrate Christian charity. They did not even
let political good sense guide them; for after all we *were objectively allies* in

a struggle against a common enemy. While we bled and died, their attitude was at best indifference, and all too often "friendly neutrality" to the Germans. "Let the Germans do this dirty work for us." And there were far too many cases of willing, active, enthusiastic Polish assistance to the Nazi murderers.

There was, of course, a handful of noble Poles, but nobody listened to them; their voices never carried over the barbaric yawp of hatred. Heroically they managed to save some individuals, but they could bring no mitigation of Nazi ferocity. The very bases of our faith had crumbled: the Polish fatherland whose children we had always considered ourselves; two thousand years of Christianity, silent in the face of Nazism; myths of our shared lie-ridden civilization. We were despairingly alone, stripped of all we had held sacred.

We hounded ourselves with our own guilt. Terrible as the pogrom was, had there been at any point a solution we had neglected out of ignorance, weakness, or cowardice? Could we have thought of something which might have saved us? Suppose that Czerniakow, before killing himself, had summoned the ghetto to resistance. Would the ghetto at that point have been capable of organized armed resistance? Not even the greatest optimist among us could answer that question affirmatively. We had lost our political and intellectual leaders. The majority of our young men, including the most militant, were in exile in the Soviet Union. Three years of hunger and epidemic had brought a sharp rise in male mortality, so that there were, when the Resettlement Operation began, four women to every three men. The ghetto had been systematically ground down for three years, by savage Nazi discrimination and repression, by famine and disease, by traitors among us, by the ghetto police, by the Gestapo, by the misgovernment of the Judenrat, and finally by the April and June massacres. No, at the time of Czerniakow's death, the ghetto would not have been ready to offer mass armed resistance.

Militarily, the uprising of a single quarter in a great modern city—without a trained army or military organization, without arms or a chance of obtaining arms, without natural cover in which to hide, or means of retreat and maneuver—holds no prospect of the slightest success. Such a quarter could be promptly brought to its knees by cutting off food supplies, turning off the water. And it is easier still when the men rebelling are undernourished and heavily burdened with women and children.

There were other factors. Nothing in Jewish history had prepared the ghetto for armed rising. The ghetto Jews were not warriors. For more than two thousand years the Word had been more highly respected than the Sword. We were the descendants of that people who had created the image of the lion and wolf lying down with the lamb, of swords being beaten into ploughshares. The history of the Jews in Diaspora was a history of being driven from place to place, too often locked up in ghettos, subjected to periodic persecution and pogrom; it was not conducive to development of the military virtues. Heroic armed exploits by Jews in the Diaspora had been the exception, not the rule.

Not that Jews lacked courage. Jewish participation in the underground revolutionary movement in tsarist Russia and in the political life of interwar Poland supplied abundant examples of bravery and dignity. The Sholom Aleichem *batlanim* and *luftmenschen,* Marc Chagall's surrealistic fiddlers, Franz Kafka's neurotic intelligentsia, and Martin Buber's exotic Hasidim were undergoing revolutionary change in the prewar years. They were becoming disciplined workers organized in trade unions, educated in the revolutionary traditions of the 1905 uprising, developing armed self-defense groups against pogroms, becoming a people of Zionist pioneers and toilers. But, despite all that, they were not prepared for military action against the Nazis. The unmerciful use of collective responsibility by the Germans kept even the most hotheaded in check. This use of terror had begun immediately after the occupation: on November 22, 1939, the Germans shot 53 Jews from the house at 9 Nalewki Street; in January 1940, they shot 100 Jewish professionals—physicians, lawyers, and engineers; on April 17, 1942, they shot, in the street in the middle of the night, 52 people suspected of underground activities; on June 3, 1942, 110 Jews were executed in Babice.

The feeling we had for the Germans cannot be oversimplified into hatred. Hatred we felt, but the chief emotion was terror. We couldn't think of the Germans as human beings. They were mad dogs unaccountably loosed from the chains of history and morality. You don't hate a beast of prey, you feel loathing and terror. We feared the Germans with a dreadful, paralyzing panic stronger than the fear of our own deaths. During the final liquidation of the ghetto, a Jewish woman, on her knees, begged a Polish policeman, "Shoot me! Shoot me. I'm more afraid of the Germans than of dying." One day a German came to take a Jewish child from its mother. When she pleaded for its life, he said, "If you can guess which of my eyes is artificial, I'll give you the child." She looked intently at him and said, "The right one." Astonished, the Nazi replied, "That's so, but how could you tell?" After hesitating for a moment, she told him, "It looks more human than the other one."

The basic factor in the ghetto's lack of preparation for armed resistance was psychological; we did not at first believe the Resettlement Operation to be what in fact it was, systematic slaughter of the entire Jewish population. For generations East European Jews had looked to Berlin as the symbol of law, order, and culture. We could not now believe that the Third Reich was a government of gangsters embarked on a program of genocide "to solve the Jewish problem in Europe." We fell victim to our faith in mankind, our belief that humanity had set limits to the degradation and persecution of one's fellow man. This mentality underlay the behavior of the Jewish leadership at the very beginning of the resettlement, when the overwhelming majority voted against armed resistance. Some felt we ought to wait for a joint rising with the Poles. Others were resigned to sacrificing 70,000 Jews rather than jeopardizing the entire community of 400,000—the Nazi policy of collective responsibility was very much alive in our memories. Still others were religious Jews, committed to the tradition of *Kiddush HaShem:* a martyr's death sanctifying the Name of God. They believed that, when the enemy came for us, we should be dressed in our prayer shawls and phylacteries, poring over the holy books, all our thoughts concentrated on God. In that state of religious exaltation, we should simply ignore all Nazi orders with contempt and defiance; resistance and violence only desecrated the majesty of martyrdom in sanctification of the Lord's name. I heard the following unexpected argument in favor of nonresistance.

"Try to imagine Jesus on the way to Golgotha suddenly stooping to pick up a stone and hurling it at one of the Roman legionnaires. After such an act, could he ever have become the Christ? Think of Gandhi and Tolstoy, too. For two thousand years we have served mankind with the Word, with the Book. Are we now to try to convince mankind that we are warriors? We shall never outdo them at that game."

Last, there was the fact that there can be no struggle without some hope. Why does the man unjustly condemned to death fail to turn on his guards as he is led to the gallows? Why did the three thousand Turkish prisoners Napoleon ordered drowned put up no resistance? Why did fifty thousand French Huguenots permit themselves to be slaughtered in a single night by French Catholics? And what of the Armenians?

There is no precedent for the eventual uprising of the Warsaw ghetto because it was undertaken solely for death with dignity, and without the slightest hope of victory in life.

As the ghetto came slowly back to life, smuggling was resumed, but now it had a very different character. Every day thousands of Jews marched out of the ghetto to work in establishments located on Aryan territory and each of them was a walking dry-goods store. A man put on four shirts, one over the other, several pairs of shorts, trousers, and socks. There might be bed sheets wrapped around his body under his clothes. Women workers concocted fantastic costumes and turbans, which served to get upholstery and curtain fabrics out of the ghetto. These bulging figures moved slowly and looked anxiously forward to the moment when they must pass the guards at the gates. "How's the guard today?" they'd eagerly inquire of Polish workers entering the ghetto with their special passes. When the reply was, "What a guard!" and underlined with a broad smile and a raised elbow, spirits lifted perceptibly. But there were also the trying days when guards searched everyone carefully, beat up people, and brutally stripped women naked in the guardhouse. The life of anyone caught smuggling hung by a hair.

In the course of the working day the various smuggled articles were sold on the Aryan side and workers came back to the ghetto with bread, fats, sausage, and other foods artfully concealed on their persons. An art of "packaging and containment" was gradually evolved, based on careful study of the guards. They rarely searched a man's cap or a woman's hair, so small objects and paper money could be hidden there with fair safety. Extremely valuable things were swallowed or stuffed into the rectum. The more intimate female garments and the portion of the back just under the nape were also usually safe places. One of the most successful ruses was to put some small object into one's overcoat pocket and then throw the overcoat open saying, "Search me." Guards usually ran their hands up the body, but left the outflung overcoat alone.

Lunch pails with false bottoms were helpful. A smuggler would be careful to leave some portion of his lunch, preferably some soup, in the visible upper part. Another trick was to fill lunch pails with so-called stinkies, a vile-smelling fish then on the market. Not all such stratagems worked, however. For a time, Lena's pharmacy was opposite the main gate and she was in a position to see how severely smugglers were treated when caught. On one occasion guards caught a boy trying to smuggle in a revolver. He was made to stand for hours against the wall with his arms upraised before his body was riddled with bullets.

Large-scale smuggling also flourished. The kerchief industry prospered and shops, with their "legal" exports, also managed to divert a proportion of their production to be sold on the Aryan market. Brushes, hardware, and paper products were sold in that way, too. Jewish police formed a gang to steal valuables, especially furs from the *Werterfassung* warehouse on Niska Street. Thus, while the Germans were sending the most valuable ghetto properties back to Germany and selling the less valuable things to Poles at the Tlomackie Street synagogue, which they had turned into a warehouse, the ghetto Jews were unofficially selling everything else that remained in the ghetto.

In October 1942, our printshop was issued a small quota of special passes, which entitled the bearer to move about the ghetto freely during the day. Because no one was eager to use them, Rachman gave me one. I walked about the ghetto for days on end, ostensibly on the lookout for raw materials from which kerchiefs might be made, and contacting buyers for the finished goods. On one of these jaunts I dropped into the Judenrat building and saw a great pile of immigration certificates to Palestine. Unfortunately they had arrived too late to do us any good; the addressees were already dead.

I went everywhere and looked at everything with an insatiable curiosity. Surely, for the few weeks that the passes were valid, no one knew the ghetto better than I did. Although the occupants of each shop area lived an isolated life, people's moods and experiences were much the same everywhere. They mourned those who had been killed; they counted their losses; they shed many tears for those who were left behind—themselves. I felt I was taking my last look at a dying world.

When the autumn rains came in October, the blood was washed away from the ghetto streets. Winter was coming and it got dark earlier. Our flat was cold and uncomfortable, the plumbing balky and frequently broken, and there was no one to fix it. There were new tenants in the attic overhead, a carpenter and his wife, his mother, and their little son, who was only a bit older than Wlodek. The carpenter's brother, a former Jewish policeman, also lived there with his wife. Often when I got back from the day's work, the two boys were playing, and my son was screaming, *"Juden raus! Alle Juden runter!"* They were playing the resettlement game. Sometimes Wlodek would dress up in my broad belt, and carry his toy gun, his high childish treble proclaiming, "I'm a German! I'm Geipel, and I'm going to Berlin tonight." Then turning to his little friend, he would roar, *"Jude, raus!"*

Occasionally, at least, Wlodek's games were more humane. He would make a bundle of his things, sling it over his back and say that he was setting out to see the world. I would wave good-by and when Wlodek was about to go out the door, Lena would burst into tears. "Boo-hoo. My little boy is leaving me. What shall I ever do all alone without him?" At that, Wlodek would turn back, spread his arms helplessly, as if to say, "What can you do? She's a poor weak woman," and then in a very grown-up masculine voice declare, "You see, she's crying again." And the scene would end in a joyful reunion.

Moments like those were rare and short-lived, however. Sorrow hung over the ghetto. Even during the worst suffering there had been jokes. Now our sense of humor had almost entirely deserted us, although there was still some gallows humor. One of the macabre puns then circulated was a play on the words *afterlife:* "Do you believe in the post–cattle car life?" (The Polish expression for the afterlife is *zycie, poza grobowe*, life beyond the grave; the Jews changed the last word to *wagonowe*, cattle car.)

But a crisis was in the making; the steel was being tempered. Those who were strong grew stronger; those who were weak were breaking down altogether. National destruction, the agony and impotent shame of seeing one's brothers murdered, the defenselessness, the smoke of Treblinka, and the curses of those who had been loaded into the cattle cars all fueled the fire in which the armed uprising of the ghetto was forged. Two organizations of militants were to lead the battle. One, the ZOB *(Zydowska Organizacja Bojowa)*, or Jewish Fighting Organization, was headed by Mordecai Anielewicz. Organized officially in October 1942, the ZOB was made up of various anti-fascist Zionist groups which had organized and mounted the assassination attempt on Szerynski. The nucleus of the ZOB consisted of a group of kibbutzim: HaShomer HaTzair, Dror, Gordonia, and Akiba, all of them quartered in Mila Street. There were also members of the Polish Workers Party (the Communists) and so-called wild groups, organizations of individuals without any political complexion or party affiliation, banded together to resist the Germans. Other organizations joined, uniting in a so-called Jewish National Committee, which with the Labor Bund subsequently became known as the Coordinating Commission. Besides Anielewicz, the key ZOB members were Hersz Berlinski, Itzhak Zuckerman, Marek Edelman, and Michal Rosenfeld.

While the ZOB had an outspoken anti-fascist character the ZZW *(Zydowski Zwiazek Wojskowy)*, the National Military Organization, headed by Pawel Frenkiel, was composed of revisionist *(Irgun Zvai Leumi)* members. Less popular than the ZOB, it was better organized and trained in military matters. Its headquarters and arms cache were at 7–9 Muranowska Street. In addition to Frenkiel, its leaders were Nathan Szulc and Lejb Rodal.

Our biological existence had been threatened and at last we fought for our lives. While some of the ghetto youth, obsessed by memories of terror and loss, were becoming demoralized, and others took to nihilism and hedonism, a new type appeared—Jewish young people who held their heads high, prepared for anything that might happen. Rightly or wrongly, sensibly or not, faithful to Jewish tradition or against it, this portion of the ghetto youth had come to a decision: they had taken enough; they would take no more.

The turning point was the assassination of Jakob Lejkin, deputy chief of the Jewish police, carried out deliberately after the ZOB formally sentenced him to death. A lawyer by profession, Lejkin had demonstrated his zeal during the resettlement and thereby made himself doubly hated. He was a small man and inordinately ambitious, and the ghetto had nicknamed him Napolejkin. Sentence was carried out at five one afternoon in Lejkin's apartment in Gesia Street by a young militant, Elias Rozanski. The news spread like wildfire and, unlike the attempted assassination of Szerynski two months earlier, this act did not pass unnoticed. There was now a strong desire to bring Jewish traitors to justice. Not long after, another militant killed Israel First, head of the Judenrat's economic bureau; he was a Gestapo agent and liaison between the occupation authorities and the Judenrat. Szmerling, the ghetto police officer who was chief of the cattle car loading at Umschlagplatz, escaped the same fate only because he had broken his leg and was home under heavy guard for three weeks.

The ghetto followed these actions with an increasing sympathy, which obviously marked a new spirit and frame of mind. There was no lack of volunteers to bear arms. Young people of both sexes, burning with a desire for revenge and filled with enthusiasm to resist, flocked to join. But how, in our wretched predicament, were all these eager young people to be armed? The official Polish underground *Armia Krajowa* (Home Army), which was under the orders of the Polish government-in-exile in London, for a long time refused to give the slightest assistance. Only after long, repeated demands did it supply even a minimal quantity of small arms. The Polish left-wing underground organizations (People's Guards and the Socialist resistance groups) were somewhat more sympathetic, but they were weak and had little in the way of arms and ammunition. In this respect the ZZW was luckier than the ZOB because former comrades-in-arms on the Aryan side supplied some guns and ammunition, and also helped in other ways. Still there was a great shortage of competent instructors and trained cadres in the ghetto.

As a result Jews attempted to arm themselves individually from the Aryan side where some weapons and ammunition were available. Both organizations bought weapons, as did individuals and other groups. Smuggling the weapons into the ghetto was a serious problem. They either had to be thrown over the walls, usually in Parysowski Square, or brought through the gates by individuals. The ZZW got its guns and ammunition through a tunnel between its headquarters and another house on the same street on the other side of the wall. Molotov cocktails—which a young Jewish engineer Michal Klepfisz had been taught to make by Polish Socialists on the Aryan side—were manufactured inside the ghetto. Yet to the very end the ghetto was left almost altogether to its own devices. Neither in fighting for survival nor in dying with dignity did it receive appreciable outside help.

With returning strength and determination, ghetto activity also took other forms besides preparing for armed resistance. Escape occupied the thoughts of many people. The simplest way out was to seek shelter with Gentile friends and acquaintances who were willing to give it—with or without money. Some Poles made a business of sheltering Jews. Another device was to pretend to be a Gentile when seeking accommodations with a Polish family and never to betray one's identity even to one's hosts.

A handful of Poles were sympathetic, eager to fulfill their Christian and patriotic duties, either from ideological, personal, or monetary motives. But the great majority looked on indifferently. They felt that the Germans were solving their "Jewish problem" for them. Though the Germans were doing it brutally, they said, it was effective; Poles, with all their Slavic softheartedness, could never have brought themselves to do the slaughtering. In short, however heartbreaking to watch, exterminating the Jews was necessary. Then there were the *shmaltzovniks,* the blackmailers and professional trackers-down of Jews in hiding, a fairly numerous and busy group drawn from the most vicious, semicriminal elements in the Polish population. Packs of these jackals lay in wait at every gate hoping to catch someone leaving the ghetto illegally, and when they did, they milked the victim of everything he owned before turning him in to the Gestapo to be murdered. In addition to the ordinary hoodlums, there were a number of "ideological" anti-Semites who informed or betrayed out of conviction, out of hatred for Jews. Among these, Polish police and firemen were especially assiduous and succeeded in betraying large numbers of Jews to the Gestapo. Such anti-Jewish dregs terrorized many decent Poles, making them exceedingly cautious in dealing with Jews because they might at any moment be denounced by these hoodlums as "lackeys of the Jews" and "traitors to the Polish people."

What happened during those tragic days in Aryan Warsaw led many a Jew to return to the ghetto, disillusioned and embittered. They chose to be with their own people, even to die with them, rather than undergo the humiliation and persecution they had to suffer outside the ghetto walls. A good many Jews would have preferred to escape to the woods where they could fight the enemy openly, living and dying as Jews rather than assuming false Gentile identities, but the region around Warsaw offered little opportunity to do so. There was almost no natural cover nearby and little help from the Poles, so that for the overwhelming majority of ghetto Jews escape to the woods or to Aryan Warsaw was not a practical solution.

CHAPTER 3

THE REVOLT

IN THE FALL OF 1942, there was a feverish campaign to construct safe hideouts inside the ghetto walls. These were called "bunkers" in ghetto slang, and many an engineer or contractor derived his entire business from orders for such private shelters. There were literally hundreds of different types and the inventiveness of the builders seemed almost inexhaustible. Basically, a bunker was a hidden space with no visible entrance. Underground bunkers in cellars were accessible only through long tunnels through which one had to crawl on hands and knees. Some even had emergency exits. Some were palatial shelters with beds in tiers, ample food and water, electric lights, and even radio sets. Shelters were dug under courtyards where garbage cans were kept, under courtyard toilets, and other places normally so repulsive as to offer security. Secret rooms were built in apartments with entrances through large armoires—there were no built-in closets in Poland—or by swinging a big tile stove aside on hidden hinges. Entrance might be through coalbins. Many shelters were simply walled-up alcoves consisting of space hollowed out between two apartment walls. Bunkers were built to hold anywhere from five to fifty people, but when danger came, no one worried about the planned capacity of a hiding place.

Another category of shelters was the nest-type, built in attics and giving builders a free field for fantasy. Our bunker was of this kind and came into being when the carpenter who lived above us reminded me one night in November that everyone was building a hideout and suggested we do likewise. I agreed and we set to work. Across from the attic apartment which the carpenter's family occupied was space for drying laundry. We put up a wooden wall exactly like the other attic walls and cut that space off from the staircase. That was our hideout. To enter, one had to make one's way on the outside of the building through a narrow level passage between the drainpipe and the sloping roof. We blocked the opening into this passage from the inside of the building with a big container of sand left from the firefighting equipment issued during the defense of Warsaw in 1939, as well as with a pile of old rags. Even if anyone moved the rags and sand, they would still have to find the camouflaged door and know how to open it. Beyond that first camouflaged door, a low tunnel, which could be negotiated only on hands and knees, led to another camouflaged door behind which the shelter itself was located. We planned it for fifteen persons and to us it seemed foolproof. All users-to-be shared equally in financing the project.

Besides building shelters, people were also frantically making passageways between rooms, apartments, staircases, cellars, and attics, thereby linking houses until eventually we could move around an entire residential block without once going into the street. By that means the ghetto became an enormous honeycomb connected by hundreds of invisible arteries.

The Germans, too, were busy preparing for their next move. Their opening gambits were psychological, intended to set our fears at rest and simultaneously to lure into the open any Jews still in hiding. Summoning a Judenrat delegation, the Germans ordered it to submit a ghetto production plan through May 1943, and also urged upon it the importance of opening some cafés, a moving-picture house, a theater, and some children's homes. Several children who until then had been detained at Umschlagplatz were released. There were other indications that the whole Umschlag itself might be liquidated. The Germans issued an amnesty for all Jews presently living outside the ghetto provided that they returned before the end of November 1942. Though the Jewish population was no longer taken in by these maneuvers, a considerable number of Jews did return to the ghetto, because of the constant blackmail and persecution on the Aryan outside. Current German strategy went further in encouraging illegal Jews to come from their hiding places by permitting the *Werterfassung* to take on workers in all their shops without the usual difficulties and formalities. The staff in our printing shop, for example, swelled from 38 to 100. The stationery department in particular grew in size because it used unskilled workers and anyone who paid Rachman a certain sum could get a job. He passed the money on to Fogel, the right-hand man of Obersturmführer Franz Konrad, Geipel's successor as the SS man in charge of ghetto looting. At the end of 1942, the *Werterfassung* numbered several thousand workers.

During the weeks after the great deportation thousands of these illegals tried to legalize their status. I did everything to legalize Lena, but not even my friendship with Dr. Milejkowski and the fact that as a pharmacist she had a food-ration card sufficed. Eventually it turned out to be a blessing and saved our lives but at the moment this additional insecurity became an unbearable strain on Lena's frayed nerves.

One day, instead of the usual SS man, two German Army MPs were assigned as escorts on our daily march to and from the printing shop. This caused a great deal of talk. According to some it meant that the ghetto was passing into the hands of the Wehrmacht and that, after all the quarreling between the SS and the Wehrmacht generals, the latter had finally won out. The German army needed skilled Jewish labor, this line of reasoning went, and we would now be working for it, and wouldn't have to worry about survival. According to others, however, it meant that the situation on the Eastern front was so desperate that all SS men were being sent there and no one was left to guard us except the older, home-service types in the regular army.

Though such rumors circulated from time to time, and may actually have reflected real friction between the SS and the army—a quarrel which the SS won—they may also have been inspired by the Gestapo to lull Jewish vigilance.

In any event the appearance of these Wehrmacht MPs raised ghetto hopes for a while because most of them were older, relatively decent men, who reminded us of soldiers of the First World War. When I occasionally spoke to the two assigned to us, I learned that they came from Magdeburg and had been Social Democrats. "What the Nazis did to the Jews is the greatest piece of military sabotage in history," one of them said to me. A little man with an intelligent, foxy face, he was indignant. "I was in Warsaw in 1918. I know Polish Jews and I remember how much they can do for our war effort. Hitler simply threw a tremendous military asset out the window."

When the other soldier was alone with me, he said, "We certainly didn't want it like this." And he added, "I'd like to see all those heroes showing what they can do at Stalingrad."

"How did the German people ever let themselves be deluded like this?" I once asked him.

"*Die Jugend* . . . the young people," he explained. "They seemed to go mad. I didn't recognize my own son and I never dared speak openly with him the way I'm talking to you."

Two weeks later the Wehrmacht men were gone as abruptly as they had arrived. Early in December a new Judenrat announcement was issued, signed by Judenrat Obmann, Marek Lichtenbaum. The SS officer in command, Obersturmführer Mende, had telephoned to say that it had come to his attention that rumors of a new resettlement and other changes in the status quo were circulating in the ghetto. Mende authorized the Judenrat to deny all such rumors in his name as "not corresponding to the truth." Jews, Mende assured us, had nothing to fear. Czerniakow had made a similar announcement less than six months before; this new pronunciamento dispelled the short-lived optimism the appearance of the Wehrmacht had engendered.

The printshop was now assigned to a new SS man, named Emil, a native of Constance, on the German-Swiss border. One of his favorite topics was how the German-speaking cantons of Switzerland would be *anschlussed* as soon as the war was won. "It'll only take a phone call," he gloated, in happy anticipation of that day.

One day, while our column was returning from work, two SS officers stopped us in Nowolipki Street and, paying no attention to Emil, they took every cent we had. Though as Jews we had no right to have any money whatever, Emil reported what had happened to his superior, Konrad, and two days later we got most of our money back. Konrad's idea apparently was that nobody had the right to get at *his* Jews.

The Leszno Street printing shop was only one short block from my old apartment in Orla Street and I was constantly tempted to visit it because I had left my diary there. I had kept it faithfully for more than two years and I wanted to preserve it and bring it up to date. However, close as the flat was, to go there would be taking my life in my hands because it was strictly out of bounds. I might be shot on sight. One day in November I finally plucked up the courage and ran up the old familiar stairs and through the silent building. In the apartment there was plenty of evidence that we had had uninvited visitors. It was hard to recognize the place in which we had spent so many happy years; it looked like a forgotten, unkempt cemetery. My desk was still there and I went through all the drawers, but could not find the diary. I searched the entire apartment, but no diary. I ran across an album of family photographs with Wlodek's baby pictures and just as I was leaving the apartment with that under my arm I caught sight of a little book lying under the dining-room table. I went back and picked it up. It was a Polish passport made out to a Jan Trzeciak. How had such a document, made out to a person I'd never heard of, gotten into my apartment?

When I brought the photographic album home, Lena was horrified and berated me for risking my life for some old pictures. As long as people were alive, she reminded me, one could always take more photographs.

Things were happening all around us. While the pharmacy was still on Gesia Street, Lena had mentioned being approached by young men from the underground for first-aid equipment. Every so often they came back to ask for more bandages, gauze, cotton, and iodine, and soon the supplies they required reached such considerable proportions that Lena took the precaution of handling them secretly.

One day when I did not go to work, Lena came back to the apartment very excited. With her was Izak Dorfman. We had lost track of him months before after his telephone calls from Lublin, and now he was in Warsaw, safe and sound. His story was fantastic and I am ashamed to say that I discounted half of it as pure imagination. Izak had survived the Lublin Resettlement Operation and found himself first in the Majdan Tatarski ghetto, and then in Majdanek. There he was housed in what had formerly served as stables. The brutality of the guards was incredible and many inmates died. Prisoners who hid money and precious stones were hanged if caught. A loaf of bread cost 100 zlotys and a lunch of bread, butter, and meat cost a twenty-dollar gold piece.

When the typhus epidemic broke out that fall, the Germans treated it with brutal simplicity: prisoners were made to run a gantlet and anyone who stumbled, fell, or did not run fast enough was beaten to death. This effectively weeded out the typhus patients. Roll calls lasting several hours, during which inmates had to stand at rigid attention, cut down the remaining sick and weak ones.

Every morning prisoners were driven into Lublin by truck to work on a construction project and there Izak, who had managed to get clothing and documents from a Polish civilian, succeeded in escaping. He then walked all the way to Warsaw and was now living with his girlfriend, Zosia, on the Aryan side. "Don't believe any German promise. Not a single Jew is going to survive," Izak warned us. "Our only chance is to get out among the Aryans: anything else is certain death. Don't stay here another minute: get out of the ghetto!"

It was going to take six months more for me to grasp that, far from exaggerating, Izak was understating the case. At that time I was still skeptical.

Another frequent visitor was Franciszek Malec, a Polish letter carrier whose way of getting into the ghetto was to show a letter addressed to someone living inside the walls. Because of his mailman's uniform, the guards always let him pass. The same letter served more than once. He knew the Zandbergs who lived in the back room of our apartment and was helping them to prepare their escape. He got Aryan documents for them, carried some of their possessions out of the ghetto for them, and sold their valuables so they could get money, because he could smuggle things out under his heavy cloak and in his mailbag. He also performed similar services for other people in the ghetto. A cheerful, jovial man, he brought us heartening news of the war from outside and smuggled in underground newspapers. In that way we learned that the tide was turning against the Nazis and that resistance to them was increasing all over Poland.

The last weeks of that tragic year 1942 were comparatively quiet. There were still killings, of course—for being caught on the streets during working hours, for smuggling, for engaging in illegal business activities, for being found in the wrong building (visiting a wife or a husband or a relative, for example), or arbitrarily, for nothing at all. Klostermeyer's street patrol now included a huge dog, trained to attack people, capable of knocking a man down and holding him down by sinking his teeth into leg or thigh. Klostermeyer made a little game of it. If the victim did not remain rigidly at attention, smiling, head bared, while the dog worried pieces of his flesh off—if the victim made a gesture to resist the beast or tried to run—he was "shot trying to escape." But to those of us who had seen the worst of it, this was a time of comparative calm, though Pinkiert was still kept busy every day.

On December 31, ten of us sat down for a modest celebration, not knowing that six of us would never see another New Year's Eve. We were not even that optimistic; we thought it would be the last for all of us. Since we all lived in the same building the curfew did not bother us, and since we had access to the pharmacy's "medicinal" alcohol, we had plenty to drink and got very drunk. There was only one toast, the traditional Jewish toast, nor was any ever more apt: *Le'Haim* (To life).

The year 1943 began with foreboding. "They're busy again at Umschlag." "Ukrainian and Latvian guards have arrived." "The Vernichtungskommando is on its way to Warsaw." "Final liquidation of the ghetto. No one will be spared." *"Judenrein!"* On January 9, Heinrich Himmler and his staff inspected the ghetto. An armed group of SS officers led by Police Chief Odilo Globocnik, protected by small armored cars bristling with machine guns, escorted the SS chief as he raced through the streets. His inspection took only minutes, but we all knew what it meant: Himmler had last visited the ghetto in July.

I plunged into a long period of darkness punctuated only by a few flashes of consciousness: I had caught typhus. Our old friend Dr. Izak Lichtenberg looked after me. His whole family had perished in the deportations and he suffered an anguish of loneliness. He could get through the days by keeping busy, but the nights were torment. He rose unrefreshed every morning faced with the prospect of another day and then another unendurable night filled with the unanswerable questions: Why? What for? He clung to me like a drowning man, came to see me at dawn and dropped in at intervals throughout the day, staying for hours at a time. His treatment was old-fashioned: leeches under the ears, glucose injections, doses

of Pyramidon. Typhus has no known cure. Mine was a severe case. I ran high
fevers when I was delirious and raved much of the time. My subconscious
mind ran rampant:

*An old man in burlap kneels at the foot of a broad staircase. His long hair and
beard, streaked with gray, float in the breeze. On his head are ashes, the symbol of
mourning, and his hands are raised in prayer. I am looking at myself. How very
old I am!*

   *Miriam Orleska dances forward among skeletons, her face set in the lines of
sorrowing Rachel. Her eyes are empty, but directed into mine, and she raises a long
white hand to point to me. Her voice is horrible, her tone accusing: "He is still alive!"
The voice of Moskowicz follows immediately: "His wife is living, too!" The voice of
Councillor Gliksberg comes next, like a stern judge's: "And his child is alive, too!"*

   "For not having attained the honor of Kiddush HaShem, *" Moskowicz
solemnly intones, "for having been sentenced to live instead of sharing the fate of
the community, we banish him from our midst. Henceforward he shall walk the
lonely path of the man who has no people. I formally exclude him from our flock
and summon you to say the prayer for a son denied the privilege of dying with his
own.* Kaddish. *"*

   *I try to cry out, "No, no, I am wholeheartedly with my people. It was blind
fate that permitted me to go on living," but my voice makes no sound and Moskowicz begins to sway, praying fervently for my soul. The others intone a solemn amen
and turn their backs on me.*

   *An old man steps forward carrying a large cross. His face is that of a con-
vert to Christianity who used to work for* Caritas. *He falls to his knees and strikes
his forehead against the ground. Passionately he recites aloud:*

> *Our Father in whom I do not believe,*
> *Hallowed be Thy name;*
> *Thy Kingdom come,*
> *Thy will be done, in earth as it is in heaven.*
> *Give us this day our daily life,*
> *Have mercy on the souls of murderers,*
> *And forgive them their trespasses,*
> *For we cannot.*
>
> *Forgive them for they know not what they do,*
> *And we can neither forgive nor forget.*
> *We do not ask mercy, Lord, for ourselves,*
> *Who were burned at the stake in Belzec*

And gassed in the chambers of Treblinka,
Who died in the cauldrons of the ghettos,
Who perished of typhus and hunger,
For Thou hast not granted us Thy mercy,
And Thou knowest not what Thou hast done.

The sound of galloping horses drowns out these voices, and an army bugle sounds. The strains of a Polish battle hymn fill the air. Kapko, in Uhlan dress uniform, gallops by on a beautiful brown horse, holding an automatic rifle with both hands and spitting bullets to right and left. With a contemptuous glance at me, he shouts, "You're not human beings, you're dirt! I told you to run off and join the partisans!"

I wave desperately to Kapko, begging him to take me with him, but he has galloped on.

The strains of "Eli, Eli" soar and shiver my spine. The half-mad Rubinstein goes through wild Cubist capers and shrieks: "All are equal. None shall survive. He's cheated us all. He has broken the Covenant! He's the God of Treblinka!"

Aunt Sarah looks at me from her deep, long-suffering eyes, her features inscrutable: "It is written in the Holy Books," she says, "that a time will come when the living will envy the dead."

It was Jozef Zandberg's turn to open the pharmacy that morning and he had not been gone more than a few minutes when he came running back up the stairs, pale as a ghost. "The guard at the ghetto gate has been doubled, and they're not letting the working parties through to their jobs. Something's up. I don't like the smell of it. Let's go up to the attic. Hurry!"

I was still running a fever and had to be helped out of bed. Half-dressed I was hurried to the attic, but how they got me through that narrow tunnel I don't know. When I came to, I was on a mattress on the floor and our tiny hideout was jammed full of people, many of whom I didn't recognize. The carpenter was closing off the entrance, and Lena was saying over and over again, "I'm so grateful it was Mr. Zandberg's turn this morning. I would never have noticed the extra guards. I would never have noticed. We'd all have been done for if it had been up to me!"

It was January 18, 1943, the day the second Resettlement Operation began. After an hour or two we heard a commotion in the courtyard and the hateful shouting once more: *"Alle Juden runter! Alles runter!"* A long silence, then the rhythmic thud of heavy boots on the staircase. It stopped. They were at the second floor. We heard gun butts splintering doors.

Silence. Then the boots on the stairs again. Third floor. Banging on the doors, the splintering of wood, a woman's shrill scream. Fourth floor. Banging on doors, but no splintering of wood. Again the boots climbing. They were approaching the attic. We could hear voices. My throat was dry, I couldn't breathe. No one in our hiding place seemed to move a muscle. They were on the landing now and went into the carpenter's apartment. We heard a young Ukrainian voice bark, "*Nemá* (Nobody there)."

"*Keine Juden?*" A German voice from the landing below.

"*Nein,*" the Ukrainian replied.

The boots tramped downstairs, away from us. I was drenched with sweat. At that moment we heard two shots, clear and distinct, followed immediately by automatic-rifle fire. Then another burst. A little later, an explosion. All quiet again, though from time to time there were distant detonations we couldn't identify.

About an hour later, Ola Kacenelenbogen rushed up to our shelter and berated us loudly. In the fuss and struggle of getting me upstairs, she had been overlooked. No one had alerted her to the roundup, and she and her family were taken completely by surprise when they heard the spine-chilling "*Alle Juden runter!*" from the courtyard and then the boots on the staircase. With extraordinary presence of mind, Ola had hurriedly donned a white apron and nurse's cap and at the first sound outside her door had calmly opened it and said, "*Kein Eintritt! Fleckfieber!* (You can't come in. Typhus)." The Germans had jumped back from the doorway; typhus was one of the few things they feared.

As before, the roundup ended at sundown and that night we all came out of our shelters. The entire ghetto was stirred by the electrifying news that a real battle had taken place at the corner of Niska and Zamenhof Streets. Members of the Jewish underground had stood off the SS with guns, grenades, Molotov cocktails, and pickaxes. About twenty Germans had been killed. There had been nests of resistance in our own building and in the adjacent one at 56 Zamenhof. (The two were connected by a secret passage.) The men had waited for the Germans to get inside the courtyard before they opened fire from two sides. Similar resistance had taken place in Leszno, Nowolipie, and Smocza Street shop areas. We were overjoyed, though the news sounded too good to be true.

The new Resettlement Operation was headed by Brand and SS Hauptsturmführer Theodor van Eupen,[8] commandant of the death camp at Tre-

---

8. SS-Hauptsturmführer Theodor van Eupen, was in fact the commandant of Treblinka I, a forced labor camp for Jews located about a mile from the killing center.—Editor's note

blinka. German headquarters was in Muranow Square and they had tanks, small artillery pieces, automatic rifles, and hand grenades.

My sister Roza had been looking after Wlodek while I was ill with typhus, but that night she came to see us and brought him back with her. When the roundup began she had gone to the shelter in her building, a hidden room entered by moving to one side a huge tile stove specially hinged for the purpose. Wlodek had behaved with perfect understanding of the situation and had not made a sound. He had in fact been much calmer than many of the adults, who were near hysteria. Nonetheless, Roza's neighbors, who owned the shelter jointly with her, resented Wlodek's presence and insisted she take him back to his parents. Children were, of course, a great problem in hideouts and their presence sometimes led to quarrels and fistfights. Neighbors had even forced mothers to strangle their children when they cried, and when the mother resisted, had done the job themselves.

Wlodek stayed in the bunker with us for the next three days of the January operation. He behaved like a little soldier throughout. We had more than thirty people in our shelter, originally planned for fifteen, and every bit of floor space was taken. Some of the people were not neighbors, and some were complete strangers who had been surprised in our building by the roundup.

There was a lot of shooting the second day and that was when my illness reached its crisis and my temperature began to go down: I was out of danger then—at least from the typhus.

From everything we could learn it seemed that the operation was making little headway. The underground's open resistance and the passive resistance of the rest of the people was accomplishing the impossible. After four days the second resettlement was called off without having attained its objectives. In many cases only a few underground fighters had been enough to save everyone in a big apartment house. After the first shot the Germans were afraid to search cellars and attics: they merely shouted into the courtyards, fired a few shots, and then withdrew.

About the only people they had managed to round up this time were those who still had faith in the power of their "valid" documents, and who went down to the courtyards when ordered to do so. No one asked to see their papers then; they were simply herded off to Umschlagplatz. Many Judenrat officials and workers met their end in this fashion, among them our old friend Dr. Izrael Milejkowski. Only when he went down to the courtyard of his apartment house did he realize that his immunity as a Judenrat member no longer obtained, and then he shouted, "Murderers! Our blood will be on your heads!" The surviving Judenrat staff blamed the depletion in their ranks on Abram Sztolcman, the council's vice-chairman, who had instructed all officials to report to the Germans in obedience to issued orders. He had assured them that they would be perfectly safe.

Six thousand people perished in the January roundups, but this time the Germans paid in killed and wounded. We were a changed people now. We had no more illusions about German plans for us. During the first resettlement a "valid" document had occasionally worked; during this second one, a really good shelter had served; but when the next wave of deportation came, documents and shelters might be of no avail. We knew, too, that just as we had learned the Germans' tactics, they would soon learn ours. Ghetto dwellers made proud pilgrimages to places where blood on the snow marked scenes of successful Jewish resistance. The self-pity and resignation which had tormented us after the cauldron were burned away; we were now living torches of revolt.

Typhus left me very weak; I felt weightless and everything seemed unfamiliar. About the well-known typhus convalescent's ravenous appetite, I could do little; I could not afford to stuff myself and for days I went around hungry. My sister Roza came to the rescue with thick soups and horse-meat steaks—horse meat was the only readily available meat and it was smuggled in quantity into the ghetto. Soon I felt better, though for a long time I was weak.

On the surface the ghetto seemed normal: work parties went out the gate every morning; the Judenrat agencies functioned as usual; shops were busily productive; and the pharmacy remained open. But just below the surface feverish preparations were under way for the ghetto's last battle. The Poles we came into contact with now looked at us with new eyes, though, as in the past, you could still hear conversations like this one around the gates:

"That windbreaker's a nice coat. Sell it to me. I can give you bread, lard . . . and I'm willing to pay you well for it."

"It's winter. It's cold. I need the coat myself."

"What does it matter? They're going to make soap out of you anyway. Sell the coat to me. Why should a nice coat like that go to waste?"

Such things were said neither as a taunt nor in hatred. The facts were only too evident: the Jews were too stupid to understand their situation and it was necessary to hammer it home to them. After the January resistance, however, we occasionally heard Poles say things like, "Bravo, little Yids! That's the way. Stand right up to them!" Or, "They're eating you for lunch and saving us for dinner!" Or, "As soon as those sons-of-bitches have finished you off, it'll be our turn." The new spirit in the ghetto seemed to have made a great impression on the Poles, though we knew that the resistance had been fantastically exaggerated on the other side of the walls. Also such comments were the exception; the great bulk of the Polish population had not changed its attitude. The ZOB was still unsuccessful in its efforts to obtain arms from Polish underground groups, and there was no perceptible decrease in the blackmailing and informing on Jews outside the ghetto.

Our own first thoughts were to improve our bunker. We installed electricity, piped in water, and improved the camouflage of the entrance. We set up a system of permanent lookouts on the stairs and in the courtyard so that next time no one would be taken by surprise, and we shared all-night duty in two-hour shifts. A set of alarm bells was installed in every apartment and the signal could be given by pressing a single button downstairs. Instructions were to alert everyone at the slightest suspicious occurrence.

The same thing was going on all over the ghetto. Shelters were being built, which were expected to hold out for weeks and months, and some to last to the very end of the war. Everyone was discreet about where his shelter was located and how entry to it was gained. Most of these bunkers turned out to be living tombs, though we were not able to foresee that.

Lena and I thought constantly of how to save Wlodek. We knew now that being a Jewish child was a death sentence for him, and for us, and we went over in our minds the list of our Aryan friends and acquaintances, singling out the few who might be willing to help us. When Izak Dorfman and Zosia came to see us, he renewed his entreaty that we do something and do it soon. Zosia, who was very fond of Wlodek, said she would take him any time we said the word, but Izak was opposed to any such arrangement because the risks were too great for the child and for them.

I began writing letters asking those I had singled out among my Aryan friends to help me save my son. I asked nothing for Lena or myself, only their help in saving the life of an innocent boy. Every letter had to be delivered by hand—there was no longer mail service in the ghetto—and this was difficult to manage because people were reluctant to accept letters from the ghetto delivered by strangers. Blackmail might all too easily be the result. For that reason I alerted my friends in advance by telephone whenever possible, using the phone at the TOZ offices at 56 Zamenhof Street. I could get to it without going outdoors, using the secret passages, but the phone was in constant use and I had to wait for hours before I could put through a call. Smugglers used it to contact their Aryan confederates, and others had purposes like my own. The ZOB also had calls to make on that telephone, and only trustworthy persons were permitted its use.

Since not all my Aryan friends had phones, I often had to call on Kapko at his office to ask him to send Kazimierz, a man in his employ who had formerly worked for us, as a messenger. Kazimierz was one of the finest individuals I have ever known, and a man to whom I am profoundly grateful. He would go to the individual I wanted to talk to and ask him to await a call from me at Kapko's office at some convenient day and hour. Then I had to call Kapko back the following day to learn what, if any, appointment Kazimierz had succeeded in arranging. Kapko had business partners from whom he wished all these things to be kept secret, but he was cooperative about carrying out my requests. Often, appointments were made and for one reason or another could not be kept. The whole procedure was laborious and time-consuming in the extreme. And when I finally did manage to speak to a friend on the phone, I then had to persuade him to meet me at the Leszno Street printshop, which was now outside of the ghetto walls. There was no risk to any Gentile going there because they could always pretend to be trying to buy Jewish rags, but many were nevertheless afraid to go there. I spoke to many friends: some agreed to come but never did; others did come but would not or could not help; and finally only one real possibility for saving Wlodek began to take shape—the Maginskis.

Stefan Maginski had been one of the members of the group with whom I had fled Warsaw in September 1939, and he and his wife had visited us just prior to the ghetto's being walled off. Originally from Lvov, Maginski was a highly educated man, and a very able journalist, with a special talent for presenting complex problems in a simple direct style. He was a romantic and chivalrous gentleman, warm, human, friendly, and fond of a drink; indeed, he was his most charming after a few drinks, teasing, witty in a mordant way, and full of esprit. He had nothing of the narrow-minded or doctrinaire about him in politics and his generous nature always put him on the side of the underdog. Twenty years my senior, he used to treat me a little like a younger brother. He was fond of me, and I liked and respected him.

While Stefan was exiled in Russia during World War I, he had fallen in love with Marysia Laudyn, a young actress, who had been a real beauty and still was a handsome woman. Wholeheartedly devoted to her, he always remained a bit astonished (secretly) that she had agreed to marry him.

She complemented her husband's charm and intellect with her own warmth and feeling, and they made an extremely attractive couple. They had no children.

After several telephone conversations, Mrs. Maginski agreed to meet me in Leszno Street and on the appointed day Lena and Wlodek joined the printers' column when we marched off to work. When Mrs. Maginski appeared, I took her to one of the empty apartments in the printshop building and there, with Lena, we discussed the entire matter. Mrs. Maginski told us she had a friend in the country who would be willing to take Wlodek for a very modest payment. He would be well taken care of there, and she, Mrs. Maginski vouched for the honesty, decency, and responsibility of the people concerned. She said she couldn't take Wlodek herself because she and Stefan were too old to blossom forth suddenly with a five-year-old child; besides, they were up to their ears in underground work. The amount of money was, indeed, modest, no more than taking care of Wlodek would actually cost. Happily, we had the money because, somewhat earlier, in an effort to earn some cash, I had gone into partnership with Izak Rubin in smuggling out of the ghetto some of the kerchiefs made from pillowcases. We had been quite successful and as a result I was able to pay for Wlodek's care for several months in advance. With unerring instinct, Wlodek did his best to win Mrs. Maginski and she was very taken with his charm. She agreed to make the necessary preparations and promised to come for him in a week or two.

A short time afterward, Dr. Lichtenberg committed suicide. Even after I had recovered from typhus, he had come to see us often because he found it increasingly difficult to be alone. The night before he died he had looked at us imploringly, not quite daring to ask to stay the night. The next morning we learned that he had taken cyanide.

One day I went to the Brushmakers' to see my wife's brother, Adek, who was sick. As I walked down one of the corridors in his building, I saw a mimeographed poster on the wall. It was an appeal to resist the Nazis. It said that this was no time to think of saving one's own skin, but a time to think of the future of the Jews. Even those able to escape the ghetto should stay on instead and fight. It was signed by the Jewish Military Organization (ZZW). That was the first evidence I had seen with my own eyes that an underground other than the ZOB existed. Soon there were to be more such indications.

More and more the ZOB had become the sole spiritual authority in the ghetto. The wealthier people were taxed by it for arms and ammunition, and to maintain fighting groups. Most people contributed willingly, but the unwilling were forced. People were pleased to learn that Judenrat members, Jewish policemen, and shop managers were all being made to kick in to support the underground. More gratifying was the story of Judenrat president Lichtenbaum, who had refused a ZOB order to contribute 50,000 zlotys. The ZOB held his son hostage, and within twenty-four hours Lichtenbaum had paid the sum in full—and made no mention of it to the Germans either. The underground also carried out a number of "expropriations." They raided the Judenrat treasury, held up the Nalewki Street bank, and executed a number of other such operations. In that manner considerable sums were accumulated.

On the way home from work one day I had a serious talk with Izak Rubin. Though only twenty-two, he was a young man of superior qualities and had matured greatly in the recent weeks. Tall, broad-shouldered, and very handsome with his blond hair and blue eyes, he looked like a Slav. We called him the "blond Izak" to distinguish him from his cousin and childhood friend, the "black Izak" Dorfman. I had known Izak Rubin from childhood and had great confidence in him; in ghetto slang, Izak had *blit* (blood) or guts. He loved me like a brother and would have given his life for Lena and Wlodek. One day black Izak Dorfman had visited us with his girlfriend Zosia, and they had brought along with them a very good-looking girl, a friend of Zosia's named Janka. When she met blond Izak, she urged him to go back to the Aryan side with them, but he had refused to consider his own safety until the rest of us were able to settle our problems.

The day before, Izak told me, he had met Zygmunt (Zalmen) Frydrych. Zygmunt also had Aryan features, had known Izak from childhood, and had a high opinion of and full confidence in him. Zygmunt had been a youth leader in the Labor Bund and in the ghetto had a job in the Judenrat Provisioning Agency. An active ZOB member, he was one of the best people in the Jewish resistance. He told Izak that the ZOB had suffered heavy casualties in the January fighting chiefly because they had lacked arms, but there were also other causes: poor liaison between combat groups and lack of military training. "The merest German private," he said "knows more about organizing warfare than we do." Zygmunt asked Izak to join the ZOB, saying that they needed men like him, and Izak replied that he'd be happy to.

One of the conditions of membership was living together in common quarters, but Izak felt he could not comply with that condition. Also, he belonged to no political party, and barracks were assigned along party lines. Not because political differences mattered at this time—we were united in the face of death as we had never been united before—but because those with similar political backgrounds knew and trusted each other, and trust was absolutely necessary in such conspiratorial work. In addition, since Izak had such an Aryan appearance, Zygmunt thought he might use him for special assignments. These considerations led to a decision to have Izak organize his own resistance group at 44 Muranowska Street, but Zygmunt warned that he would have to get hold of his own arms. Izak suggested that they use the printing shop as a liaison point, and Zygmunt agreed, provided that Izak could organize a unit based there as well.

Izak was terribly wrought up by the conversation, and he made up his mind to leave the ghetto to see what he could do, but first he wanted to help us make arrangements for Wlodek's safety. Next, Lena and Roza had to be provided with secure hideouts on the Aryan side, and only then could we plan to do something for ourselves.

For weeks I had been phoning Kapko, trying to persuade him to meet me, but though helpful in reaching others, he was reluctant to come to Leszno Street himself. At long last, however, he relented, and I spent the night before our appointment putting my ideas in order and preparing a speech. Kapko was unchanged. His business was thriving and he had made a great deal of money. There was something guarded about him, something I couldn't put my finger on. The former cordial sincerity, the directness, was missing. He seemed depressed, restless, eager to be gone. But there was no time for psychological analysis; I had to speak my piece and do it quickly. I began by observing that the tide of battle had turned and that since Stalingrad our ultimate victory was sure. It was only a question of time. Unfortunately we in the ghetto would not live to see the German defeat, for we were doomed. Unless, of course, our brothers outside the ghetto came to our aid. "Help us," I begged him. "In the name of the past, in the name of humanity, of our struggle against a common enemy, yes, in the name of Christianity." I spoke passionately, stumbling over my words, but I could see I was not being persuasive enough. Kapko nodded, smiled sympathetically, and now and again gripped my hand, but I could tell I was not getting through to him. He assured me that he'd do all he could, that I'd hear from him soon, but that his people were terrified. Blackmailers and informers were everywhere, and they were all afraid of their own shadows. Kapko avoided my eyes and kept staring into the distance. I knew I had failed.

Then, suddenly, I remembered the dream which had so terrified me during my typhus fever, and words began to pour out as if someone else were speaking through my mouth. "Kapko," I said, "it's fine that you're making money and willing to help people less fortunate than yourself. But you must realize we are coming to a time when none of that is enough. Money makes enemies. You can be certain that dozens of pairs of eyes are watching you, keeping track of your every movement, your slightest peccadillo. Sooner or later you'll be called to account.

"Sergeant Stanislaw Kapko, member of the Warsaw Municipal Council, vice president of the Union of Noncommissioned Officers, member of the Polish Publishers' Association," they'll say, "what did *you* do for Poland in the days of Auschwitz and Treblinka? Where were you, a born leader, when Poland was lying bruised and bleeding under the invader's heel? You were a *businessman!* You were making *money!* Is that what your combat record was?"

I had touched a live nerve. Kapko's reaction was instantaneous. He glowered, following what I was saying with an expression close to pain. But something inside me had to get spoken.

I reminded him how when we had fled in September 1939, with defeat bitter in our mouths, he had been a man of vision, believing in the future. He had talked of guerrilla warfare, but none of us had understood him then. Now, with victory coming closer, we were ready and eager for his leadership. Dozens, hundreds, thousands of desperate people were willing and eager to fight. We had nothing to lose. We were ready for anything.

I cannot remember all I said, but when I had finished, Kapko was weeping, so overwhelmed that for a long time he could not speak at all. When he finally did, he raised his right hand and with bloodless lips he whispered, "So help me God!" When he regained his composure, he thanked me for having brought him back to himself, for having helped to save his soul. When we parted, he said he would have a plan of action drawn up within the week, and then he embraced me. I was overwhelmed by the meeting, too; the violence of his reaction as well as the things I had found myself saying left me deeply shaken.

Spring came timidly that year as if it did not belong in the ghetto. Piles of dirty snow were slow to melt, and the few trees took a long time to bud. The only joyous note was the sun, which burned brightly and steadily every day. Once more the axe was to fall, heralded as usual by a gigantic German lie. Now recovered from his hernia operation, Walther Caspar

Toebbens, the ghetto's chief German industrialist, added to his duties of ruthlessly exploiting his Jewish slave labor the position of head of the new Resettlement Operation. The SS had retired from the stage, we were told, and we were Toebbens' "own" Jews. By order of Himmler, Toebbens told "his Jews"—in a kindly, paternal tone—Warsaw was to be made *judenrein*, literally cleansed of the Jews. We were not, however, for a moment to suppose this meant Treblinka or Majdanek. Instead, all machinery and personnel were to be shifted to Poniatowa and Trawniki, labor camps in the Lublin district. There, Jewish workers, their wives, and children could live out the war safely in the wholesome country air. All German ghetto shop owners personally addressed their Jewish workers, swearing that no harm would come to a single Jew. A few Jewish shop managers were taken in and collaborated with Toebbens, but though they all worked hard to persuade us, few of us volunteered.

When the Germans actually began to dismantle the machinery in some shops, there was sabotage. Shops and warehouses were destroyed or badly damaged. Underground activists beat up a number of the foremen, and one manager who collaborated with the Nazis was shot dead in the street in broad daylight. On the walls of buildings the inscription "Poniatowa and Trawniki equals Treblinka!" was scrawled and the ZOB issued a proclamation warning that the new program was simply a continuation of the planned extermination of the Jews. "Hide your wives and children and take up arms!" the underground advised, "Only resistance can save the remnants of the ghetto's people!"

One day in March, Rachman and our SS man summoned me to the office and handed me a page of German copy to be set on my Linotype. It was Toebbens' appeal "To the Jewish Munitions Workers of the Jewish Quarter!" *(An die jüdische Rüstungsarbeiter des jüdischen Wohnbezirkes!);* Jewish workers were asked to volunteer for resettlement to Poniatowa and Trawniki. In it the Nazi occupation authorities for the first time entered into polemics with the ZOB, warning Jews not to trust anyone but the German shop managers, and declaring that the ZOB was misleading them with false promises. I pulled three extra copies of the document and that night passed them to Izak to take to our liaison man with the ZOB.

A day or so later I met Leon Berkowicz in the street. Before the war an owner of one of the city's biggest advertising agencies, and also part owner of a chemical plant, he had seen active duty in the September campaign as a commissioned officer under General Bortnowski and had distinguished himself at the battle of Kutno. During the first Resettlement Operation his chemical factory had been taken over by Toebbens. Berkowicz had an excellent reputation as a sensible and honest man, and I considered him a friend. He told me he was on his way to see me. He had a proposition for Lena to go to Poniatowa with him to organize a pharmacy there. "I can guarantee you good living conditions and even a chance to make some money on the side."

"Are you out of your mind? Do you really expect us to volunteer for Poniatowa?" I asked.

"What else is there to do? They'll deport us from Warsaw in any case. Don't have any illusions about that. We have only two choices: escape to the Aryan side, or Poniatowa. Personally, I prefer the latter to continual blackmail and living like a rat in a hole."

"Don't you realize Poniatowa is a trap?" I remonstrated. "Do you trust Toebbens?"

"Yes, I trust Toebbens. I know him personally and I think he's telling the truth. Oh, he's no better than Brand, but he's making too much money from exploiting the Jews to be eager to get rid of us. He'd stop at nothing to keep his shops going and he's got more influence than you think. All those SS murderers are his partners, or in his pay, from top to bottom."

"Didn't you see what the ZOB said?"

"They're a bunch of romantic kids. I have had a little experience with soldiering and I know just how hopeless the chances are of standing off the Germans in the ghetto. There'd be nothing left except a pile of rubble. I'd rather leave voluntarily than be dragged away by force. At least I'll be able to take some of my belongings with me."

Berkowicz came to see me several times thereafter for my answer, and he grew quite bitter at my persistent refusals. Daily, more and more people were getting out of the ghetto. In March, the Zandbergs and two other families got out with Franciszek's help, as did Lena's brother Adek and his wife Bronka. Their living quarters had been arranged by Franciszek's "partner," a streetcar conductor. As news of Franciszek's powers spread, total strangers began to call on me to ask about him, but at the end of March he stopped coming to the ghetto entirely. Several times I had suggested to him that he could make a good deal of money by smuggling arms into the ghetto, but he always declined with an embarrassed, "Too risky."

Those who could not think of escape dreamed only of getting weapons. It became an obsession: people would part with everything they owned to get hold of a pistol or a single hand grenade; to lay hands on a *spluwa* (Polish slang for a "rod") became everyone's idée fixe. Even such an obdurate civilian as I was, who had always severely criticized militarism, got the fever. But behind it was a new psychology manifested in remarks heard everywhere: "Let's give them some of their own back." "One German, at least, for every Jew." "This time we won't give up so easily."

In January, Ada Kacenelenbogen, whose parents had sent her out of the ghetto after the July resettlement, returned. She was in a state of nervous breakdown and refused categorically to leave the ghetto again. "I'd rather die with you here," she repeated, over and over, in the face of her parents' pleas and despair. She was only fifteen years old and Aryan-looking. By March she informed her parents that she had joined the ZOB. Her father did everything he could to dissuade her, in vain. "I should think you'd be proud of me, give me your blessing," she told him, "not mourn the loss of a daughter. We're all going to die anyway. I should think you'd be happy I've earned such an honor." At this, her father, Josef, burst into tears, took Ada in his arms and, crying all the while, recited the Hebrew blessing over her. Ola, the girl's mother, fainted.

But Ada was not the only one to prefer death in the ghetto to life outside. Nor was it a matter wholly of distaste for conditions in Aryan Warsaw. Many people believed that to save one's life under the circumstances was worse than selfishness: it was treachery. Underground proclamations did much to encourage this conviction, and many of the younger people refused excellent opportunities to escape individually; they would remain to fight. All they asked was arms.

I was impatient for news from Mrs. Maginski and Kapko. By the end of March, Mrs. Maginski paid a second visit to Leszno Street to tell me her friend outside Warsaw was ready for Wlodek. We had two weeks to prepare the child psychologically and materially. New shoes were a necessity. Lena had, in the interim, been teaching Wlodek the Catholic prayers. "Now, remember," she told him, "you have never lived in the ghetto and you must never use the word *ghetto*. You're not a *Jew*. You're a Polish Catholic. You must never use the word *ghetto*. Your father is an officer in the Polish army who is a prisoner of war. Your mother is living in the country, and Mrs. Maginski is your auntie." Over and over she drummed the lesson into him, but was it possible to make a Marrano out of a five-year-old child? Could we anticipate all the circumstances, the verbal traps, to which he would inevitably be exposed? Could he become so perfect a conspirator that he would never by the least word or gesture betray his origins or background? And even as we strove to assure his Gentile pose, we were bitterly aware of the tragic spectacle of a mother teaching her only child to disavow his parents, his people, and his former life.

We also had only two weeks to engrave on our hearts and minds the image of our only child. We tried not to let Wlodek feel the pain the impending separation was causing us; we didn't want him to be nervous and so spoil the whole elaborate deception. Instead, therefore, we made it into a great adventure, an exciting game, and told him that now he was "setting out to see the world." All of that he accepted calmly enough.

As things turned out we did not have even two weeks. Only seven days had passed when Mrs. Maginski turned up again at the Leszno Street printing shop, terribly upset. The Polish underground had heard that the liquidation of the ghetto would begin any day. The child would have to be removed at once. She brushed aside all our objections about not being ready. "It's now or never," she insisted, and told us she would return the very next day for Wlodek.

Roza and Izak Rubin spent that last evening with us. We all had supper together and that we did not give vent to our feeling is another example of how much human beings can endure. We kept telling ourselves how lucky we were in this impossible situation, but why did our "luck" have to be so tragic?

The next day was one of those radiant spring mornings. Lena washed and fed Wlodek. At eight o'clock we joined the printers' column and Wlodek got into the horse-drawn wagon with other women and children. Mrs. Maginski came to the printing shop at eleven. Outwardly calm, she was a bundle of nerves. Not a tear was shed. No one said an untoward word. But Wlodek, sensing what was happening, said to his mother, "Don't be sad, Mommy. You see I'm not crying a bit." Only at the last minute did he clutch his mother and ask her, with all the seriousness of which five-year-olds are capable, "Mommy, is it really true that I'll never see you again?"

"What a silly idea," Lena managed to reply. "Why, just as soon as the war is over, I'll come for you right away."

Mrs. Maginski took Wlodek's hand and walked briskly out of the building. Wlodek skipped along beside her and she didn't look back once. They crossed Leszno Street and turned into Orla, and we watched Wlodek walk with her. When both of them were cut off from our sight by a wall, a valve slammed shut in my heart. Everyone crowded around us to congratulate us. We had been very very lucky, they said. So, indeed, we had. When I marched back home that night and saw along the route many of the children, on whom fate had not smiled, I felt a rush of profound relief and genuine gratitude in my heart. There were still true Christians among the Poles, and it took genuine courage and morality to be a true Christian in that bitter time.

When we sent Wlodek with Mrs. Maginski, we seemed to touch off a movement. Many children of those who worked in the printing shop now were sent from the ghetto, and the shop itself became a transfer point for those who were leaving. Grownups, too, took advantage of our location as a relatively easy and inexpensive way of making contacts with the outside, of entering or leaving the ghetto.

A few days after Wlodek had left us, Adek and Bronka came back to the ghetto, morally and physically broken. The conditions they described were nightmarish. Franciszek's partner, the streetcar conductor, had turned out to be unreliable. The people whose address he'd given them knew nothing about them and refused to let them in. After the most earnest entreaties, they were allowed to spend one night. The next day they tried to get in touch with both Franciszek and his partner, but without success. They called on a number of friends, but no one would help. After a week of being driven from pillar to post, with their money all gone and their illusions dispelled, they decided to return to the ghetto.

Izak Rubin, blond Izak, was luckier. Black Izak Dorfman and Zosia received him with open arms, as did Janka, who had fallen in love with him. He got Aryan papers and then called on Kapko. I had warned Kapko that he would have a visit from Izak, gave him a password, and told him that he could speak as frankly to Izak as he would to me. Izak came back to the printing shop full of hope. From what he told me Kapko seemed a changed man, full of enthusiasm, projecting fantastic schemes, and he had sent a message asking me to meet him on Friday at the printing shop because he had a plan of immediate, practical action. Izak also got hold of a pistol and several clips of ammunition. Getting the weapon into the ghetto posed a serious problem and I suggested to Izak that he take it apart and that we bring it in piecemeal. Izak disagreed. He objected that this would simply multiply the chances of getting caught. "Besides," he said, "you stay out of it. It's my gun and I'll do it my own way. There's no need for two men to take risks over one gun." The next day Izak simply carried the gun, hidden in a loaf of bread, right past the guard; the loaf was wrapped in a piece of dirty newspaper to make it look unappetizing. He hid the bullets in the false bottom of a lunch pail and put some of the ill-smelling little fish in the visible part to cover it up. For the first time in my life I held a pistol in my hands. What magic in this piece of metal! With it came the knowledge that though we might die, we could no longer be slaughtered like sheep.

The Friday of Kapko's visit came, April 16, 1943, a fine sunny day. Kapko arrived with Kazimierz, to whom I gave some clothing to be delivered to Mrs. Maginski for Wlodek. Kazimierz promised to return on Monday for the rest. I also quizzed him about finding living quarters for Roza and Lena, but he spread his arms in a gesture of utter helplessness. He already had Mrs. Lande, the wife of our company's former lawyer, living in his tiny apartment, and there was no room for anyone else. He did promise to talk to his brother, Janek, who had also worked for me for some time.

Kapko and I went into a private room where we could talk freely and he told me rather solemnly that he had given a great deal of thought to what we had discussed and had come to a number of conclusions. He was ready to act and had already taken his first steps. His plan was to recruit a hundred men—a former Uhlan, Kapko spoke of "a hundred sabers"—and send them to a place in Lublin province. He hoped this could be done quite legally through the aid of a business firm with which he had close relations. This firm would apply to have a hundred Jewish workers allotted to it. They would leave the ghetto officially by truck headed for Lublin. Once there, he and his "boys" would make their escape to the woods. Should the application for a hundred workers fail to be approved, it would be necessary to set up an underground railway for facilitating individual escapes. We would start recruiting immediately, limiting ourselves to able-bodied young men, preferably with some military training and experienced in the use of firearms. A few commissioned officers were essential. No women were to be taken; old people and children were not to be considered, though some of them might be placed with his boys' families. It would be useful to have a doctor, tailor, cook, and barber.

In September 1939, Kapko's boys had buried a large cache of arms and ammunition, but it would be necessary to set up a drawing account of 300,000 to 400,000 zlotys to purchase additional arms and equipment, as well as for administrative expenses. Liaison officers would remain in Warsaw, inside and outside the ghetto, to continue recruiting suitable men. A training course would be organized and more men prepared for escape to the woods. Our first task would be smuggling guns into the ghetto, either through the printshop or some other place. Also we had to arrange places for our women outside the ghetto.

Kapko informed me that since our last talk he had had a bill of sale drawn up for the apartment house I owned, and the proceeds were to go to our military fund. We embraced affectionately when we parted, neither of us suspecting that this was to be our last meeting.

I went back to the ghetto filled with hope. Everything seemed to be going well. My luck seemed finally to have turned. Though we didn't discuss it, neither Izak nor I were keen on leaving the ghetto for the deceptions, blackmail, and extortion of surreptitious life on the Aryan side. To fight proudly and as Jews, inside or outside the walls, meant an end to evasion. The prospect of becoming partisans under Kapko's leadership was very attractive, but there was also a sense of guilt; the appeals of the underground had touched a chord of responsibility in us and we were reluctant to abandon the ghetto like a sinking ship.

Izak spent the weekend with us and we stayed up all night discussing the details of Kapko's plan. We drew up a list of men to approach first, including a number of former officers, and we decided that Izak should speak to Zygmunt Frydrych to coordinate our plans with those of the ZOB.

The next day I went to see my former lawyer, Lande. As a high-ranking police officer, he lived in the apartment house at the corner of Gesia and Zamenhof Streets. I had not seen him since the Resettlement Operation, and my visit took him by surprise. He was aware of the ghetto feeling about the police and was prickly in consequence, so that it took some time for me to get to the purpose of my call. Gradually, however, he thawed out and I gave him our plan in rough detail—mentioning no names and omitting details—and he was deeply moved. He said that many of the Jewish police were quite prepared to give their lives in penance for their tragic errors. Many, he contended, were decent people and ardent Jews, and asked only an opportunity to redeem themselves. "Just give us a chance," he said. "We want to wipe out our guilt. I myself will undertake to recruit a suicide squad—human torpedoes—to go against the Germans. German blood will wash away the crimes of the Jewish police. Now, don't smile, the Jewish policeman today is a tragic figure."

That was the day before Passover. Although we did not observe the holiday in full ritual, its spirit was very much with us. No one could remain unaware that Passover commemorated the freeing of the Jews from slavery in Egypt, and many of the verses of the Haggadah had immediate and special meaning for us in the ghetto. We also had many visitors from outside the walls, particularly people who came to spend the holidays with their old parents.

The next day, Monday, April 19, I was to be thirty-eight years old.

On that Sunday what remained of our family gathered: my sister Roza, Lena's brothers Adek and Marek and their wives, and blond Izak Rubin. We all missed Wlodek and he was the main subject of our conversation. Just before curfew we said good-by to Roza, Marek, and his wife; the others were staying the night with us. We did not know it was to be our final goodby.

The night before, SS General Jürgen Stroop had arrived in Warsaw. A man with a long criminal Nazi record, he carried in his pocket Himmler's secret orders. They said: "I order the destruction of the Warsaw ghetto."

The last act of the tragedy had begun.

This is not a history of the Warsaw Ghetto Revolt, that explosion of despair, martyrdom, and heroism which marked the death of a people. It is only one survivor's report of one shelter in one Warsaw ghetto apartment house whose fate was typical; Jewish Warsaw was consumed by fire and flame, the traditional accessories of *Kiddush HaShem*.

Late on Sunday night, April 18, 1943, Polish police began to surround the ghetto. Within an hour the underground had learned of it and declared a state of emergency. Fighters were assigned to their posts. Weapons, ammunition, and food were distributed; so were supplies of potassium cyanide. By 2 A.M. next morning (April 19) the Polish police were reinforced by Ukrainian, Latvian, and SS units, ringing the ghetto walls with patrols stationed about thirty yards apart. What we had so often expected and dreaded was about to take place: the final liquidation of the ghetto was at hand. Small groups of Jewish fighters went from house to house, informing everyone of developments, ordering people to take arms or to go to shelters.

I had just come on guard duty at our apartment house when two ZOB boys arrived. They were about blond Izak's age, perhaps even younger, between eighteen and twenty. One was tall and fair-haired, with the thin features and dreamy eyes of a poet. He wore long trousers and an unbuttoned shirt under his jacket. The other was short, chubby, with pink cheeks, dimples, and merry eyes. He wore high boots and a windbreaker. Both were bareheaded, carried rifles in their hands and grenades in their belts. They spoke softly, but their voices carried. These were our children, the doomed defenders of the ghetto.

It did not take long to alert everyone. I awakened Lena and the others in our apartment. We put on our best clothes and took the linen bag we had prepared with lump sugar and biscuits cut into small squares.

About thirty of us gathered in our shelter. In addition to Lena and me, blond Izak, Adek and Bronka, and the carpenter's family, there were other neighbors I scarcely knew. We had only a single weapon among us: Izak's pistol. Izak crouched at a peephole near the entrance to the shelter, from which he could see part of the courtyard. By dawn the ghetto was a ghost town.

We had only lately extended the entrance tunnel to the front attic of our building and it was possible, through artfully camouflaged passageways, to go to a point just above the corner of Muranowska and Zamenhof Streets. From there you could look down the entire length of Zamenhof Street to where it joined Gesia Street, and also see a large part of Muranowska Street toward the square. A special passage had been broken through the carpenter's apartment so that it was also possible to get to the north side of the building fronting on Niska Street. There the view embraced all of Niska Street, right and left, as well as Umschlagplatz directly in front of us. That same passage continued along the front of the building on Zamenhof Street and connected with number 62 where the TOZ offices were and where a resistance group was preparing for a last-ditch stand. Later that day we heard them shooting at the guards who were taking captured Jews to Umschlag.

On the second floor a hole had been bored through one of the lavatories into the next house, 42 Muranowska Street, from which, in turn, there was a passage to the next apartment house and so on down to the end of the block.

Hundreds of people living in the ghetto had been preparing for this moment, and had documents and lodgings on the Aryan side, but as always, the long-expected operation came upon them suddenly enough to upset all plans. They had expected to slip over quickly "at the last minute," but all their elaborate preparations were now useless. The grandiose plans Kapko and I had made were also useless. The back streets of the ghetto and the tunnels and shelters would be our guerrilla woods. There would we make our stand and there we would die.

We sat in the shelter, but nothing happened. Everyone was silent, caught up in his own bleak thoughts, drawing up the balance sheet of his life. We had to prepare to meet our deaths. One important thing, at least, we were thankful for: two weeks before we had been able to smuggle Wlodek out of the ghetto with Mrs. Maginski.

A few hours later, at eight o'clock on Monday morning, the shooting came close to us. The Germans marched through the gate at the corner of Gesia and Zamenhof Streets and took up positions in the little square

in front of the Judenrat offices. They put rows of ghetto police in the front
ranks, convinced that the defenders would not fire on fellow Jews and that
the Germans could thus get through to Zamenhof Street behind a human
screen. Our fighters let the Jewish police go by, but when the German troops
passed, they loosed a barrage of bullets, grenades, and Molotov cocktails.
The battlefield now became the corner of Zamenhof and Mila Streets
where resistance fighters occupied all four corner buildings and fired on
the Germans from all sides. One homemade incendiary set a tank afire,
burning the crew alive, and spreading panic and disorder among the Germans. But the German officers rallied their troops. Another tank appeared
and before long it too met the same fate. Germans, Ukrainians, and Latvians
scattered in disorder: one German, his leg smashed by a grenade, limped
to a doorway using his rifle as a crutch; another, his helmet on fire, ran
screaming around the square, a human torch. Scores of dead and wounded
lay scattered on the pavements.

We watched the battle from our attic and more than once Izak's finger
was on the trigger of his pistol, but his orders were to cover the withdrawal
of "our unarmed people should it be necessary to leave the shelter. . . ."
Guns and riding crops in hand, German officers urged on their disorganized
Judenhelden: the men who had shown so much combativeness with defenseless women, children, and old men, now broke before the fire of our resistance. Then field artillery stationed at the corner of Nowolipki Street opened
fire on the ghetto from no-man's-land, and the shelling continued intermittently throughout the day.

When we returned to the shelter, we told the others what had happened, and although we were all doomed to a terrible death, we were
gripped by a strange ecstasy. We embraced and congratulated one another;
women cried and laughed; people began to sing psalms in a low voice; and
one gray-haired man spoke the blessings aloud: "How wonderful it was to
have lived to see such times!"

Suddenly I felt beyond life and death. I felt sure we were going to
die, but I felt a part of the stream of Jewish history. We were part of an
ancient and unending stream of immortal tradition that went back to Titus
and his Roman legions ravaging Jerusalem, to persecution in Spain under
Isabella and Ferdinand, to Khmelnitsky massacres, and to more recent
pogroms and massacres at Kishinev and under Petlyura.

Later we learned from some of the fighters that the first battle had
taken place at the corner of Nalewki and Gesia Streets. A German unit,
singing lustily, had marched into the ghetto to be met by bullets, hand

grenades, and homemade incendiaries when it reached that corner. The Germans scattered, leaving their dead and wounded, and pursued by harassing fire; then came a battle of several hours' duration before the Germans finally withdrew.

Fighting continued intermittently at that corner all during Monday. Ghetto fighters kept moving from building to building, springing up in the enemies' rear to strike unexpectedly and effectively. By nightfall, however, the meager supply of grenades and Molotov cocktails had given out, and they had to retreat through the back of the house at 33 Nalewki Street into Kurza (Kupiecka) and Zamenhof Streets. Before pulling back they set fire to the big *Werterfassung* warehouse at 31 Nalewki Street where the SS stored looted Jewish property.

The shooting stopped when it grew dark, but flames and billows of smoke shot up from around Nalewki Street. When it was quite dark, we went down to the courtyard of our apartment house to wait for word from our fighters. It was about 10 P.M. when the gate opened slightly and two men in SS uniforms silently entered. They wore battle helmets and carried automatic rifles slung over their shoulders. Their high boots were wrapped in rags to silence their movements, and they called out to us in Yiddish, "Don't be alarmed, Jews, it's us." They were our boys and they gave us an account of the day's events. There had been a hard-fought battle in Muranow Square where the house on the corner at 42 Nalewki Street was held by a strong resistance group. At one stage in the battle, a German unit which had fought in the skirmishes on the corner of Gesia and Nalewki Streets had retreated to this house and the resistance fighters had attacked them from the rear and destroyed the entire unit, capturing their weapons and uniforms. After that, our blue and white flag was raised on the roof of their building.

Later in the afternoon, a second German unit equipped with howitzers and flamethrowers and bolstered by tanks had made its way to the square from Niska and Pokorna Streets. The square was defended by ZZW men under Pawel Frenkel and Leon (Lejb) Rodal, the best-armed, best-trained unit of the ghetto resistance. Equipped with rifles and plenty of hand grenades, they occupied the houses along the eastern and southern sides of Muranow Square, and from that favorable position they opened fire on the attackers. They inflicted especially heavy losses on the Germans with a machine gun in the attic of the apartment house at 7 Muranow Square, overlooking the entire plaza. By using the passageways between apartment buildings, the defenders were able to keep changing the direction of their fire and inflicted even more casualties on the Germans, who finally withdrew at sunset taking their dead and wounded with them.

But at the corner of Gesia and Nalewki Streets, our men had been forced to abandon their positions under overwhelming fire from Germans who had penetrated deep into Gesia Street and were firing on them from the rear. Most of our men were withdrawn from that area, and though they had sustained losses, the invaders had also paid heavily.

The Germans then showed their "heroic" qualities in dealing with the defenseless inhabitants of the ghetto hospital at 6 Gesia Street. The building had been shelled and set on fire after the SS had gone through the wards shooting and killing without mercy. Those patients and staff members who had made it to the shelters died in the fire.

As one fighter concluded his grim report, he observed that this was what we could all expect if we fell into their hands. He inhaled deeply from his cigarette and in its glow we realized that this was not the chubby, cheerful boy of yesterday.

Someone blurted, "Where's your comrade?" The young soldier's voice went suddenly shrill. "You won't see him again. He fell on Gesia Street." "Was killed," "perished," or "died" would have seemed almost normal at that moment when Jewish life in the ghetto was so cheap, but with his quiet, dignified choice of the word "fell" the young soldier made a lump rise in our throats. A woman next to me began to sob.

"Don't cry," one of the neighbors admonished her. "He's better off than we are. He sold his life dearly. What do we have to look forward to: being burned alive, like the people in the hospital?" He turned to the boys in uniform. "Give us weapons. We want to go down fighting, too, at least die like men."

The young man drew himself up, his voice slightly raised, and his manner showed he had thought about the issue often. "When we mourned the victims of the July massacre, we swore we would never again be led to slaughter without fighting back. You are soldiers without weapons. If you had weapons you would fight, too; fight with us to the last. Only we don't have the guns." He told us that their way of fighting was easy, the usual way, with guns. They were fighting because they were young and defending our dignity. But our way of resisting was unique; we were choosing a martyr's death. We could have surrendered; died the swift, clean, scientific death of the gas chamber. Instead, we had chosen flaming crucifixion: torment.

We felt that we were resisting Nazi military force barehanded, that our refusal to surrender was no less heroic than the armed resistance of those who fought them with guns. We were co-fighters, not just fodder, excrement, meaningless sacrifices.

Hand in hand, Lena and I slowly climbed the stairs to our attic fortress. Bound together by an evil fate no less than by our vows, my beloved wife, companion of my bad days as well as my good, was now closer to me than ever.

Army Supply II, where Lena's two brothers worked, was located in a separate part of the ghetto called the Brushmakers' area. Though Army Supply II specialized in ironmongery, and stationery plants were also there, a number of factories manufacturing brushes had given the section its name. All day Tuesday the shelling came from that direction and cast a glow across the sky. When the Germans summoned the inhabitants to report voluntarily for deportation, no more than two dozen out of 8,000 there surrendered themselves. The rest hid in their shelters. When the Germans opened their attack, the defenders, led by Marek Edelman, blew up the entrance to the building at 6 Walowa Street, which they had previously mined. Dozens of Germans perished in the explosion. General Stroop then called for artillery fire on the entire Brushmakers' area. Buildings caught fire and thick clouds of smoke obscured the heavens. Our resistance suffered heavy losses and house after house went up in flames. All day we watched the glow in the sky that told us the Germans were shelling the Brushmakers' area.

From our observation post, we could not see Muranow Square where more fighting took place. The Germans had concentrated a strong force there, with tanks, heavy machine guns, and flamethrowers. Fighting at that point was particularly violent as a result. The Germans attacked again and again, disregarding their losses, until the Jewish combatants had to withdraw, escaping to the Aryan side through their subterranean passageway.

From our observation point, we could actually see flashes of the fighting in Zamenhof and Mila Streets. We saw German Red Cross cars speeding there and back along Zamenhof and Gesia Streets, and from time to time columns of deportees were marched by SS escorts down Zamenhof to Umschlagplatz. On one occasion the resistance fighters in the building at 29 Zamenhof fired on the SS and Ukrainian escort and forced them to run. The column of deportees quickly dispersed. Other underground fighters in 62 Zamenhof also raked the escorts with gunfire.

Opposite Mila Street, on the roof of a house on Zamenhof Street, we could see a Jewish sniper behind a three-foot-high chimney that gave ideal cover as he picked off Germans. Bullets whizzed by him, but the

THE WARSAW GHETTO *in 1943*

▬▬▬ Ghetto walls   ◯ Ghetto gates   ▬▭▬ Railroad

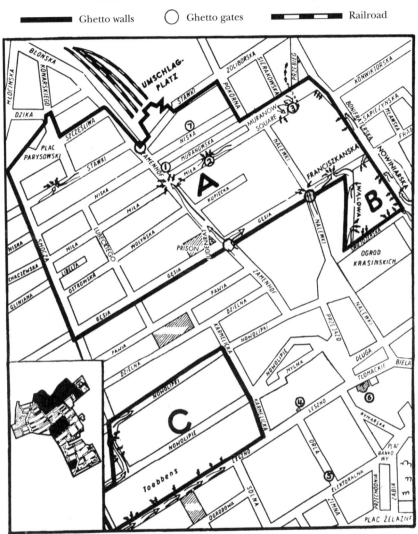

Arrows show areas of fiercest fighting (solid arrows indicate defenders' positions, open arrows the attacking German columns).

Inset: After the resettlement, the Warsaw ghetto, now less than one-quarter of its original area, was divided into four separately designated enclaves.

A. Central ghetto; B. Brushmakers' area; C. Shops; 1. Author's residence (Muranowska 44); 2. Mila 18, headquarters of the ZOB; 3. Muranow Square 7–9, headquarters of the ZZW; 4. Printing plant (Leszno 24); 5. Author's former residence (Orla 5); 6. Great Synagogue, blown up after the destruction of the ghetto; 7. *Werterfassung.*

chimney protected him. Suddenly he spun around, obviously hit, and grabbed one of his legs. After a moment, however, he reached into his bag for more ammunition and began reloading his rifle. In the interval three SS men ran swiftly down the street below and darted into a doorway on Mila Street. Perhaps fifteen minutes later the trap door on a rooftop some two buildings behind the sniper was pushed up and a helmeted German head poked through the opening. Cautiously the German peered around, saw that he had a perfect line of fire on the sniper, hoisted himself onto the roof, and carefully aimed his rifle. As he was about to press the trigger, a boy and girl appeared on a balcony across the street. With incredible speed the boy fired a shot at the SS man on the roof and the girl tossed a grenade into a group of soldiers in the street who had been laying down covering fire at the sniper to keep him behind the chimney. The girl disappeared into the building and the boy took cover on the balcony, while the SS man on the roof dropped out of sight. When the sniper heard the shot behind him, he turned quickly and a bullet from the street caught him. He dropped his rifle, his body careened around, rolled to the edge of the roof, paused at the gutter, then toppled over the edge. The boy on the balcony, riddled by a burst of machine-gun fire, collapsed over the railing convulsively, holding on to his rifle. The girl crawled back out onto the balcony, grabbed the rifle with one hand and with the other slowly and painfully pulled him inside. In a moment or two that rifle was in use again from a nearby window.

The entire southern part of the ghetto—the Brushmakers' area and the Gesia-Nalewki quarter—was in flames. Fires were breaking out sporadically in our sector, too, started by German shelling, or by grenades and satchel charges of dynamite the Nazis were using to flush resistance fighters out of their hiding places. . . .

. . . We called them Pierre and Lucy, the names of characters in a Romain Rolland tale, as they sat there in one corner of our shelter, looking into each other's eyes. In that place of death and destruction, those children, neither of whom was yet twenty, were figures of romance. Both had the beauty which suffering refines: he tall and slender with jet-black hair, pale skin, burning black eyes, and aristocratic features; she, like a young Madonna by Titian with eyes of an extraordinarily pure blue. It was obvious that they were waiting for something. After two or three days in the shelter, a Polish policeman came for them. In the deserted courtyard, he called up loudly, "Olek! Olek!" It had been planned long ago: he was to take them to the Aryan side where, since neither of them looked Jewish, they might be safe. Documents, lodgings, had all been arranged. The father of the boy had saved the Polish policeman's life at the front in 1920, and the Polish policeman had come to repay that debt.

The boy and girl left the shelter and we were all happy for them. At least they would get away; their love would survive the disaster. His mother, herself still young and handsome, said, "Go, my children. May God be with you. And remember, when it is all over, that you are Jews." She raised her hands and blessed them, and didn't shed a single tear; she smiled when they got down on all fours and crawled down the tunnel to the exit.

The next day Lucy came back, or rather our guard brought her back. He had found her at daybreak seated on the steps of a staircase across from our shelter. It took some time before we could get her story. The two of them had first been taken to a house in Szczesliwa Street where the ghetto wall ran through the courtyard. All they had to do was get over the wall. Guards on both sides had been bribed; Gavrilo, a Ukrainian guard, kept watch on the ghetto side, the Polish policeman awaited them on the outside. Lucy had seen Gavrilo looking at her in a way that terrified her, but she had said nothing. When it grew dark, Gavrilo came with a ladder, put it against the wall, and told the boy to come out and climb it. The lovers kissed hurriedly and in a moment he was on top of the wall ready to drop down to the outside. At that moment—his legs over on the Aryan side, his body still turned toward the ghetto—Gavrilo shot him down. And right there, before the dying boy's eyes, on the gravel of the courtyard at the foot of the wall, Gavrilo raped Lucy. It was night when he left her lying there, beside the body of her lover.

On Tuesday the apartment house across the intersection of Muranowska and Zamenhof Streets, directly opposite us, was set aflame. The day was windy and sparks kept blowing our way, a real danger. We went through the passage to the building next to us at 42 Muranowska. There, in one of the front apartments on the second floor, which had belonged to a member of the Judenrat, I found a telephone. I picked up the receiver and to my amazement found that the phone was working. As if it were normal times I asked for the fire department, reported the fire in the house on Zamenhof Street. In a few minutes the fire engines appeared and with their customary efficiency the firemen put out the fire. I called them on several occasions shortly thereafter and they always came without delay and extinguished the fires. Finally, however, probably on German orders, they no longer responded.

Tuesday evening abounded in sensational news. Everyone had somehow heard a rumor that the Poles had joined the Jewish uprising. Allegedly, armed Polish forces had broken through the ghetto wall at several points and were fighting shoulder to shoulder with our own underground. All Warsaw was up in arms against the Germans, led by the various Polish underground forces, and episodes of fraternization between Polish and Jewish underground fighters were movingly described. An unlimited supply of arms was making its way to the ghetto; more important, we heard that the whole world had been electrified by the news of our uprising, that the Allies had promised to parachute troops and supplies to help us.

A blood-red glow hung over the southern end of the ghetto, dark pillars of smoke swirled above it, and from that time on the acrid smoke and the stench of smoldering fires never left the ghetto. In this Dantesque atmosphere nothing seemed impossible, for nothing was more fantastic than reality.

That evening for the first time in two days we made a fire in the small iron stove and enjoyed hot potatoes and kasha from our reserve stock. And we slept in our own beds that night.

But Wednesday was no different from the day before. The Messiah did not come. Nor did any arms. Nor any help. Instead, the air was filled with sounds of gunfire and intermittent explosions. Fires were everywhere. On that day General Stroop closed in with thirty officers and two thousand combat-trained troops equipped with tanks, armored cars, artillery, flamethrowers, heavy weapons, and aerial support; he had facing him a handful of poorly trained, poorly armed ghetto fighters. Jewish losses were very heavy. Ammunition was giving out and the strategic centers of resistance in Gesia Street and Muranow Square were already crushed. Resistance fighters retreated from one position to another. Defeated in one place, they sprang up elsewhere, time and time again, but it was clear that in the end they would be defeated.

For Stroop the major problem was the tens of thousands of civilian Jews holed up in their shelters, deaf to German threats and persuasion alike. Himmler's orders had been categorical, but to break this desperate passive resistance and to dig the Jews out of their hiding places might take months. The resistance fighters understood that, too, and after two days of street fighting they shifted their tactics, saving their ammunition for defending bunkers and hideouts.

Stroop, faced with the prospect of a house-to-house skirmish for every single building in the ghetto, was equal to the challenge. In reporting to his superiors, he stated: "I decided on complete destruction of all Jewish habitations by setting fire to every single building."

Wehrmacht engineers were brought in and moved methodically from house to house, drenching the ground floors and wooden staircases with gasoline and setting fire to them while simultaneously hurling explosives into cellars and basements. Building by building, street by street, the Nazis began to raze the ghetto. That decision sealed our fate. The ring of fire and annihilation closed in on us inexorably. The ghetto was a raging sea of flame. There was no further help from the fire department and we had no way to put out the fires ourselves. We began to lose contact with the other sections of the ghetto and with nearby buildings as well. Street fighting was now rare. The Germans had set up a battery of heavy machine guns at the corner of Muranowska and Zamenhof, controlling access in three directions. Anyone who stepped out of doors within its range was instantly mowed down. And the siege tightened.

Macabre as the ghetto was during the day, at night it was a lurid phantasmagoria. Raging fires lit up the dark and the air was filled with the sizzle and crash of burning timbers. Smoke and gas choked the nostrils, searing the lungs and throat. Walls and staircases crashed, freeing clouds of dust and soot. Even buildings not yet afire became red-hot from the intense heat of the fires around them and gradually the whole ghetto became a great blazing furnace, with no fresh air, but only suffocating heat and fetid odors. The hiss of fire and the collapsing of buildings drowned out the sounds of gunfire, though from time to time the wind carried a human moan or a distant scream.

SS General Jürgen Stroop, a Roman Catholic, married and father of two children, casually wrote in his April 22, 1943, report: "Whole families of Jews enveloped in flames leaped out of windows or slid to the ground on bedsheets tied together. Measures were taken to liquidate those Jews at once."

Then came Easter Sunday. Church bells rang out that bright April morning as the God-fearing Poles of Warsaw, dressed in their finest, crowded into their lovely churches to hear once again the glad tidings—so often repeated, yet always joyfully anticipated—that he who had died on the cross for the love of man was risen from the dead. Faces brightened and hearts swelled on that feast day of the Resurrection as bells rang out and choirs chanted the glory of the Holy Trinity. My five-year-old son was among them, perhaps, his tiny treble also joining the choral response of the Easter service: *Kyrie Eleison!* He Is Risen!

Mass over, the holiday crowds poured out into the sun-drenched streets. Hearts filled with Christian love, people went to look at the new unprecedented attraction that lay halfway across the city to the north, on the other side of the ghetto wall, where Christ's Jewish brethren suffered a new and terrible Calvary not by crucifixion but by fire. What a unique spectacle! Bemused, the crowds stared at the hanging curtains of flame, listened to the roar of the conflagration, and whispered to one another, "But the Jews—they're being roasted alive!" There was awe and relief that not they, but the others had attracted the fury and the vengeance of the conqueror. There was also satisfaction.

Batteries of artillery had been set up in Nowiniarska Street and were shelling targets in the ghetto from there. The explosions of grenades and dynamite could be heard as well, as Jews scrambled from their hiding places. Pain-crazed figures leaped from balconies and windows to smash onto the streets below. From time to time a living torch would crouch on a window sill for one unbearably long moment before flashing like a comet through the air. When such figures caught on some obstruction and hung there suspended in agony, the spectators were quick to attract the attention of German riflemen. "Hey, look over there! No, over there!" Love of neatness and efficiency were appeased by a well-placed shot; the flaming comet was made to complete its trajectory; and the crowds cheered.

Traffic in Umschlagplatz was increasing. More and more columns of Jews, apparently rounded up from the shop areas, were driven through the gate in Gesia Street, down Zamenhof, to where they were loaded into the cattle cars. From our vantage point we could see Umschlag plainly, well enough to make out individuals and even to recognize some of them.

Toward evening trucks began to line up in Niska Street and were loaded with the contents of the *Werterfassung* warehouses by a working party of Jews guarded by SS men. For hours this process continued, trucks coming and going, Jews working on the double, prodded and driven by SS men. When the last truck had gone, two SS men conducted the working party to Umschlagplatz, while the remainder set fire to the buildings. That night we were surrounded on all sides by burning buildings.

On Monday, a week after the uprising had begun, an elderly Jew with a noble, spiritual face and ineffably sad eyes asked whether we would mind if he recited the *El Mole Rahamim,* the traditional prayer for the dead, for our heroes and martyrs of the rebellion. No, we did not mind. And there in the shelter of the attic of 44 Muranowska Street resounded the ancient mourning for the souls of those whose bodies would forever remain in the ghetto. The fervor was profound, and in bewailing the bitterness of fate, we prayed also for those of us whose turn was inexorably approaching, for we did not know whether there would be anyone left to say the *El Mole Rahamim* for us.

For several days we had not seen "our" fighters, and when they appeared one evening, still in uniform and still with rags around their boots, we shot a stream of questions at them: "Where are the Poles? We heard rumors of a general uprising. There were to be arms for everybody. And what about the Allies?" Liaison was inadequate and they were not informed about what was actually happening; they had heard of acts of sympathy and solidarity by Poles, but a general uprising or a major action was nothing but wishful thinking.

Fighting of a sort was still going on inside the ghetto—scattered and disorganized, but determined. Those people who had been burned out of their shelters were roaming the streets, looking for hiding places. We agreed to take ten people and neighboring shelters took some. But we stipulated that they must get food for themselves because ours had almost run out. Our fighters also warned us that under no circumstances were we to show strangers the entranceways to our shelters. The Germans were holding a number of Jews and under dire threats forcing them to spy out and report the location of shelters. Extreme precaution was imperative.

At that point I met Szymon, the leader of the fighting group operating from that part of our building which fronted on Zamenhof Street. A former laborer on projects outside the ghetto, Szymon commanded a group of four rifles, men younger than he, but just as close-mouthed. They occupied a third-floor flat with one room camouflaged off. They had a few girls with them, their wives and children having been rounded up and deported while they were away at work during the first Resettlement Operation. It was they who had fired on the guards leading deportees to Umschlagplatz, but now they were saving their ammunition until the Germans came to get them. When the systematic firing of houses had begun, they had considered escaping to the Aryan side and trying to join the partisans in the woods, but the plan seemed impractical. Moreover, they had women and older people with them, so they were staying and would fight to the last bullet. They agreed to take in a dozen of the newly homeless.

The next night our fighters brought a group of fifty people, refugees from Mila Street whose homes had gone up in flames. Two of the new-comers took us aside and told us some of the bloodcurdling details. Their building had been set afire by an artillery shell, and as the flames spread, people hiding in the shelters had been forced into the stairwells and court-yards. The fighters defending the building had given orders to evacuate it when suddenly piercing screams were heard from one of the apartments. These were finally located as coming from behind a wall, but no entrance could be found. When at last the fighters smashed an opening through the wall, they were engulfed in smoke and flames. Disheveled creatures crawled out on all fours. Most of the people were terribly burned, the most tragic a young girl whose legs had been charred to the bone. Their shelter had been built over a windowless alcove, whose ventilation had been through a narrow opening just below the ceiling. The only entrance had been by a trap door situated in an identical alcove on the floor above, but it had been barred by an iron bedstead which had apparently collapsed as a result of the heat, preventing the trap door from being opened.

It was now Tuesday, April 27, the ninth day of the uprising. Our end was very near. Early that morning violent shooting broke out in Niska Street. Dispatched to reconnoiter, Adek brought back the information that the street was full of Germans, shooting and throwing grenades into buildings. The entire length of Niska Street was one billowing sheet of smoke and flame. The fighters put up a fierce defense and our own build-ing had joined in the shooting. We all were suffering from lack of sleep and food, but we were at high tension, gripped by a kind of ecstasy that made any effort seem within our capabilities. We knew our turn would come right after Niska Street's, but to die along with our native city seemed natural.

We heard shots in the courtyard and the baleful, *"Alles runter! Alle Juden runter!"* So it had come. Forty people held their breath and listened for every sound below. The summons was repeated several times, then silence. The noise of windowpanes being smashed. Izak peered through the peephole and whispered, white-lipped, "They are pouring gasoline and setting fire to the staircases and apartments on the ground floor. . . . Now they are coming across the courtyard."

In perhaps half an hour the heat had become unbearable and thick billows of smoke began to fill the shelter. Our turn had come. "Everybody follow me!" Izak called out in a terrible voice and ran for the exit. "We're evacuating this shelter!" Below there was the sound of gunfire. Everyone rushed the narrow exit. No, not everyone. Nearly half our companions had not budged. They had chosen to take their potassium cyanide, and now they looked on with the gentle indifference of those who are no longer of this world, who can no longer be touched by such things as Nazis. *"Shma Yisroel,"* thundered the old Jew in a powerful voice none of us suspected his frail body could contain. And the voices crept through the shelter like a puff of wind: *"Shma Yisroel!"*

When we had made our way through the exit and found ourselves in the stairwell, the smoke and flames were just reaching the attic. Below was an inferno of fire. Our only way out was by the roof. We climbed the ladder, pushed open the trap door, and crawled over the roof to the trap door in the next building. We raised it quickly and jumped down: Izak, Adek, Bronka, Lena, and I.

This building, 42 Muranowska Street, was not yet on fire. Not a soul could be seen, all the inhabitants were in their shelters and hideouts. The house's weird silence and emptiness was like a cemetery, like ours had been an hour before. We went down to the cellar, through passages and tunnels to the rear of the building. In one of the empty apartments, on a password given by Izak, the tile oven turned on its hinges and opened the entrance to a camouflaged shelter. The shelter was cleverly built, supplied with all conveniences including running water, but nonetheless it was clear to us that it was a deathtrap. As soon as the Germans set the house on fire, the shelter's ingenious rotating oven mechanism would be heated out of shape and would not open and the occupants would be fried to death. But though we tried hard, they would not be persuaded. An awful premonition seized me and I could hardly wait until we left.

Again we sneaked through attics and staircases, tunnels and passages, and hid in cellars to which I felt instinctive revulsion. We planned to get as far from our burning apartment house as possible and to cross to the odd-number side of the street under cover of night. The backs of the odd-side houses abutted on the backs of the Mila Street houses. Our aim was to reach a house down Mila and across Nalewki Street where there was a secret passage out of the ghetto. By the time we reached the middle of the block, it was almost night. We were exhausted and our measly ration of biscuits and sugar lumps left us hungry.

When it got dark we set out to reconnoiter. Across the pavement was an empty plot, the remains of a building bombed out in 1939, an ideal spot for crossing the street, we thought. The problem was to find a shelter or a fighting group on the other side of the street, and we didn't have much time. German columns were moving down from both ends of the street and were bound to meet very soon. Before dawn Izak went on a scouting mission, promising to be back within three hours no matter what the outcome of his search. When he was not back at six, we could not contain our anxiety. In daylight the streets were covered by the cross fire from the German machine-gun embankments, and no one could move. We were without weapons and without a shelter.

Events overtook us. . . . Again the barking machine guns downstairs and the heinous command to surrender. Broken windows, grenades, and gas bombs; smoke and flame. Already experienced in what those sounds portended, we instinctively ran up the ladder to the roof, to the trap door of the neighboring building, and dived down. We had made it: out of the frying pan into the fire. The two German columns had met halfway and this building was already aflame, its staircase in even worse condition than the one we had just left. Smoke filled our lungs and blinded us, and we were half suffocated. Instinctively we decided to go back up to the roof, but there was no ladder. We hesitated only for the fraction of a second, then Adek climbed up on my shoulders and reached the roof. The two women pushed me up to where I could grab his outstretched hands; then we both pulled Bronka and Lena up, all but suffocated by now.

Warsaw roofs are steeply pitched, covered with tin, with a board that runs along the peak the length of the building, from trap door to trap door, from chimney to chimney. These rooftops are the exclusive domain of chimney sweeps, and figure prominently in little boys' dreams. We straddled the board and just sat there, intoxicated with the bright April sun we had not seen for ten days, greedily filling our lungs with fresh air: it was a moment of ecstatic relief. Below us the inferno raged. We could feel the whole building tremble with internal convulsions, the crash of timbers and the mounting roar of fire. The fair face of my son suddenly peered at me through the smoke, his head framed in golden curls: "Will I ever see you again?"

"Lena," I whispered. Never had I seen a human face change so swiftly; suddenly as I stared at it, my wife's face was drained of blood, of life. She said, "Oh, no!" and turned to look at the trap door.

Catastrophe had overtaken us, indeed. In the scramble from the shelter, the little bag Lena wore around her neck had worked loose and was gone. It contained our last defense, our last refuge: cyanide. With it we remained masters of our life and death. It had been our most precious treasure, our final bulwark of hope. Its loss was the last straw: I tasted worm-wood and gall.

But the fire wouldn't wait. I summed up the situation. We had two alternatives. Either we jumped from the fourth floor, or we burned alive up there. All were silent, defeated, expressionless. "It's so hard to die!" Bronka suddenly cried out with new strength. "Just look at this beautiful sunshine. . . . At least let's try to get down. There's always time to die." It was as if we had been waiting to hear her words. Down we went, pell-mell through smoke, flames, leaping acrobatically over collapsing stairs and dodging falling beams. Filthy, covered with soot from head to toe, we ran out the doorway.

Vae victis!

In the courtyard a German officer in combat helmet and goggles stood with several soldiers. His left hand was raised in the air and he was studying his wristwatch intently. "You certainly had pigs' luck," he said when he saw us, half with approval, half with regret. "A minute more and it would have been too late." At that moment another group emerged from another doorway. The officer lowered his left arm and a burst from a sub-machine gun mowed them down like wheat in a field. They were a minute too late. . . .

The Germans led us through the archway out into Muranowska Street. A sizable group of Jews were assembled from the neighboring apartment houses, among them our neighbors, the carpenter and his wife. They had their little boy with them, but there was no sign of their old mother. One of them told us with tears in his eyes that she had remained upstairs: cyanide.

Several SS men were guarding us, and a young girl standing nearby was very nervous. Imploringly she turned to one of the SS men and asked, "For God's sake, a cigarette!" He was still young. He did not hit her or curse at her; he said nothing and acted as if he hadn't heard. He walked away, paused, then walked back and past the girl without looking at her once. Casually a cigarette fell to the ground at her feet.

Another SS man kept staring at Lena. He walked to her and looked straight into her face for a long time. "What's your name?" he asked finally. She gave him her married name. He looked at her again, then walked away without another word. She had recognized him. They had been classmates at the university studying pharmacy, and she knew he was a *Volksdeutsch*. Had she given him her maiden name, he might have remembered, he might have helped. Perhaps his conscience troubled him, or perhaps it was just idle curiosity.

Finally we were lined up in ranks of five, and heavily guarded by SS men we made our way along the well-worn last bitter mile of Warsaw Jewry toward Umschlagplatz. When we passed Niska Street, the fighting was still going on; from roofs, from the windows of burning buildings, from doorways. Suddenly Lena clutched my hand and squeezed it with all her might. A bloodcurdling scream rang out from an upper-story window filled with flames where a woman appeared holding a child by the hand, and toppled down to the street. That was our last sight of the Warsaw ghetto.

That same day SS General Jürgen Stroop reported: "A total of 2,560 Jews were rounded up today within the former residential area, of whom 547 were shot. In addition, an undetermined number of Jews perished when their hiding places were blown up or burned."

When a hopelessly sick and very dear person dies, the human heart, even when prepared for the inevitable, is shocked into apathy, accepting the obnoxious but astute and centuries-tested funeral ritual. Not until the coffin sinks into the pit and the first clods of earth drop on what was once a beloved human being does the heart leap like a wounded bird. Only then is the finality of the loss, the dread meaning of the word "never," clear.

And so it was now. I was a living stone. But when the tremor shook the train that meant its wheels were turning, and the locomotive jerked powerfully, it was as if I were realizing our defeat only then, for the first time, and my heart constricted in ultimate despair.

CHAPTER 4

IN THE KINGDOM OF DEATH

WE MADE UP OUR MINDS that if the train went toward Treblinka, we'd jump off; death by a bullet seemed preferable to the gas chamber. If, however, the train went toward Lublin, we'd see what fate held in store. We lay on the dirty floor of the freight car, packed together with other deportees, the tension and fatigue of the past fortnight having at last caught up with us. Listless, emptied of feeling, we lay there utterly exhausted. Someone gave us a piece of dried bread, then a lump of sugar. We weren't even hungry; we no longer cared.

The red glow of the burning ghetto followed us as our train crossed a bridge over the Vistula and circled Warsaw, moving slowly, laboriously, switching from track to track on its way to the East Station. The glow grew distant and darker. We clattered over a viaduct and then the train unmistakably headed south, toward Lublin. We didn't have to make any further effort; we could just lie there on the floor.

Right after sunset there were noises near the little window of our boxcar. In the darkness a young man calmly gave instructions to a girl. "I'll lift you up. First stick your legs out the window. Let yourself down slowly. Hold on to the edge of the window, first with your elbows, then with your hands, while you try to find something to support your feet on the outside of the car. Then, let one leg swing out. Turn your body in the direction the train is going and jump off to one side, spreading your arms and fingers, and bending your legs. After you've rolled down the embankment into the ditch, wait for me there. If I don't come for you in a half hour, you're on your own." A last embrace. He lifted her to the window and a moment later we heard her body thud against the ground and then similar sounds of other bodies hitting the earth. Suddenly there were shots from the roof of one of the cars where Ukrainian guards were posted, then automatic rifles barking from other cars. The train rumbled on. Those who managed to jump off were left behind, but now it was too dangerous to make the attempt.

In the dark we moved through the suburban area on the Otwock line where "all Warsaw" went for summer vacations. Here lifelong friendships were formed; here young people dreamed their dreams of conquering or liberating the world; here they made their first timid flights into poetry. Here, a girl named Lena had smiled at me for the first time. . . .

A trip that normally took three hours took us six or eight. We lost all track of time, the night seemed endlessly long, and then the train ground to a halt, lights flashed outside, there was the noise of people scurrying, and then the doors of the cars were unbolted with much clanking. Rude voices shouted, *"Aussteigen! Alles aussteigen!"* ("Get out! Everything out!")

We jumped out of the cars. Guards herded us together with shouts and blows. In the darkness people called to one another, lost each other, then discovered each other again. One man ducked under a car, perhaps to relieve himself, perhaps in an attempt to escape. A gun flashed, a shot resounded; the victim did not even cry out.

We were driven to a large building at the head of the train. There were few lights, but we could see thousands of people crammed into immense halls, and jammed up and down the length of staircases. We were at the old Lublin *Flugplatz* (airfield). Lena and I held on to each other tightly. Finally we found a spot in the corner and lay down on the stone floor. Our post–cattle car life had begun. . . .

Outdoors the morning was derisively beautiful; the weather had been like that through the entire cruel month of April, the time of our destruction. We found ourselves among thousands of others, most of whom had been on the same train we had. The sea of heads moved aimlessly: some indifferent, resigned, some nervously excited.

Police duties had been entrusted to Jewish prisoners of war of the 1939 campaign whom the Germans had not released at the end of hostilities. They were well fed, wore Polish uniforms, and had been brutalized by four years of captivity during which time the Nazis had murdered or tortured to death almost 90 percent of their original number. They spoke Polish and Yiddish and usually addressed us with, "Hey, you Jewish son-of-a-bitch!" The airfield echoed with their barking, but they did not otherwise molest us.

Gradually we learned about our place of deportation. The so-called concentration camp of Lublin was divided into three parts: the Flugplatz, located on the grounds of the Plage-Leskiewicz airplane factory, inoperative since the war; the SS workshops at 7 Lipowa Street, to which Jews qualified as skilled laborers—smiths, mechanics, shoemakers, tailors, carpenters, and so on—were assigned; and the concentration camp proper of Majdanek, generally referred to as the KL *(Konzentrationslager)*. All "transports" were unloaded at the Flugplatz, which served both as a depot and distribution center. From there, Jews were also sent to labor camps at Poniatowa, Trawniki, Budzyn, and the peat bog at Dorohucza, all in the vicinity.

Early in the morning an SS officer made a speech telling us that this was a labor camp, that those who worked hard would be treated fairly, would be fed and clothed, and would survive the war. Two sturdy-looking, well-dressed Jewish girls, summoned for the purpose, eagerly confirmed his promises, but we were not reassured. After the speech we were told to sit on the ground and SS men gave orders to the Jewish POWs. Soon cries resounded: "Electricians needed at Trawniki. Electricians wanted at Trawniki. Report with your wives. . . . Tailors, carpenters, shoemakers . . . to Poniatowa, to Trawniki, to Schultz, to Toebbens. . . ." Adek, sitting next to us, began to get restless. "Shouldn't we go with the electricians?" he said. I asked if he knew anything about being an electrician. He replied that anyone could be an electrician. He could fix small things and we could always "organize" something; it was always better to have a trade. I refused. I wouldn't volunteer for anything. It was hard for Adek to make up his mind, but when the call was repeated a second, then a third time, he jumped up and implored me: "Come on, let's stick together. It'll be easier if we don't separate."

I stuck to my decision. Adek grabbed Bronka by the hand, and they ran in the direction of the cars. They waved to us from the moving train. When they had gone, we met the carpenter and his wife who had lived next door to us in Muranowska Street. They told us happily that they had met an acquaintance who had found a place for them in the Lipowa Street workshops, that they were going there now and taking their child with them.

A young woman was pushing her way through the crowd near us and a little girl ran after her, weeping and sobbing, "Mama! Mama!" The woman did not look back but pushed ahead and the little girl screamed louder. Suddenly a POW came up, sunburned, tall, formidable. He grabbed the woman by her shoulder with his left hand, and slapped her with his right hand, yelling, "You Jewish bitch, are you running away from your own child?"

She reeled under the blow. Then, her face distorted with pain and anger, she shouted, "Let me go, you beast! That isn't my child. I have no children. You mind your own business! How dare you hit me!"

"Is this your mother?" the POW asked the little girl.

The child, no more than three years old, nodded.

The POW slapped the woman again. "You were willing to screw and bring bastards into the world and now you don't want to croak with her? You goddam bitch, you whore!" He slapped her again and again.

"She isn't mine. I'm twenty-two. I want to live," the woman tried to argue, but she weakened under the blows. In the end, she broke down, grabbed the child in her arms, and pressed it to her breast. She was whimpering now, and stood like a statue of suffering, resigned to her fate.

The crowd began to stream toward the largest building. An open space was formed where we were ordered to form ranks of five. Lena and I kept to the rear and could not see what was happening at the head of the formation. Then another order was shouted, "Men and women, form separate ranks." I took Lena's hands, her eyes looked with love into mine. A last kiss. Not a single tear was shed. She held her head high to give me courage. A surge of the crowd separated us. Two strangers stood beside me, we were ordered to clasp hands and a moment later the gigantic procession began to move slowly forward.

When I reached the corner of the building, I understood the terror I had seen in everyone's eyes. On both sides of us stood SS guards with grenades in their belts and submachine guns at the ready, holding barking police dogs straining at the leash. Never had I seen a collection of such murderous, degenerate human faces. The SS guards closed in around the column and moved us toward the Chelm highway, where we turned and walked eastward away from Lublin.

We had walked less than a mile when several older men began to lag behind. That was what the SS men were waiting for. A police dog leaped and knocked one wretched old man to the ground, dug its teeth into him, and other dogs attacked the remaining laggards. The SS men gave the dogs time to have fun with their victims and then finished off the old men with a shot or a blow of a rifle butt. The cries of people torn by dogs and the sound of shots was our marching song the rest of the way.

After an hour's march the column turned off the road to the right. We walked a few hundred yards more and found ourselves in a strange settlement with many wooden sheds. We were led to one on which there was a big sign, *Effektenkammer.* The first fifty were driven inside, the rest of us waited. Was this it? Our hearts pounded, our breathing became more difficult. In a few minutes, men were running stark naked out of the shed; singly and in groups they vanished into a brick structure some fifty yards farther ahead. Finally, it was our turn. When the shed was full, the SS man ordered us to strip. We were allowed to keep only our eyeglasses, suspenders, or belts. Money and valuables were to be thrown into special wooden boxes that lay all over the room. Those attempting to conceal valuables, they warned, "would be shot on the spot." Two SS men circulated among us, hurrying laggards with shouts and blows.

"Can we keep our papers?"

"*Nein.*"

"The photo of my child. My only child."

"*Nein.*"

A last glance at the faces of your loved ones. Papers and photos were to be thrown onto the floor; since they had no value, they didn't go into the boxes.

When everyone was undressed, an SS man yelled, "Now get the hell out of here, you dirty Jews, and take a bath—in the next building." So this was to be it. We could not keep our pulses from pounding. We ran through a low door into a big room with a concrete floor. A great many people were clustered around a dozen or so barbers who with clippers were removing all the hair from people's heads and bodies. The barbers were Jewish camp prisoners, too, and we showered them with questions which were all the same: "What is it like here?"

"It all depends. . . . If you can get 'organized,' you might be able to stand it."

Someone began to scream that we were in a gas chamber and they were going to turn on the gas any minute. People stampeded for the door, but new arrivals pushed them back. The barbers swore it was a lie and took the occasion to ask the men whose hair they were cutting, "Have you got anything up your ass?" More than one was naive enough to admit he had concealed valuables there. The friendly barber would then "save his life" by extracting the hidden treasure from his rectum. "We're never searched, you see, because we're part of the personnel. But if they find anything like that on you, you go straight to the gas chamber."

"You mean the SS men look up your ass?"

"Sure. Don't you think they've heard of such tricks? They've got special flashlights."

At the far end of the room stood a young SS man with a riding crop in his hand. All those who had been shaved had to run up to him with raised hands, spread fingers, and mouths open. The SS man looked each one over cursorily and then, with a flick of his riding whip, pointed to one of two doors, one to the right and the other behind him. When I ran through the right-hand door I found myself in a shower room; the water was turned on, and we were given a piece of soap with which to wash. After a few minutes we were driven, still naked and dripping wet, to an adjoining room where a few camp inmates stood behind a counter distributing clothing. Everyone was given a set of clothes, which included cap, coat, trousers, shirt, underwear, socks, and wooden shoes. The clothes were handed out without regard to size and anyone who asked for something smaller or larger was told contemptuously: "You want a punch in the nose?

Keep moving. . . ." Or else, more kindly, "What do you think this is, you poor bastard, a haberdashery? Listen to this man-about-town: he wants to die in a tuxedo!"

We were pushed on by the continuing stream of newcomers behind us, so that we could not, in any case, linger very long. Once beyond the door of that room we were outdoors, where we donned our rags. When I looked at my companions, what I saw was like a macabre costume ball, like the crowd of beggars in *The Dybbuk*. New arrivals were given the worst old clothes; anything halfway decent they might have been wearing on arrival was sent to the *Vaterland*.

We now learned that the other door, the one behind the SS man, actually led to the gas chamber. We had been no more than two yards from it. While we were taking our showers, the less fortunate had died in agony.

I had felt nothing, absolutely nothing. A complete vacuum. I analyzed myself with detached curiosity. I expected myself to react, to feel something, to revolt, or to collapse. But the only response was purely physical: breathlessness and nausea.

Once again we were made to fall in, in ranks of five, and were escorted down the main road to the camp. At regular intervals, there were watchtowers manned by guards with submachine guns, and the entire camp was surrounded by two barbed-wire fences. When we came to a gate, one of our escorts barked something to a sentry and we were permitted to enter a large square area in which wooden barracks were clustered. We had arrived in the kingdom of death, in the third field of the Majdanek concentration camp.

Majdanek was hell. Not the naive inferno of Dante, but a twentieth-century hell where the art of cruelty was refined to perfection and every facility of modern technology and psychology was combined to destroy men physically and spiritually. To begin with, in accord with Germanic efficiency—*Ordnung muss sein!*—the new shipment of prisoners was taken to the camp office *(Schreibstube)* where "scribes," mostly Czech and Slovak Jews, sat behind tables. One of them carefully filled in a long form for which I had to supply my name, date of birth, occupation (I said printer), and then came the question: "When were you arrested?" I looked at him surprised. Was he trying to mock me? Could it be that he didn't know? "Well, when were you arrested?" he repeated impatiently.

"We weren't arrested. We were rounded up during the uprising."

"All right, all right," he said, in a bored voice. "But when?"

I gave him the date. He handed me the form he'd filled out and told me to go to another table. I glanced at the form and had only enough time to read a few words at the end. They gave me a jolt: "SD (for *Sicherheitsdienst*, the Nazi security police) . . . sentenced to life imprisonment. . . ." I handed the form to the clerk at the table indicated and he gave me a numbered piece of canvas. I looked at my number: 7,115. From that moment I ceased to be a man, a human being; instead I became camp inmate 7,115.

After the formalities, we were driven to an empty barrack where a few moments later our new master appeared: the Barrack Elder *(Blockälteste)* of Barrack Number Five. Short, heavy-set, and a former policeman, Mietek Szydlower was a native of Lodz who had been sent to Majdanek from the Warsaw cauldron in September 1942. With brutal frankness he told us what it was like there.

"This is a KL," he said. "Remember those two initials, KL. . . . *Konzentrationslager.* This is a death camp, a *Vernichtungslager.* You've been brought here to be destroyed by hunger, beating, hard labor, and sickness. You'll be eaten by lice, you'll rot in your own shit.

"Let me give you one piece of advice: forget who and what you were. This is a jungle and here the only law is the law of the strongest. No one here is a Mr. Director or a *Herr Doktor.* Everyone here is the same; everyone here is shit. All are going to die."

"There's no hope?" someone asked tremulously.

"Ten percent of you may survive. Only those who can get a special job have a chance. Those who have gold, jewels, money, can buy jobs. For the others, only one hope: to organize."

That was the second time I had heard the magic word and I thought it referred to a highly clandestine but ubiquitous organization of the just, which protected the most deserving or the most wronged. But Barrack Elder Szydlower quickly dispelled my romantic fantasies. In camp slang, "to organize" merely meant to look after number one. It was to steal soup from the kitchen, for example; but to steal bread from a fellow inmate, however, was to really steal.

"And another thing," Mietek added, "It's important to keep your eyes and ears open all the time. We have a saying here: You'd better have eyes in your ass."

We were all hungry. We hadn't eaten, couldn't remember our last meal, but we were too late to be fed that day; there hadn't been time to put us on the rolls properly. We'd start eating the next day, we were told. Later we learned that this too was another example of organization—by camp officials. Several hundred stolen suppers meant a handsome profit for them.

The barrack was a long wooden shed originally intended as a stable for horses, easily verified by the *Pferdebaracke* inscription over the doorway and the ramps instead of steps at the entrances. A narrow glass opening ran around the building just under the roof to let some daylight in, but there were no windows in the usual sense. Triple-decker bunks stood against both walls and a narrow aisle was kept between bunks and walls, a broader one between the two rows of bunks. At the far end of the building was a second entrance, usually kept locked. Near the main entrance were the bunks of the barrack elite: the Barrack Elder, the Scribe, and a few orderlies *(Stubendienst)*. The Barrack Elder was master of life and death of his subjects. The Scribe kept the rolls, the life-and-death statistics of the barrack. He recorded the daily increase *(Zugang)* and decrease *(Abgang)*, or transfer *(Verlegung)*, whether to another barrack, camp, or hospital. He also noted "natural" decreases, i.e., by death. The orderlies kept the barrack swept and in order, and saw to it that no one stayed hidden there during the day. Occasionally they also acted as the Elder's deputies in handing out food rations. Soon after our arrival a new official was appointed to beat up inmates at the Elder's orders, a job usually given to Soviet prisoners of war. In our barrack the job was held by an athletic native of Leningrad named Andrej. In the next barrack it was another Russian, Ivan. Andrej was normally quiet and rather goodnatured; but when he was "on duty," he would grow excited and could be terrible.

All these "authorities" were subject to the central authority of the *Lagerschreiber,* or Camp Scribe, who had a dozen clerks working for him. Together these were the clerical office (Schreibstube). The Lagerschreiber's principal assistant was the official who assigned inmates to specific work parties, the so-called *Kommandos.* As a member of a Kommando, each prisoner was subject to another hierarchy of masters. Each Kommando had a Kapo, or head. The term was thought to be derived from the Italian *capo* (head); but others maintained it was an abbreviation of *Kazetpolizei*, or *Konzentrationslager Polizei.* The Kapo also had assistants called *Vorarbeiter* (foremen) who in their turn had assistants called *Schieber* (pushers). Although these were all prisoners, too, they had the power of life and death over the workers assigned to them. At the very top of the concentration camp hierarchy was the so-called *Lagerälteste* or camp warden, also a prisoner, but invariably a German.

These various prisoner authorities were themselves ruled by a parallel

SS organization. Every barrack had its own SS barrack leader, every labor project its own SS men, and at the top of their hierarchical pyramid stood the *Lagerführer,* or Camp Commandant, generally a high-ranking SS officer.

Majdanek was divided into five "Fields," each in reality a separate camp, consisting of a gigantic rectangle surrounded by barbed-wire fences. A few yards from the wire, wooden signs warned: "ATTENTION! DEATH ZONE!" The wire was electrified and anyone who touched it was electrocuted. At the four corners of the rectangle stood watchtowers with armed guards at the ready. The first field housed the central camp offices and the files; the second field was occupied by highly skilled prisoners employed in the camp workshops; the other laborers were crowded into the third and fourth fields, between which there was a large area called Coal Field or In-Between Field. Field Five was reserved for women prisoners. Fields Three, Four, and Five were filled with inmates destined eventually for the crematoria.

Field Three, where I was assigned, had twenty-two numbered barracks, all of the same design, around a large central open space—except for Barrack Nineteen, the *Gamelbaracke.* Entrance to that was obscured by a high wooden fence so that one couldn't see what went on inside, but we soon learned that it was where the old and weak inmates were housed, the vestibule to the gas chamber. To the right of the entrance to the field was the field office barrack, inhabited by the "aristocracy of the field; to the left were the automotive workshops *(Fahrbereitschaft).* The last barrack on the left was the kitchen serving all five fields; across from it was the L-Barrack, which contained washrooms.

In Barrack Number Five we were given sacks and told to go out and fill them with straw. Those were our mattresses. We were each then assigned a bunk. When the soup, bread, and margarine were brought in for the regular inmates, we newcomers ran to the washroom to get a drink of water to stay our hunger, but the crowd around the faucets was so great that we had little hope of getting close to them.

At 9 P.M. we were driven inside the barracks and at 9:30 the gong sounded to mark the end of the day. Anyone caught outside after that time could be shot on sight by the guards on the towers. The lights inside went out except for a few small bulbs, but we were not to have a quiet night's sleep. About 10:30 P.M. the noisy *Wagenkolonne,* the working party which took rations from the kitchen to the other fields, came in. Though this assignment was hard work, those on the work party were given double portions of food and allowed to catch up on their sleep during the day. Moreover, they earned money by such chores as delivering messages between one field and another, carrying greetings or gifts from husband to wife, or vice-versa. The majority of these men would not have exchanged for anything in the world their privilege of visiting the women's field three times a day. The Wagenkolonne turned in quickly, but then the parade to and from the latrine began and kept up for the rest of the night.

What was called a latrine consisted of a wooden box with handles at both ends similar to what hod carriers use to transport cement. Only one such box was assigned to each barrack, which might house two or three hundred inmates, and sometimes as many as five hundred. The overwhelming majority of the camp inmates suffered from diarrhea and almost everyone also had weakness of the bladder, so that the latrine was soon filled and overflowing. The stinking puddles on the floor were nauseating and when men had to wade through them barefoot because they had been thoughtless enough not to put on their wooden shoes, it was worse. But barefoot or shod the inmates trotting to and from the latrine soon tracked the entire barracks up with filth. To add to the dreadful stench the crowd around the latrine was usually noisy, and for our first few nights at Majdanek we found it very hard to bear. Afterward nothing could disturb our sleep.

At 2:30 A.M. the Wagenkolonne left for work, and an hour later, at 3:30 A.M., the gong announced the beginning of a new day. The orderlies yelled, "Everybody up!" and we barely had our eyes open before Andrej was running back and forth pulling sleepers out of bed by their legs, clouting some over the head, speeding along the dawdlers. Over and over again, in his comical mixture of Polish and Russian, he threatened, "You're going to get twenty-five lashes on your bare ass. . . ."

And so the nightmare began first thing in the morning. German *Ordnung* demanded that our bunks be made up in strict military style and rigidly perfect. Since the majority of inmates had no military or even scout training, the demand was rarely met. Though Barrack Elder Szydlower daily rewarded the two best bedmakers with an extra portion of bread, he simultaneously punished at least a dozen by depriving them of their portions. When that proved ineffective, he ordered those whose beds were improperly made to be flogged. The barrack orderlies took immediate advantage of this—"organization"—and for a modest payment in margarine, soup, or a slice of bread, they exempted the untidy or made up their bunks for them.

After making our beds we rushed to the L-Barrack to wash. We soon learned that the washrooms, like everything else in Majdanek, were instruments of torture. Crowds pressed around the building in such numbers that they had to be held back by Kapos with clubs in their hands. When you did finally manage to get inside and get close to a faucet, you were likely to be attacked by one of the many Kapos or orderlies standing there. Anyone taking off his shirt was especially liable to be beaten. "What do you think this is, a Roman bath? Or a beach?" A punch in the face was the usual accompaniment to such comments. If, prudently, you kept your jacket on and simply splashed your face, the Kapo would shout, "You filthy shitface, don't you know how to wash?" And you got your punch in the face anyway. Every day men came back from the washroom bleeding from the blows on the head and face, and before long the intended aim was achieved: the number of visitors to the washroom dropped to a minimum and the orderlies no longer had to work so hard cleaning and polishing it. Prisoners themselves, they consequently did not have to be so frightened when the SS inspectors came around, for the SS men had no special consideration for the buttocks or necks of camp "officials."

At 4:30, "coffee"—a light mint infusion without nourishment and with a repulsive taste—was distributed. We often took a few swallows and used the rest for washing, but not all of us were able to do without this poor substitute for coffee and consequently many inmates ceased to wash. This was the first step to the grave. It was an almost iron law: those who failed to wash every day soon died. Whether this was the cause or the effect of inner breakdown, I don't know; but it was an infallible symptom.

After coffee came the daily roll call, in which inmates lined up in ranks of five, dressed and redressed to military perfection, and interminably counted and recounted. The actual number of prisoners had to dovetail with the theoretical number computed by the Barrack Scribe. Prisoners who had died since the previous roll call also had to be counted present, so their bodies were dragged out of the barracks and placed on the ground next to their live comrades. When everything had been checked, with continuing screams and blows, the barracks staff took its place in front of the assembled ranks. Two *Blockführers* marched briskly from barrack to barrack, and at their approach everyone froze at attention and held his breath. The Barrack Elder always gave the command in an especially dramatic way: *"Block fünf. Achtung! Mützen . . .* (the pause always seemed to last an eternity) *. . . ab!"* Then he stepped forward, reporting the number of prisoners present. The SS men would inspect the ranks, take their own count, and then pass on to the next barrack.

When the numbers did not tally, there was hell to pay. The barrack staff scurried around like rats and they were urged on by SS men with kicks and blows. The barracks were thoroughly searched and woe to the wretch who had fallen asleep, fainted, or was simply too weak to stir. They fell on him like a pack of mad dogs. If the barrack staff found him before the SS men got there, he had a chance; but once the SS men arrived, he was as good as dead. By the time he was dragged out and propped up in formation he was half dead from the beating he had been given. As soon as roll call was over he was publicly hanged for "having attempted to escape."

Most often, however, when a man had to be searched for, he was beyond the reach of the SS. He would usually be stretched out staring up at them with fearless, glassy eyes, teeth bared in a mocking grin that no SS man's fist could wipe away. They would kick and curse him nonetheless, but he was beyond their power.

When roll call was completed, the order, *"Arbeitskommandos formieren"* rang out. The formations would then scatter, and in the big open area dozens of work parties would form and be marched out of the gate under the leadership of the Kapos. Slowly the square was emptied and the barracks staffs would go back inside to their duties. Only the newly arrived who had not yet been assigned to Kommandos were left behind. For these there was no hiding or resting in the barracks. Whether in broiling sun or pouring rain, it was forbidden to be in the barracks during the day and new arrivals were forced to spend the entire day out of doors. They would be divided into groups of fifty with a Kapo in charge and the drilling would begin. This pitiful and comic spectacle of ragged men in wooden shoes trying to imitate well-drilled military formations was continued beneath a barrage of blows, curses, and orders. The Kapos, young and well fed, did not tire quickly and depending on their mood—and the frequency with which SS men appeared on the square—drill might be more exhausting and sadistic on one day than on another.

When the Kapo was in a bad mood or desirous of showing his zeal to the SS men, formations did everything on the double, push-ups, knee-bends, and all the rest, without letup all morning long. The sun rose and beat down pitilessly, we grew increasingly exhausted by the exercise; we were tormented by hunger.

At last noontime came and an hour break for lunch. We stood in formation in front of the barrack awaiting the return of the work parties. The barrack staff brought kettles of soup from the kitchen and set them up in a row, and we stood in line and one by one went up to the kettle. One of the orderlies took a bowl from a pile, and the Barrack Elder in person ladled some soup into it. One by one the inmates grabbed the bowl with the steaming soup and greedily began to drink it while walking away. There were no spoons at Majdanek: with time, you might organize one, but in the interim you drank the hot soup directly from the bowl and you did it in a hurry because the bowl might be needed for someone else.

The soup line always moved fast. Several hundred starving men kept the closest and most suspicious tabs on the Barrack Elder as he plunged his ladle into the kettle and filled bowl after bowl. To distribute soup from the kettle was a great art and a great mystery. Theoretically, each inmate was entitled to a liter of soup and the ladle did, in fact, hold one liter. But all the Barrack Elder had to do was step up the pace of his serving, tip the ladle ever so slightly to one side or another and he pinched some of the soup from each theoretical "full" liter. Several hundred such fractions add up to a considerable amount of soup. In most cases the thicker and more nourishing ingredients in the soup fell to the bottom of the kettle and the top was little more than water. Naturally the Barrack Elder always left the thickest part of the soup at the bottom for himself, for his own turn came last. Often he would work it so that the spoon literally "stood up" in the bottom of the kettle. A rude voice would yell angrily, "Stir the soup goddamn it!" The Elder would seem to give the soup a good swirl with the ladle, but he would be careful not to stir very deeply so that his own share would be nonetheless nourishing for all of the showy exhibition.

Only the newcomers waxed indignant about this; the old-timers knew better, and didn't try to buck the system. Their strategy was based on the type of soup being served. For potato or turnip soup, where the best settled at the bottom, one tactic was necessary; for cabbage or nettles, where the "best" remained on top, another was called for. Each kettle held fifty liters, and for potato or turnip soup, they placed themselves in line at the end of every fifty men, while the newcomers surged forward to be served first. In these matters, the experienced inmates acted with great shrewdness, and one of them initiated me into the soup strategy shortly after my arrival, my basic course in the *Konzentrationslager* University.

After everyone had had his bowl of soup, the Barrack Elder granted his favorites the privilege of scraping the bottom of the kettle and licking it clean, and there was constant competition for that privilege. This one-hour break for soup, served and consumed outside the barrack, was the only break during the workday.

Field Three housed from 5,000 to 8,000 inmates, and during my first lunch break I looked around eagerly for men I had known in Warsaw. I found many and from them I learned that the workers from our printing plant had been sent to the Flugplatz only a few days before me; they had been assigned to Poniatowa, Trawniki, the Flugplatz, and Majdanek. They had been deported with the personnel of the *Werterfassung,* and only Rachman and a group of nine men had been left behind to dismantle the presses and prepare them for transport by rail. The *Werterfassung* authorities had decided to move the printing plant to Radom and as soon as the machines were installed and ready, all the printers now in the camps would be sent there to operate it. Some of the printers told me that Rachman had given a high-ranking SS officer 100,000 zlotys so that the printshop would be moved to Radom and our printers assigned to it.

After the Kommandos had been formed and marched away for the afternoon work, the newcomers were ordered to the barracks to be shaved and to have numbers sewed on their clothes. The barracks barber turned out to be my regular barber from Leszno Street, a man named Stopnica. The man who sewed on my number was the well-known Warsaw tailor, Nisson. Inmates were not yet issued striped uniforms in those days but instead wore cast-off civilian clothing; down the back was a wide red band and the letters KL, with similar stripes on the trouser legs down the front of the left leg and the back of the right one. Inmates who failed to report to the authorities when these stripes faded risked being hanged "for planning to escape."

Each inmate also had a black number on white canvas sewed over the left breast of his jacket and below it a colored triangle with a letter inside designating nationality: P for Pole, U for Ukrainian, F for Frenchman, and so on. The color of the triangle indicated the nature of the inmate's "crime": political prisoners had red triangles, common criminals green, saboteurs black ones, homosexuals pink, religious objectors purple, and Jews yellow triangles. Neither Germans nor Jews wore letters to indicate nationality. The Jews were a group apart and the yellow triangle was a sufficient badge in itself. Only we, the Jews of Warsaw, were singled out for special "distinction": besides the yellow triangle pointed upward we had on top of it a red triangle pointing downward. Together they made a red and yellow six-pointed Star of David which stood for "the Jewish Bandits of Warsaw."

After being shaved and having our numbers sewed on, we were sent out of the barracks to continue drilling. This time we were to learn to take our caps off together, and the practice gave opportunities for endless sadistic beatings of those who put their caps back on a second too soon or too late.

Beating and being beaten was taken for granted at Majdanek, and was an integral part of the system. Everyone could beat an inmate and the more experienced inmates never questioned why. They knew that they were beaten merely because they happened to run into someone who wanted to beat them. In most cases, the beating did not even involve personal anger or hatred; the authorities hated their victims as a group because when you wrong people for no reason, sooner or later you must come to hate them. It is difficult for man to endure the idea he is a beast and maltreats another human being without cause; therefore, he eventually discovers justification for his behavior and imputes the fault to his victim. Thus, beating was part of the system. Thus, also, the victim was expected to take his licks standing rigidly at attention. Attempts to avoid blows, to cover one's face or head, were treated as additional offenses. Some made the mistake of smiling stupidly as if they understood the "joke" being played on them, as if they appreciated the authorities' "sense of humor," which served only to irritate the beaters further. Worst of all were the beatings undertaken for sheer distraction, for there the morbid imagination of the executioners knew no bounds. Some derived their greatest pleasure from refined torture and were delighted by the professional approval of their colleagues. Some were motivated by sadistic curiosity: they wanted to see how a man suffers and dies. Still others achieved a sexual enjoyment from the last fatal spasms of their victims.

One Kapo, for example, lay in wait near the camp latrine, hidden behind a brick pile. When he saw an inmate running for the latrine he would jump out of his hiding place and call the prisoner to him. The unfortunate victim, repressing the pain in his bowels, would stand at attention while the Kapo showered him with questions. "Where are you going, you son-of-a-bitch? Who is your Kapo? What Kommando? Where were you born?" By that time the poor wretch would be writhing with pain. Then the Kapo would make him do calisthenics, making him squat in deep knee-bends until the poor man could no longer control his sphincter and "exploded." Then the Kapo would belabor him with kicks and blows until, bruised and bleeding, covered with his own excrement, the victim would be allowed to drag himself to the latrine.

Another Kapo specialized in torturing alleged escapees. All over the area were scattered large cement pipes a yard in diameter. Occasionally, an inmate ready to faint from exhaustion would seek refuge from the hot sun or pouring rain in one of those pipes, where he would usually fall asleep. Which was precisely what the Kapo was waiting for. He would sneak up to the pipe and arouse his victim with a bloodcurdling yell. The prisoner would leap out of the cement pipe and run for his life, the Kapo screaming in hot pursuit. Soon other Kapos and SS men would join the hunt and prolong it deliberately until their victim was surrounded. His pursuers would merely stand there for a time, watching the inmate's agonies, his heaving chest, his maddened eyes, and the smile on his face, the inexplicable smile of a man who knows his end has come but somehow cannot believe it.

Then one of the pursuers would step forward for the kill. The step signified that the victim was his, and his alone, and none of the others would touch him. If the man playing the part of the matador was one Kapo, a native Viennese, he would knock the prisoner down with a lightning blow and then, with a balletlike motion put his heel against the man's throat. His specialty was strangling prisoners with the heel of his boot, and he would stand erect in the pose of a Roman gladiator enjoying the approval of the other Kapos, who would speak admiringly of a "good, clean job." A real master, a strangler who did not need to dirty his hands. If the matador was another Kapo, named Janusz, his method of killing was different. He would throw himself on his victim and lie on top of him, almost caressingly wrapping his fingers around his victim's throat. To the uninitiated, it might seem that the two bodies were throbbing in erotic ecstasy, and in fact the Kapo did have an orgasm at such moments, while his companions looked on in snickering admiration. This might happen once, or even twice a day.

But most beat their victims because it was the custom of the place. At Majdanek no one could be neutral: either you were victim or executioner. Anyone in authority who failed to take advantage of his privilege to beat inmates undermined his status in the camp elite. Later, we learned that the elite of our tormentors was far from homogeneous; within the hierarchy there were complex factions and conflicts.

At 6 P.M. the Kommandos began to return and the gate became lively. Every few minutes a Kapo—some in red cavalry breeches—drew up before the guard, stood at attention, and reported that his team was returning in such-and-such numbers and the guard would scrupulously write that down in his book. Some teams came back like victorious armies, ranks swaying evenly and rhythmically, files on parade. Others came back as from a pogrom, uneven ranks of emaciated and exhausted men driven by the kicks and curses of their foreman and Kapos. At the end of such processions usually came the corpses, carried on stretchers by their comrades. The work parties assigned to road building, about which there were blood-curdling stories, produced the most corpses. Not only was road construction beyond the strength and endurance of weakened, undernourished men, but the worst sadists were the Kapos and foremen on those Kommandos.

The camp was, in fact, a small city, and continually expanding. Admin-istrative work alone required considerable staff. The kitchens, for inmates and SS took a small army of potato peelers, dishwashers, cooks, and food handlers, as well as the special detail which carried the rations to the various fields. The camp kitchen in our field served at times as many as 30,000 inmates. Workers were required for new buildings, new roads, fences, water conduits, and all the rest. Workshops of all kinds employed tailors, me-chanics, cobblers, seamstresses. Only a small part of workshop production went to fulfill camp needs; most of it was devoted to cleaning up and re-pairing objects looted or confiscated by the Germans so that they could subsequently be sent to the Reich. Hundreds of inmates worked at sorting, disinfecting, and storing the property taken from new arrivals, and choosing the best of it for shipment to the *Vaterland.*

A special team was permanently employed to empty the gas cham-bers and dispose of the bodies. The normal problem of the murderer— what to do with the body—was one of Majdanek's most difficult "technical" problems, and the task of disposing of the dead frequently lagged behind the constantly stepped-up "output." Some dead were buried in the old-fashioned way, in enormous mass graves in the Krepiec Woods—the work of the so-called *Waldkommando* (the forest detail)—and some were burned on special grills in a provisional crematorium—the task of the *Himmel-kommando* (the heaven detail). Bones were ground up and mixed with ashes and the latrine excrement to be used eventually as fertilizer. A special *Scheisskommando* (the shit detail) cleaned up the latrines and carried away the excrement. Of all the work parties this was considered one of the most desirable: men assigned to it were given better rations and the SS men left it alone because of the stench.

In time, special Kommandos were organized to go into Lublin every day to perform various kinds of work. Their workers were dressed in striped uniforms. Getting on those Kommandos was very difficult because the op-portunities for smuggling, getting additional food, and simply for getting out of camp appealed to everyone.

Those inmates without a regular work assignment were the labor re-serve. They spent their time drilling or doing calisthenics in the square, or engaged in work to embellish the camp. The Germans considered this work very important, and flower beds were planted next to every barrack, and the expanse of lawn, with a pool and fountain, at the main field entrance required constant care.

The quietest, least trying period of the day was the two-to-three-hour period between the end of evening roll call, held shortly after 6 P.M., and the gong announcing the end of the day. First, food was distributed. One three-pound loaf of bread was assigned to every eight inmates, or six ounces per person. On Monday we might receive a slice of horse-meat sausage, supposed to weigh about two ounces. On Wednesday, perhaps, a spoonful of beet marmalade, and on Friday, a small piece of cheese. Three times a week we got a half-ounce of margarine, twice a week half a liter of mealy porridge, and once a week a handful of boiled potatoes.

Breakfast was a bowl of mint infusion; lunch a bowl of soup made of turnips, cabbage, carrots, nettles, or other weeds, plus some potatoes. There might be some meat in the soup, but it was invisible to the naked eye. On rare occasions one could see a microscopic "eye" of fat. The bread contained so many kinds of ersatz that it too had very little nourishment. The evening meal was always the day's main meal.

Majdanek's diet was a principal and planned weapon in the extermination of its inmates. But not even all of those starvation rations got to the inmates. A long chain of go-betweens preyed on the defenseless prisoners and stole their food in a thousand ways. Barracks staff carried to its apex the fine art of cheating on weight and volume. The rest went to camp staff or was sold, so that inmates never received even the small amount they were theoretically entitled to. Those who had money could buy anything they wanted—butter, bacon, salami, vodka, cigarettes, warm clothing, even chocolate—luxuries which came from food parcels or were smuggled into the camp.

In May 1943, Gentile Poles were still housed in the same barracks as Jews and were allowed to receive letters and parcels from their families; we Jews were not. Compared to us they lived royally. Part of the food they received they sold or exchanged, another part was stolen by officials. The addresses on some parcels were illegible, or had fallen off or been torn off, and some addressees had already died. Officials often deliberately damaged parcels in order to steal their contents. Civilian foremen from Lublin were sometimes employed on the Kommandos and they smuggled into camp food which they sold to their underlings. A kilo of bread, which cost 4 zlotys in Lublin, cost 100 to 150 zlotys in the camp.

Although every inmate was carefully searched before being sent to the showers, some did manage to smuggle in jewels, bank notes, and other valuables, many by concealing them in dentures or in the rectum, or simply by swallowing them. Through intermediaries these valuables were subsequently exchanged for food or used to organize jobs on desirable Kommandos or in the camp administration. Consequently, most of the valuables ended up in the pockets of camp personnel, Barracks Elders, clerks, and employees in the labor office. One Barrack Elder was denounced to the Germans and when his bunk was searched, the SS men discovered a bottle which contained diamonds, and six pounds of gold coins and other gold objects. He was hanged. As everywhere else, stealing was permitted at Majdanek, but if you were caught, you paid for it with your life.

Thus, there was a camp "upper crust," living moderately well, while the mass of inmates suffered constant hunger which drove men insane, turned them into subhumans with contorted intestines. Hunger cannot be described or explained; those who have never experienced it cannot understand that a hungry man is a disgrace to the dignity of the human species. To let go of your food at Majdanek, to put it down for a moment was to lose it. At first, some prisoners tried to save part of the bread issued at night in order to have something to eat in the morning. Bread put aside that way regularly vanished during the night, and we soon realized that the only safe storage for food was our own stomachs. So we ate everything at night and next morning had only the repulsive mint concoction to get started on.

After two or three weeks of the regime at Majdanek, sex problems disappeared. Women lost their periods; men lost their urge. Whatever sexual life remained was the province of the better-fed camp functionaries. They could buy girls for a slice of bread, they could have affairs with women functionaries, they could pervert little boys.

During suppertime inmates were permitted to walk around the field and to meet friends from other barracks until at 9:30 the gong summarily announced the day's end. Attached to the giant gallows that stood in the center of the square, the gong reminded us twice a day where we were.

My first reaction to Majdanek was relief: we were at the very pit of wretchedness and nothing worse could happen. All our desperate struggle against our fate, our attempts to escape, to run, to hide, was behind us. The burden of responsibility for the lives of those I loved had willy-nilly been taken from my shoulders; I had done what I could, but their fate no longer depended on my efforts. My situation had been drastically simplified; all I now had to worry about was my own survival.

I still felt some of the exaltation of the last days of the Warsaw ghetto. That desperate fight still cast its retrospective glow. I felt I was a witness to disaster and charged with the sacred mission of carrying the ghetto's history through the flames and barbed wire until such time as I could hurl it into the face of the world. It seemed to me that this sense of mission would give me the strength to endure everything.

But I was underestimating Majdanek. Hell has no bottom. During the first days there I felt so many blows upon my head that I was completely crushed. A group of us again remained behind when the Kommandos left and we marched and ran from one end of the field to the other, from kitchen to fountain and back. Near the fountain, the Lagerälteste was amusing himself with his daily victim. He wore a green triangle, indicating that he was a common criminal, but this did not prevent him from repeating proudly, *"Ich bin ein Germaner,"* or from being friendly with the SS men. Often, at random, he would grab someone and throw him into the pool, and whenever the man's head came up for air, he would club it or kick it back under the surface. The convulsive floundering of the drowning man filled him with ineffable joy and he invited SS men or even other inmates who happened by to share in his delight. The fun often ended tragically: the victim either died on the spot, or emerged so weakened from the ordeal that he contracted pneumonia and died in a few days.

Always near the Lagerälteste was a fourteen-year-old Jewish boy called Bubbi. In velvet shorts and military boots he wandered around Field Three with his little riding crop and even Jakob, the most hardened Barrack Elder and the terror of Majdanek, looked at Bubbi with horror. In a moment of confidence our own Barrack Elder, Szydlower, told me the boy's story. Bubbi had been sent to Majdanek from Lublin with his parents in the resettlement of autumn 1942. The Lagerälteste had liked his childish face and chosen him as a minion. Among the German inmates who were the Majdanek elite—some of them had been in camps since 1933—homosexuality was widespread and they often picked boys from among the deportees. After Bubbi had been so selected by the Lagerälteste, the boy had been "knighted" and raised to the rank of a Kapo. For the ceremony the boy's mother was brought from Field Five, his father from an adjoining barrack, and in the presence of the SS authorities and the camp elite the boy hanged his parents with his own hands. The Lagerälteste was very proud of his minion's exploit and pronounced him a *psychischer Germaner* in spite of his Jewish origin.

Bubbi used to loll around the field nibbling on cherries or slowly eating a ham sandwich in front of the starving prisoners. Thousands of hungry eyes followed him, though reason dictated that one ought not look in his direction at all for fear of catching the little monster's attention. But Bubbi found his own victims. His greatest pleasure was to select an especially tall inmate, order him to squat down until his face was level with Bubbi's own, and then Bubbi would spit cherry pits in the prisoner's face, aiming at his eyes. The prisoner was expected to smile broadly to show he was entering into the spirit of the little game. Bubbi would giggle and laugh happily, smacking the prisoner across the face with his riding crop, and when he lost his balance and fell over, Bubbi would be beside himself with joy and would occasionally give his victim a cherry, first putting it into his own mouth and then spitting it into the prisoner's. When Bubbi ran out of cherries, he filled his mouth with water and spat it over his victim's face. This might go on for hours until the victim fell exhausted.

The SS had other distractions, too. At any moment the gate might open and a motorcycle driven by an SS man in a white sweater would roar in at top speed. This was Obersturmführer Anton Thumann, commandant of Field Three; driving his motorcycle full speed into a group of marching prisoners was his favorite diversion. When ranks of prisoners scattered at the sight of the death-dealing vehicle, Thumann would single out a couple of them for punishment, rope their hands to the motorcycle and drag them after him, gradually speeding up until they were no more than torn flesh and crumpled bones and the barracks square was crisscrossed with blood.

One day some of us were watching one of these exploits when three SS men came up. Our Kapo suddenly ordered us into formation near one of the barracks. The first rank of five was ordered to spread out, leaving an interval of about ten steps between them, and to march to the center of the square. There the Kapo ordered them to run toward the kitchen. Clumsily, in their wooden shoes, the five men began to run, supposing it to be a race to amuse the SS men. Then a shot rang out from the tower at the other end of the field, followed by a second and a third. The five men dropped flat on the ground, but the Kapo ran at them waving his blackjack and four of them leaped to their feet at once while the fifth man lay there groaning. He was yanked to one side and the Kapo ordered another file of five to run. Four men dropped at the shots and the fifth ran on like one possessed. Then the four got up; none had been wounded.

I was in the sixth row. The practice in firing at moving targets kept up and our turn was next. I was covered with cold sweat. There were more and more victims and when my turn came a veil seemed to fall over my eyes. Mechanically I marched to the center of the field and turned to the right. "Run!" the order was barked. I felt I was choking. My mind was a blank, my reactions purely physical. I was hunchbacked with fear; there was an unbearable itch between my shoulder blades. Suddenly I felt a horrible pain and a stiff neck. "Bang!" All my muscles abruptly relaxed and I dropped on my face. I opened my eyes. I was not hit. The Kapo was running toward us, his blackjack swinging. I jumped up and raced to one side where the earlier survivors stood. Next to me a tall man said in an undertone to the man next to him, "Chaim, does blood stink?" Chaim didn't answer, only shook his head. "In that case," the first man replied, "I've just shit. Thank God." The others glared angrily at him because they didn't like his using such a stupid old joke at that time—and because he was not the only one in that condition.

Target practice continued for another half hour, with variations. The guards on the tower now fired at the man who ran fastest, then at the one who was last, now at the one in the center of the group, and then at those on the sides. Sometimes no shots were fired when men began to run, but when the last five started there was a burst of submachine-gun fire and all five men fell to the ground.

But the fun would not have been complete and the Germans would not have been Germans if no "moral" was drawn from the activity. The inmate who had not dropped to the ground at all was given a double soup ration and from among the "Jewish cowards" who dropped unwounded, an SS man picked one to be punished. *"Komm her Dreckjude, wirst umgelegt."* (Come here you shitty Jew, I'm going to lay you out!) The victim knelt, face to the wall, his eyes closed and the SS man held a pistol to his temple. A shot sounded and simultaneously another SS man smashed the kneeling man on the head with a two-by-four and knocked him unconscious. A few moments later when the victim opened his eyes and looked around him bewildered, the SS man said, choking with suppressed laughter, "You see, you're in the next world now and we're the bosses here, too. And you're still the *Dreckjude* you've always been."

That afternoon I had to help unload trucks and carry new stools into the barracks. About forty of them were brought in and placed in the center aisle, one next to every other bunk. During roll call our Barrack Elder Szydlower made a brief speech: "Listen, you sons-of-bitches, today new stools were put in the barracks. I am warning you, may God have pity on any one of you who tries to sit on a stool, lean against it, or eat on it. The stools are there for decoration, not for your comfort, and I don't want to have to answer for every spot on them and I don't want the orderlies to have to clean up your shit. If I catch anyone sitting on a stool I'll unscrew his legs and he'll get such a shellacking that he won't sit down for the rest of his life."

After supper Szydlower sent for me to tell me that my middle-tier bunk was now assigned to some "big shot," and I'd have to take one of the top bunks a few rows back. At first I didn't care, but around midnight I was awakened by something wet on my face. The barracks was full of snores and the latrine stench. Outside it was raining heavily and there was a hole in the roof right over my bunk. I moved to the edge of the bunk, but soon it was completely drenched. I got no sleep and finally the gong ended my torment.

Something different was in store for me. After roll call, when the order resounded to form Kommandos, the scribe called out the numbers of those inmates assigned to road building, but many of them began to gripe and one had a hysterical fit. He threw himself on the ground, tore his shirt, screamed he would rather be killed on the spot. Others showed the marks of the previous day—a black eye, welts from a riding crop, a bandaged hand. Several Barracks Elders and a Kapo came to the assistance of Szydlower and the "mutiny" was swiftly quelled. "As punishment," thirty additional men from our barracks were assigned to the road-building work party, including me. We joined a large column which soon was marched through the gate, and we sank up to our ankles in the clayey ground still sodden from the all-night downpour. Our wooden shoes stuck to the clay, making every step an effort. Small wonder that road building was a recognized necessity at Majdanek. We marched past Fields Two and One and found ourselves in an open area next to the Chelm highway. Before us were the guardhouse, the kennels with 200 trained police dogs, and the Political Department, whose mention gave political prisoners the shakes. Nearby was a house said to be the camp garrison's bordello.

We were split into a number of small groups, mine assigned to loading stones onto a cart that was mounted on rails and stationed at the top of a small hill. When it was filled with stones, a prisoner got up behind it to steer it. Other prisoners gave the cart a shove and the driver went down the hill, braking the cart with the help of a heavy pole wedged between the back wheels and the body of the cart. In the same way he had to bring the cart to a halt at the bottom of the hill, where another work party unloaded the stones and then four prisoners, of whom I was one, had to push the empty cart back up the hill. Two young Soviet prisoners of war, supervised by a Kapo and an SS man, were our foremen. During the morning all went well, but in the afternoon the SS man and the Kapo for some reason became enraged and began to belabor us with riding crops and sticks, shouting in broken Polish and German: "Quick, quick. Shove hard, you lazy bastards."

The foreman emulated them and soon we were running up and down hill under a steady stream of blows. The Russians joined the game wholeheartedly, enjoying the beating and adding their native Russian obscenities to the continual stream of *"Dreckjude," "Judensau,"* and other imprecations screamed by the Germans. One of the Russians ran up to the man next to me and smashed him in the face with his fist. When I looked at him surprised—could he be the same man who had spoken so gently that morning?—the Russian screamed at me, "You Jews won't work. In Russia, too, you always pick the cushy office jobs. Well, now we'll teach you a lesson!"

I had made a mistake in attracting his attention. After a moment the cart was ready to descend again, but this time the driver didn't manage to slow down. His pole broke, the cart jumped the rails, turned over, and spilled the load of stones. The driver had jumped off right into the arms of the SS man and was killed on the spot for "sabotage." When his bloody remains were shoved aside to be carried back to camp after work, the Russian pointed to me and said, "You take his place."

I had never done anything like that in my life. With terror in my heart, I tried my best . . . and to my surprise was successful. Every time the cart got safely down the hill, I was soaked with sweat and shaking with tension. That evening when our column returned to camp, four stretchers with the dead made up the rear, two of them from our barracks. I could barely stand on my feet at roll call. We were counted, as usual, and the numbers tallied. The Barrack Elder glanced at the corpses sympathetically because they had died conveniently. The barracks staff hated to have inmates die at night, for then they did not profit from the deaths. This way the Barracks Elder and his cronies got the dead men's shares of the supper ration, since the supper roster had already been closed for the day. To die during the night was an uncomradely act and the disappointed jackals showered abuse on the corpse in the morning.

Our misfortunes were not yet over for the day. A slip-up somewhere had left the over-all roll call for Field Three short. In Majdanek, where the main activity was the extermination of hundreds of thousands of people, the slightest bookkeeping error sent everyone scurrying as if the fate of the Third Reich were at stake. At such times the roll call might be prolonged for hours until the missing inmate was found, or the error otherwise accounted for. This time we did not have to wait long. In about half an hour a prisoner ran in through the gate followed by an SS man belaboring him with a club. "Aii, I'm dead. I'm not alive!" the victim screamed at the top of his lungs. The poor man did not know how close to the truth he was. It turned out he had been in the latrine when his Kommando had been ordered back to camp. By mistake he had fallen in with another team which ended up at Field Four. He realized this at the gate to Field Four and reported to the sergeant on duty there. Nevertheless, he was summarily sentenced to be hanged for "attempting to escape."

All barracks were ordered into a formation around the gallows. The doomed man, surrounded by SS men, was so bewildered and frightened that not until the last moment did he seem to realize what was happening to him. Only when he was standing on the gallows stool and an SS man put the noose around his neck did he come to his senses. Then with all his strength he kicked the hangman in the face with his wooden shoe. A moment later the stool was out from under him and the victim swayed in the wind. Only then, in impotent rage, did the SS hangman throw himself on the hanged man, punching him wildly. Six thousand exhausted, hungry men watched in silence. Finally there was the anticipated call, *"Essen holen!"* (Chow!) and with a sigh of relief the formation dispersed.

During the eight weeks I spent at Majdanek I saw five public hangings in Field Three. There were three other "attempts-to-escape" victims, and the last was the execution of the Barrack Elder whom I have mentioned, hanged for concealing gold pieces and a bottle of diamonds. Inmates remembered him for his constantly reiterated motto: "Don't forget, you must die so that I may live."

On the night of my first road-building experience, again I could not sleep. It rained and my bed was soaked; I was tormented by rheumatic pains; I had caught cold in the bladder and kept having to run to the latrine all through the night; in the morning I could barely drag my body to roll call. Again I was assigned to the road-building Kommando. This time we were to dig ditches for sewers, and each group of five prisoners was alloted a length of ditch to dig. My group included two sturdy, well-fed young Polish laborers, two emaciated Jews from the last Warsaw shipment, and myself.

The Polish boys worked so efficiently that our group did better than the others, our sector was ready before the midday break, and the Kapos and SS men who strode back and forth passed us by and did not beat us. After soup, our group was ordered to dig a lateral trench to the main conduit. Our Kapo nudged me, picked up a stick, thrust it into my hand, and said, "You'll be foreman!" The Polish boys glared at me angrily, but dared not protest. Flashing their shovels, they set to work again efficiently, but the two Warsaw Jews at the other end of the ditch could barely move and every other minute they had to stop for rest. The Poles grumbled loudly: "Look at those goddamn goldbricks! No wonder the Germans exterminate them like lice." Gradually, they grew bolder and began to urge me on: "What are you standing there for? What kind of a foreman are you? So now we have to work for these dirty Jews? Why don't you use your stick on them?"

I tried to appease them, but failed. When I urged the Jews to greater effort, they replied that I was as much an anti-Semite as those Polish brutes. I knew that to save my own skin I ought to hit them, but I simply couldn't do it. In a camp swarming with sadists and murderers waiting only for a pretext to indulge themselves, and many who did not even need a pretext, I was sure that I would be maimed or killed. What was I to do? I began to shower abuse on my mutineers: "You so-and-sos, shut up, and get back to work!" The Poles and Jews responded in kind, and our Kapo ran up. *"Was ist los?"* he yelled. Examining the ditchdigging at the Polish end and at the Jewish end, he ordered me to bend over and a merciless blow set my whole body afire. A moment later I was in the ditch with a shovel in my hands and a new foreman, one of the Poles, stood over me, brandishing his stick. "You shitty intellectual, so you want to play the good guy, huh? Well, if you don't want to smack them, you'll have to work for them!" I dug with such a passion that the Pole was amazed; I dug as if my salvation depended on it, and my two Warsaw colleagues, encouraged by blows, were working harder, too.

I dragged myself back to camp that night like a beaten dog. When I went into the barrack, Szydlower jeered at me. He had heard about the incident. "Next time you'll know better," he laughed sardonically. "I, too, thought in the beginning that the world would come to an end if I smacked someone, that I was a traitor to humanity, to my people, to God knows what. Jews are sacred, Jews are martyrs. How could I lift my hand against them? But I got used to it. Jews are just shit like everybody else." The two Warsaw Jews who had brought it all on me listened with cynical approval. "Everybody knows you can't be an asshole in the KL. A schmuck of a Jew is worse than an apostate. If we get a stupid foreman, why should we work ourselves to death?"

That night it poured again and I lay on my bunk, groaning, in what was no more than a mud puddle. Every muscle and joint of my body ached, and I still had a cold in my bladder. I was close to a complete breakdown. What hurt me most was the attitude of the two Jews I had tried to be decent to. I could not keep up the struggle any longer. I would have welcomed death; I would even have killed myself if the effort had not been too great. I was at my lowest ebb. "You're *kaput*," I said to myself. "They've finished you off in three days. *Kaput!*" My instinct of self-preservation summoned up visions of Lena and Wlodek, and of those who had died in the ashes of the Warsaw ghetto and whose last testament I had determined to transmit to the world, but in vain: my will was broken.

I slept fitfully, in starts, and gradually the will to live won out over my torpor. I was lucky. Had the breakdown come two weeks later I would no longer have had the inner resources to resist, but Majdanek had not yet sucked out my last ounce of strength; there was just enough left to tip the scales. "I am going to live," I said to myself. "Let them jeer, let them call me an asshole, but I will not beat anybody up." Half unconscious I climbed down from my bunk and sat with my back against the wall where the rain could no longer soak me, and so spent the rest of the night until reveille sounded.

Before roll call I went to the Scribe, a man I'd known before the war, and asked him not to send me on the road-building Kommando because it was beyond my strength. He looked at me closely, but said nothing. It was a cold morning and I shivered in my wet clothing: I could barely stand at attention. The Scribe assigned me to do garden work near the barracks, the lightest work in the camp. I had to weed the lawn and remove all refuse from it. I picked up every piece of paper, stone, weed, then watered and smoothed the ground. I spent most of the day on my knees. The day grew warmer, too, my wet clothes steamed in the sun, and the warmth assuaged my rheumatic pains.

"I must do something," I kept saying to myself. But what? I had to get less dangerous and exhausting work. But how? Beginning with the Scribe Weinkiper and Barrack Elder Szydlower, all the people who might help me looked at me with what I can only describe as embarrassed compassion. The Barrack Elder in Number Six barracks, who was a prisoner of war, and who was looking for an office worker, told me candidly, "I have at least twenty inmates who'd gladly give me a ten-dollar gold piece to get this job. Have you got anything to offer? If you have, we can talk. If you haven't, you're wasting my time. I'm too poor to afford gifts. I might do it for my brother, or my best friend, but for a stranger . . . ?"

In despair I took a step so bold that later I never did understand how I dared it. The ruling caste among the camp inmates during that period were Czechoslovak Jews. They controlled the central office jobs, kitchen jobs, and most other key jobs. They had been sent to Majdanek in May 1942, when the camp was "ruled" by Jewish prisoners of war from the Polish army, soldiers who had fought in the 1939 campaign against the Wehrmacht. Originally there had been 12,000 Czechoslovak Jews there but by May 1943, only 800 were alive. The survivors spoke of the past with horror, of roll calls that lasted all night in winter cold so that in the morning the ground was littered with frozen bodies, of the ruthless slaughter of the sick and weak, of endless beatings for the slightest infraction, of unremitting hunger. And all those Czechoslovak Jews remembered was that their torturers had been Polish Jews. Though they knew their tormentors were only tools in the hands of the Germans, their resentment persisted. Those who had survived were the strongest, toughest, and shrewdest, and gradually they had managed to move in on the better jobs as the Polish prisoners of war were sent into Lublin. They were able to do this because most of them spoke fluent German.

In the main office of Field Three, the Lagerschreiber, who was next in rank to the *Germaner,* was a Czech Jew named Horowitz. Small, bald, with a low forehead and jutting jaw, yellowed skin and a bristling beard, he treated the new shipments for the crematorium with contempt rather than hatred. Occasionally he made short speeches at roll call to inform the inmates of the latest orders and, although no one understood the language, he spoke Czech, usually opening with "Pricks!" *(Hújove!)* After summing up the order in Czech, he translated it into German. He did not torture inmates, but he was short-tempered and did occasionally strike out at or kick a prisoner.

I made up my mind to ask Horowitz for help. As he was coming into the administrative barrack, I stopped him and in one breath told him I was an editor and journalist by trade, and that I felt I had a duty to survive to tell the world about the murder of the Jewish people. I appealed to him to help me to survive. When I finished my outburst, I closed my eyes, expecting to be beaten. When I opened them again, Horowitz was looking at me kindly. "Strange," he said in German, "before the war, I, too, was a journalist. I edited a monthly issued by the Ministry of Foreign Affairs in Prague.

I understand you. I'll help. Go back to your barrack. Don't worry." He asked for my number, the number of my barrack, and my name. I looked at him incredulously. He smiled and repeated, "Go back to your barrack. And don't worry."

When I got back to my barrack, the Scribe informed me that the big shot who had taken my bunk had been transferred to another barrack and I could have my old bunk back again. But when the road-building Kommando returned that night, carrying two dead, my spirits sank again. There was wailing and lamentation, and finally Szydlower made up his mind to take a drastic step. After roll call he negotiated with two Kapos of the road-builders' Kommando and concluded a deal which he announced triumphantly to us. For a regular tribute of one bread ration a week—in our barrack of 300 men that meant 40 loaves of bread—the Kapos promised to beat the workers more moderately, and not to death. Needless to say, Szydlower got his cut of the 40 loaves. But even that enormous (by Majdanek standards) bribe did not stop the murders. After two days of relative calm, the torture and murder resumed, allegedly because of intervention by a third Kapo, and the transaction came to nothing.

Szydlower had figured out that it was more profitable to rule over a gang of well-placed inmates than over wretches. Though he would not have hesitated to sacrifice an inmate's life to make his own easier, he was ready to help us as long as our survival did not threaten his interests. With new shipments from Warsaw arriving daily, more men were needed in all branches of the camp administration. Szydlower got busy at the employment office, headed by another native of Lodz, a lawyer, and one night announced that he had succeeded in placing about fifty of us in the kitchen as potato peelers.

The very word *kitchen* was a magnet to which everyone was attracted. Szydlower picked out the neatest-looking inmates, and I was one of the lucky ones. We marched eagerly to the kitchen barrack and were met by the foreman of the potato-peeling room, a man generally called Lieutenant Franto, because he had been a lieutenant in the Czech Army. I spoke to him and in him gained a protector. The only Jew in the town in which he lived, his Jewish ties amounted to the fact that once a year, on Yom Kippur, he took his family in a horse-driven carriage to the nearest town where there was a synagogue.

The camp kitchen was in an L-shaped barrack, divided into three rooms: one where potatoes were peeled, a washing-up room which also served as a storeroom, and the kitchen proper. To the last we were forbidden access. At the head of the kitchen department was an SS man with a number of assistants, a crowd of Kapos and foremen and Schiebers. Our work was organized so that on each side of a trough of potatoes a group of ten inmates sat peeling. There were troughs at intervals of every two yards. The peeled potatoes were thrown into a small vessel with handles which, when filled, was taken to the wash-up room where a clerk recorded the number of vessels brought in by each group of peelers.

We began work the next day and a few days later our group included teachers, lawyers, rabbis, and other intellectuals, among them my old friend, the historian and former deputy to the Polish parliament, Dr. Isaac Schipper.

After the days spent in calisthenics and drilling and on the road-construction gang, sitting down in a warm room and doing light work was heaven. We were particularly grateful when the weather was bad outside. Yet even here we had to work without letup. The output of each group was carefully watched, and the group which daily peeled the most potatoes received an extra ration of soup. We had to be careful not only to deliver our daily quota of peeled potatoes, but we had to make sure that the parings were not too thick. Anyone caught peeling potatoes uneconomically lost the job. Moreover, we were searched every day to make sure that no one smuggled either potatoes or peelings out with him. Because the rabbis, Dr. Schipper, and I were scarcely expert potato peelers, we resorted to a stratagem: in cooperation with some of the other potato-peeling groups, we "borrowed" one filled vessel every day so that each group had its turn at getting the additional soup ration. Thus, even we finally managed to organize something. But like the rest, we were hungry, and being so close to food, smelling its tantalizing odors all day long from the kitchen, was an added torment which gave us dizzy spells and painful stomach spasms.

Aside from the higher-ups, the dominant figure in the potato-peeling room was a former Polish police officer named Germasinski. Dark, squat, with a square-cut face and turned-up nose, Germasinski was, under the guise of joviality, a menace. He had two favorite games. One was to hide and watch the potato-peeling brigades. When he caught someone slowing up or talking to his neighbors, he would throw a potato at the man's head. If he managed to hit his target, joyous shouting and laughter rang through the room. His second game was more dangerous. There was a big water basin at the back of our room and Germasinski would sneak up on his victim and suddenly push his head into the water and hold it under. If the SS man in the kitchen ran up, lured by the victim's struggles and Germasinski's maniacal laughter, the game would end tragically. The victim would be ducked again and again until he drowned. The other prisoners were forbidden to stop working or to look up and watch while that sadistic exhibition was being perpetrated: we had to sit there pretending that nothing was happening.

In the adjoining room, where the potatoes were rinsed before being taken to the kitchen, all the jobs were held by a well-organized group of young Belgian Jews. They spoke French among themselves, lived in the same barrack, and shared all their possessions.

The kitchen proper was run by Slovak Jews, most of them from Carpatho-Ruthenia, superstitiously religious and simpleminded. They took special care of rabbis, so that in Field Three rabbis had a good chance of surviving. From these men the two rabbis who worked with my potato-peeling group often got extra portions of thick soup, slices of salami, meat, and margarine, which they hid under their coats. One of the rabbis ate everything he got; the other, a taciturn man involved with his private concerns, exchanged everything—even his soup ration—for bread and boiled potatoes. The former said that Jewishness allowed one to eat nonkosher food if one's life was endangered; the latter merely smiled and remarked that if such was the will of God, he would get by on dry bread rather than eat nonkosher food. The law allows, but does *not compel* such observance, he said.

The Slovak Jews favored children as well as rabbis. There still were a number of children at Majdanek, boys between ten and fourteen who had escaped being gassed on admittance. Most of them were employed by the Schreibstube as messengers—*Laufer.* All day long one saw them dashing back and forth in the various fields, their young voices crying, "Barrack Scribe Number Six wanted at the office!" "Barrack Elder Number Eleven go to the employment office." Some had fathers among the prisoners and took care of them affectionately, as if they themselves were grownups and their fathers children. Even the most hardened Majdanek old-timer had a soft spot for the Jewish children, a species being made extinct before our eyes by the Germans. Some of the prisoners showed their affection in the most curious ways, such as teaching the boys obscenities and terms of abuse. When the children used such words, their mentors purred with pleasure.

But some children were not so fortunate. A few days after my arrival I saw eleven-year-old Uri Horensztein, son of one of the Judenrat secretaries who, before the liquidation of the ghetto, had lived in our apartment house on Muranowska Street. Though Uri was big for his age, he had been pampered by his mother and now cried all day for his parents. Because of his experiences and the drastic change of diet, he lost control of his bladder and wet his bed nightly. The Barrack Elder assigned another boy of his own age to keep him company, but the other boy proved no help; instead, he abused Uri, beat him, mocked him, stole his food, and made fun of his bed-wetting in front of everyone. Finally, the Barrack Elder sent the boy to the Gamelbaracke[9] where the Lagerführer found him one night and personally hanged him with a belt.

By being assigned to the kitchen detail I was better off than before, but I was still tormented by hunger, and in the face of that basic animal deprivation, food became the only subject of conversation, the master of our thoughts. During the endless morning roll calls, Szulc, a former well-known Warsaw restaurateur, would describe in detail all the dishes that had been prepared in his restaurant—the gefilte fish, the long salamis, the roast geese, the cakes and rich desserts, the varieties of bread and rolls—and we would listen fascinated. To prolong that dream of paradise lost, one of us would ask in an undertone, "And what menu would you suggest for today, Mister Szulc?" He would then improvise a menu and we would owe him for a delicious if imaginary banquet, for he was no ordinary chef; he was a poet and psychologist of food and dining.

Every few days I contrived to run into Horowitz, though such accidental meetings often took hours of planning and waiting on my part. He would wave to me and say, "I haven't forgotten you. You must be patient." In the end I couldn't stand it any more and I told him how I was suffering from hunger. The next day he told Szydlower to give me, in addition to the soup from the kitchen, a portion of the soup distributed in the barrack as well. That was little enough, but at the time I would gladly have sacrificed all the treasures of the Louvre for that small supplement to my daily diet.

"Shipments" continued to arrive from Warsaw, day and night, and the camp swelled. Barracks supposed to hold 200 were housing 400 and 500, with many sleeping on mattresses or on the floor. Every transport brought further news of the destruction of the ghetto. After the houses were burned down, the Germans had mopped up. Using trained dogs and special microphones placed against the walls, they had methodically searched the ruins for still undisclosed hiding places. When they found one, they destroyed it with grenades and poison gas. The Jewish police was

---

9. *Gamel* is Hebrew for camel. The occupants of these barracks were called camels because of their thin arms and legs, and swollen knees and elbows.—W. D.

finished; what was left of it had been massacred in the courtyard of Pawiak Prison and in the doorways of the house on Dzielna Street across from the prison. The Germans did retain a number of Jewish prisoners to take along on their mopping-up operations. These had to cry out in Yiddish outside the ruins suspected of containing shelters, "Come on out, Jews! Your salvation has arrived!" Some crawled out, dazzled by sunlight and stunned by fresh air after the weeks of darkness. Filthy and unshaven, they looked like animals. Occasionally these were still sent to Umschlagplatz, but most often they were shot right there, before they had recovered from the shock of coming into the open.

A sixteen-year-old boy among the new arrivals told us calmly how he had lured out the occupants of a shelter in 36 Zamenhof Street. "But later," the boy complained, "Jews wouldn't come out any more, so the Germans sent me to Umschlag." From among the inmates listening in gloomy silence to the story, a boy of about the same age jumped forward and began to punch the other boy's face. "You dirty rat. We shot at Germans from that house, and you . . . ! My mother was in that shelter in Zamenhof Street." My beloved sister, Roza, had been in a shelter in that building, but was it the same shelter? The infuriated avenger was finally pulled off the young traitor. . . .

New prisoners who arrived after office hours were sent to spend the night in the area called the Coal Field, between Fields Three and Four. They were ordered to lie flat on the ground, and warned that anyone who raised his head would be fired on. The deportees lay there all night, drenched by rain; cold, hungry, afraid to stir. One of the printers' groups, which included Mrs. Igdal and her small daughter and Levinson and his eleven-year-old son, spent such a night in the Coal Field. Levinson, a shy, plain man, was a bookbinder and the scene so upset him—he had lost his wife in the first Resettlement Operation the previous August—that he kept staring into the darkness crying, "Europe, where have you gone to?" He was never himself after that, but was drunk whenever he could find alcohol, and always writing poetry.

In the morning, when the men were separated from the women, Mrs. Igdal took his son with her and her little girl. Mrs. Igdal, the wife of a Warsaw printer, was a tall, blonde, handsome woman who, when we were arranging for Wlodek to leave the ghetto, had refused to make such arrangements for her daughter though she had plenty of money with which to do so. "What happens to me will happen to my child," she insisted.

To the great surprise of the Majdanek old-timers, all women and children of this transport, including Mrs. Igdal and the two children, ended up in the women's field instead of in the gas chamber, as was the usual course of events. (Levinson and Mr. Igdal were sent to Field Four.) Such a thing had never happened before in Majdanek. In addition to that, for the first time in the history of Majdanek a section of Field Five was reserved for women with children, and the latter were given rations of milk every day. The wife and child of one of our barracks orderlies, Sztabzyb, were also in Field Five and Sztabzyb pulled every string he could to get letters to them, to send them bread, and so on. Old-timers shrugged and said that the Messiah must have come. Rumors began to circulate that Majdanek was about to be converted into a labor camp where all inmates would be employed and receive wages, canteens would be set up to sell food, and the terrors of the *Vernichtungslager* would soon be a thing of the past. Everyone willing to work would live.

Then, one day, all the women and children were loaded on trucks and taken ". . . to another camp where the living conditions were better." Igdal believed that fairy tale for many weeks, but Sztabzyb knew the truth immediately, and the rest of the barracks staff fought to keep him from hanging himself. For a day and a night he lay on his bunk sobbing, and then he got up and went back to work.

A few days later Jozef Kacenelenbogen, my old Muranowska Street neighbor, showed up at our barracks, shrunk to half his size. His story was brief and shocking. After Jozef and his wife, Ola, had left our shelter, their daughter, Ada, who had lost contact with her fighting group during the ghetto battles, rejoined them. Eventually, all three of them were sent to Majdanek and spent a night in the Coal Field. At daybreak Ada lifted her head to look around, a shot rang out, and a bullet went through her skull. She did not even have time to groan; she was dead. Her parents were inconsolable.

Although the mornings were exceptionally cold, the camp authorities ordered us to appear for morning roll call barefooted and bareheaded now: spring had come. We stamped our bare feet on the frozen ground, but it helped very little. I had an abscess on my right foot from wearing the wooden sabots and I could stand on it only by putting socks under my soles, though this was punishable by death. The abscess weakened me to the point where sometime in May, I fainted during roll call. Fortunately my neighbors noticed and held me up. That evening I went to the infirmary and the doctor berated me for bothering him with such trifles. He did finally agree to lance the abscess, without either anesthetics or disinfectants, and he was surprised that I was able to stand it, because the abscess was almost an inch deep.

At long last, Horowitz came one day to tell me he had gotten me the job he'd been waiting for. He took me to a field near the entrance where a single barrack stood surrounded by a high fence. A square sign before it had the inscription: *Fahrbereitschaft*. Inside, he introduced me to the Kapo, saying, "This is your new Schreiber." To me, he said, "Well, now you're in. But I haven't been able to organize anything for Schipper. No one wants him because he's too old."

The Fahrbereitschaft was Majdanek's motor pool. In the barrack was a repair shop with every trade connected with automotive repair represented by at least one specialist: mechanics, glaziers, locksmiths, electricians, painters, carpenters, leatherworkers, and the like. Two noncommissioned SS officers, who looked like twins, were in charge, and they had a Kapo, a Scribe, and a messenger boy. Most of the staff were Poles, there were a few Slovaks, and only two or three Polish Jews, thirty people in all. The Kapo, a Warsaw-born Pole, received me politely, but without enthusiasm. He looked over my clothes and said that first they'd dress me up. We went to the storehouse, where I was given a decent suit that almost fit me, clean linen, and a pair of real leather shoes of the right size. After washing myself and putting on the clean clothes, I felt like a pasha. I had caught cold standing barefoot on the frozen ground in the icy temperatures, and my nose was running. Timidly, I asked the Kapo for a handkerchief and, to my surprise, was given one.

Horowitz had done his level best. I hadn't known there was such a paradise at Majdanek. My companions were decent and courteous. A loaf of bread was divided into four portions instead of eight. You could eat as much soup as you wanted and nobody cared because most of them received food parcels from home. The barrack was heated by an iron stove. We talked about politics and other general subjects. Finally, we got up at 5 A.M. instead of at 3:30 and roll call took no more than a few minutes. Most phenomenal, there were no members of that Majdanek scourge: lice! In short, it seemed like heaven.

I worked in a glass-enclosed booth where my job was to record the numbers of incoming and outgoing cars. When one of my SS men appeared, I had to run outside, stand at attention, clicking my heels, and report the number of cars which had entered or exited, and how many were in the motor pool at the moment. A couple of passenger cars, some trucks, and one covered van standing to one side, which people described in a whisper as "the gas chamber," made up the motor pool. The van—the Russian expression for it meant "soul-destroyer"—was, indeed, the first Majdanek gas chamber. Victims had been locked inside and killed with carbon monoxide. Fahrbereitschaft vehicles brought in food and other supplies and took out Majdanek's principal product: corpses. Trucks were rarely used to carry prisoners to the gas chambers: they could walk there, it saved gasoline.

The idyl was short-lived, however. I spent three days at the motor pool, during which I ate my fill, picked up some physical and moral strength, got myself thoroughly washed and cleaned before, on the afternoon of the fourth day, the two SS men suddenly appeared with another prisoner and told me summarily to get out. They ordered me to take off my precious leather shoes, gave me the much smaller wooden ones of my successor, then took me out to a field and assigned me to a ditch-digging Kommando. The whole event took no more than three minutes and no words were wasted in effecting the action. So ended my career as a Majdanek Scribe.

After work that night I went back to the barrack, where I found that everyone already knew of my demotion. What caused it, who was responsible, I never learned. Horowitz didn't go into details, but kept repeating, "You've been jinxed, but perhaps we'll find something else." Later I looked back on the experience as a stroke of luck. Had I kept my soft job, I might have stayed at Majdanek and shared its fate.

For the time being, however, I was thoroughly miserable. True, I had been left with my decent suit and what was, for a prisoner, a small fortune: I had my rag of a handkerchief, a piece of string, and a pencil stub. But I had lost my job in the kitchen and the double ration of soup that went with it, so I had to start all over again from scratch. Franto promised to take me back into the kitchen as soon as there was an opening, but at best that meant a whole week. My body had already gotten accustomed to a more abundant diet and I suffered more acutely from the return of hunger pangs than I had before.

A few days later I was once again set to work on the lawns, this time near the outside border of the camp. Majdanek covered a large area, nearly 250 hectares (or more than 600 acres), its external boundaries guarded by the so-called *Grosse Postenkette*, a chain of sentries based on a system of bunkers. Around the individual fields and the administrative buildings was the *Kleine Postenkette*—the guards on the watchtowers. Close to the Grosse Postenkette the ground was marked off into squares of sod two feet by two, and three to four inches thick. Our task was to cut the turf from the ground and take three or four squares of sod at a time back to our field, where they were carefully pieced together to form a lawn. We soon learned that the grass was edible and we came back with mouths full of a sticky green paste. The very act of chewing had a calming effect, and we could fool our stomachs that way for a bit.

Once, as I was kneeling in the meadow, carefully separating the squares, I suddenly saw something gray nearby. I looked more closely: it was a frog. At first I turned away in disgust. Then I looked again. The frog did not seem so repulsive this time. Were not frogs considered a delicacy in France? I rebuked myself for thinking such thoughts and closed my eyes to avoid the temptation. A moment later, when I opened them again, the frog was gone. My neighbor to the left looked at me arrogantly and then smiled. . . . His jaws were working rhythmically.

The hell of Majdanek went right on as savagely as always. When we came close to the Postenkette, our guard would ostentatiously take a big slice of bread or piece of meat from his knapsack. When a hundred eyes were staring at it, he would throw it just beyond the Postenkette. "Whoever gets it," he invited, "can keep it." The majority smelled a rat and weren't taken in, but someone was always tempted. When two prisoners reached the meat or bread together, they would fight each other savagely for the booty, and the sentry would shoot them both just a moment or two before they stepped back over the line. . . . "Attempted flight." The SS man would then remove the fatal bread or meat from the dead man's grasp and carefully put it back into his knapsack.

This was a daily game. When there were no "volunteers," the SS man would encourage hungry inmates not to be "stupid," and would assure them that nothing would happen to them. If only one man volunteered, he would be permitted to cross the boundary both ways and to consume the morsel. That was intended to punish the "cowards." If no one volunteered at all, the SS man would pick a victim himself and usually let him return alive. The inventiveness of the SS sadists created endless variations of torture, for what kept the killing from becoming monotonous for them was watching the fear and the death agonies of the victims.

Generally, obscenities were used so abundantly at Majdanek that often you did not hear a decent word for hours on end. Some of the officials always addressed the prisoners with, "Hey, you whore!" When once I asked one of them "Why *whore?*," he replied contemptuously, "Anyone of you can be bought, like a whore, for a bowl of soup."

When I got back to Field Three, Adzik Kipel, one of the men on the Wagenkolonne, came to see me. He saw Lena every day on his trips to the women's field. She had been appointed Barrack Nurse and though she was suffering from hunger, she did not have to work out-of-doors. Not only did he have news of my wife, but he told me to go to the barbed wire after roll call because an "acquaintance" wanted to see me.

At one end of our field was the latrine, two parallel boards over a foul-smelling ditch. It had no roof or walls, and the stench was awful, but we got used to it and it became a place to rest and a center of social life. Here, we exchanged the latest gossip and news. The latrine accommodated some forty people at a time and, as the number of prisoners in Field Three then was between 5,000 and 6,000, it was constantly crowded, all the more so because being there during working hours and roll calls was forbidden. All day long a Soviet prisoner of war was stationed there, stick in hand, to prevent us from using the "temple of reflection." He was a gentle man by nature, but to all entreaties he had one unvarying answer: "I want to live just the way you do. I get an extra portion of soup for doing this." Since most of us had dysentery, the ban kept many of us miserable and many of us had to use our trousers.

Behind the latrine double strands of barbed wire separated Field Three from Field Two. Throngs of prisoners stood on both sides talking through the wire, throwing messages through, or pieces of bread attached to stones. Such talk was, of course, strictly *verboten,* and twenty-five lashes on naked buttocks was the penalty for being caught. When I came to the wire, standing there in front of me, on the other side of the wire, was blond Izak Rubin.

"Izak," I cried out, "What are you doing here?" I was stunned. Apparently my appearance had changed for the worse considerably because Izak did not at first recognize me. When he did, he told me what had happened to him after he left us and went on his scouting mission. He had managed to cross Muranowska Street to Mila Street, and was on his way back when the two German columns had joined. It was too late. When he returned, the house was burned out and no one was there. Later he had joined the fighting groups and taken part in several skirmishes, and a week later he had escaped to the Aryan side where Janka had received him with open arms. With black Izak he hid in a specially arranged cellar shelter, but after only a few days he was captured. Either they had been denounced, or it was a routine roundup, but both Izaks had been deported to Treblinka. The whole transport was unloaded outside the camp—the first time such a thing had happened at Treblinka—and the three hundred strongest men were sent to Lublin. When the two Izaks realized they were being taken south, black Izak decided to jump off the train and, during the night, succeeded in doing so. The guards on the roof of the cattle cars had opened fire and kept blond Izak from following, and he thought black Izak had probably been killed.[10] Blond Izak was assigned to Field Two, was relatively well off, and said he would try to get some extra food smuggled in for Lena.

I was so absorbed in his story that I forgot to keep "eyes in my ass," and a Ukrainian Kapo took down my number in his notebook and was continuing to look for other transgressors when suddenly I noticed him. "Wait," I told him, and ran back to the barrack. When I got there, I cried out for a helping hand, and a decent fellow prisoner I knew only by sight took out four lumps of sugar and gave them to me. I ran back and handed them to the Kapo. He tried to bargain and I cut him short. "Be thankful for this," I said. "What more can you expect from an ordinary prisoner?" He agreed to cross out my number and I was greatly relieved. I was certain that I could not have survived twenty-five lashes.

Every night the list of culprits was read out at roll call, and they were publicly flogged on a specially built trestle over which the prisoner had to bend, sticking out his backside. Two men held him and a third—sometimes the Germaner in person—beat him mercilessly with a leather strap studded with nails, a strap that literally tore out chunks of flesh. Particularly cruel was a certain SS man nicknamed Dziobaty[11] because he was pockmarked. The screams of those being flogged were heartrending, and many died on the spot.

I now had a debt of honor to pay. The four lumps of sugar had saved my life and I somehow had to pay my benefactor back. I went to the camp "stock exchange" situated in front of the kitchen barrack. Hundreds of prisoners were always there waiting for some miracle to happen, and lively trading went on. Some had soup to sell in exchange for bread, others swapped bread for margarine, etcetera. I spent two hours carrying out a series of transactions, which I shall always consider my greatest commercial exploit. I helped one man get soup for bread, another to get cigarettes for soup, and so on, until I emerged with two cigarettes clear profit. Two

---

10. Not until 1955 did I learn that Izak Dorfman had somehow made it back to Warsaw, though wounded in one leg, and with Zosia's help had survived the war. He was still alive in Poland in 1965.

11. Literally, pecked full of holes.—Editor's note

cigarettes were the equivalent of four lumps of sugar and when I handed them over to my benefactor, I was very proud of myself.

All roads in Majdanek led to the crematorium. Starvation made us increasingly less resistant to disease, and tasks we could have performed with ease only four weeks before were now beyond our strength. Like most of the inmates I had swollen legs, the result of undernourishment and poor metabolism. (Only a few days before, the prisoners at roll call had been ordered to roll up their trouser legs so that the SS men could see whose legs were "too swollen.") Everyone sat and pushed a finger into the swollen leg or legs to see how quickly the depression would come back to normal. Many prisoners had faces terribly swollen from exposure to the sun, faces like pumpkins with narrow slits for eyes.

We were melting away. There was once again more room in the barrack. People suddenly disappeared. If they died in their barracks, they were removed discreetly by the Himmelkommando, but most of them went to their deaths through the *Gamelblock*, Barrack Nineteen. At Auschwitz inmates reduced to extreme emaciation, literally nothing but skin and bones, were referred to as *Muselman;*[12] at Majdanek they were called Gamels. All other barracks sent their Gamels to Barrack Nineteen, from which they went to the gas chamber.

Usually they were taken there at night, but once I saw the operation in broad daylight. The shout *"Barrackensperre!"* echoed through the field and we were driven into our barrack, and the doors bolted. Through a crack in the wall we saw a long procession of living skeletons slowly emerging from Barrack Nineteen on their way to the gate. It was the way we would look in another two, four, or six weeks: it was the way it all ended. Majdanek was an industrial factory for producing corpses: death, the destruction of the greatest number of prisoners in the shortest time at the lowest cost was Majdanek's purpose. Life was treated as something ephemeral and unimportant, as essentially worthless; in fact, contemptible. Death was our constant companion and not a terrible one, for quite often one wished passionately for it. It was life that was terrible, the long, agonizing process of parting from it after it had been shorn of dignity. Life in Majdanek was reduced to its basic elements, without the nuances and shadings that make up normal life and give it charm. Here the doomed devoured each other, and even the privileges of the diabolical camp hierarchy offered no im-

---

12. Because of their vacant, trance-like demeanor.—W. D.

munity. One day Horowitz came to our barracks, unceremoniously dropped his trousers and showed Szydlower his backside, black and blue, and furrowed like a freshly harrowed field. It was the Germaner's work. "The only difference between me and the most wretched Camel," Horowitz said bitterly, "is that I will die with a full stomach."

Szydlower had his turn shortly thereafter, too. One day we were assigned to carrying rocks from a gigantic pile in our field where other prisoners had put them the day before. Each of us picked up one large or two smaller rocks and then the whole column marched some distance behind the women's field and put the rocks in another enormous pile. Through the barbed wire we saw women sitting on the latrine and, far from arousing frivolous or obscene reactions, this spectacle inspired only deep hatred against the Germans for the debasement. Moving the rocks served no useful purpose except to give an occasion for maltreating the prisoners, who were punished for not lifting heavy enough rocks, for dropping rocks, for stumbling, and so on. The work was especially dangerous that day because one of the SS men assigned to our group was the notorious murderer, Dziobaty.

One of the men working near me was a weak-looking individual who—while the more experienced prisoners picked out huge flat rocks that looked impressive, but weighed little—picked up only small rocks, ignoring his neighbors' advice. Eventually the foreman noticed him and made him pick up an enormous rock. The man bent under its weight and said apologetically, "I can't carry anything heavy, I have a hernia."

"What's he saying?" Dziobaty was suddenly next to the foreman.

The foreman told him.

"Oh, a hernia, *Ruptur,*" the SS man said sympathetically. To the prisoner he said, "Show me, I've never seen one."

Flattered by the SS man's interest, the prisoner complied and lowered his trousers. The SS man bent forward, then swung his foot back and with all his might kicked the man in the genitals with his hobnailed boot. The animal shriek that resounded froze the whole column and faces of curious camp officials appeared in front of every barrack. Blood poured from the body of the prisoner, who now lay writhing on the ground, howling like a dog. Dziobaty, overcome with rage, began to kick him over and over again, roaring, *"Du dreckiges Arschloch, verfluchter Judenschmarotzer. . . . Ruptur hat er!"* (You shitty asshole, you goddamn Jew parasite. . . . He's got a rupture!") The body finally lay still.

The dramatic finale of the episode took place that afternoon when one of the camp messenger boys ran to our barrack to bring his father a parcel. Szydlower didn't have the heart to tell the boy what happened, but finally he came out with it. For a long time the boy refused to believe it even while staring at his father's mangled corpse. Then he ran out in front of the barrack, raised his fists to heaven and screamed; "You whore! You whore!" He threw himself on the ground in despair and kicked the earth and scratched it, crying "Father, Father!" After a while he fell silent, jumped up and like a dog ran back to the Schreibstube.

A short time later Szydlower was called to the Lagerälteste's office. When he came back, he could barely drag his legs. The Germaner had questioned him briefly and sentenced him to twenty-five lashes "for neglecting the care of prisoners in his charge, and for assigning them tasks beyond their strength." The messenger boy was given moral compensation for the loss of his father in the form of the privilege of administering the first ten lashes. This probably saved Szydlower's life. However much the boy tried to avenge his father, he was not a professional and his lashes were not dangerous; ironically, Dziobaty administered the remaining fifteen. Szydlower was beside himself with rage, and decided to teach all of us a lesson. After roll call we were driven one by one into one corner of the barracks; there Andrej grabbed us by the neck and forced us to bend over while Szydlower in person, alternating with the orderly Feldman, gave us each five blows "to avenge the wrong done him." So, democratically, justice was spread over all of us equally and the death of an innocent prisoner avenged.

About this time I was assigned to the kitchen again and there, had many talks with Dr. Schipper. I had met him first in 1930 when we worked on the newspaper *Nowe Slowo,* and had seen him many times in the ghetto. Even the potato peeling was now beyond Schipper's strength; he suffered cruelly from hunger and often during morning roll calls lost consciousness altogether. To make matters worse he had a young relative at Majdanek about whom he was greatly concerned. The young man was charming, intelligent, but disfigured by horrible pus-filled ulcers on his face, and though Schipper tried to help him get a "soft" job, he never succeeded, because everyone was repelled by the running sores.

Schipper was an embittered man. He believed that the money the ZOB had collected in the ghetto should have been used to organize the escape of the most socially valuable elements to the Aryan side rather than spent for arms. But he disliked talking about such things; instead, he preferred to talk about the war situation. He managed to get a Polish newspaper from Lublin every day and was well informed of current developments.

One day he told me proudly that the island of Pantelleria had been occupied by the Allies. For an instant his face lit up and then he said sadly, "And what of it? Pantelleria is far away, God's in His heaven, and here lies death in wait for us at every corner. Any day may be the last one for us."

One night after roll call Schipper came to visit me and we had a long talk. He told me that he had been opposed to the ghetto's armed uprising, but that the destruction of Polish Jewry did not mean the destruction of the Jewish people; it was merely one episode from the historian's point of view, terrible to be sure, but comparable to other disasters in Jewish history.

"But surely," I asked, "you don't believe that the way Polish Jewry passed from the historical scene is a matter of indifference to the future of our people?"

"No, it isn't," he replied. "It raises general problems involving the most profound motive forces of history. The last word has not yet been said about the historical antithesis between the warrior and the martyr. The defenseless martyr attains heights of dignity which will forever remain beyond the scope of the warrior, however brave. And what should be the historical testament of Polish Jewry be, the clanking of arms, like everyone else, or the power of the spirit? The testament of the heroic warrior or of the saintly martyr?

"Even more important, everything depends on who transmits our testament to future generations, on who writes the history of this period. History is usually written by the victor. What we know about murdered peoples is only what their murderers vaingloriously cared to say about them. Should our murderers be victorious, should *they* write the history of this war, our destruction will be presented as one of the most beautiful pages of world history, and future generations will pay tribute to them as dauntless crusaders. Their every word will be taken for gospel. Or they may wipe out our memory altogether, as if we had never existed, as if there had never been a Polish Jewry, a ghetto in Warsaw, a Majdanek. Not even a dog will howl for us.

"But if *we* write the history of this period of blood and tears—and I firmly believe we will—who will believe us? Nobody will *want* to believe us, because our disaster is the disaster of the entire civilized world. . . . We'll have the thankless job of proving to a reluctant world that we are Abel, the murdered brother. . . ."

Early in June I was summoned to the Schreibstube and officially informed that a request had been received from Radom to send all Jewish printers there, with their wives. I asked Horowitz whether I had to start proceedings on Lena's behalf, or if she would be sent with me as a matter of course. He said the request covered her, but just to be on the safe side, he'd get in touch with the office in the women's field.

We felt like celebrating. The whole field was electrified by the news. So it was possible to get out of Majdanek alive. Unbelievable! Rachman had saved us after all. . . . Every day or two the printers were called to the Schreibstube, their names taken, lists drawn up, numbers checked. One day a messenger came to the kitchen barrack to summon me. Several other printers were waiting in front of the barrack and as we set out, an SS man came out of the kitchen. He stopped us. "Where are you going?"

"We've been summoned to the office. We're printers. . . ."

The word *printers* was like a red flag to a bull. Enraged, he fell on us, punching and screaming, "Printers! It's because of you we have this war and all our misfortunes. Hanging's too good for you. Without you there wouldn't be all that propaganda against us. Get out of here before I kill you."

In the office we were told that we would depart the next day. Our last night in Majdanek. Everyone envied us and tried to say something warm or pleasant by way of farewell. But a sad joke one inmate made kept coming to mind: "At Majdanek life is one long Jewish holiday. We live in tents as during the Feast of Tabernacles; we are dressed as for a Purim carnival; we eat as on Yom Kippur; and our mood is always that of Tisha B'Av."

But they would not let Lena go. Although the terms of the request from Radom were explicit, despite Horowitz's assurance, the camp bureaucracy adhered to its own rule: Majdanek would not release anyone if it was possible to keep him or her. My joy at my own impending departure was thus poisoned by having to leave Lena in the slaughterhouse. But somehow I had to get to say good-by to her. The only way was to get myself on the Wagenkolonne that every morning took "coffee" to the other fields before roll call. I appealed to the foreman of the Wagenkolonne, but he looked at me angrily and said, "They've taken my wife away and I don't even know where she is, and now you want to say good-by to yours. You're sentimental. Good-by! Beat it, or I'll break you in half."

I had no choice but to go to the Kapo, who agreed at once, but the foreman's expression left no doubt that I'd have a hard time. At half past two in the morning I set out with the Wagenkolonne for the kitchen. The kettles were ready and we loaded them on a flat wagon. Every kettle weighed more than 100 pounds. Two prisoners stood on the wagon while two others handed the kettles up to them. The men who did the work regularly were better fed than I and used to it, and I was panting with the effort after I had lifted only a few kettles. The more so because the foreman was watching me like a hawk. At one point my hands went numb and with every clumsy movement, hot liquid scalded them.

At last loading was over. The wagon normally drawn by two horses, one on either side of a single shaft, was now drawn by some prisoners, while the others pushed. It rolled heavily across Field Three, out the gate, and on to Field Five. An SS man drove us, not sparing the stick. The prisoners, too, were in a hurry. The moment we reached the women's field, all of them including the foreman and SS man vanished inside various barracks and left me and another "sucker" to unload the kettles. Every one of them had a wife, sister, or mistress there, and a mass of parcels, letters, and oral messages to deliver. I had informed Lena of my visit the day before and a few moments later she came out with a friend. They stood about ten yards away from me while I got down on my knees and pretended to be adjusting the wagon's shaft.

Lena looked beautiful. She was wearing a man's jacket, was suntanned, and had thinned down. She told me she had done everything possible with the field office, but though the wording of the Radom request was clear and the other printers' wives had backed her up, the office stubbornly maintained she was not specifically mentioned in the list. "I hear that shipments are about to leave for other camps," she said. "Should I join them or stay here?"

Once I got to Radom, I would move heaven and earth to get her out of Majdanek, and I was sure Rachman would do his best to help me, so I gave her the answer that poisoned my life thereafter and that I will regret to my dying day: "Stay here. I'll get you out. Otherwise, how will I ever find you?"

For a long time we looked at each other in the growing daylight. I couldn't utter a word. And there was nothing to say. "But our boy *is* safe, isn't he?" Lena finally said, smiling. That last look I engraved on my memory, my wife standing against the background of the barrack in the pale pink light of a Majdanek sunrise. Her eyes were bluer than ever, her face more beautiful. So much love and sadness were in her expression that I wanted to beat the frozen earth of Majdanek with my head and burst into animal howling.

Then she threw me a lump of sugar, her farewell gift, and so we parted, without tears, without a kiss.

On June 15, 1943, all the printers in Fields Three, Four, and Five were assembled in Field One, where the central offices were. We had not seen our fellow workers from the other fields since the tragic days of April, and we greeted each other like long-lost relatives. We were sent to the bath-house, then to the storeroom, where we were given decent clothes. We felt ourselves the favorites of fate. When we got back to the offices, the chief Lagerschreiber, a smiling and amiable German, checked our numbers against the records. We showered him with questions of how things were at Radom.

"They can't be any worse than here," he answered. "At least there's no crematorium there. Moreover, you can take your *shiksas* along!"

I stepped forward and said, "How about my wife? Her number is 8,222. She's entitled to go with me, but they won't let her go."

He checked his files and said, "You're right. I'll settle the matter for you. . . ."

Lena was not the only one whose name was not on the list. A number of others had also been omitted. One printer named Szaja Szarfstein was listed, but his name mistakenly spelled *Szyja* Szarfstein. It so happened that there was a Szyja Szarfstein in the camp. Though the latter was not a printer and though all the printers swore that Szaja was one of them, that minor typing error cost Szaja his life, and saved Szyja's.

We were ready, waiting for our food rations, when the phone rang. The Schreiber lifted the receiver and after a lengthy conversation told us that Radom wasn't ready for us yet. When they were, he'd let us know. Our hearts sank. We had to leave our new clothes at the office and go back to the fields in our old rags. We were welcomed with a certain amount of malicious pleasure, and for the first and only time I heard the Barrack Elder, Jakub, laugh. His stony face became positively animated and he could hardly conceal his satisfaction. "They thought they'd get out of Maj-danek," he gloated. "You get out of this place only via the crematorium chimney. . . . " His faith in the inviolability of Majdanek's laws, shaken by the prospect of our departure, was now fully restored and he looked on us almost benignly.

We were cast into the depths, and it was agonizing to get used to the idea that hell was beginning all over again. A few days later our departure turned out to have been really postponed and not canceled. An order from the office called for the printers to be ready to leave at any moment, and the Barracks Elders kept us confined to the barracks all day. I had kept after Horowitz, urging him to do something for Lena, but though he prom-ised to do his best, he always added, "You don't know Majdanek. . . . "

A week later we were told that 1,000 prisoners were to be sent to the Hasag Armaments Factory at Skarzysko-Kamienna. Selecting them took a whole day and prisoners, naked to the waist, were paraded before a table where an official noted the numbers of those qualified for departure. On the night of June 24 those selected, and the printers as well, were crammed into Barrack Twenty-Two. There, squeezed together like sardines, we spent our last night at Majdanek. From outside came the sounds of sporadic shooting, the electrified barbed wire kept humming in the wind, and the camp slept its heavy, nightmare-plagued sleep. Finally, the gong on the gallows announced the dawn of a new day. After roll call and after the Kommandos had gone off to work, we were herded out of the barrack and formed columns in the eternal ranks of five, the printers in a separate unit. Each of us received a three-day ration of bread and margarine, and a slice of sausage.

There was no more talk of giving us new clothes and leather shoes: we left Majdanek in our rags. It was a painful lesson to me because after our first trip to the office, when we told how we had been given new clothes, my old acquaintance, Stopnica the barber, persuaded me to swap the clothes I had been given at the Fahrbereitschaft for his own lice-ridden rags. "After all," he insisted, "you'll get new clothes anyway." I finally let myself be persuaded and now I was left with his repulsive rags.

Horowitz looked me over with the eyes of an expert, and laughed. "You've made it just in time. You're a complete Gamel."

The column started. We passed through the gate of Field Three. We waded through mud puddles, passed the road-construction area, the administrative building, and came out on to the Chelm highway. Marching in step, escorted by SS men, we left Majdanek behind us, but my elation was spoiled. What of Lena? Suddenly the head of the column stopped and slowly, very slowly, reluctantly, began to turn back. We were panic-stricken.

A thousand hearts stopped beating. "Majdanek never lets go its victims . . . except through the chimney." Behind me someone began to sob. Was it possible? Our terror lasted only a few moments, but it seemed an eternity. We turned off into a side road and in less than a half hour we were in Lublin standing before a long freight train, next to a car with the chalked inscription, "Radom." People called to us from an adjoining car, fellow printers rescued from Poniatowa, Trawniki, Dorohucza, the Lublin Flugplatz, and Lipowa Street.

The moment we were inside the freight car we fell on our three-day food ration and devoured it. Loading took another two hours, and we could hear the SS men yelling, ordering the railroad workers around. At last it was quiet, then a long drawn-out whistle, and the train began to move, but even as we moved away from the Valley of the Shadow of Death, the rhythmic clatter of the wheels seemed to be repeating, over and over, "Le—na, Le—na, Le—na. . . ."

CHAPTER 5

RADOM, OASIS OF TEARS

THE TRIP FROM LUBLIN to Radom took less than three hours. When we were ordered off the train at a railroad siding, the sun shone brightly. Two SS men accepted the shipment, although we were 101 prisoners instead of the 100 they had been told to expect. Our fellow printers in the adjacent car, who had been assigned to labor camps near Lublin, looked very different from those of us from Majdanek. We were living skeletons, shabbily dressed in ridiculous clothes; they wore their own clothing, they looked strong and healthy, and we later learned they had even been able to keep some of their personal belongings. We were marched through back streets into the town, and the few people outdoors vanished the moment we came into sight. We finally arrived at a street whose entry was blocked by a closed wooden gate. A Jewish policeman opened it and the column entered the ghetto of Radom, officially called the Radom Labor Camp.

The narrow street, Szwarlikowska Street, was lined with little houses as warped and twisted as those in Chagall paintings. Peering out the windows were the faces of the Jews of Radom, silently greeting the new arrivals. They received us with mixed feelings, the strongest of which were horror and compassion. It was inconceivable to them that people could have been reduced to the state we were in. They interpreted the transfer of the printing plant from Warsaw to Radom as a good omen, and the transfer of prisoners from the KL to Radom also seemed reassuring evidence that for the time being the city was safe. Simultaneously, the news of the Warsaw Ghetto Uprising had reached Radom, and the city's Jews were afraid the "Warsaw bandits" might start trouble there. Radom's Jews lived in terror, and with good reason: of a prewar Jewish population of 30,000, a bloody succession of manhunts and resettlements had left only 3,000.

The main Radom resettlement had taken place in September 1942, at the same time as the one in Warsaw. Subsequently, Radom had gone through a number of minor but very bloody selections, operations, and massacres, and still fresh in everyone's mind was "Operation Palestine" of March 1943, when the Gestapo called for registration of all Jews who had papers to go to Palestine, or who had relatives there. More than 100 Jews reported. They were loaded onto trucks with their belongings, taken to a nearby woods and executed by firing squads.

Jews who survived the slaughters had been shipped to the labor camp we were now in, and were employed in its workshops as tailors, metal-workers, cobblers, and so on. The labor camp was under the command of SS *Untersturmführer* Schippers, who ran it with the help of the ghetto police. But here the people did not hate the police. Along with a number of other camps in the Radom district, ours was subject to the overall authority of SS General Herbert Boettcher, to whom all SS and police in the region were responsible. Organizationally, Radom was an outside branch *(Aussen-lager)* of the Lublin KL, whose other branches included Blizyn and the camps on the right bank of the Vistula—Poniatowa, Trawniki, Dorohucza, Budzyn. As was the case in Warsaw, all Jews were SS property and hired out to various companies which paid the SS five zlotys per day per laborer. To administer the confiscated Jewish enterprises, high-ranking SS officials had created the Osti *(Ostindustrie Gmbh)* corporation, later renamed the *DAW (Deutsche Ausrüstungswerke).*[13] Like the Warsaw *Werterfassung* the Osti-DAW took over the possessions of Jews who had perished, and therefore the "shops" in Radom and the printing plant being transferred from Warsaw belonged to the Osti. Among the shareholders in Osti were General Boet-tcher and Hauptsturmführer Dr. Max Horn. Leon Weinburg, a Radom Jew, was head of the Osti office and de facto head of the labor camp.

The sorely tried Jews of Radom received us cordially. They wanted to know everything that had happened to us, what it was like at Majdanek, who we were, where our families were. An elderly man named Joel, who had somehow managed to save some remnant of his fortune and was thus enabled to live in a patriarchal style, invited me to his home for dinner. Six of us sat down at his table that night. The lady of the house blessed the candles because it was Sabbath evening, and then we were served soup with noodles; boiled chicken was put on the table, and it was hard to believe that only that morning we had been in Majdanek.

We were quartered in the homes of Radom Jews, some of them still in their prewar apartments. With Samuel Kassirer, a Warsaw printer, a quiet and decent man, I occupied a kitchen in the ground-floor apart-ment of a widow who lived on Szwarlikowska Street with her daughter, son, and son-in-law. A few days after we arrived, the shop workers donated two

---

13. The Deutsche Ausrüstangswerke (DAW, German Equipment Works) was actually founded in May 1939. This SS-owned firm exploited the labor of inmates of concentration camps. The Ostindustrie Gmbh (Osti) was founded on March 12, 1943, specifically to exploit the surviv-ing Jewish laborers in district Lublin for deployment in the German war industry. Osti was dissolved after the mass murder in November 1943 of most of the remaining Jews residing in Lublin district.

days of their rations to us, and so for two days we were treated to generous meals served by the ladies of Radom on the shop premises. The cordi-
ality shown us was even more precious than the food. In addition, since
most of us needed medical attention, the Jewish community rose to the
occasion on that score, too. Thanks to the hospital under the management
of Drs. Neufeld and Boim, only one of us died and the rest were restored
to health.

Full of new strength I took vigorous steps to get my wife and friends
transferred from Majdanek. With several other former inmates, I drew up
a list of eighteen people, with Lena and Izak Rubin at the top. With two
fellow printers I took the list to Leon Weinburg and speaking in the name
of all the printers, we told him the people listed had been left behind by
mistake or because of red tape, and stressed the need for swift action. Every
day they stayed in Majdanek might mean death for any one of them. Weinburg promised to take care of the matter. Encouraged by his friendliness,
I told him that if he wanted to do something important for the Jewish
people at large, he ought to include Dr. Schipper's name on the list. He
agreed heartily and took down all the relevant data on Schipper.

I was full of hope, expecting to see them all arrive any day. Next I set
out to find an Aryan address through which I might contact Warsaw by
mail. Here Joel helped me. He had kept up contacts with Gentiles and
after a few days I had an address. I was afraid to write to the Maginskis, but
I did write to Kazimierz, giving him a brief account of what had happened
to me and asking for news of Wlodek.

The printing shop was to be housed in a former two-story school
building, but the machines had not yet been shipped. We also had to wait
for the printers who remained in Warsaw with Rachman and Keisman.
After about ten days the machines finally arrived. They had been adequately
crated and our job was to give expert help in setting them up in the school
building. Our mechanics had remained in Warsaw with Rachman, but we
feared delaying any longer so we installed the machines ourselves. Fortunately, the smaller presses and Linotype were almost ready for immediate
use, but we had trouble with the flat-bed presses, though in the end we
managed to get those set up, too. In moving the Linotype, one of the big
springs snapped. The Germans said sullenly that there was no hope of
importing another from the Reich. My life depended on that spring, for
if there was no Linotype machine there would be no need of a Linotype
operator. In the end, the spring was welded together in a nearby workshop

and I put it back on the machine with my bare hands because I had none of the necessary tools.

The printing shop was a fifteen-minute walk from Szwarlikowska Street, and we were taken there every morning under the escort of two or three ghetto policemen. The rear of the ground floor had the flat-bed presses; another room had other presses, a paper cutter, perforators, and similar items. The Linotype was installed in the front room and next to it was the composing room. The second floor was the stationery department, which employed mostly women, and the bindery, which manufactured albums, boxes, and so on. A stamping-engraving shop was also on the second floor. Paper and cardboard were stored in a small adjacent building.

Two weeks passed and still nothing from Weinburg. Whenever we questioned him he said he was expecting to hear any day. Finally, one night after work, we went to his house and pressed him for action, and he admitted that he'd lost the list. I was furious. Indignantly I told him he was playing with eighteen lives and every day's delay might mean another death. He agreed to accept another list and to send it right off. When we left Weinburg, my two companions, neither of whom had any family in Majdanek, reproached me for being so blunt with him. "Don't you realize that Weinburg is powerful here? We understand that you want to save your wife, but you have no right to risk all our necks!"

Next day Weinburg assured us he had sent the list off. But as the days passed he continued to put us off and in the interim my companions grew more and more lukewarm about the whole thing. While this was going on the families of the ten printers still in Warsaw with Rachman and Keisman were also urging Weinburg to find out what had happened to them. Though this dispersed our efforts, and I realized that things looked bad, I did not lose hope because Weinburg continued to be reassuring. I simply could not believe he would take a matter involving the lives of eighteen people lightly.

Toward the end of July I finally got a reply from Kazimierz. It moved me to tears. He wrote that he was glad I was alive, for they had given me up for dead, and that "Wlodek is a constant ray of sunshine. He is well and cheerful." I recited those words over and over to myself, and raked myself because Lena couldn't read them. But the letter also brought bad news. Kapko had been arrested and murdered by the Gestapo. Whether his end had any connection with our plans, or had some other cause, I never learned.

SS officers from Osti dropped into the printing shop frequently to keep an eye on our progress, and we always asked them about the ten men in Warsaw and the eighteen people in Majdanek. Finally, after many evasive answers, one said to Goldman, the printshop foreman: "There was a mistake with them. Instead of Radom, they were sent to Treblinka."

"My son is in Treblinka, too," Goldman said, looking hopefully at the SS man.

"How old is he?"

"Twelve."

"Well, they have good schools at Treblinka," the SS officer said, without batting an eyelash. "Later, maybe we can get him transferred here, but things are difficult right now."

Incredible though it seemed, the barefaced lie raised Goldman's spirits greatly.

One day a number of high-ranking SS officers headed by Boettcher himself arrived at the printshop. The printers were ordered to assemble and Boettcher asked how they were getting on. Goldman, wearing a white linen suit made for him by the Radom shopworkers, replied calmly that everything was going well, "but if the ten men from Warsaw came, it would be easier."

"If they don't come, can you, or can't you, get the printshop working?" Boettcher asked, his cruel conqueror's face impassively handsome. I looked at his eyes and saw the gas chamber. We could smell Majdanek in the air . . . if we were not ready.

"Oh, of course," Goldman replied without the slightest hesitation, "the printing shop will be operating within ten days."

"Very well, then, I give you ten days."

The printers never arrived. What had happened was that one July afternoon, after the machines had been crated and shipped, the SS man escorting them back to their quarters had given them a long burst in the back from his submachine gun. And so all ten had died, Jona Rachman and Abram Keisman among them. We missed them all, especially Rachman, who had organized the transfer to Radom, seen to it that the printers were released from the death camps, and so saved all our lives.

What most impressed the Germans who visited our printing plant was the Linotype. This mechanically ingenious device attracted them, for the Germans have great respect for machines and mechanical skills. Some of that respect for the machine even rubbed off on the Jew who had mastered the complicated Linotype and could operate it. Haunted by the stereotype of Jews as parasites and Shylocks, here they were confronted by a Jew who was a highly skilled craftsman. I had to explain the mechanism to them in detail and when I presented one of them with a lead slug with his own name cast on it, he looked at me as if I were almost a human being.

One day Dr. Max Horn visited and I took advantage of the occasion to tell him that eighteen of our fellow printers, and my wife, had been left at Majdanek. He was outraged and exclaimed, "How could they be so stupid!" He asked me to draw up a list of the missing printers and to send it to him: he would take care of the matter immediately. Next day he had the list, but I never saw him again.

I alternated between despair and sudden flare-ups of optimism. Every promise of aid filled me with naive hope; every delay cast me into profound depression. I couldn't understand how my companions, those who had miraculously escaped the hell of Majdanek, could walk about calmly, smiling, eating, yet knowing their fellow workers might be dying in the most horrible circumstances. Surely some energy and resolution might yet save them, but no one wanted "to take the chance." My eyes were finally opened by Moniek Rotstein, eldest of a numerous and sympathetic clan. A physical wreck, suffering from tuberculosis, Rotstein had a marvelous Talmudic mind. A just man, but cynical about the human race, he had an analytic perspicacity and critical boldness that did not draw back from the most sacred traditions or conventions. His opinions were so often precisely the opposite of the generally accepted ones that he was nicknamed *Moishe Kapoyer,* Moses Upside-down. He was apparently the only one among us who realized how tormented I was, and who sympathized. One day, when I confided in him about my efforts on behalf of Lena and the others, he looked at me with compassion—or perhaps it was irony—and said, "Maybe I shouldn't say this to you, but I'm like that, so I'll say it anyway. Your wife isn't coming here, nor is anyone else from Majdanek. Are you so blind that you can't see that this scoundrel Weinburg sold your wife and the other Majdanek people to rich Radom Jews? Why should he bring Majdanek inmates here when he can get a fortune for their jobs in the printing shop?"

It was the terrible truth. The people of Radom thought the printshop was a safe place and, before we realized it, it was swarming with rich Radom Jews who had never been near a printing shop before. Weinburg was careful to assign three or four real printers from Radom, too. He also got his own wife and their fourteen-year-old son into the shop, a sister-in-law with two little daughters, a nephew, and so on. More than that, he had a dozen of those who arrived with us sent away to other jobs to make room for his own protégés. He might have done the same thing for the eighteen in Majdanek, but he had instead cold-bloodedly sentenced them to a horrible death.

I had by now seen enough, both in Warsaw and Majdanek, not to condemn lightly people who fought for their lives with the utmost ruthlessness. But Weinburg's cool, premeditated act shook me to the roots; it seemed to me the lowest pitch of vileness. The Nazis were willing to let my beloved Lena go, but she was going to die because of Jewish machinations, and that was a thought I could not bear.

"For God's sake," I said to Rotstein, "what can I do?"

"*You* can't do a thing," Moniek answered coldly. "You can only fight them with their own weapons. If you had money, you might offer a higher price for your wife's life than they are willing to pay for her death. Threats will get you nothing. Radom is too small. They'd hand you over to the Gestapo without a moment's hesitation.

"You have just one chance—but *you* will never take it. Go to the Germans and tell them everything. The Germans would liquidate all of them, of course, but there is no guarantee that they would bring your wife here. But even if you were certain they would, you're not the kind of man who could pay that price. We live in an age of beastliness. Hitler unleashed the lowest instincts not only in Germans, but in all the peoples who fell under his domination, both as individuals and as groups. All you can do is suffer with your wife."

I saw Lena waiting in the hell of Majdanek to have me get her out. I had told her to stay there and wait for me. I had deceived her, betrayed her, killed her. My words were a death sentence. Would she think I'd forgotten her? Telepathically, I tried to beseech her across the miles: "Hear me! Run away. Run away!" I thought too of Izak Rubin, dear as a brother to me, and heard him calling across the barbed wire, "Remember, I'm counting on you!" How could I let them know *not* to wait, to get out on the first shipment if they could? When I asked one of the rich Radom Jews who had a job in our printing shop to forward a letter to Majdanek—he had contacts in Lublin—he named a price that was beyond belief.

And, in the interim, life in Radom went on normally. The men I worked with had left Majdanek behind; only I was doomed to stay there forever. The first honeymoon of Radom's sympathy was over and many of Radom's Jews were surprised to discover among our prisoners a few men who had somehow managed to keep hidden gold and diamonds, who were even richer than they were. And those of us who complained of never getting enough bread or soup apparently had always been beggars and complainers. "He who takes doesn't tire easily," they declared sternly, "but he who gives can have his fill quickly enough." Nevertheless, at bottom, they were decent people and we made lifelong friendships with many of them.

Exactly ten days after Boettcher's visit the shop was ready to work. A foreman was appointed to head each department: typesetting and printing under Goldman; bindery and stationery under Wlodawski; stamping and engraving under Cypel; and Igdal was made manager of the storeroom. Over all of them Weinburg appointed one of his protégés, a Radom printer named Wolf Saltz, a loud-mouthed creature who always gave us trouble. He was given the title of Vorarbeiter. Above him was a German civilian, Hans Bartz, a native of Hamburg, and in time he had an assistant, an ethnic German from Riga, SS Corporal Fechner, a binder by trade who had been brought up among Jews and spoke excellent Yiddish with a ripe Lithuanian accent and an abundant mixture of Hebrew words.

He rarely beat anyone and never displayed cruelty, but it was obvious that he would have murdered any of us without a qualm had he been ordered to do so.

Hans Bartz was an entirely different kind of man, the first "different" German we had encountered. He had great sympathy for us. He had himself been interned in a concentration camp and advised us to escape if possible, for nothing good could be in store for us in a camp. "I'd gladly help you to escape, but I warn you not to try to hide in the woods around Radom. They're full of Polish nationalist guerrillas who are supposedly fighting the Germans, but they consider it their first duty to murder Jews who have escaped from the camps or the ghettos. They'd as soon cut your throat as look at you." This was unfortunately an accurate description of the conditions, and we were ashamed to have to be warned against our fellow countrymen by a German. He spoke with contempt for our Ukrainian and Lithuanian guards, too, using for them the term for British colonial troops, *Askaris*.[14] In the fall, when a sack of potatoes was allotted to him, he distributed them among the workers in the shop. Also, he gave us the heartening news that Hamburg had been completely devastated by Allied bombing raids. "Some of the street signs with the street names are left, but there are no streets. It's all just a pile of rubble."

Printshop workers fell into three distinct groups: a core of professional printers; a large group of rich Jews from Radom, some with their wives and children, including Weinburg's family and the families of our three Jewish policemen; and the women working in the bindery and stationery depart-

---

14. *Askari* was the term first used by German colonial administrators for native African auxiliary troops. This term was applied to the auxiliary police force trained at Trawniki and recruited from Soviet prisoners of war and civilians from the west Ukraine and southern Poland because their original purpose was to serve as "native" auxiliaries in the occupied USSR.— Editor's note

ments. Friction among the groups developed from the outset. For the rich
Jews the printing shop was simply a refuge; they were interested only in
keeping out of sight and eating well. They started cooking first thing in
the morning and were eventually given a separate kitchen. They dodged
the dirty work, like carrying coal or paper, and behaved like privileged
characters. There were also violent quarrels among some of the women
and their foreman who kept them under too rigid discipline. But most disputes derived from the inadequate rations. Most of the former Majdanek
prisoners and many of the others had no money with which to buy food
to supplement their meager diet. We had to organize additional sources
of income. Some women baked pastry, which they sold in the shop and in
the ghetto; one man with a pleasant voice gave concerts for the natives of
the Radom ghetto, but most of us dealt in clothing and in smuggling.

Between the privy and the smithy in the courtyard behind the printing
plant was an open space about ten yards wide fenced off by barbed wire;
this area became a trading exchange where the Gentile natives of Radom
came to do business with us. We began to take old clothes from the ghetto
on consignment and to buy food that we smuggled back into the ghetto.
But while the professional printers were busy working indoors, the parasites
had plenty of time for trade and consequently we would get back from the
shop hungry while they had been stuffing themselves all day. More and
more frequently the professional printers found themselves forced to stand
for hours near the barbed wire, dangerous because an unexpected visit
from the Germans would have dire consequences. As a result, when someone showed up with bread or butter to sell, the printers would leave work
en masse to buy before the parasites got it all.

To end this state of affairs, we created a food cooperative, probably
the only one of its kind in a concentration camp. We divided all the personnel into groups of ten, with a leader for each group. A few of us were
kept on duty at the smithy and bought food for all with the money we had
managed to bring with us. One would negotiate with the suppliers, the
others would carry purchases to the smithy and from there to the printing
shop where we used one room as a storeroom. Each group reported its
needs in the morning, and purchases were made accordingly. We ordered
bags of bread, kasha, vegetables, and by eliminating competition and buying the food in bulk we got better prices and more accurate weight. Food
was then reweighed, rewrapped, and distributed equally to the various
groups. One man was appointed head of the cooperative and he arbitrated
disputes. Group leaders got daily bills, which had to be paid the next morn-

ing. Working capital was supplied by shares of 100 zlotys each which could be paid in installments. The cooperative worked very efficiently for almost a year, assuring us a sufficient supply of food and eliminating the major cause of dispute and conflict.

Only two men caused us trouble in connection with the cooperative's business. One was a Jewish policeman assigned to us, a coward, perpetually in fear of a German patrol catching us. When he saw us carrying big bundles, he always yelled angrily, "That's all we needed, people from the camps!" forgetting that without us he would have no safe job. And when he saw one of us dart out of ranks to drop a letter into a mailbox—Jews were forbidden to send or receive mail—he screamed, "Do you want to get me shot? Don't you realize that I'm responsible for you?"

The second, incomparably worse, was our Vorarbeiter, Wolf Saltz. Stupid and coarse, his new power went to his head. Flattered by the attention and the company of Radom's erstwhile rich, who kept him well fed and frequently drunk, Saltz forgot he had been a common laborer. Having lost his wife during the resettlement he now lived with an intelligent young girl and never tired of telling us the most intimate details of his sex life with her, and boasting of his exploits. With a foolish smile, he would repeat again and again, "When did I have it so good? When did I eat chicken and cake every day?" But if he caught one of the Majdanek inmates baking a few potatoes or cooking some beans, he shouted like one possessed! "What do you think this is, a restaurant? Did you make snacks for yourself at Majdanek? They brought you bums here and now you think you're people. . . . You want something to eat? Fry your own shit, you goddamn beggars!"

In the main, however, our life at Radom was without major conflicts. We had quarrels and intrigues; there were friendships and flirtations, and a number of the women who came with us turned out to be pregnant, but they were given abortions or their children were stillborn. In that little world my grief cut me off from the others. Contact with Warsaw was broken. I couldn't get a new mail drop, and Joel refused absolutely to help me again. Gradually I fell into a state of torpor, and I would sit for days at my Linotype machine, staring at the keyboard, while in my ears sounded the words of the ghetto song:

> Treblinka village,
> The last resort for every Jew;
> Whoever comes there, remains there:
> Remains forever. . . .

Only Moniek Rotstein would join me there and whenever he did, we talked for hours on the same subject: How had all this happened to us? What had brought it on? Moniek had not been through the final holocaust of the burning ghetto. He had been at the *Werterfassung* in Niska Street. He didn't hide, but reported when ordered for deportation and was sent to the camp at Trawniki with his wife, brother, and sister. Things had been bad there, but nothing like Majdanek. He had not suffered as much as I had in the past months and, unlike me, he was able to muster a realistic view of things that bordered on cynicism.

When I told him of the Ghetto Uprising, he asked ironically, "And did you think that was all as it should have been?"

"What do you mean?"

"That fighters equipped with weapons, who had the chance to die like men or break through to the Aryan side should have ordered you to stay in the ghetto until you were burned alive? Was that an ethical decision?"

"What else could they do?" was my rejoinder. "It wasn't their fault that there weren't enough guns to go around. If only the attitude of the Poles had been different!"

"And what did you expect them to do? For years the Poles have been dreaming of getting rid of the Jews and now, at last, Hitler does it for them, does it far more effectively than they ever could. At bottom they're delighted, however horrified by the inhuman cruelty. The Krauts devouring the Kikes: what could be sweeter? Why didn't the Germans dare to build gas chambers and crematoria in other countries? Because they knew that anywhere but in Poland the people would resist, that no other nation in Europe would tolerate such an abomination on its territory. In Poland there hasn't been a single guerrilla attack on a concentration camp for Jews, not a single attempt to stop a train carrying Jews to the gas chambers. Why? Because from the first the Poles accepted the Nazi line on the Jews. To them Jews have never been part of the Polish nation; patriotic solidarity doesn't apply to them, and they don't fall under the commandment to love thy neighbor. In Poles, Christianity only goes skin-deep anyway; beneath are bottomless pits of paganism.

"Also, a Pole who shelters or helps a Jew is subject to the death penalty. They themselves are terrorized, and there aren't many heroes. If the shoe had been on the other foot, would we have acted differently? Would we have risked our lives to save theirs?"

I said that rarely in history had Jews been in a position to help others, but it was a fact that during the 1863 Polish uprising against Russia many

Jews risked their lives to help the insurrectionists and there was no known case of a Jew betraying an insurrectionist to the Russians. I admitted that the Poles were terrorized, but I insisted that they were a courageous people, and were threatened with death not only for sheltering Jews, but for many other things—smuggling, slaughtering cattle, failing to deliver their quotas, trading in foreign currencies, not to speak of things such as political activities, reading underground literature, listening to foreign broadcasts, and so on—and that they kept right on doing them. Why was it that only helping Jews scared them? I didn't blame the individual Pole for this, but their leaders—government, political parties, intellectuals, the Catholic Church—who had failed to create the proper climate. A Pole didn't hesitate to slaughter a pig, because that was praised as a patriotic virtue, but saving a Jew was a sin and disgrace. Even while the ghetto was going up in smoke, Poles watched, but made no attempt to offer armed help. By its passivity the underground leadership condoned the Nazis' action and exonerated the Allies for adopting the same passivity.

"Don't misunderstand me," Moniek replied. "I wasn't trying to justify the Poles. They'll pay plenty for their attitude in the end. Not that I believe in historical justice, but no nation escapes the consequences of its actions. That's my 'boomerang' theory of history. Our tragedy has now become the tragedy of European civilization. When the Poles wake up it will be a terrible problem to them—and to the Germans, too. In twenty years, young men will discover that their fathers were murderers and they'll ask them, 'What were you doing then?' They'll never recover from the terrible guilt.

"And now that all the nations have been shown that you can murder millions with impunity, the question will eventually be asked, 'If Jews only yesterday why not Americans, or Catholics, or Chinese tomorrow?' How can Christianity survive the discovery that, after a thousand years of its being Europe's official religion, Europe remains pagan at heart? I don't know whether the Pope has made an effort to come to our defense. I don't think so. I don't believe in the wrath of God, or that there is such a thing as wholesale redemption or wholesale damnation, but Christ is crucified daily and rises again. Man is neither evil nor good. In every one of us is a Christ and an SS man. And each day the SS man crucifies the Christ inside us because evil is more militant and aggressive than good, because mankind is frail and fearful, because evil is contagious always, but most when it is organized and institutionalized. The struggle against evil never ends."

"But, Moniek, you haven't answered the most important question. Why? For God's sake, why, why?"

"If you look for an answer in terms of morality or metaphysics, you won't find one. If you ask why Hitler acts as he does, we can make some guesses. But first you must keep in mind that Hitler is not a political leader, but the head of a criminal gang, that his lust for murder is stronger than the dictates of reason or self-interest."

Moniek believed that murdering the Jews would *not* be advantageous to Hitler or to Germany *in the long run*. But in the short run, he saw anti-Semitism serving as a cement that joined the criminal elements in all the conquered countries and made them Hitler's allies, thus paralyzing resistance to the Germans. Looted Jewish property was a magnet which attracted millions brought up to believe in the myth of the Jewish wealth. Every single family in the Reich or in the occupied countries had profited either directly or indirectly from looting Jewish possessions. Millions of jobs Jews had formerly held in eastern and central Europe had gone to Germans. By continuing the techniques of murder and robbery the Germans intended to destroy the intellectuals and middle classes of the countries they'd conquered, reducing the natives to laborers and peasants.

"Then why leave any of us alive?" I asked.

"That serves a triple purpose," Moniek replied. "The Reich needs labor and the SS makes that concession to the Wehrmacht—skilled Jewish workers. Second, Jews are used to organize the loot and put Jewish enterprises back into operation. Third, these SS gangsters don't want to get sent to the front, and this way they can stay behind and get rich at the same time. To them, at present, the Jews are a godsend, and they will do their best to keep us alive. It's even possible that they're holding on to us as their alibi before world opinion if they lose.

"But what is most important is this: our survival is temporary. We are doomed, and our death is only a matter of time. . . ."

We talked like that for hours, days, weeks on end. The months went by, and soon the summer was over, the days grew shorter, the leaves withered on the trees. One rainy October day, unable to endure it any longer, I went to see Bartz. I knew he was sympathetic and loved children. I told him I had a son with Gentiles in Warsaw, and that my wife was at Majdanek. I asked if he would help me get her out of there. He told me I was lucky about Wlodek, that he would do everything in his power for Lena, and that he would let me know as soon as he learned anything. Days and weeks of nagging anxiety passed and when I questioned him, his answer was that he hadn't found out anything yet. Then he began to avoid me.

Early in November, the Szwarlikowska Street camp was liquidated and all but a few hundred workers moved to the camp in Szkolna Street, miles away, on the other side of the railroad tracks, where previously only those employed in the munitions factory were housed. New barracks were thrown up to serve as living quarters and as workshops. The printing plant stayed where it was, however. There was also an administrative barrack and one for the SS. For some weeks the new camp was separated from the munitions factory camp by a barbed-wire fence, which was later torn down. For the former Majdanek inmates it was just another move, but the Radom people were severely shaken by it; they realized that the period of relative safety for them was over.

Our belongings were taken to Szkolna Street in trucks, but we went there on foot. We found Weinburg and a couple of policemen guarding our things, and each of us picked his own out of the pile and walked off. Suddenly a policeman ran after some boy, caught him and brought him back to Weinburg with his bundle. As the policeman beat him up the boy explained, weeping, that he had made a mistake because his bundle looked exactly like the one he'd taken. But Weinburg coldly handed the boy over to an SS man named Richard Rokita. A moment later we heard a shot and then the SS man ordered the policeman to remove the body. The boy was buried on the far side of the road

With the move to Szkolna Street, the *Arbeitslager* Radom became a *Konzentrationslager,* officially an extension of Majdanek. We had to surrender our civilian clothes and were given striped uniforms though I managed to steal back my own clothes when the SS guard looked away for a moment. We no longer lived in apartments but in barracks. By comparison with Majdanek, however, it still seemed like a boardinghouse. Roll calls took place at 7 A.M., lasted only a few minutes, and involved no fuss about small inaccuracies. At first families were able to live together, but later women were assigned to separate barracks.

Only days after we were installed, we were ordered into the usual ranks of five and a careful selection was made by the SS men headed by Obersturmführer Wilhelm Blum. As always the victims were chiefly older people and mothers with children. They were locked up in a separate barrack guarded by SS men and Ukrainians. The rest of us were driven through a narrow passage between the barracks to the other side of the square. There were a few children in the printing shop, one of them a sweet little girl whose mother appeared to have lost her mind and stood there helpless, eyes vacant. When we were ordered to march, Mrs. Rachman took the little girl under her long skirt, we surrounded her, and by walking slowly managed to get through the dangerous narrow passage. Only after we were safe did the mother come to and, weeping wildly, throw her arms around Mrs. Rachman.

But we couldn't do anything for one of our coworkers, a young woman named Ruta Oknowski, who had her son Olek with her. Her husband had been killed in Warsaw, and Ruta with her child had been able to slip into a group sent to Poniatowa. Later she joined the shipment of printers to Radom. Ruta was a pale, handsome woman with a classical Greek face and a perfect profile. Bartz frankly admired her and even Fechner treated her kindly, but now he pretended not to see her. He remained aloof and impassive when she and her boy were led away with the selected.

After two long hours Ruta and Olek reappeared on the safe side of the square, terror still in her eyes. When she had recovered sufficiently, she told us how she had, after desperate bargaining, bribed a Ukrainian guard with a gold bracelet so that he had let her jump out the window and take Olek with her. At one point Olek had become so exhausted from the fear and tension that he had said: "Mommy, maybe it's enough. Let's cuddle together, close our eyes, and go to see Daddy. . . ."

Later, the several hundred people in that barrack were marched to Biala Street and murdered without the help of gas chambers.

Olek Oknowski was a year older than Wlodek, and talking to him was almost like talking to my own son. I became very attached to him and in my loneliness my feeling for the boy was very precious. Like his mother, Olek had raven hair except for one lock in the front turned completely gray. Ruta either misinterpreted my affection for the boy, had compassion for my ordeal, or, impelled by her own loneliness and desire, saw in Olek a bridge to a more intimate relationship. Had I been certain Lena was alive, perhaps I might have succumbed to the temptation, but now the thought was a sacrilege, a betrayal of the dead I could not countenance. I tried to explain that to Ruta one evening and the next morning her eyes were red and swollen from crying. A few days later she became "cousins" with the pockmarked Kapo from the *Effektenkammer* (clothing warehouse), who kept her in organized gewgaws, and I was left even more lonely without the pure childish affection of Olek.

The regime grew stricter; a new team of SS men moved into the camp and the number of SS guards in the printing shop was increased. For a while we had difficulty buying food for our cooperative but eventually we "tamed" the new SS men and on occasion they even helped us carry the bags. Bartz was transferred elsewhere and Fechner became sole boss of the printing plant. Though he was a scoundrel, we reached a *modus vivendi* with him in which he received gifts both in kind and in cash, and as a result conditions in the printshop went on much as before.

Two of our new SS men, Rokita and his comrade, appropriately named Moerder, provided us with plenty of cruelty and bloodshed. They loved to exercise us on rainy days, when they could order us to fall face down in the mud. Rokita would then launch into a long harangue about how the prisoners forced him to cruelty and bloodshed; he himself was a quiet, peaceable man. "I told you plainly to fall on your faces, and now I see one of you who's no farther down than his knees. He just kneels there staring at the mud as if it was fire and brimstone. I repeat my order and he still doesn't obey. I must teach him a lesson and hit him over the head or shoot him, because clearly what he is doing is disobedience, sabotage. Then there are protests. And whose fault is it? Mine? No, *your* fault!" His tirades always ended with that catechism, with the same question and the same answer: *your* fault.

Moerder liked to remind us of his name. Depending on his mood of the moment, he would say, "My name means *murderer* and I *am* a murderer," and he would shoot to kill. Or, "Yes, my name means murderer, but I am not a murderer," and then the prisoner would escape with only a cruel beating.

The new SS men were always interested in the printshop. One day, after talking to one of them and casting a slug of type with his name, I asked him where he had come from. He said his team had arrived straight from Lublin, and he added, "The Lublin KL is kaput. All the Jews there were destroyed."

"But why?" I asked.

"Weapons were found hidden among the prisoners. They were going to mutiny!"

Stimulated by my unconcealed horror, he told me in gory detail of the black Wednesday of November 3, 1943, of the Majdanek massacre. In Field Five (the women's field) at Majdanek, there was an L-shaped barrack at the right edge. One wall of that barrack, which faced the barbed-wire fence, was removed, the wire was cut, and for three days 300 prisoners working in two shifts were made to dig three ditches 2 yards deep and about 1,000 yards long. Approximately 100 SS men were then lined up in two rows to form a gantlet, and groups of 100 Jews at a time were made to undress, run the gantlet to the L-shaped barrack, and from there to the ditches, men and women separately. SS men drove them into the ditches with rifle butts, forcing them to lie flat. Other SS men standing above them raked them with automatic-rifle fire. The next groups were forced to lie down on top of the corpses of the previous ones. The killing went on for two days, from 6 A.M. to 5 P.M., with SS men relieved at two-hour intervals. During this process, two trucks were drawn up blaring gay ballads, marches, songs, and dance tunes through a loudspeaker to drown out the victims' screaming. And afterward the Polish inmates celebrated and got drunk because the Nazis had killed their Jews.

"Let me tell you," the SS man concluded, "that was something; eighteen thousand people killed in two days. All the Jews of Lublin, the Flugplatz, Lipowa Street, the KL—all five fields—everything. . . ." He stopped. "Did you have any relatives there?" he asked, an afterthought.

I shook my head. "No," I said.

I had been hit at the core of my being. Night descended and I had no will to live. Every night I died with Lena, held her hand as she was flogged and driven by the SS men; I jumped into that last ditch with her, and I was with her when she looked up at the sky from the bottom of that ditch hoping to catch a glimpse of God and seeing only the face of her murderers. And I relived Izak's death as well. He had waited for me, too; and I had also let him down. Every night they haunted me, every night I died with them on a cold November day in Majdanek. The thought that Lena *might* have been saved were it not for a Jewish scoundrel made it all the more unbearable. I mourned her with all my heart, reliving our life together, regretting the moments of separation, the joys I had neglected or failed to give her. And most of all I lacerated myself with the thought that I had doomed her with my careless words, advising her to stay at Majdanek so that I would be able to find her. I would not have to look for her now: she was in a mass grave with 18,000 others.

I could not get to sleep at first, and when finally I did, exhausted, I woke up screaming from some nightmare, such as the little boy being dragged away by the Gestapo and crying, "O Daddy, why did you go away and leave me?"

Suffering rises in you higher and higher, becomes more and more painful: it gets to your chest, goes up to your throat, your mouth, and finally fills your whole head. Then nothing matters. I reached that point: I let myself go completely; I wandered about like a ghost. I was plagued by boils which broke out all over my body, swelled with pus, burst, only to reappear at some new place. Phrases, stale with centuries of use, commonplaces that mean nothing to the fortunate, suddenly took on new, urgent meaning for me. *"De profundis clamavi. . . .* O merciful Lord, how I invoked You, I unbeliever. . . . *Contra spem spero. . . ."* I understood; I remembered the date: November 3 was burned into my brain in letters of fire. Yet in the silence of my heart I prayed; at any moment I'd wake up, and the whole nightmare would have disappeared.

Everyone in camp had lost someone and all bore their grief in silence. Another's tears met with understanding, but not with sympathy: one unhappy man doesn't pity another, is not moved by another's misfortune. Yet how little sometimes suffices to save a perishing man: a glance, a word, a gesture. Once I gave a fellow prisoner a boiled potato and he never stopped thanking me for having saved his life. Another time I helped someone to regain his feet after he had fallen during a march. He not only reached our destination alive, but survived the war; and he maintains that without my help that one time he would never have gotten up, he would have been killed where he lay. In the camp it was easier to get a piece of bread than a kind word. Prisoners helped one another as best they could, but they shied away from sentiment. Help, yes; compassion, no. Even help was extended harshly and when you thanked a prisoner, his almost invariable reply was, "Aw, kiss my ass!"

What brought me back to life, pulled me up out of the depths of despair was warmth, compassion, kind words the Melcers gave me. They acted instinctively and I think that even they did not realize the full extent of my agony beneath the pretense of indifference, or how far I had already gone off the deep end. What exactly they did I cannot describe, and perhaps it cannot be expressed in words. Their small kindnesses, their naive confidence that we would all survive, their occasional smiles, their simple words that fell like manna on my anguished heart. What brought us together was the common fate of our children, hidden in Warsaw with Gentile families, the experiences we had endured in the past year, and our indifference to the intrigues and gossip which dominated camp life. Adam Melcer worked in the room near mine as a compositor, while Julia kept the ground floor clean. She talked to me even when I didn't answer; they both asked me to eat with them and, when it was time to go back to the barracks, they waited for me and walked with me. I slept nearby and they would gently shake me half awake when I moaned too loudly in my sleep. And slowly, as if returning from a long journey beyond the frontiers of life, I recovered.

The road back to the Szkolna Street camp from the shop was longer than to the old one in Szwarlikowska Street. As usual we marched there in ranks of five accompanied by a tune whistled by Kapo Wiktor. He whistled beautifully and the SS men liked him so much they made him Kapo of the printing shop. One night when we were marching back to the barracks in a heavy autumn fog, so thick it was difficult to recognize a man a few feet away, someone said, "This is perfect weather for the Jews hiding on the Aryan side in Warsaw. The devil himself wouldn't recognize them now. . . ." Just then a Radom civilian walking by on the sidewalk, as if in answer to the comment, called out in Yiddish, "Keep up your courage! Don't give away your ration card!"—the old Warsaw slogan. That living proof that there were Jews still alive on the Aryan side lifted our spirits immeasurably. But a few days later something happened that electrified us.

At work Julia Melcer was asked to go to the barbed wire to see someone just arrived from Warsaw. She supposed it would be the Gentile woman who was sheltering her daughter, and ran out immediately. Moments later she was back and asking her husband, Abram Kotlar (our bookkeeper, her brother-in-law), and me to go out with her. At the barbed-wire fence we found a young Gentile-looking girl in her early twenties. We were thunder-struck when she said, "I have been sent to you from Warsaw by the Jewish National Committee and Coordinating Commission."

She told us that when she had asked to see the Jews of Radom, she had been sent to the Jewish public baths. When they heard who she was and where she had come from, the people were frightened to death and sent her to the printshop, saying that there she would find people from Warsaw.

"I've come to encourage you," she said. "Try to hold out. The Jewish underground will do everything it can to help you. If you have children hidden on the Aryan side, we'll help you with money. For the time being we don't have much, but we'll soon have more. We can give you funds, and Aryan papers."

The girl was the legendary "Wladka," the heroic courier of the Jewish underground. We had no reason to question her identity because Julia Melcer had known her personally under her real name, Feiga Peltel. Wladka gave us 10,000 zlotys to be distributed among the poorest prisoners and asked us to draw up a list of all Jews now in Radom and to send it to her. Melcer's Polish friend was to serve as our mail drop if we wanted to get in touch with her. We also gave her the addresses of our children in Warsaw, but I gave her not the Maginskis' number, but Kazimierz's. The reason was that for some time I could not remember whether they lived at 52, 42, or

54 Pius Street, and that weakening of my memory tormented me. I despised myself, considered it a betrayal of my own child, but the fact was that because of what I had gone through I could not remember the number with certainty.

Wladka's visit was a tremendous boost to our morale. To realize there were people who had not forgotten us, that there was still someone left to tell the postwar world of our fate, was to have a beacon in the stormy seas. And Wladka, that lovely girl, still almost a child, who struck no heroic poses, reminded me of those two young fighters on Muranowska Street: she was our flesh and blood, our hope and pride. We were once more part of history, no longer anonymous fodder for the crematoria, and we held our heads higher, our shoulders straighter.

We formed a committee which included the two Melcers, Abram Kotlar, the printer Samuel Kassirer, and myself, and were surprised to discover how many inmates refused to join because they were afraid. We distributed the money among the neediest, and the news of our contact with the Jewish underground lit up almost everyone's face. We went to work to draw up a list of the inmates of our camp, but it was not easy. There were more than 2,500 names and, of course, we had no typewriter. When we asked the camp Scribe to give us a list of the inmates, he was so frightened that we had to threaten him to keep him from reporting our request to Weinburg. But on the wall of each barrack a typewritten list of occupants was posted and we stole these lists, completing and correcting them where possible, and sent them on to the Jewish National Committee through our mail drop.

The new year opened dismally; in January 1944, the dismantled barracks of Majdanek were shipped to our camp. Hundreds of inscriptions were scrawled on the boards, greetings from beyond the grave, but though I pored over the messages for hours on end, I found no name I knew. From time to time also, small shipments of prisoners arrived. One day, walking in the square, a stranger stopped me with a hearty, "How are you?" He sounded like an old friend, but I told him I'd never seen him before in my life. "You don't recognize me?" the other said excitedly. "I knew you at once. I'm the policeman who came for your son in Mila Street, remember?"

His audacity stunned me. Pale and emaciated, he stood there, his goggling eyes humble. When I could finally speak, I said, "Why you dirty bastard, I'll knock your teeth out of your head. . . ."

"Oh, now, don't be in such a hurry to beat me up," he said pathetically, shriveling up. "I got my share of what was coming to me. I lost my wife and three children. . . . Strange as it seems you're the only man close to me, the only one I've met who knew me way back then. . . ."

My fist dropped. He stood there, head bowed, like a beaten cur. And that was the way I renewed my acquaintance with Hersz Nachtigal.

CHAPTER 6

PILGRIMAGE THROUGH DARKNESS

SEVERAL RADOM JEWS made up their minds to escape from the printing shop; during my stay there were three such attempts, but all ended tragically. The first was in November during the liquidation of the Szwarlikowska Street ghetto when Leon, a Radom Jew employed in the shop, vanished. Friends told us he was hiding in the house of a Gentile. His girlfriend, Klara, a very popular nurse in the camp hospital, unable to endure the thought that her beloved Leon had left her in a time of danger, thereupon took a fatal dose of luminal. Three days later his body, stripped of all his possessions, was found in a side street and the Gestapo ordered the ghetto police to bury it. Another attempt by a man named Cukierman ended the same way.

One of the workers in the shop was Weinburg's nephew, a twenty-year-old named Emil. He became close friends with a Bialystok boy, a recent arrival, and both decided to escape. As a rule, Fechner made an inspection tour of the printshop every morning, going from room to room, and whenever he saw people talking, he would say in Yiddish, "What is this, a *cheder*, or a synagogue?" He expected my Linotype to be flawlessly clean and I had to make it "shine" like a samovar. Fechner would rub any dark spot on the Linotype, then wipe his finger on my forehead or nose. If the finger left the slightest trace of oil or dirt, I had to clean the machine again.

After his tour, he would go to his office, eat an ample breakfast, take a nap, and make no further appearances for the rest of the day. One day, however, he suddenly summoned the foremen to his office and in a trembling voice told them his pistol had just been stolen. It took the foremen only a few minutes to discover that Emil and his friend had fled, and obviously had taken the pistol with them. Foaming with rage, Fechner threatened to report the escape to the Gestapo, and warned that we'd all be punished severely. But he calmed down when he realized that if the Gestapo found out, he might himself be sent to the front. We came to an agreement: we would buy Fechner a new pistol in return for his not reporting the escape. He demanded an exorbitant price for the pistol, but some of the wealthier Radom Jews put up the money.

The boys' escape impressed us, but in a few days we learned that, after wandering in the nearby woods, they had sought shelter in the former Szwarlikowska Street ghetto. From there they got in touch with Weinburg, asking him to help them get back into the camp, but Weinburg refused. A day or two after that the runaways were caught and killed by the Gestapo.

A while later a mass escape attempt was discovered by accident. A heavy truck about to enter the camp suddenly tilted over as the roadway beneath caved in. SS men, investigating, found that a long tunnel had been dug, which led from the privy in one barrack to a spot beyond the barbed wire. Only a few yards more and the tunnel would have extended to the far side of the highway, but those who had dug it apparently had lacked the planks necessary for shoring, or had made some other error. As a result they had weakened the road surface too much for it to bear the weight of the truck. A number of inmates had worked on the tunnel for weeks, digging secretly and disposing of the excavated earth by throwing it into the latrine ditch. Food had been prepared and stored, and others were ready to join them in the break. People in the barracks had noticed that food and some other objects were disappearing, but attached no importance to it. One of the participants turned out to be my "old friend," the former policeman, Nachtigal. A number of those involved were arrested, but though at Majdanek they would have been publicly executed, here the SS contented itself merely with painting red spots on their foreheads at a special roll call.

Meanwhile the printing shop production changed. In 1943, we had done mostly commercial work and official forms for Osti and other SS agencies. But early in 1944, we received a large order from Majdanek for tables showing rationing figures for incoming and outgoing shipments. All our efforts to work out from the tabular data what was going on at Majdanek—the actual number of prisoners, for example—ended in failure. More and more frequently now we got requests for SS command and police posters. Occasionally we even had to work on Sundays, and a group of us would be marched on the double to the shop to print German and Polish posters announcing hostages taken or executions imposed. Poles were being executed for illegal slaughter of cattle, smuggling, sabotage, possession of weapons or radio receivers, for belonging to the underground or partisan bands, and so on. But Moniek Rotstein was right: few Poles were willing to risk death to help Jews.

One day Rotstein came to my room and said, "Do you want to see an SS man crying? Go to the paper warehouse." There, I found an SS man on guard duty, tears rolling down his undistinguished face. He did not try to wipe them away or conceal them: he just stood there, weeping. I asked him what was the matter and he told me he was an ethnic German from Transylvania and his wife was Jewish. He had long been urged to renounce her, and the day before he had been given an ultimatum: either he gave her up or he would be interned in a camp himself. He had until nightfall to make up his mind. Through his tears, he asked, "How can I give her up? She is the mother of my three children." He wept all day; the next day he was gone.

Another revealing incident took place one day while we were marching back to our barracks. Two Wehrmacht soldiers saw our column and stopped to insult the SS escort. "You sons-of-bitches! *Judenhelden!* You got yourself safe jobs while we go to the front to get killed! You filthy SS swine!" The SS men replied in kind and the exchange of abuse continued, to our considerable satisfaction, until one SS man was about to open fire with his automatic, but just then an MP patrol on motorcycles roared up and separated the warring heroes.

The former Majdanek inmates stuck together, often reminiscing about our last day there, when we had dreamed of a loaf of bread. Now one former Majdanek inmate, Adzik, had a bar set up under a bunk in one of the barracks where he sold vodka he had smuggled in to "wash down our grief." A shining example to his customers, he was usually in high spirits by the time we marched back from work every night, and he would sing this edifying song:

> Let heaven's will be done,
> To it we must ourselves resign.
> And those who do not like it so,
> They can all kiss my ass. . . .

But more often our mood was gloomy. Sudden searches at the entrance gate would rob us of our food purchases. On other occasions, for one reason or another, there were no ghetto food buyers and we had to "eat our merchandise and capital," a couple of raw eggs, some raw bacon, and onions for supper. Worse, all our bunks were searched from time to time and our belongings stolen. Since that took place while we were at work, we never knew whether it was done by the Germans or our fellow inmates.

One day Mrs. Melcer excitedly told me that her child was coming with her Gentile Polish friend to visit. The two of them, the Melcers' child and the friend, would stroll back and forth in front of the shop while Julia and her husband watched from a second-story window. They actually carried out the plan, and the parents watched the child, holding their breaths, tears of sadness and joy mingling on their faces. We in the shop looked on fascinated. I would have given much to be able to see Wlodek, but could never have dared so sentimental and dangerous a luxury.

Early in the summer of 1944, Wladka paid us another visit. Graceful, pink-cheeked, one strap of her blouse torn and hanging rakishly down off her shoulder, she looked so attractive that the young SS man on guard duty near the barbed wire was fascinated. Ostensibly, she had come to sell us a big loaf of bread; actually, our Aryan identification papers were inside the bread. We took her inside the paper warehouse where we could talk without interruption. Although Wladka had delivered the precious documents, she stressed that the Jewish underground could not provide any places to live in Warsaw, so if we wanted to escape, we had to arrange that on our own. She had also brought us money, 50,000 zlotys, which seemed to us a colossal sum. And finally she told us that they were now in a position to supply us with weapons. The magic word *weapons* made my heart leap painfully, but it was nothing more than reflex; it was too late now. A year in the camps had destroyed our zeal of April 1943; the frustration of the ghetto holocaust had left us bitterly realistic. We were wretched, defeated men who no longer cared whether we died in an aura of heroic resistance, or went up in smoke through the crematoria chimneys. To fight for life or death, yes; to fight only for death—no more! Heroic demonstrations seemed pointless; objectively, in the conditions of Radom they would only be a provocation.

Wladka kept repeating, "Don't be afraid of Jews. Every Jew is your brother!" But we knew better. We knew that after looking death in the face day after day, some of our brothers had been transformed into our worst enemies: terror had made them into Judases.

Practical considerations also played a role. Where could we hide weapons? We spent our days in the printshop and our nights in the barracks, and even if we found hiding places, should we hide our weapons in the barracks or in the shop, or divide them equally between both places?

The woods were the only answer and, since Wladka's first visit, there had been some among us who strongly favored escaping to them. But the woods around Radom were infested with partisans of fascist and anti-Semitic hue, and being murdered by them held no special attraction. Surely there must be another kind of guerrilla, like those mentioned by the German posters we were printing. We had to get in touch with them. We asked Wladka if she could give us contacts with the Polish underground in the woods. If she could, many of us were eager to escape and join them. But on that score Wladka was very definite: the Jewish underground could do nothing about contacts with the Polish guerrillas. It could supply us with weapons; for the rest, we were on our own. Julia Melcer was the first to speak. "In that case, we must just wait. We can't make a decision now." Sullenly, we were all forced to agree with her. Wladka was surprised. "You really *don't* want weapons?"

We said good-by to Wladka in front of the warehouse. She was about to leave when a little Gentile boy—he could have been no more than twelve—suddenly grabbed her, yelling, "A Jewess, a Jewess!"

Wladka didn't lose her presence of mind. She took the boy firmly by the hand and pulled him forward angrily, "You're coming to the police station with me, you little brat! I'll teach you a lesson!" The boy began to struggle, finally wrenched free, and took to his heels.

We immediately took steps to distribute the money; we decided to give 500 zlotys to each person, enough to restore the strength of the under-nourished, and to buy some new clothes. In addition to the printers, we helped the workers in the ammunition factory with whom we had as yet few contacts, and some new arrivals from Budzyn who had come to the Szkolna Street camp in March. Among them were many people from Warsaw, and two old acquaintances, Dr. Rubin Tylbor and Dr. Ludwik Fein. The latter soon became a close friend of mine and through him we distributed the money to the newcomers. In giving it we were guided primarily by the recipient's need, but we excluded policemen, former policemen, foremen, and our own Kapo. Two of us made each presentation and each recipient was told of the origin of the gift and sworn to secrecy. We helped almost 100 people that way and kept a few thousand zlotys in reserve. I used my money to buy a pair of good leather shoes from one of the people in Radom. Those shoes were later to save my life, but at that time it was the moral and morale values that lifted our spirits even more than the money.

About a week after Wladka's visit, at the monthly meeting of the co-operative's administrative board, the roof fell in. Vorarbeiter Saltz showered me with abuse. It turned out that our shop officials had learned of Wladka's money and resented not sharing in it and also having been kept in the dark about it. Saltz, with characteristic delicacy, suggested that I had taken more than my share of the money—"You're so rich," he said, "that you don't give a shit about our whole miserable co-op!"—and he declared that I would be removed as head of the cooperative and would be kept under strict surveillance by the policemen and the Kapo. The other foremen did not take the floor, but silently nodded approval. I replied briefly that the decision to exclude foremen had not been mine alone, that I had not been alone in the distribution of the money, and that they would all do better to keep their mouths shut.

The situation was tense. Once our secret got out, we could never be sure whether one of our "singers" (informers) would hear about it and carry it to the Germans. Fortunately, the authorities knew of only two "culprits," Melcer and me. For the time being, Kotlar and Kassirer were not suspected. We believed that Saltz must have been told by someone who had received money from us, and we soon discovered who he was. It was clear, however, that he had talked out of sheer naivete, not from malice, and without the slightest notion of the complications his indiscretion would cause.

From that time on our Kapo never left me for a moment at work; he even accompanied me to the privy. As a result I could communicate with Kotlar and Kassirer only after working hours. The Kapo smelled a rat somewhere and told me bluntly, "I won't do anything against you, but if you're planning to escape, I'll stop you unless you take me along with you."

Although we had Aryan documents and a bit of money, we had as yet no way to escape and no concrete plans. Shortly after Wladka's visit the guards around the printshop were reinforced and two SS men, instead of one, now stood at the gate. Until now escaping had not been too difficult, but things began to move at an accelerated pace. Searches became more frequent, both at the gates and in the barracks. One day, on returning to the barracks, I found Dr. Ludwik Fein pale and trembling. While he was at work someone had taken his entire fortune of 10,000 zlotys, which he had hidden in his pillow. We gave him 500 zlotys from our reserve fund.

The newspapers reported the attempt to assassinate Hitler on July 20. A few days later rumors circulated that the Soviet Army had occupied Lublin, reached the Vistula, and would shortly take Radom. Suddenly we were not taken to work in the printing shop, and guards on the towers were on the alert day and night.

On July 26, 1944, the entire Majdanek garrison arrived in Radom, 600 strong, all with the faces of murderers. Next morning the population of the Radom camp, about 3,000 in all, was lined up in ranks of five and marched out of the camp. The evacuation, the first of many such, had begun; now we were made acquainted with still another kind of murder: the death march.

The swaying ranks crossed the railroad tracks and marched through the town of Radom. Crowds of Poles silently watched the procession from the sidewalk, only occasionally calling out to one of us, "Are you all right, Rivka? Hold out, it won't last much longer!" Or, "Hey, Abram, don't worry, our men aren't far now." Several prisoners, natives of Radom, dove into the crowd and mingled with the Poles, and some of them survived the war.

We came out on the highway and I blessed Wladka for my good shoes. The Melcers, Ludwik, and I kept close together. Our reserve funds, 3,000 zlotys, had been left in the printing shop under the stove and we had very little money, but under our striped uniforms we wore civilian clothes and carried our Aryan documents. We were determined to escape at the first opportunity. We headed westward over fields and through infrequent patches of wood. It was very hot and we were thirsty, but were forbidden to break ranks. When we passed a well, two men under guard were sent to get water. They could not bring back enough for all of us, but if anyone tried to go to the well on his own, the SS men escorting us shot without warning.

As it grew harder to walk, women with children, the old, and the sick lagged behind. Some sat on the edge of the road, indifferent to everything. Following the column were wagons with provisions and one which cheerfully picked up the sick and exhausted. From time to time it would turn off the road and we would hear gunshots in the distance. Then the wagon would return empty.

Before sunset we halted in a large field of stubble alongside the highway. We camped in the center of it surrounded by a circle of SS men. We were even forbidden to go to the latrine; those who had to relieve themselves did so on the spot. In the morning, when we set out again, the SS went over the field with bloodhounds to make sure no one had dug himself in. Nevertheless, we heard that several people had succeeded in doing so and thereby escaped.

Our next halt was beside a little river near the town of Opoczno. Ludwik nudged me: we could hide under the bridge. A few moments later a shot rang out behind; someone else had had the same idea. On another occasion we rested, leaning against a hedgerow and wondered if we could just duck into it, and crawl through to the other side. But there were SS men on that side waiting for people who had thought of that. Whatever occurred to us as a foolproof way of escape turned out a few moments later to be the end of those who put it to the test. Our escorts apparently knew all the tricks.

On the third day of the march we reached Tomaszów Mazowiecki. Here the women were separated from the men, and the scenes of parting were painful. We tried to discover our destination, but no one seemed to know. Finally, one of the SS men told us we were headed for the Lodz ghetto.

The three-day march had already taken 120 victims.

Women and children were confined in the city jail and the men in the Tomaszów factory for manufacturing artificial silk. There were hundreds of hiding places in the large factory hall, but the SS officer in charge warned us that all pipes and underground passages were being filled with poison gas. We tried to talk to the factory workers, but they were unfriendly. Though we had almost no property, the Radom people carried money, valuables, clothing, bed linen, and many other things. We made friends with one Radom mechanic who had a set of tools with him, and he agreed to stick with us.

A few days later freight cars were made up on a factory siding and we were loaded into them. Our car door was left open on one side and an SS man sat on the floor with his legs outside. The space immediately behind him was left empty and the rest of us were crammed on either side of the car. The train started late in the afternoon, and from the position of the sun we figured out that we were headed not toward Lodz but south toward Auschwitz. Gloom descended: the name Auschwitz alone had a depressing effect.

Ludwik and I were in the back part of the car, and there, he, the Radom mechanic, and I had a council of war. Behind us was the conductor's booth from which steps on both sides led down from the car. All we had to do was saw an opening in the back wall of the car, crawl through it into the booth, go down a few steps, and jump off the far side of the train. The SS men were posted on the other side and there was a good chance we wouldn't even be noticed. When night fell, the mechanic set to work, and we sang in chorus to drown out the noise of the saw.

Suddenly there was a commotion. One of the men near us complained in Yiddish that he was from Minsk, spoke no Polish, and had no place to escape to. We would run away, he said, while he would have to remain and be hanged because of us. He wasn't going to let us do that to him. A muscular boy from Staszow, lying next to him, grabbed him and began to choke him, but the Minsk man's son rushed to his father's aid. Such a hue and cry arose that an SS man fired a shot in our direction. We told father and son that we would give them bread if they went to the other side of the car and left us alone. They agreed. We went back to work, but the people on the other side of the car complained loudly that they had no room as it was and did not want "immigrants." The two men from Minsk returned, but by then day had begun to break and we had to give up our attempt.

The train slowed down and in the distance buildings and factory chimneys loomed. Finally we were in front of a large wooden gate surmounted by an arch which had on it in huge letters the inscription, *Arbeit*

Macht Frei. The train passed through the gate, switched back and forth for a while, then stopped next to a platform. We were in Auschwitz. On the platform were a few perfectly healthy-looking inmates in striped uniforms. Not for some moments did our escorts order, *"Aussteigen!"* but before I got out of the car, I looked at my beautiful Aryan identification papers, tore them into little pieces, and scattered them around the car.

We got off, formed ranks of five, and were kept standing like that for a long time. We tried to talk to the inmates on the platform, asking what it was like, and only got the answer: "Don't you know: Auschwitz!" Beyond the barbed wire, among some sallow-faced figures, children were running about. "Gypsies," a voice informed us. When the Auschwitz inmates saw that we also wore striped uniforms, they lost all interest in us; arrivals from another camp were not likely to have any valuables or food. A few ranks in front of me I saw Moniek Rotstein, his face the color of parchment, his eyes dead and indifferent. He could barely stand and had to be held up from both sides.

Three SS men came up the platform. There was the cry *"Achtung!"* and we snapped to attention. The SS officers stopped at the head of our column, then walked around it, studying us in silence. When they had completed the circuit, one of them called out, "Those who are sick, weak, or worn out from the trip, step forward! They'll be taken to the camp."

I saw Moniek Rotstein straighten up with what seemed like his last strength. The two Frenkel brothers, seventy and seventy-two years old stepped forward; they looked like twins, only one was a bit taller, and they held each other by the hand. Slowly they walked up to the SS officer and stopped. They knew what they were doing, but they had had it.

We stood like that for about another hour until the order came, *"Einsteigen!"* We climbed back into the cars and after another two hours the train slowly started to back up. *Arbeit Macht Frei* had disappeared in the distance. Auschwitz didn't want us: we were being taken elsewhere. "Well, we spent a couple of hours in Auschwitz just looking around, but we really didn't like it so we decided to find some more amusing place." That was the kind of thing we said to each other at the time. But later we learned that the women who had been separated from us were taken from Tomaszów to Auschwitz and left there.

Our train was moving west and soon we would be out of Poland, out of the cradle of our birth which had become our mass grave. We traveled for several nights and days. We passed through some Czech towns, halted on a siding in Vienna, and when we asked our SS escort where we were heading, he replied laconically, "Natzweiler, Alsace." Just why that made us happy, we couldn't say, but we had persuaded ourselves that our chances to survive were greater in Alsace. We were famished, but the worst part of the journey was the filth. There was no place to wash and we were lice-ridden. When at last we were disembarked somewhere in Germany and taken to a shower, we revived.

We were in a camp of civilian laborers from the East, the so-called *Ostarbeiter* who had volunteered or were forced to work in the Reich. Among them were many Poles and Jews with Aryan documents. In the shower room Ludwik met one of those Jews with Aryan papers, a woman, but they did not exchange a word; she merely stared at him fixedly. Before the war she had been a nurse and worked with him.

Moniek Rotstein never reached our destination; he died in the crowded cattle car somewhere between Auschwitz and Württemberg. He was buried in Württemberg and, though it would not have mattered to him, I was glad that he had not gone up in crematorium smoke, and that he was interred according to the rites of a religion for which he had ceased to care.

That same day trucks took us to our final destination, a camp near the town of Vaihingen, between Stuttgart and Karlsruhe, small, set on clayey soil, which autumn rains turned quickly into one huge puddle. The printers stayed together and were given two adjoining rooms in the same barrack, a much better one than we had had in Poland. A corridor ran down the middle of it and on either side were separate rooms with bunks. Each room held about 30 to 40 people, and had windows and doors. We took Ludwik along with us into one of our rooms. At the center of the camp stood the privies, elegant affairs with seats and a roof. On the far side of the highway stood little houses where the civilian laborers—Poles, Ukrainians, Russians, and Frenchmen—lived.

After a quick roll call the next day, various German civilian foremen appeared to recruit manpower. Faithful to my principle never to volunteer for anything, I was arbitrarily assigned to a Kommando. We were arrayed on a slope and ordered to dig ditches. The German foreman had never before worked with slave labor and was amazed at our low output. At first he urged us on good-naturedly, repeating, *"Bewegung! Bewegung!"* but later he fell into a rage and beat us.

When we were marched out to work for the first time, the few people on the streets avoided us. Before our arrival, the citizens of Vaihingen had been informed that a shipment of criminals was on the way and had been warned to be careful.

An underground explosives factory was being built for I. G. Farben-industrie at Vaihingen, in an abandoned quarry. What had formerly been a steep outcropping of rock had been hollowed out in the years of quarrying and the gigantic cavity was to house a factory that would thus be naturally protected from Allied air raids. Work went on at several levels. At the top level were railroad sidings, supplies of cement, piles of boards and other building materials, tool sheds, and stocks of supplies. At the very bottom of the quarry, rock was being drilled and concrete foundations laid. There was a tunnel down to the lower level, but to get back up again you had to climb a broad flight of steps several stories high. There were intermediate levels along the way with batteries of small locomotives, flat-cars, and cranes for removing debris and hoisting steel beams.

I worked at all levels of the quarry and at all kinds of jobs, I carried bags of cement, hastened by the riding crops of SS men; I steered the little locomotives and flatcars; I split rocks with a pneumatic drill. And I worked day and night shifts. I was now an old-timer, resistant to pain and cold; inured to beating, opprobrium, and heavy labor; insensitive to pain and unhappiness. All I retained was the newspaperman's greedy curiosity, the desire to see and find out everything, to engrave in my memory this Dantesque world from which humane emotions had been eliminated.

As in Radom there was a group—camp attendants, craftsmen, hospital staff—who never left the camp. They had brought along possessions which they gradually exchanged for food. Although the food at Vaihingen was not bad, there was not enough of it and those who wanted to survive had to find additional nourishment. I had a few suppliers who entrusted me with things they wanted to sell, and that way I made some money in "commissions." One Russian woman asked me to get her a bed sheet for which she'd give me a pound and a half of bread and ten apples—items which were currency at this camp. That evening I bought a bed sheet for a pound of bread and seven apples. Next day when I brought the sheet to the Russian woman, she was delighted, and of her own accord added a pound of bread to the bargain. There was a great demand for leather brief-cases. Poles were particularly eager to own them and paid high prices. All the briefcases in that camp must at one time or another have passed through my hands. Once I was badly cheated. I took a pair of trousers belonging to an inmate, sold it to a German foreman for several loaves of bread, to be paid one each day. The foreman paid the first loaf and then I couldn't find him. I did not know his name, only where he worked, but whether he was transferred, or fired, I never learned. However, I had a very unpleasant scene with the tailor who had given me the trousers and who would not believe me when I told him the foreman had vanished. On another occasion, while I was working at clearing railroad tracks, I cashed in twenty apples, of which five were my profit. I asked the Kapo to keep them for me and gave him one apple for his trouble. He put the bag of apples on the step of a railway car. After a while one of my fellow inmates told me the Kapo was going to the bag too often and I was barely able to rescue my capital in time: but he had eaten up all my profit.

While there was little beating in the camp itself, a notorious SS man, Moeller, was much in evidence at the quarry, especially on the upper level. He liked to boast that he was the "bonebreaker of Sachsenhausen" and he beat inmates unmercifully. One day a German foreman scolded me for having stayed at the latrine too long and I looked sullenly back at him. "How dare you look at me like that, you insolent Jewish pig!" he yelled. Before I had time to assure him of my great respect for him, Moeller had sneaked up on me, hit me on the head and thrown me face down on the tracks. I spit out my broken teeth, and stood at attention, but Moeller had already gone. The foreman had not expected me to be punished so severely and began to apologize and explain that after all there was work to be done.

One day, while I was assigned to the task of taking nails out of a pile of boards, I found a Warsaw man named Edek working beside me, and it turned out to be one of the pleasantest days I had in the camp. Before the war, Edek had worked in the Warsaw office of Warner Brothers and he knew all the newspapermen, so we found that we had many acquaintances in common. He was a delightful conversationalist and we talked of Polish and Russian poetry, recited poems, and dreamed of publishing in the postwar world a magazine like *Life* or the *Saturday Evening Post*.

There were so many doctors among the inmates that Ludwik did not get a job in the camp hospital; instead he was put into a first-aid tent at the upper level of the quarry. Soon Germans and Ostarbeiters were coming to him with their ailments, although as a Jew he was forbidden to treat them. Each of his "patients" brought him something in payment and soon he had plenty of food and, more important, tobacco. At night, after we had eaten, Ludwik would solemnly take a pinch of tobacco and a paper from his pocket and carefully roll a cigarette. Someone would quickly give him a light and Ludwik would make a ritual of smoking with eight pairs of eyes watching his every move. Slowly, he would take three or four deep puffs and then hand the cigarette to the man beside him for a couple of puffs, then on to the next man—a ritual observed in complete silence.

One day while I was digging in the quarry alone, a German civilian walked by, stopped and stood about a hundred yards away from me. Suddenly, in the unnatural silence, he began to whistle the first bars of the *Internationale*. "Arise ye prisoners of starvation, arise ye wretched of the earth. . . ." So struck was I by this song of international solidarity in that pit of hatred that when he stopped, I whistled the second verse. When I stopped, he picked up the third verse, and so our whistled dialogue continued until the anthem was finished. On his way out, when he passed by me, he smiled and whispered, "Keep your chin up. We're not all like them. We'll help you." He said something else, but it was in Swabian dialect and I couldn't understand him. I never saw him again.

I liked to work with the drill though it shook me up, but I really suffered when one day a fragment of rock flew up and smashed my glasses. Without them I might easily stumble over the edge into the quarry abyss. Also, with Moeller roaming the project like a vulture, I ran the risk of not being able to see him in time, thus exposing myself to a beating. I rushed to the office to report the mishap, and was promised that the SS man at the hospital would be able to get me a new lens in town. But when several days had passed and nothing happened, I went from barracks to barracks in despair, offering bread for a lens. One irascible inmate finally offered to fix me up and from under his pillow took a bunch of lenses varying in size and thickness. After half an hour, I found a suitable though badly scratched and dirtied lens, but it was no time to be fastidious. The price was exorbitant, two loaves of bread to be paid in installments, and before concluding the deal my creditor went back to my barrack with me to check up on my credit standing. Only *after* he was satisfied that I was a good risk did he let me have the lens.

Our morale was kept up by the increasingly frequent Allied air raids. Sudden drawn-out siren howling would interrupt our work day and night, music to our ears. We took shelter in the tunnel between the lower level of the quarry and the road and sometimes had several hours of rest there before the all clear sounded.

Apart from that we had one consuming interest: food. When the day shift passed the night shift, the question always was, "What's for supper?" The night men would give the details, sometimes graphically raising their elbows and saying, "Such soup! The spoon stands up!"

Apples are abundant in Württemberg and the road we took to the quarry was lined with apple trees, in that season bent under the weight of the ripe fruit. Every morning hundreds of apples lay on the ground and it drove us wild to look at them. Sometimes it was so irresistible a temptation that we broke ranks (and discipline) and ran to pick up the tempting juicy fruit, or jumped up to snatch it from the branches, unmindful of the rain of blows from the SS escort.

One day in October a fellow prisoner brought back from town a newspaper which knocked my precarious mental balance out of kilter. The copy of the *Vaihinger Zeitung* passed from hand to hand until it finally reached our group. On its front page was an article on the Warsaw uprising, the first news we had had of it. The article was full of abuse of the Poles and read: "... the wind blows through the deserted streets of Warsaw, and the ruins of the former capital of this unreasonable, ungrateful nation. ... Where Warsaw once stood today an empty field of rubble stretches, and only the savage howling of the autumn gale offers up prayer for the 200,000 people heedlessly sacrificed by the insane megalomania of its criminal leadership. ..."

Until then I had been able to keep my most nightmarish fears at bay. I had repeated to myself, mechanically, that I had a child in Warsaw and that I must survive in order to find him after the war. I had not permitted myself to doubt, for I knew that once the dam of purpose was broken, I was lost; but now under the impact of that newspaper report, all my defenses broke. Fate was robbing me of the last straw to which I could cling; the one hope that linked me to life was dissolving. All I could see was the windswept Warsaw streets and somewhere under the rubble my son, deserted by his parents, alone in the hour of terror before death.

Once again I felt I was dying, and darkness fell over my mind. My comrades made fun of me, arguing that there were a million inhabitants in Warsaw and even according to the German statistics "only" 200,000, or a fifth, had perished. That gave me an 8 to 10 chance, they said. "May we be that lucky! Why should your son have to be one of those killed?" Indeed, why should my boy be among the minority? One part of me grieved for Wlodek; the other behaved as if nothing had happened.

Fall brought cold winds, early evenings, and days of rain. The clayey ground turned into an almost impassable sea of mud. The rocky ground of the quarry finally got the best of my leather shoes and I caught cold in the bladder again. As at Majdanek I had to run to the latrines several times during the night, about a hundred yards down the corridor and a hundred back each time, and the nights were cold and damp. Many of the other inmates suffered the same complaint and some were so weak that they urinated before reaching the latrine. Some peed in their food bowls, which they then carefully washed each morning before eating from them, but most simply let go on the floor. This so enraged the SS man who was our Block-führer that he swore if he caught anyone doing that, he'd cut his balls off. Once he woke up the entire night shift of our barracks and ordered every one of them to get down and lick up the urine on the floor of the corridor.

Coming back from work one day I ran into one of our printers, who was working as foreman of a night shift at the concrete mixer, which earned him an extra bowl of soup. As he saw me dragging my feet wearily over the ground in my torn shoes, he shook his head and said, "You're in bad shape, Berg." When we were told that work on the construction project would soon be cut down, and that some of us would be sent elsewhere, I was glad. Since I was a diligent worker, I found myself one of the first listed by the foreman for transfer. Ludwik shared my feelings about the transfer, but later told me he had changed his mind and advised me to try to remain in Vaihingen.

Next day I fixed it up with the Kapo and for a portion of bread he agreed to remove my name from the list of those to go, and put it back on the list of those who were to stay. I breathed a sigh of relief, but when I got back to camp after work that day, the situation had again changed. Ludwik had learned that a certain Dzialoszynski of Budzyn was to be Lagerälteste of the shipment and he would probably give soft jobs to all his Budzyn cronies. This would make Ludwik head of the hospital. I ran back to the office, but it was too late: the list had been turned over to the Germans and there was no room for me. As I stood there in the corridor, dejected, a young boy approached. He was weeping. His family had been murdered, he told me, and he had only one brother left. Now he was being transferred and his brother was remaining in Vaihingen. I had a brainstorm: "Let's swap places," I said.

I could barely keep the boy from kissing my hands. We summoned my creditor and in the presence of witnesses my future "heir" undertook to pay the bread installments I still owed for my eyeglass lens. His brother fixed it up with our Lagerälteste so that when he called out the numbers of those to be transferred I would step forward and he would simply not notice it: the Germans did not know us by name anyway. And so it was done. When the Lagerälteste called out, "Number 1398, Donat," the name by which I was henceforth to be known, I took my place in the column to be shipped out. Soon we were marched to the freight cars.

Later we learned that two weeks after we left, all work on the Vaihingen construction project ceased and the remaining workers were sent to extract mineral oil at Kochendorf. Among those sent was the boy whose place I had taken and his brother. All of them died in the killing labor of that impassable swamp, except one man: the Kapo. Goldman, our former printing foreman, was also there and when he reported to his SS man that he had lost his shoes in the mud and asked what to do about it, the SS man said, "Go hang yourself!" Goldman took off his belt and obediently hanged himself. Officially, I died there, too. Had it not been for that chance, last-minute encounter, I would have shared their fate. *Hic obiit Berg, Donat natus est;* here Berg died and Donat was born.

Our train rattled on for several hours and late at night stopped in front of a long barracks. A man in a *Luftwaffe* uniform opened the car door and looked as surprised as we were. When we asked what kind of work was to be done there, he shrugged and said that there was no work there. The next morning we discovered that there were 560 of us and that we were at Hessenthal-Schwäbisch Hall, near Stuttgart; like Vaihingen, it was a branch of the Natzweiler concentration camp system. It was a tiny camp, five barracks all told, and situated on a hill between the highway and the railroad tracks. The Lagerführer was one August Walling, a former airman, now an SS sergeant. The Lagerälteste was Dzialoszynski, who gave the easy jobs to his former Budzyn comrades. Ludwik and Dr. Emanuel Gross took over the infirmary, the so-called *Revier,* and a few days later Ludwik got me appointed as a medic. Gross was one of those who had received 500 zlotys from Wladka's cache in Radom and he, too, supported my candidacy.

The infirmary staff consisted of two doctors and three medics, the other two medics being Edek and my "old friend," the Warsaw policeman Nachtigal. Later, the staff was augmented by two more men: Ilya Karlovich Dvorkin, a native of Omsk, Siberia, who served as orderly; and Toporek, a young native of Lodz, who had had some first-aid training. Though Ludwik was senior to Emanuel, both in age and medical experience, Walling took a liking to Emanuel and made him head of the infirmary. Ludwik felt slighted, which led to sharp and sometimes amusing differences between the two doctors.

The infirmary consisted of four rooms, two of them wards in which patients lay in triple-decker bunks, a third which served as a consulting room, and the fourth which was our bedroom. Two bunks, one double- and one triple-decker, were set up there for the two doctors and three medics, and Dvorkin and Toporek slept in the barracks with the other inmates.

It took no more than a few days for Emanuel to obtain from the Lagerführer two concessions, which were masterpieces of camp diplomacy. First, patients were granted additional rations, including sugar and cereals; second, the infirmary staff was also given these added rations. This meant a great deal, for it freed us from the task of organizing food. Every night, therefore, I drew up a list of patients to be confirmed by the Lagerführer, and taken to the kitchen.

A fairly large Kommando was assigned to local quarries, and smaller work parties to special jobs. By special request one boy was allocated to the local butcher, worked in civilian clothes, and was treated like a member of the butcher's family. After the war he married the butcher's daughter and stayed on there.

Only the kitchen help, office clerks, infirmary personnel, tailors, and shoemakers stayed in the camp. The rest of our shipment was assigned to do heavy work at the big military airfield at Hessenthal, a huge aerodrome with many hangars, repair shops, an ammunition depot, and a large hospital, as well as several buildings where military personnel and their families lived. The infirmary sent me to the airfield where I was to serve as *Feldsanitäter* (field medic). On my sleeve I wore a white armband with a red cross, and I was later able to organize a genuine mess kit and a large knapsack on which I painted a red cross.

Every day, after a quick roll call, we were marched from camp to the airfield, a distance of three and a half miles. Our route took us through the main street of Hessenthal, and the column of prisoners in military formation, followed by a medic, greatly impressed the Germans, but there were also civilian faces which peered out at us from behind their curtains with horror and with sympathy.

My office at the airfield was in the ammunition depot. There, for safety's sake, the furnace had been set into a specially built recess which I used as an office. It was warm and dry, and the fact that the whole building might blow up at any time, and that the recess had no door, did not disturb my peace of mind. On the shelves next to the firewood I laid out the first-aid materials and medicaments I had brought along in my bag and waited for patients. And there were always patients. Occasionally, a genuine accident occurred on the airfield or in a workshop. One of our printers fell from a scaffolding and suffered such severe injuries that he was operated on immediately at the airfield hospital. Another printer broke his leg and was put into the local military hospital for several weeks alongside wounded German soldiers and Canadian prisoners of war. When I visited him, he gave me a truly royal gift, a genuine Old Gold cigarette given him by one of the Canadians. But most of the cases were minor cuts, scratches, and the usual camp disorders: dysentery and malingering. In bad weather my office was besieged by drenched, shivering *Häftlings* who simply wanted to come inside long enough to get warm and dry. They were a danger because if the Germans discovered that my place was being used to shirk work, it would have been liquidated on the spot. In the end, we reached an agreement—five minutes to dry and warm; and though some prisoners made scenes, the rest kept to the agreement.

I was the only prisoner who had freedom of movement at the airfield, though I always had to have a plausible story prepared if challenged. I soon learned that the airfield offered great organizational opportunities. Fall came late that year and was relatively mild, so there was a bumper crop of apples. To our delight there were also many air raids and, when the alarms sounded, workers were hastily led off the roads into the fields where there were piles of ripe apples on the ground and many heavily laden fruit trees. Often I went back to camp with my knapsack full of such excellent vitamins, but man cannot live by apples alone, and there were other opportunities.

After a few days we were put under the supervision of airborne troops headed by *Oberfähnrich* (Ensign) Fischer. If it is possible to use the term "friendship" to describe a relationship between a Warsaw Jewish ex-journalist and a German airborne trooper in 1944, we became friends. But probably the word sympathy is more accurate. Oberfähnrich Fischer developed a sympathy for me. We were the same age, born in 1905, and that probably helped. A native of Constance, where he had worked as an architect, he insisted, when he learned I had completed my studies in chemistry, on addressing me as Herr Doktor.

He seemed to know about the fate of the Jews, but when I told him some of the details, he was deeply shaken. Over and over he repeated, *"Mord, nein, das haben wir sicher nicht gewollt."* (Murder, we surely didn't want that.) When I questioned him as to how it had all come about, he said that he wasn't and never had been a Nazi, and certainly did not approve the Nazi extermination solution for the "Jewish problem." "But the world should understand what Hitler meant to us," he explained. "In nineteen thirty-three I was twenty-eight years old and had an architect's diploma, but because of the Depression I had never had a job or earned a penny. Do you know what it's like for a young man to live without hope, without a chance to make a living? Hitler gave us work, and more, he gave us hope. No price seemed too high to pay for that. No one turns down hope. So we followed him. . . ." Even as late as November 1944, Fischer still believed that the Third Reich would be victorious; he had confidence in "our new weapons."

Every day at exactly 10 A.M., Fischer appeared in my office to bring me his bread ration, and that went on for months. Each time his airborne troopers received their soup, a thick nourishing broth, he summoned me in a loud voice, *"Sanitäter!"* and I was given a mess tin full of that body-building fluid.

During that same period I got to know our Kapo, Bronek, one of the most original characters I have ever met. A peculiar combination of Mongol, with high cheekbones and narrow slanted eyes, and the Hassidic face, he was also a peculiar mixture of asceticism and sensuality. Most interesting was his outlook on life. Before the war he had been a guard in a well-known insane asylum at Zofiowka where he had been convinced that the whole world was mad and that by virtue of his professional experience he had acquired the key to madmen's souls—what he called the "right approach." "There are two types of madmen," he philosophized, "the quiet ones and the raving ones. The quiet ones bother nobody, but the others are dangerous. There are only two ways of dealing with them, a punch in the nose or a strait-jacket. Our tragedy is that the Nazis were the violent type and we had no means of punching them or strait-jacketing them. The worst thing, of course, is to give a raving lunatic a submachine gun. That's why we can't do anything about them."

Bronek had great respect for the camp privileged, whom he called "the tribe of Levites," and the utmost contempt for the rest of the inmates, whom he called "hangers-on." When he learned that I enjoyed Fischer's sympathy, Bronek's respect for me grew, all the more so because he couldn't understand our rapport, and my own conduct was a complete contradiction of all his principles. For instance, I never approached Fischer without first having been summoned, least of all when there was soup distribution. And then, of course, Bronek always managed to be at my side so that he, too, got a portion. Nor could he understand why I often gave my soup to the "hangers-on," who had nothing to give me in return. Bronek had never done anything in his life disinterestedly: he never gave something for nothing, but he never beat anyone for nothing either. He had no compassion for those he struck, but he was not wantonly cruel. When he cursed inmates, he never showered them with obscenities as other Kapos did; instead, his swearing had a "guiding idea": for example, "May you be given a big pot of steaming soup so thick that the spoon is dented by the pieces of meat in it, and may the Lagerführer stand next to you and beg you, 'Eat your fill, it's all yours,' and may you inhale the marvelous aroma and lie there paralyzed in every limb so you can't touch the soup!" Or, "May you have dysentery and bleeding hemorrhoids so that you have to run to the latrine all day long, and there, have to wipe yourself with sandpaper."

He explained his outlook in these terms. "What is the difference between a prostitute and a whore?" he would ask. "To be a prostitute is a profession, but to be a whore is a trait of character. A prostitute can be honest, and a respectable woman a whore by nature. The same goes for Kapos. I am a prostitute Kapo, some are whorish Kapos. If all of us are to die, I want to suffer as little as possible; if only one of us is to survive, I want to be that one. No matter what the cost.

"At first I tried to be fair to the hangers-on, but little by little I got to hate them. If you abuse someone long enough, you begin to hate him. That's the scoundrel's self-defense. So he convinces himself of his superiority, and begins to hate and despise those he wrongs."

Only once did I see Bronek cry, when he told me how he lost his wife and child. He had been a policeman in the ghetto and would rescue people from the Umschlag when they paid him enough. One day one of his colleagues who had not filled his quota took Bronek's wife and child to the Umschlag. Bronek's first wife had been taken at Otwock, and this was her sister, so the policeman took her on the pretext that the marriage was not legal. When Bronek raced to the Umschlag, the cattle car was just being shut and bolted and his wife managed to wave to him from a distance. "And she smiled, you hear, she smiled at me! Because I was greedy for money and wasted my life I couldn't even protect the only two people I really loved. . . ."

One day Fischer came to the airfield with a happy expression on his face and shared great news with me. "Well, it's the end now. A great offensive. The front is broken. . . ." It took me several minutes before I realized that he meant a German offensive and that at last the "secret weapon" would defeat the Allies. My heart sank. Fischer looked so triumphant, so self-confident that something extraordinary must have happened. It was the Battle of the Bulge. But I never did get to see how he felt a little while later, for shortly thereafter he was promoted to lieutenant and transferred to Prague.

Gradually I built up regular contacts with the airfield hospital. I visited it daily on one pretext or another, and rarely came away empty-handed. I was not too tormented by hunger, but I was always psychically hungry;

all my thoughts revolved around food. Though the hospital staff was not wallowing in luxury, what they had seemed like wealth to me. The personnel treated us kindly and I remember particularly two women, one an elderly attendant everyone called Mutti and a tall, handsome nurse named Elizabeth. On my expeditions to the hospital I was usually accompanied by fourteen-year-old Beryl, limping and cross-eyed, who had by a miracle survived all the selections. A very smart boy, he had instinctively guessed that associating with me would profit him, and he became my "adjutant." He always brought tears to Mutti's eyes by telling her fantastic stories about his hardships, so she would say, fondly stroking his shaven head, *"Ach, du armes Wesen!"* (You poor thing!) Beryl was himself moved to tears by his fate and often carried away by his own play-acting. Usually he pretended to be twelve, and on one occasion went so far as to claim he was nine, but when Mutti looked astonished, he shrewdly corrected himself to say that he was nine when he lost his parents. . . .

The hospital supplied considerable additions to our daily diet, but even that was not enough for Beryl. He was perpetually starved. Around the airfield were villages with red-roofed houses and every one of those roofs evoked a mirage of a table set with pots of steaming boiled potatoes. Beryl was one of a pack of dauntless desperadoes who daily sneaked off the air base to raid those tempting red-roofed houses. Though such a crime was punishable by death, the houses drew the boys like a magnet, stronger than reason. Once one boy was caught and Walling drew his own pistol and shot him, at the same time warning the Lagerälteste that he would be answerable if there were repetitions of such incidents. Beryl and some of his comrades were given cruel hidings, but they had no sooner recovered than they went off to the farmhouses once more. For a time they were confined to camp, but it started all over again, until finally, on Bronek's suggestion, the *Oberkapo* made a deal with them. Each could have a double soup ration if he promised not to make any more excursions. The boys agreed, of course, but still sneaked out to be fed by the farmers, and this went on to the very end. Interestingly, the German farmers never refused to feed the boys; they gave them soup and potatoes, but seldom bread. I suspected Bronek of conniving with the boys to protect them on their expeditions for a share in the loot.

Eventually our technique of organization expanded. More and more often soldiers and civilian foremen brought us their shoes to repair and I took the shoes back to camp where our cobblers repaired them in their workshops against payment in kind. I got a percentage of this, also in kind, and thus after some time I became the proud owner of a pair of solid, leather shoes. From time to time Germans who came to me with minor injuries gave me a cigarette or some bread for treating them. On one occasion a sergeant with long-standing syphilis asked me to supply him with the appropriate medicines, but despite all my efforts to accommodate him—he was ready to pay the fantastic sum of 24 pounds of bread!— I was unable to get the proper drugs.

Gentile workers of several nationalities were also employed at the airfield. One large group was composed of Russian Ostarbeiter who had been deported to the Reich by entire villages, and who now lived with their wives and children in the neighboring village. One of them came to see me many times and told me about their life. Though the Russians were deportees, they lived with their families, were free to visit their friends and go to other villages on Sundays, and we considered them quite privileged. With the Italian prisoners of war I spoke in broken French and sign language. Our relations were friendly and everyone understood me when I said, *"Benito kaputo."* There were also many Polish laborers on the nearby farms and they never lacked food. We got on well with all of them since we were at the very bottom of the hierarchy of oppressed. Each group showed us sympathy, partly because it was a great solace to men who feel wronged to know that there are others even more wronged, more wretched, even more to be pitied.

Every nationality had its characteristic way of helping. The Germans were unsentimental and businesslike: *"Ein bisschen Suppe?"* the hospital cook would say, and a moment later we had two voluminous canteens filled to the brim with soup. The Italians were not too prosperous themselves, and their soup not much better than ours; still, whenever they managed to save part of their ration, they called us with as much enthusiasm and fanfare as if they were announcing the war's end. And they also always encouraged us, replying to our *"Benito kaputo"* with *"Hitler kaput!"* Nor were the Russians well off, but they put all their hearts into the gift of soup. With a big smile they'd ask, *"Supu, brat, zhelayesh?"* (How about some soup, brother?), and our hearts as well as our stomachs were warmed.

Gifts sometimes came from unexpected quarters. One morning a civilian foreman I had never seen before rode up on a bicycle, looked cautiously around, then handed me three pounds of dry bread crusts from his dispatch case, and rode away. The camp inmates who visited me that day were pleasantly surprised to be given some crusts of bread, and the continual presence in my mouth of warm chewed bread made me feel blissful. On another occasion the ground crews at the ammunition depot where I had my office gave me a large kettle of soup because it was too sugary for their taste. It was a godsend because that day their "soup" was oatmeal sweetened with sugar. I thought it was marvelous, but because I couldn't eat all of it, I tried to find some especially hungry work party to give it to.

After the Kommandos returned from work, the sick were received in the infirmary, which filled the two hours before supper. Emanuel treated the countless abscesses, scrofulas, and carbuncles from which the inmates suffered because of filth and malnutrition. Edek, tall and handsome, impressive in his white gown, helped him and soon we jokingly called him *Herr Dozent*. Ludwik handled the internal complaints and I assisted him. I kept the records, noted the diagnosis, the method of treatment, and the disposition of a case. The doctors could exempt a patient from work or admit him to the infirmary—the dream of every inmate. Unlike the large death camps, we had no selections here, so that prisoners were not afraid that going to the hospital would lead to the gas chamber. They dreamed of the hospital as a place to rest, gather their strength, keep warm and clean, and be fed. Toporek, Dvorkin, and Nachtigal did the infirmary's chores and later I learned that Nachtigal also performed a confidential task which grew in importance as the mortality rate among inmates increased: he pulled out the corpses' gold teeth. He did this late at night and so discreetly that I caught him at it only once and then purely by accident.

Our evenings were quiet, undisturbed by violence. The horror of Majdanek receded slowly into the past and though we were certain that we would never see the end of the war because the Germans would liquidate us before then, we did not at that moment feel threatened. And so we had plenty of time for grief and tears, for mourning, and reflecting on our tragedy. Because we were old-timers now we did not indulge in sentimentality or outbursts of emotion: we discussed things dryly and matter-of-factly; but at night, alone in the dark, we wept, and in the morning arose with tears still undried, fragments of our nightmares still clinging to us. If outwardly we seemed impatient and irascible, inwardly we were gnawed by sorrow and yearning. We were ashamed to display our feelings in front of one another and it was easier to make a sacrifice or do some favor for someone than to speak kindly to him. We joked and told stories, but our jokes were pitiless and vulgar, our laughter brutal and obscene. Occasionally we recited poetry and told stories: Chwat, a law student, was a walking anthology of Polish poetry from Mickiewicz to Tuwim; and Edek told us endless tales of actors and film stars, some true, others made up for the occasion. Some of the inmates also sang Jewish folksongs and sentimental Russian ballads, and there was one song they repeated often, about how someday there would be the same sky for all men, for all races.

The sky closed down, low and milky, and flogged by winter gales, the leafless trees were bent and forlorn, scratching bare branches against the inhospitable air. It was the first day of a new year, 1945, and the year began in an unusual way. The first Saturday snow fell very heavily and didn't stop for twenty-four hours. We found ourselves blanketed by three feet of snow, more than even the oldest natives had ever seen. On Sunday, camp inmates, civilians, and soldiers stationed nearby were mobilized to clear the airfield, but despite all our strenuous efforts, the field was not operational for several days. That Sunday a soldier I treated for a minor cut rewarded me with six cigarettes and we had a real smokers' banquet. A few days later the snow thawed and we were back in a mild Württemberg winter, but now other things began to take place. Our camp was transferred to the authority of the Todt organization and our SS escort was augmented by a *Sonderkommando* composed of Dutch, Croatian, and Byelorussian Askaris. Whether due to weather, transportation breakdowns or the new authority, our food deteriorated a great deal. Bean soups once thick enough to make the spoon stand were now things of the past. Though conditions were far better than in the death camps, more and more men were getting sick. Whereas the camp had been sending 500 men of its full complement of 560 to work daily, now no more than 300 could be mobilized, the remainder having been exempted by our doctors. The airfield administration threatened to cancel their contract with the SS, and Walling, who was living in clover with his mistress, was abruptly faced with the prospect of being sent to the front. Foaming with rage, he threatened the doctors with harsh penalties and finally fixed a maximum of permissible daily exemptions for sickness. We could treat just so many inmates as patients, not one more.

Now every morning there were dramatic scenes when work parties were made up. Kapos drove the men into ranks with kicks and blows, and every night the infirmary was besieged by sick inmates. The doctors despaired: we had almost run out of medicines; the number of hospital beds was small; and the number of exemptions for sickness had been reduced by order of the Lagerführer. In nine out of ten cases all the men needed was a few days of rest and more and better food, for they had reached the limits of their strength and endurance, but those were precisely the things the infirmary could not provide. To make matters worse the camp was swept by a plague of dysentery caused by the extreme exhaustion. The wasted bodies were simply unable to assimilate their food; it passed through them as through a sieve, yielding no nourishment, so that in addition they were still wracked by pangs of hunger. Those with dysentery melted down like candles, relieving themselves in their clothes, and swiftly turned into stinking repulsive skeletons who died in their own excrement. We had no charcoal; all we could do was to char bread.

The only medicine we had in anything like adequate supply was aspirin, and we had it in three forms, acetylsalicylic acid, Bayer's tablets, and a Dutch brand. Ludwik, to keep up patient morale, devised the ruse of giving them aspirin under different names. Men began to die like flies, as if their strength had altogether given out. Great inventiveness was required to vary the "cause of death," and I wrote such things as "general weakness," "pneumonia," "acute heart trouble," "anemia," anything except the true cause: starvation. The dead were buried on the slope of a hill just outside town, and Schwäbisch Hall, where there never had been a Jewish cemetery, now received a permanent monument from the Polish Jews. When we left the camp two months later, a quarter of our original number lay in the 140 graves there.

The *Leichenkommando,* which we called the "funeral society," was headed by a pious old Jew named Grossman, the father of one of our Kapos. During the day bodies were carried to a shed behind the barracks and every night Grossman and a helper loaded them into a cart and took them to the cemetery. Sometimes, when the final agony lasted for several hours, Grossman grew impatient and cursed the dying man. One Friday night, when I got back from the airfield, I found him kicking a man who was not swift enough in giving up the ghost. "You scoundrel, you piece of carrion," Grossman yelled, "don't you see it's getting dark and that soon it will be Sabbath? What are you waiting for?" Finally the dying man gave up, and was quickly loaded into the cart and the funeral procession moved briskly out the gate toward the cemetery.

After years of witnessing death en masse, we were once again faced with the mystery and tragedy of individual death. People slipped away, each in his own fashion, without violence, torn away from life slowly, reluctantly. Some tormented bodies resisted annihilation for hours, struggling hopelessly against their invincible adversary. Life is loud, but death silent. When the groans, rales, coughs, yawns, hiccups ceased, we knew the end had come. After Walling shot the boy who sneaked out to get a meal from a farmer, he sat for hours at the boy's bedside, observing the young organism's struggle to survive. When the boy eventually recovered, Walling brought him apples to eat. Walling also sat watching for long periods of time the death agonies of Majewski, a Pole who had been a professor of geography in Cracow. Majewski struggled courageously, but his age betrayed him, and he was buried in the Schwäbisch Hall cemetery, a better fate, after all, than the crematorium chimney.

From time to time we heard news of how the war was going, and occasionally even got our hands on a newspaper. In that way I learned that Warsaw had been liberated, which would mean that my son, if he was still alive, was free. The Western front moved closer to us daily and, though we were convinced the Nazis would do away with us at the last moment, we entertained a secret hope that when the time came they might be too busy to do so. Every Jewish life saved, every inmate wrested from the jaws of death was now a victory in our own little war against Hitler, and took on an enormous importance: we fought for the life of every patient with a stubbornness which only a short time before would have struck us as quixotic. We did so to such a degree that one of our male nurses who always scolded patients—"What the hell are you trying to prove, that we'll survive the war? Like hell you will!"—now kept his mouth shut.

Spring came early and was unusually warm that year. Sirens sounded more and more often, the bomb-heavy planes came in at much lower altitudes, and the violent explosions in the distance heartened us. Our airfield's turn came one Sunday in March when suddenly all the camp sirens began to wail together. Flight after flight, squadron after squadron of the big bombers moved across the sky in combat formations, majestic and formidable. Dull explosions shook the air and columns of fire and smoke rose from the direction of the airfield. We watched entranced at the spectacle of destruction at last being visited on the heads of our assassins.

Next day when we were marched to the airfield, it was a shambles, with enormous craters where runways had been, great piles of masonry and iron beams scattered all over the area. Hangars had been hit and their metal skeletons stood twisted against the sky. Several bombs had fallen among the buildings where the military personnel lived; there had been many casualties and those buildings were now completely evacuated. But though the damage was nothing like what had happened to the Warsaw ghetto, it did satisfy some of our thirst for vengeance.

Bronek, the Kapo, was given a team of specially selected strong men to clear out those houses. Because there were still a number of victims under the debris, I was assigned to the team as medic. Our boys worked with great gusto, hoping to find considerable amounts of food, but they were disappointed. What there was—furniture, bed linen, kitchenware—had little value for us, and we could use only such personal linen and clothing as remained. Though the loot did not amount to a great deal, rummaging through the German dwellings—a *Werterfassung* operation in reverse—gave us great satisfaction. We divided the loot fairly and put the bodies into a cellar, handing them over to the Germans in installments in order to prolong this more than ordinarily pleasant work. One of the men found a man's torn-off arm and remembered that some days earlier we had disposed of a body with the right arm missing. The man took the arm to Bronek who coolly put it in the cellar and said in his customarily polite way, "You idiot, what the hell's the matter with you? We'll discover that arm and turn it in when I think it's advisable. For the time being, not a word to anyone about it." Only when our work was almost completed and all the ruined houses had been meticulously searched, was the arm turned over to the Germans.

A few days later another Allied air raid destroyed the Schwäbisch Hall railroad station. All the citizens of the town and the camp's inmates were mobilized to clear the rubble, but the authorities apparently decided that, even at that critical juncture, close contacts between civilians and camp inmates were undesirable; we were taken off the job the next day.

Defeat hung in the air, but though the Third Reich was in its death throes, it did not collapse. It held the German people in an iron grip; they followed orders and kept their mouths shut, they submitted to Ordnung and *Befehl* without a murmur, and to the last moment they put up not the slightest resistance to authority. Nevertheless, from the trees in the town there were bodies swinging, hanged in the last spasm of Nazi terror. The authorities took these drastic steps because of defeatism, because of lack of faith in the Führer, or for what they called sabotage. The bodies hung like that for several days, swaying in the wind, as a warning to others.

For us the prospect of liberation was a heady brew. Not that we really expected to see it personally, but this was our war with Hitler and we wanted to survive to spite him, to feast our eyes and spirits on the spectacle of his downfall, to witness the whole evil power of the Third Reich in a heap of rubble. Yet, in front of the houses we sometimes saw children at play, clean, fair-haired, well-mannered children of a nation of murderers. Their fathers and brothers had murdered our children, but as I walked through the streets of their town and saw those trusting, defenseless little ones, I became acutely conscious of the fact that we could never bring ourselves to murder them when the hour of revenge came.

Wlodek would now be seven years and three months old, with blond hair and blue eyes like the little German boy I watched on the corner. My wound was reopening. Every time the wind blew from the east, it seemed to bring the sound of distant moans and whispers for help. Alone among strangers Wlodek had to carry on with as much cunning and intelligence as a seven-year-old could muster while I, far away and helpless, could not offer him a father's protection. "Son, be alive," I prayed, "so that you, at least, will know the victory and the revenge."

Some Nazis didn't attempt to conceal their intentions for us. A few days after the air raid, one of the younger noncoms in a ground crew, blurted out passionately, "I can't understand you Jews. Why don't you kill yourselves? Don't you realize that we'll exterminate every last one of you before this is over, whether we win or lose? Not a single one of you will survive. Don't have any illusions about that. Isn't it better to commit suicide than to go on living like a slave when you'll get a bullet in the back or the gas chamber anyway? We are never going to surrender. We'll go up to the mountains and fight on to our last breath, with our bare hands and to the last man if necessary. But what are *you* waiting for? If you Jews had any pride instead of being a horde of slaves, you'd take my advice."

With equal candor I told him that my faith forbade suicide, but that even more basically we Jews would not do their work as murderers for them. The fate of a handful of Jewish survivors now had only symbolic significance, but we were getting more joy than they realized from watching German faces as Hitler's forces were being driven back on both fronts. Why should we deprive ourselves of at least that pleasure? "We know what you'd like to do with us, but things may not work out just as you plan. You may not have the time, you may be frightened by the punishment waiting for you, drawing closer every day. Now if I were a Nazi, I *would* kill myself. You started out to build a thousand-year Reich, but what you've accomplished is to condemn the nation you're supposed to love to a thousand years of guilt. . . ."

Impending liberation on the one hand and the threat of impending extermination on the other drove a number of inmates to rash action. One spring day two prisoners did not march back to camp; instead they hid at the airfield and during the night set out westward in the hope of meeting the liberating armies. They were brothers, tailors from Radom.

Their freedom and our hope lasted exactly two days, and on the third they were caught, executed, and their bodies sent back to the camp. German civilians had refused to give them any shelter.

Apparently fearing new escape efforts, Walling made a speech at morning roll call, telling us that our lives were in danger because the front was approaching, that we would be safe only under the Reich's protection, and that the camp authorities were going to do everything possible to evacuate the prisoners in their charge to places where they would not be disturbed.

Such symptoms of impending defeat filled us with joy, but a new and alarming danger threatened us from within: typhus. Though we showered regularly and disinfection teams worked without respite, the lice were steadily multiplying. Men were sometimes so maddened by vermin that they rushed to the infirmary, threw themselves on the floor, tore off their clothes, and cried out hysterically, "Poison us! Put us out of our misery! Or get rid of these lice!" Even those of us who worked in the infirmary, where we had plenty of hot water and soap, could never completely rid ourselves of vermin. Every time we examined our clothes we found nests with eggs and big fat adult lice. On the day the airfield was bombed by Allied planes, we ran to the barbed wire the better to see the explosions. There on the wire blankets were suspended to be aired and we were astonished to see them literally crawling with lice. The sight was so revolting that it almost spoiled our pleasure in the air raid.

The early unusually warm spring did the rest. People flooded into the infirmary by the dozen; to avoid panic we called their illness a spring epidemic of flu, but we were aware that typhus had broken out in the camp. We knew if we told the Germans, the 400 inmates would be executed and the barracks burned down. A simple, drastic, and probably effective solution. Though we tried to conceal the typhus outbreak and to keep up the myth of a flu epidemic, every day we were still sending to the airfield laborers who could easily spread the typhus. If that happened, the authorities would retaliate the moment they discovered the true situation. But how could we isolate and quarantine the camp?

The infirmary staff held a secret meeting with the camp administration, all of them prisoners, and the unanimous decision was that to conceal the typhus was the lesser evil. We officially informed Walling that a flu epidemic had broken out and that the contingent of workers we were supplying would be drastically reduced for a number of days. We made the same announcement in each barracks and simultaneously decided to invoke

Draconian measures to delouse and disinfect the camp. We therefore also told Walling that during this period, when most of the workforce would be in camp, we would carry out an intensive spring cleaning. He liked the idea and agreed.

The operation had three phases. Every inmate had to be bathed and deloused; all clothing had to be disinfected; and all straw mattresses and blankets absolutely cleared of lice. The last was the most urgent task for the rest would be pointless unless it worked well. We decided that if nothing else worked, we would burn the mattresses; sleeping on bare boards would be better than sleeping on lice-ridden bedding. But the prisoners put up unexpected resistance and refused to surrender their mattresses. They showered us with abuse and threats, and said we were trying to kill them.

In a few days 75 percent of the inmates were sick. The epidemic did not spare infirmary personnel, and both our doctors, Emanuel and Ludwik, were laid low. Only I was immune, having had my typhus in the ghetto two years earlier.

Two days later, with the epidemic at its peak, Walling informed us that he had received orders from the central camp of Natzweiler to evacuate us. There was no one I could consult; everyone was in bed with a high fever. The war news now spoke of places no more than two days' distance from our camp and we heard that the French were fighting in our sector with special ardor, so there was reason for delaying action. I made up my mind to take the risk, and I bluntly informed Walling that typhus was rampant in the camp. To evacuate was out of the question, for we could not drag several hundred typhus patients across all Germany when any one of them could spread the disease. The only thing to do, I suggested, was to quarantine the camp, stop sending workers anywhere, and disinfect everyone and everything as thoroughly as possible.

Walling agreed and we went to the airfield where he informed Dr. Haller, chief of the air-base hospital, of the situation. Usually Dr. Haller treated us correctly and I counted on his backing. That very afternoon he visited our infirmary, examined Ludwik carefully, took his temperature, made a tour of the barracks and declared emphatically, "This isn't typhus." Ludwik began to explain that he had treated thousands of cases in the ghetto and that we were dealing with a classic epidemic of it. Dr. Haller, who had never seen an actual case of typhus, knew it only from textbook descriptions and replied that he could find no red spots on the bodies, spots which should be the size of peas. Moreover, he insisted that no one could survive typhus with a temperature above 104 degrees Fahrenheit, yet though we had had higher temperatures than that, we had not had any deaths. Seeing that we were in trouble, I improvised a "scientific" theory according to which Eastern Jews, because of exposure to typhus over generations, had developed a resistance, which Western Europeans did not possess and that as a result they suffered a milder form, with small, less visible spots and a lower mortality rate. But Dr. Haller was not convinced. I persuaded Walling to call Natzweiler and request that the SS doctor be sent down. Two days later he appeared, took one quick look at the patients, and said, "No doubt about it, *Fleckfieber!*"

My prestige with Walling rocketed skyward. The camp was sealed off at once, and we began to burn the mattresses, ignoring the furious protests of the prisoners. To set an example, I had my own mattress burned first. I went to the air base to get disinfectants and my heart almost stopped when I saw the three large drums marked with the big white letters: *Zyklon B.* The same chemical used to exterminate people in the gas chambers was now going to serve to exterminate lice and save people.

It was at this juncture that I called on Nurse Elizabeth at the airfield hospital. I told her I was afraid that the camp would be liquidated and none of us left alive. "Now," I said, "I have a child in Warsaw—"

"In Warsaw?" she interrupted. "Why didn't you tell me before this? My brother is a Wehrmacht officer there, and he might have helped you. . . ."

It was hardly the moment to tell her I wouldn't have trusted a Wehrmacht officer with the address of my son, so I replied that Warsaw was now occupied by the Soviets, but that what I wanted was something quite different. "I have a sister in Palestine," I said. "I'd like to leave a letter for you to mail to her when the war is over."

Elizabeth burst into tears and through her sobs said that when a man usurps powers that belong only to God, what else can we expect?

"Will you promise to send the letter?" I persisted.

"Of course," she said. "Why, it's your last will and testament!"

Next day I brought her a short note written in German and addressed to my sister, telling her that my son was in Warsaw and to get in touch with the Maginskis and Kazimierz for news of him. When Elizabeth took the letter she burst into tears once again. (A few months after the war's end she forwarded the letter to my sister Aida, who had escaped in 1939— which seemed like decades ago—and had made her way to Palestine.)

I carried out the delousing operation with extreme ruthlessness and fortunately the epidemic was relatively mild. After two weeks the tide began to turn, the number of new cases began to drop, and a new problem arose, the ravenous appetites of those recovering from typhus. I asked the Lager-älteste for extra soup rations for the convalescents. He looked at me as if I'd lost my mind. "What do you think this is, the Joint Distribution Committee?" But in the end he complied.

When I walked into one of the barracks with the extra soup, I caused a sensation. A crowd of hungry prisoners surrounded the kettle, everyone pushing his bowl into my hands. The sick and weak were driven back and in a moment the whole pot might have fallen into the hands of the stronger, but no less hungry prisoners, except that I put the lid on it and sat down on top of it. "Take it out!" I roared at my assistants. "Barrack One will not get extra soup today!" There was sudden and absolute silence. The orderlies pushed the crowd back, those entitled to extra portions lined up and each got his ration. A few times I had to stop the distribution when the line moved too close. I insisted on a full yard of free space in front of me and I got it, but for some time afterward I was nicknamed "Yardaway." For all my precautions a few clever operators still managed to get two portions of soup, and others simply stole the extra ration of those who were too weak to defend themselves. One man took the soup intended for his fifteen-year-old son, who was too weak to get up from his bunk, and drank most of it while carrying it back to him. He had for a long time been systematically stealing his son's bread, and other items of food. (The man survived the war, but his son later died during the evacuation of the camp.)

The additional food both strengthened the bodies of the convalescents and their morale. For the first time someone was looking after them in a relatively disinterested way. Not even the men who carried the pots for me were given such extra portions; theirs was only the much-appreciated privilege of licking the kettle clean.

My energetic measures produced results of which I was quite proud. The typhus epidemic which had knocked out a whole camp did not result in a single fatality. The inmates looked like shadows, dragged their feet and stopped to rest every few minutes, but at least they were out of bed at last. We did have a number of cases with secondary complications: polyneuritis, partial paralysis, and so on. Ludwik, in his delirium, had called loudly for beer. "It's appalling that a man with a university education shouldn't be able to solve the problem of a bottle of beer," he would cry out indignantly. "It's shocking! What am I a doctor for?" Though we couldn't get beer for him, we were able to get some pickles for Hirszfeld, who had been dreaming about them and who remembered those pickles to the end of his life.

Meanwhile Walling went right on talking about evacuating the camp, but as the front moved closer transportation was becoming increasingly disorganized. There were no freight cars and we began to hope that we would somehow succeed in sticking it out where we were until liberation. Then, one day, an SS man appeared from Natzweiler with orders to evacuate us, and one glance at him was enough to dispel any illusion: he was a typical SS gangster. Front or no front, victory or defeat, the Nazis would always find the time, the men, the transportation to carry out the essential task of driving the Jews from place to place, and to their deaths. To our horror, the SS man had a freight train standing at our siding two days later. Only the empty freight cars were backed into the camp, while the front part of the train and the locomotive remained outside the gates. The other cars were full of prisoners from another camp. Early the next morning we got into the cattle cars and at the last moment the SS man noticed that a "deserter" had remained in the shed for the dead, so I had to jump out and load the corpse onto the train. Meantime my car had been bolted, so I had to go into another one with people I'd never seen. The camp gate was opened, the two sections of the train were coupled, and the train began to move eastward lest its valuable cargo fall into the hands of the approaching Allies.

Five months before, when we first arrived in Hessenthal, there had been 560 of us. When we left in March 1945, there were slightly more than 400 left. There were thousands of small camps like ours all over Germany where inmates worked in factories, on construction sites, military projects, and so on. The big death camps used assembly-line methods of extermination; the little ones were less spectacular and noisy but just as dedicated to killing off their prisoners. Now, the small camps were being evacuated and their survivors shipped to the central extermination points.

We had traveled less than a mile when we heard planes overhead. Deafening explosions shook the train, and a hail of stones and debris smacked against the walls of our cars. The drone of the planes grew fainter, then stronger again, and we heard the barking of machine guns, then antiaircraft guns, and a moment later the roof of our car was riddled with bullets. Splinters showered into us and prisoners began to moan and to scream. The idea that we might be killed by an Allied bomb when victory seemed so close was absurd and impossible. We pounded against the bolted doors and finally helped a young boy out the small cattle car window who succeeded in opening the door. We rolled out like potatoes from a sack, began to unbolt the doors of the other cars, and were met by a volley of bullets. The SS men, who had jumped off the train when the enemy plane first attacked, were hidden in the shrubbery a few hundred yards away from the track and were firing at us for leaving the train without permission. We scattered in all directions. The bomber circled above us a few times, then spiraled westward without meeting any resistance; apparently the flier considered his mission accomplished.

In a clearing we joined the prisoners who had been in the front half of the train and past agonies were revived as we recognized them as natives of Warsaw deported after the 1944 uprising. Faraway Warsaw, which we had never forgotten, caught up with us in that clearing in Württemberg. Warsaw, that crucified city, we could not stop mourning, no matter how hard we tried. "Warsaw is no more," the other men told us sadly. "Nothing is left. Gone, all gone. . . . You have a little boy there? In Pius Street? May God have pity on you!"

They told us the story of the tragic uprising and how, virtually un-armed, they attacked the Germans and were bled white while waiting in vain for the powerful Red Army across the Vistula to come to their aid. Sadly they recounted how even the Russian artillery batteries had kept silent. I remembered Moniek Rotstein's boomerang theory of history: the boomerang never fails. The Poles had stood by and watched us being exter-minated by the Nazis, and less than a year and a half later the boomerang came back to them; they had left us to die alone, and the Russians stood by and watched them crushed by the Nazis.

We spent the rest of that day and night in the smashed train. Before nightfall the SS brought back a prisoner who had taken advantage of the confusion to escape to a nearby village. They stood him up next to the edge of the large crater the Allied bombing plane had left and a Transyl-vanian guard shot him for "attempting to escape." The man did not even groan, just fell grotesquely backward, like an expert diver, and rolled down the slope. The SS man walked away without looking back. We rushed down to the victim and he was still alive, so we carried him back to the train and dressed his wound. The bullet had gone right through him, but later that night he was already asking for food. Next day he was back on his feet. When, a few days later, I told the SS man that the prisoner he had shot was still alive, he nodded and grunted, *"Gut!"*

The day after the bombing several trailer trucks came and picked up the baggage and the sick. The rest of us, formed into ranks of five, began to march. The Oberkapo of the other camp, a German prisoner, happened to be a namesake of our August Walling, and the two soon became great friends. We marched slowly, but the men, only recently recovered from the siege of typhus and gravely weakened by it, kept dropping out of the column, and trucks had to stop from time to time to pick up these stragglers.

Night was falling when we reached a large railroad station, but there were no trains. The most seriously ill were left at the station on the stone floor, ostensibly to be shipped to a hospital in the Tyrol; the rest of us were marched off into the night. After about an hour we neared some marl pits and were ordered to lie down in the ditches on the slopes. The SS men warned us that anyone who stuck his head out would be shot at. The ground was wet and slippery and we had to cling to the sides of the slope in order not to lie in the water at the bottom of the ditches. It was an ordeal, but in spite of the discomfort and the sporadic gunfire, we managed to sleep. By my side a frail adolescent boy wept in a thin voice, "I'm cold! I'm so cold!" Eventually he, too, was overpowered by sleep, and huddled on the ground. When, at dawn, stiff and covered from head to foot with clay, we climbed out of the ditch, the boy still lay at the bottom: he was dead.

We came to a village where we were confined in two big barns. After a short while peasants brought kettles of boiled potatoes. The prisoners stood in line and everyone got a few potatoes in his mess tin or cap. At first the ration was six potatoes per person, then it was reduced to five, and finally to four. Those who had been served went into the other barn. But then new carts came up with colossal amounts of potatoes, the rations were increased to six, then to eight per person. When those who had received only four and five potatoes heard that, there was a riot. An indignant crowd went back, broke into the first barn, and rushed the kettles. SS men with sticks and rifles split open a few heads and soon restored order. I happened to get one of those blows and when I came to, one of our doctors was dressing my scalp.

I resumed the march with a bandaged head. Ludwik was suffering from polyneuritis and every step hurt him. We held him up from both sides and stumbled on. Now and then a prisoner dropped exhausted, never to rise again. He would be picked up by a truck and his corpse left in the next village for the village mayor to bury.

When it became dark, we stopped once more. The men were driven into a barn which was soon so full that the SS men had to kick prisoners to drive them inside. Men climbed up to find a place to sit on the beams below the roof, they filled every nook and cranny, but new waves of prisoners kept being sardined in. And all of it in complete darkness. When the doors were finally banged shut, the barn was a seething cauldron and the continuous noise, like a surging sea, was punctuated by screaming. It was a nightmare. Crammed in, horrified and stifled, the prisoners cursed and swore, trampled on one another, bit and scratched and shoved, and fought for a little space. When the sea of misery and hysteria grew momentarily quiet, someone would suddenly fall from one of the beams above and crash onto the mass of bodies below. Groans, curses, and screams would break out again and the SS men would throw open the door and fire their submachine guns at random into the barn to quiet them. Those killed fell heavily against their neighbors, the wounded screamed, and from the shoving mass of writhing bodies came a hysterical howling.

The infirmary personnel were lucky. At the last minute Walling ran into Emanuel and ordered us all to sleep in the entrance hall of the farmer's house. Horrified, we lay there listening to the ebb and rise of the sound in the barn. Sometime during the night a young SS man stuck his head in. Smiling amiably, he remarked that Emanuel was wearing excellent shoes. They had been made for him in the camp workshop only a few weeks earlier. When Emanuel did not take the hint, the SS man told him bluntly that he wanted to swap shoes with him. Emanuel turned pale, but began to pull off his beautiful military boots. Someone asked why he didn't complain to Walling instead. "Do you want him to catch me in some corner later and cut my throat?" Emanuel replied. "I won't risk my life for a pair of shoes." The exchange was quickly effected and the SS man was friendly to us to the end of the march.

In the morning when the barn was emptied, even the SS chief was taken aback at the sight of the dozens of corpses entangled in convulsive embrace, frozen in most unnatural positions, mute testimony to what the prisoners had endured before being choked, crushed, trampled, or shot to death. Those who came out of the barn alive had a wild look in their eyes and were incapable of walking. Several wagons had to be brought up before the march could resume. We looked like a procession of ragged and filthy skeletons scarcely able to drag our feet. A week before, by dint of great effort, we had rid ourselves of our lice, but the few days with inmates of other camps had given the lice ample opportunity to reconquer the ground they had lost.

From Walling we learned that our destination was Dachau. We marched all day long, with short breaks for rest, and when we went through a village the farmers looked at us in pity and fear. Some threw us bread, but generally they were too frightened. The SS knew there was little time to lose, the front was moving closer and we had to be preserved from the freedom that rode hard on our heels. We knew that we were going to march all night when we were ordered, at dusk, to camp in a meadow near the road. It was dark when we set out again and people at once began to drop from exhaustion. I was close to the end of the column with Nachtigal and next to us was the SS man who had taken Emanuel's shoes. The first to fall was a boy from Radom. A charitable farmer gave him a small piece of bread and he bit into it, but had no strength to get up. Our SS man kicked him, but the boy didn't move. The SS man turned his machine pistol at the boy. "Just a moment," the boy said, "let me finish the bread."

"What a swine!" the SS man said indignantly. "I'm going to shoot him and all he thinks about is his lousy piece of bread."

The prisoner finished his bread and did not stir. He merely closed his eyes. The gun barked. The SS man bent to see if his victim was still alive. His long military coat opened a bit as he bent down and we saw that under his uniform he was wearing civilian clothes.

Forty times that night blood soaked the edges of the road. At first we tried to help our exhausted comrades, holding them up, dragging them along with us, but the SS man gave us a "friendly" warning. "Don't," he said. "You won't help them and you'll drop yourselves and get what that boy got." Of their own accord some prisoners walked to the edge of the road and sat or lay down in absolute prostration. Others fell on the asphalt road and ranks opened and flowed around them. When the column had passed, the SS man would give the body a submachine-gun burst and waved his hand casually to signify that the corpse was to be pushed into the ditch that ran parallel to the road. Some resisted, in a last upsurge of strength; some clung to the new military boots and the coattails that covered the civilian clothes; one victim even grabbed the barrel of the gun; and some few implored the SS man to let them rest for a minute so that they could muster enough strength to continue.

Over all the roads of the Third Reich during its last days just such processions of slaves moved, evacuated ahead of the approaching armies of liberation. All the soil of Germany was soaked with the blood of such victims from all parts of Europe. They died as they were forced to run away from freedom and liberation with the last wretched shards of their lives, driven into such hells as Dachau.

Is it possible to imagine anyone longing to get to Dachau? We homeless prisoners on that pilgrimage of death dreamed of Dachau as a homeless dog dreams of his kennel. And our prayers were finally answered. The darkness on both sides of the road grew thicker as we entered a city in flames from a recent air raid. We halted in a square lit by the glow of burning buildings and fell onto the pavement and slept like beaten animals.

It was still gray when we were loaded into freight cars, and once more we had to include those who had died as well. We managed it, but why were the corpses so heavy, as if they had been turned into lead, and the heads especially like blocks of granite? At last I climbed into one of the cattle cars, where I had a portion of the floor to myself, and once again Emanuel and Ludwik, Edek and other familiar faces were beside me. We had survived the death march . . . and we were on our way to Dachau. "How I hate to be driven to Dachau!" Edek said, making a face. We replied with tired smiles that Dachau or no, we were still alive. Somehow, during that gruesome night, Ludwik's polyneuritis disappeared and he felt completely recovered.

The order came at last: *"Aussteigen!"* We jumped out, formed columns, and immediately the air-raid sirens began to howl. We watched what we later learned was the daily air raid on Munich, and it cheered us; now we were really convinced that we were still alive. The bombers went over in one big formation, made a circle, and went in again, and there were explosions and columns of black smoke.

A sign at a crossroad read: Dachau-Allach. We passed through a woods, suddenly found ourselves in the rubble of an enormous industrial plant, the famous BMW (the Bavarian Motor Works), where here and there a building wall or the remains of a lathe stood stark and lonely.

Walling halted us at the gate to Dachau: he had completed his mission.

Allach, a subdivision of the huge Dachau concentration camp, was situated close to the village. It was the first camp I had seen with brick barracks. On our arrival, Jews were separated from Gentiles and the latter, joined by many of our own people, were taken to an adjoining section of the camp. Our barracks were built with stone floors, but had no bunks so we spread straw and slept on that. Before turning in we were disinfected and bathed, and our heads were shaved by a Salonika Jew, one of the few survivors of Greek Jewry.

The part of the camp we were in was small, with only a few barracks. It had an excellent washroom and toilets, quite unlike the outdoor latrines at Majdanek or the privies at Radom and Hessenthal. There was an immense kitchen, a big disinfection barrack, and an infirmary. The area adjoining ours on one side was occupied by Gentile Poles, on the other by the women's enclosure, and both were separated from us by barbed wire. Every day old-timers met their sweethearts at the wire, and from time to time a mysterious hand opened the gate and a handful of fortunates sneaked into the women's field with gifts for their ladies in exchange for one "shot," or portion, of lovemaking.

In addition to ourselves, our enclosure contained mainly Hungarian Jews. The washroom walls were covered with signs in Hungarian we could not read. We soon discovered that the de facto authorities at Dachau were a secret international committee of prisoners, most of them Communists. Though the population was Jewish, most of the jobs were held by Gentiles. Our Barracks Elder was Walter, a German Communist and veteran of many concentration camps; our Scribe was a Belgian said to be the Secretary of the Flemish Communist Party; a Serb partisan was also part of our field, as were a number of French *maquis*. In contrast to our previous provincial camps, Dachau had the atmosphere of a big international hotel.

At 6 P.M. dinner was served: half a liter of water with carrot peelings in it, plus an almost microscopic slice of bread. Someone asked whether they were weighing the bread by the karat. We exchanged agonized glances: the war was nearing its end and we might die in Dachau of starvation almost at the last minute. Walter explained that there had until recently been plenty of food, but that the shipments and parcels had stopped a few weeks ago. Everywhere the Hungarians clustered together discussing something with great animation. *"Istenem! Kicsi kényer . . . kicsi kényer!"* they kept repeating, which we soon learned meant "My God, not enough bread!"

One advantage, however, was that we were not obliged to work. Except for a brief roll call we could take our ease. But hunger bit at our vitals.

I was standing in front of the barracks with Edek when various of the camp "notables" came up to us. Amazed and incredulous they learned from us of the Warsaw Ghetto Uprising against the Nazis. A young man, handsome as a film star, came over, a Gentile Pole from Cracow named Soszko. When he heard that I had been a newspaper publisher and Edek in moving pictures, his eyes lit up. Before the war he had been a press photographer and he knew my paper well. He had dreamed of becoming a moving-picture cameraman and Edek said that it was easy to arrange, but how could we survive on this lousy diet? We were all sure to die.

Soszko admitted pensively that things had grown worse recently, but then came the revelation that he was the kitchen Kapo. "Come see me some evening," he said before leaving, "and I'll give you something. Come just before curfew, when the guards are relieved." We couldn't believe our ears.

The next night Edek and I set out to try our luck. A guard was pacing in front of the kitchen barrack, apparently unaware that curfew was about to sound. When he glanced at his watch and ducked around the corner, we ran inside. "Soszko? Just a minute." A little later, Soszko appeared, smiling, friendly. It was all just like a movie. "How are things?" he asked, "Holding out?" We muttered something. Soszko took us to his little room and we stood there bewitched. A normal cozy room with a couch and books on a night table, photographs and other pictures on the walls. Out of the closet, Soszko took a *whole loaf of bread* and a *whole one-pound brick* of margarine, which he handed to us in the most natural manner. "Hold on. You've got to hold on. It won't last too long now."

We had to hurry back because curfew would sound at any minute. We ran out scarcely able to believe our good fortune, and carrying our treasures carefully hidden under our striped uniforms. We were veterans of camp life and we knew better than to take risks. When the lights were turned out, we slowly consumed the bread and margarine as we lay back in the straw on the stone floor. The margarine went through my body like magic balm, reaching into the farthest joints of my bones and oiling them. We didn't leave a single crumb of bread or of margarine, and then we fell blissfully asleep, sated.

Our two doctor friends were given jobs in the infirmary, and Edek was assigned to the disinfection barracks. A short while later Ludwik got me a modest job sweeping floors in the infirmary, but I didn't keep it long. About ten o'clock one morning the infirmary Kapo came in to make an inspection. A Dalmatian with a peach-bloom complexion, he was one of the handsomest men I had ever seen. I reported to him and within ten minutes achieved the most dizzying promotion of my life. Because of the new shipment and many other new arrivals, the infirmary was being enlarged and he needed another scribe; consequently, he appointed me. The infirmary serviced the various other fields as well as our own and as a result we saw there almost all the nationalities of Western and Eastern Europe. Most of the illnesses were of the usual camp-variety: dysentery, sores, and ulcers. Those who died were placed in a pile behind the infirmary every morning and trucks took them to the crematorium in the main camp. They were typically *"Muselman"* corpses, skin and bones, fetid and repulsive skeletons in striped uniforms.

The infirmary provided me with nourishing food and, more important, a clean bunk in the same room with the doctors where I could enjoy the conversation of civilized human beings in what leisure we had. The older doctors were Hungarian Jews, highly educated men. There was also a young Norwegian physician who told me how in his town the Norwegians had helped their Jewish fellow citizens. One night, with the help of the police, they had smuggled all the Jews there across the border into Sweden, beyond German reach. When I asked him how the Nazis had got him, he was a bit embarrassed and replied that he had spent the night with his girl-friend; when he returned home it was too late to join the others.

At night, after work, Edek and I called on Soszko and he never dis-appointed us. Always he had a kind word and some food. We wanted to repay his favors by finding him customers who were ready to give gold for bread and margarine (even as late as 1945 some inmates still had some gold), but he refused, saying that he was not trying to make any money. If he had wanted to, he could have had plenty of gold from others in exchange for the food he gave to us.

One day I went to see the infirmary Kapo on business and found him at breakfast. He was drinking black coffee and eating crackers and orange marmalade. I was shocked. Here was a man who could have had his fill of bread and margarine, and instead contented himself with crackers. It seemed like blasphemy or perversion to me. He lifted his head from the *Völkischer Beobachter* and said, somewhat shaken, "Did you know that Roose-velt has just died? But everything is going well at the front."

Our luck was short-lived. After ten days we were informed that half the inmates were to be evacuated. The Hungarian doctors decided that they would stay and without consulting us put us on the list of evacuees. Frankly, we had nothing against that. We knew from experience that it was better at critical moments not to stay with the weak and the sick, for they were the first to be liquidated, and hospital staffs often shared their fate.

Once more we were on the move. We got into a clean, dry freight car, but at the last moment were told that it was for the sick and we were, instead, put into an open coal car. Our escort was a seventy-five-year-old Pole from Poznán, mobilized into the *Volkssturm*. The commandant of the train was an SS officer whose conduct through the trip was above reproach. For three days and nights our train rolled over the rail network of south-ern Bavaria under a ceaseless rain, our destination presumably the Tyrol. But all lines leading there were occupied by other traffic and in the end we got stuck on a siding and did not budge for forty-eight hours. We were drenched to the bone and had virtually no food. Ludwik had a tube of her-ring paste and our meals consisted of hot water with a bit of that paste. It didn't nourish us, but at least we had something warm.

On the highway that ran parallel to the railroad we watched the spectacle of the German rout. A continuous procession of soldiers moved eastward, individually and in groups, some with full packs, others without weapons. Wehrmacht infantrymen, *Waffen* SS and the gray-uniformed airborne troops mingled with civilians. They walked or rode on bicycles, motorcycles, trucks, and sometimes on horsedrawn peasant carts. Their faces showed only sullen exhaustion. They were continually harassed by Allied planes, just as we had been harried by theirs in September 1939. When the planes attacked, the people scattered into the fields for cover, and threw themselves into the muddy ditches. When the planes left, the stream of armies in retreat would fill the highway once again.

We saw small black dots in the distance, growing by the minute, and then their outlines became clear. A group of tanks in good order were advancing, almost as if on review, two at a time, their guns belching fire now and again, the noise drowning the rhythmic clanking of their treads. Slender boys in khaki uniforms rode on the tanks with Tommy guns at the ready. When they came to the clearing where our freight cars were halted, they paused. We were a strange army, indeed, in our striped uniforms. Their commanding officer looked at us for a moment, horror written all over his face. Then he saluted us and extended his arm in welcome, smiling.

We were free.

It was April 29, 1945, exactly two years to the day since I had arrived in Majdanek.

The soldiers of Patton's Third Army were shaken as the filthy skeletons in striped uniforms embraced them, weeping, kneeling to kiss their hands, mumbling incomprehensible thanks. In that hour of liberation we wept as we had not wept during all the years of martyrdom; we wept tears of sorrow, not tears of joy. Our liberation came too late; we had paid too high a price. Only a few of us, in spontaneous gratitude, rushed to our American liberators to thank them; the overwhelming majority went to the supply cars and were soon parading around with a loaf or two of bread under their arms.

The Third Reich had collapsed before our eyes. The hour of revenge we had dreamed of during the long night of death and humiliation had come at last. Germany lay before us defenseless, and fifteen million slaves now had their opportunity to revenge themselves upon their masters. But no night of long knives, no orgy of revenge took place. What might have been a mighty blood-bath settling of accounts, which no conscience would have failed to recognize as just and long-delayed, spent itself in a feeble wave of looting. When we went to the nearby village of Staltach, the women and children were hiding in cellars and ditches. We pulled them out, frightened and trembling, but we could not collectively punish a people. We had the souls of slaves, of cowards; we were crippled by two thousand years of pogroms and ghettos, two thousand years of the Sixth Commandment had tamed and blunted in us that natural virile impulse of revenge. The sublime words, "Thou shalt not kill," which had been our shield against murder and persecution became the shield and protector of a nation of murderers and our alibi for our own cowardice and weakness.

The sons of the "master race," who had only the day before been so arrogant, were now as excessively abject and groveling in their humiliation. Every one of them was an anti-Nazi; every German family had sacrificed some member to the maw of the concentration camps; and no one, of course, had ever known anything about the most horrible of Nazi crimes. The fair-haired Valkyries, only the day before yesterday the proudest representatives of the superior Aryan race, today eagerly sought opportunities to commit what once they had called the crime of *Rassenschande*—for a cigarette, or even for nothing. When we learned that some of our prison comrades had been unable to resist the temptation, we refused to have anything to do with them. "After what we've been through, to sleep with a German girl!" Edek said indignantly. "I'd do it only if I had a barbed-wire prick!"

But at bottom the Germans did not feel guilty because of the devastation and suffering they had inflicted on the world, their consciences did not give them any torment for the nauseating and enormous crimes they had perpetrated; at bottom they had only one complaint against Hitler: that he had lost the war. A significant verbal repartee took place, scrawled on the walls of Siegestor in Munich—where Hitler staged his first, unsuccessful Beer Hall *Putsch* in 1923. Someone chalked an inscription on the wall:

Dachau, Buchenwald, Auschwitz—
Ich schäme mich Deutsch zu sein.
(I am ashamed to be a German.)

Two days later that inscription was erased and replaced by:

Schiller, Goethe, Wagner, Kant—
Ich bin stolz Deutsch zu sein.
(I am proud to be a German.)

From Staltach we moved to the village of St. Heinrich on Starnberger

Lake where we doffed our uniforms and got civilian clothes. Then we moved on to Bad Tölz, where we were quartered in the big SS barracks, and finally we moved on to the *Flakkaserne* in Munich.

The war ended on May 9, but it was eight weeks before I gathered enough strength to set out for home. During those weeks I kept asking myself why I was putting off something that was my elementary duty, something I thought I wanted to do with all my heart, but I couldn't answer the question. The truth is that I was afraid. For years we had feared death, and now those of us who had survived the holocaust feared life. I was afraid of my new freedom; I had lost the habit of freedom in the ghetto and the camps. I was afraid of returning to normal life and its activities because they seemed like desecration of the memory of those who had perished. Whenever I heard the laughter of children, I remembered the children who would never laugh again; whenever I saw an attractive woman smiling, I was reminded of Lena who would never smile at me again. The old European adage that new life springs up out of the graves of the dead did not apply to me: the "new life" was beyond my powers. What I would have liked to do was bury myself in a monastery and spend the remainder of my life in solitude and mournful meditation, or better still become a watchman in a Jewish cemetery where I might be alone with the spirits of the dead, surrounded by a life that was gone forever, and cut off from the world of the present to which nothing linked me and in which nothing attracted me.

But most of all I feared going home. I was afraid that when I did, my last ties to life would be irrevocably broken. There would be nothing left. Hoping against hope, believing against the accumulation of evidence, I kept telling myself that somewhere my motherless son waited for me and that illusion kept me alive. It was not a joyful hope; it was my recognition of paternal duty. But I trembled to put it to the test, for the fear kept returning like an ague that there was no one waiting for me anywhere, neither with tears nor with flowers; no one and nothing left, only rubble, not even graves to visit.

Russians, Czechs, Frenchmen, Dutchmen were all going home now, to rebuild their ruined houses, to reknit their family ties, to take up their lives once more. They went back with their eyes fixed on the future; they mourned their dead, but they looked forward with hope, to new births, to new marriages, to new life. What would we look forward to? What was there for us to return to? And where?

I relived every step of the last five years, tormented by nightmares and visions; and I had endless conversations with my absent loved ones. I flayed myself with a thousand ifs, the thousand ways in which the implacable course of affairs might have turned out differently, and a procession of shadows passed before my eyes. Lena, my Lena. My sister Roza, lovely as her name. Why hadn't I died with them? What was best and noblest in my people had been destroyed. Why was I permitted to live? I belonged under the ashes of the ghetto, or in Treblinka, or Majdanek. Or was that all itself a nightmare and would I awake to find my son's blue eyes staring into mine, and Lena bending over him as of old, turning her face to me and smiling . . . ? But no, our life was not an American film with its happy ending: it was a European tragedy.

On July 5, 1945, I set out for home at last, with Edek. Kotlar and Melcer had left the day before. Since the liberation Edek had turned sentimental; he no longer told dirty jokes, and he spoke of his wife, Hanka, with tears in his eyes. He had vowed that if he survived he would devote the rest of his life to her . . . and to her alone. We traveled on foot, on peasant carts, trucks, American Army jeeps, and occasionally trains, to the East. At Fürth we found a truck full of former camp inmates going home to Czechoslovakia, and the driver agreed to take us on the pretext that we were going to Cieszyn. When we crossed the border, I looked back on Germany and pronounced a solemn curse on it: "May that godless land and its people of murderers be forever accursed; may its bread be bitter with the blood that fertilizes its grains; may the winds forever moan with the cries of the murdered and the hateful fumes of the crematoria never depart from the land; may its name and memory be effaced from the book of history, never to be heard of again. Amen."

Our route took us through Pilsen to Prague, and the Czechs received us with a warmth and welcome I shall never forget. "From a concentration camp!" they would exclaim, wringing their hands, and they would give us places to stay, free train tickets, meals, and money. At the frontier town of Dziedzice we regained our native land, a matter-of-fact homecoming without sentimental outbursts. We were drops in the ocean of concentration camp prisoners and forced laborers flowing in from all directions. We had all suffered and there was no place for public shows of sympathy. At a YMCA hostel where Edek and I spent one night, we overheard a fellow repatriate, still in his striped concentration camp uniform, saying to an acquaintance, "I thought we were finally rid of them, but there seem to be quite a few coming back." His voice was filled with sincere concern; he was referring to the Jewish survivors of the Nazi extermination program.

The next morning we reached Katowice and as we walked the streets we were followed by a man neither of us knew. From time to time he ran ahead of us to stare fixedly at Edek and then, finally, came up to us and whispered incredulously, "Edek?" Never had I seen a man more deeply shaken. He simply stood there wringing his hands, staring wide-eyed, and scarcely able to speak. "You're alive . . . you're alive," he said over and over again. From him Edek learned that Hanka was alive, working as a secretary in the Central Committee of Polish Jews in Warsaw. We ran to the Katowice office of the Committee and in a few minutes Edek was talking to Hanka on the long-distance telephone.

The Katowice Committee gave us train tickets to Warsaw and some old German uniforms. Wearing those we left in a crowded train for the capital and, though we got seats in the same car, Edek and I were separated. We traveled all night, an agonizing night for me. I was happy for Edek, his wanderings were over at last. We had become close as brothers, having been through so much together, but now I was all alone. He was home . . . but was I? I sat in that crowded, smoky car and prayed that my Wlodek was alive, for the sake of his mother, for my sake, and tears streamed down my face against my will. When we got to Warsaw, I felt humble and subdued.

The train stopped at the West Station, which is in an outlying quarter of the city, and the crowds there were so animated it was hard to believe we were in a city that had been completely devastated. On the square in front of the station were carts, carriages, and trucks waiting for passengers. We got into a vehicle going to Praga and the drive took us along the Jerusalem Boulevard toward the Vistula. This part of the city was almost intact and gradually I began to hope that what we had heard about the city's destruction was exaggerated. But when we reached the Main Station I was as jolted as two years before when I had said good-by to the burning ghetto from a cattle car: all my despair and agony returned, all my efforts had been in vain, there was no hope because the center of the city was a burned-out cinder.

We drove along the Vistula toward the pontoon bridge which carried all traffic while the Kierbiedz Bridge was being repaired. Across the river I could see Praga, which had been occupied by the Red Army while Warsaw on the left bank was being systematically destroyed by the Germans during the 1944 uprising. Because Praga had remained relatively intact all government and social-service offices were now located there. The Central Committee of Polish Jews had offices at 6 Szeroka Street. A guard stood at the entrance and a broad staircase led to the second floor. Edek walked up first, and I stayed below, not wanting to be there when he and Hanka met.

A few minutes later I went up and Edek introduced me to Hanka. She told us that Jewish survivors were coming to the Committee from camps, from the woods, from hiding places, to report that they were alive and to find their friends and relatives. Most needed help and the Committee was compiling a careful register of all survivors. When I told her I was looking for my son, she smiled at me warmly, but her eyes were hesitant. Suddenly, she asked, "What's his name?"

"Wlodek, Wlodek Berg."

"But I've seen him; he came here a few days ago, with his mother. . . ."

My heart sank. "If he was with his mother, that couldn't be my son."

"A little, fair-haired boy. An urchin of a boy! Wlodzio. Yes, he was here with a lady, but maybe she wasn't his mother. . . . But I remember it clearly, he called her 'Mother.'" Hanka stopped, embarrassed, as if saying to herself that she must not arouse hopes in this man just in case she was mistaken. . . . "You say she's a pharmacist? I think she works for the Committee, in our own pharmacy. It's only a few steps away, 44 Targowa Street."

I don't know how I made those blocks to Targowa Street. I don't remember how I walked up the stairs. Someone opened the door for me. In the lobby, facing the entrance, no more than three yards away, stood Lena. She looked as if she was waiting for someone. My head was suddenly filled with blinding light and colored circles whirled and exploded around me. Someone held me up.

When I came to I kept saying over and over, "Do you know what happened? Do you know what happened?"

Gently, Lena put both hands on my chest, and said affectionately, "Now, now, calm down. . . ."

Next to us stood Edek and Hanka, weeping loudly, and strangers crowded around us sobbing, too.

PART II

———

OTHER VOICES

CHAPTER 7

LENA'S STORY

I WAS HORRIFIED by what Michal looked like when he came to the women's field to say good-by to me before leaving for Radom. Eight weeks of Majdanek had reduced him to a real *"Muselman,"* emaciated and pale, with legs so swollen that he could not much longer escape the gas chamber. I thanked God that he was leaving Majdanek, for I saw that he was at the end of his tether, though he assured me that he felt fine. The day he left, I was seized by terrible longing to be with him and I cried all that night.

When we first came to Majdanek the barracks had been bare and we had slept on the floors. There was no place to wash and we were not admitted to the *Waschbaracke.* We did not have enough soup bowls to go around and we had to share with one other person. I had to share mine with a Gypsy, filthy and covered with sores, who took four swallows of soup for every one I did. I was nauseated, but hunger was stronger than disgust.

A few days later I was surprised to see another woman wearing the lovely tailored suit, blue with rust-colored stripes, I had worn when I arrived at Majdanek. It had been taken away from me while I was in the shower room and now a Barrack Elder was wearing it. When I saw it on her, I appreciated just how lovely the suit was.

After a few weeks many women began to be bloated with hunger; they were covered with sores, ulcers, and rashes; the overwhelming majority had stopped menstruating. The so-called *Lagerseherinnen* (camp wardresses) circulated everywhere in the women's field. Dressed in gray uniforms, these degenerate viragos were armed with riding crops, which they used ruthlessly on the inmates.

At first I was assigned to a Kommando which planted vegetables, and the constant stooping gave me sharp pains in the back, so that I couldn't stand up straight. Later, I was made Barrack Nurse and my job was to dress minor wounds. The advantages were that I no longer had to work outdoors and that I received an extra portion of soup. I could also exempt patients with minor complaints from work. Those who were seriously ill I sent to the infirmary.

I received my baptism of fire one day when a girl with an ulcer on her leg asked me to exempt her from work. I was arranging that when suddenly our Barrack Elder, a seventeen-year-old girl from a good Warsaw family, wrenched a board loose from a bunk and began to beat me over the head and spine with it, simultaneously showering me with abuse. I was so stunned that I simply stood there, making no attempt to escape, and the girl's mother, who had known me in Warsaw, berated her. "You keep out of this, Mother," the girl threatened, "or you'll get it, too." Finally, however, the girl calmed down and from that day treated me with the greatest respect.

Two weeks after our arrival all the children were shipped out. Many mothers voluntarily accompanied them to their deaths.

Most of the camp jobs were held by Slovak Jewish women and by Gentile Polish women. They were among the oldest inmates and told us bloodcurdling stories about the period in Majdanek before our arrival and they shuddered with horror every time they spoke about one of the wardresses who was an SS member and a sexual pervert. During roll call she would pick out a girl from among those lined up who, despite the malnutrition, still had a good figure. Then she would attack that girl with her riding crop, aiming for her breasts, and when the victim fell screaming to the ground, the blows would fall on her abdomen. Finally the wardress would kick the wretched creature in the pelvis with her hobnailed boots and the girl, howling like nothing human, would crawl away on hands and knees, leaving a trail of blood behind her. The monster followed with delight every detail of the girl's agony. The victim usually died shortly thereafter of hemorrhage.

I never witnessed such a scene, but I saw countless selections; in fact, my whole stay at Majdanek was one long selection. Every roll call was a selection: women were sent to the gas chamber because they had swollen legs, scratches on their bodies, because they wore eyeglasses or head kerchiefs, or because they stood roll call without head kerchiefs. Young SS men prowled among the inmates and took down their numbers; during the evening roll call the women were ordered to step forward, and we never saw them again. Maria Keiler, a childhood friend and schoolmate, died that way. She had a scratch on her leg and an SS man took her number. When they singled her out at roll call she simply walked away without even nodding good-by. She knew quite well where she was going, and I knew it, too; I was surprised at how little upset I was.

In addition, there were the ordinary selections in which at the cry of *"Lagersperre! Antreten!"* all of us had to line up in ranks of five, stark naked, and march past one or another of the young SS men. The women who had sons older than these men were always the most embarrassed. The SS man was always flanked by two wardresses. In his gloved hand he held a riding crop and with the familiar gesture he would flick it, right or left. Stefa Feltens, the well-known pianist, was the victim of one such selection and I can still hear her heart-rending animal screams as the wardresses beat and dragged her to the group of those who were going to die.

Shortly after Michal's departure there were rumors that a big hospital was to be built in the camp and that all doctors, pharmacists, dentists, and nurses would have to be registered. Around July 15, 1943, when candidates for shipments elsewhere were chosen, women in those categories were automatically exempted. Such winnowing was done in the morning, after roll call. Jewish Kommandos were not marched off to work, and the strongest inmates who had official jobs formed a chain by joining hands in a circle around the entire field. All the other inmates filed past the SS man, who picked out the sturdiest. Each was asked her occupation and those selected were sent to the camp office, where they were stripped, passed a second inspection, and had their names put on a list for the next transport. Those rejected there were sent back to their barracks. When my turn came I was picked to be shipped, but when the SS man heard that I was a pharmacist he sent me back to the barracks. I was very uneasy, though I couldn't tell quite why. I had a job in Majdanek; I was known and respected; I never had to leave the field; I was relatively well off and got an extra portion of soup; and most important, Michal had explicitly told me not to leave the camp. Yet I was nervous because for the past two weeks the youngest and strongest of us had been chosen for shipment and the older women left behind. I didn't like that. Sitting on my bunk, wondering what to do, I suddenly heard the shout of a young Ukrainian boy who had arrived at Majdanek with his entire village. He was pointing at me and yelling at the top of his lungs: "A Jewess! She's hiding! A Jewess!"

As if in a trance, driven by some irresistible inner compulsion, I jumped off my bunk, ran out of the barrack, and slipped through the human chain. Perhaps taken by surprise, perhaps because they knew me, the women in the chain let me through. Perhaps they simply thought I wanted to say good-by to someone. I ran toward the office, but just outside I saw Ola Kacenelenbogen approaching the SS man. Quickly I beckoned to her, indicating that I was on the shipment, and I somehow conveyed to her that she must not reveal her real occupation. A moment later she was at my side, surprised but compliant.

It was the last shipment that left Majdanek. We were the last women in the last row of the column. The clerk, a Polish woman I knew, was astonished. "What's the matter with you? Have you lost your mind? You have a job, a hospital is going to be set up, and you don't want to stay. How do you know you're not going to be taken to be made soap of?"

"Never mind. Put me on the list."

"But your profession . . . ?"

"Please, put down that I'm a seamstress."

She shrugged her shoulders and put me on the list. Those chosen were taken to one of the men's fields and locked in a barrack. That night I heard unusual rustling and giggling, and before long the whole darkened barrack was full of sexual noises.

I did not sleep that night. Now that I had emerged from my trance I was horrified at what I had done, and I could not understand why I had done it. But it was too late to change my mind. Next morning I was in a cattle car heading west: we knew we were on our way to Auschwitz, but that made no impression on us. We reached there in the morning and were unloaded at the railhead, ordered to form ranks on the rail platform, and were marched off without a selection being made.

That was July 1943. Auschwitz was at the peak of its macabre career as an international death factory. To the "old camp," new ones were added: Budy, Harmenze, the Rajsko estate, and worst of all, Birkenau. Like a horrible gorging spider, Birkenau kept expanding—and that was where we went, to the *Frauenlager* Birkenau.

The formalities were the same as at Majdanek, except that the admissions barrack was called *Saune*. We were told to strip; male barbers shaved our heads and the rest of our bodies with clippers. A girl rubbed each of us under the arms and between the legs with a rag dipped in some disinfectant and then we were showered and given clothes on which there was an indelible red stripe running down the back. We were also given head kerchiefs. After that numbers were tattooed on our forearms. Several prisoners sat on low stools and as new arrivals went up to them in turn, they made adroit pricks in the skin with a tattoo needle on the left forearm. It was not too painful, but every prick of that needle pierced my heart. My number was 49397. I was also given a red triangle to be sewed on my clothing, which had the same number on it. When I looked around for Ola after these ceremonies, we could barely recognize each other.

We were then registered, since apparently we had been sent from Majdanek without documents. And so, when asked my profession, I replied, "Pharmacist." After registration, someone asked if there was anyone there with medical experience; I stepped forward with another inmate I had never seen before. We were told that we were assigned to the hospital, but first had to be quarantined. That consisted in being confined to a barrack for some time, and then we were sent to the hospital barrack but still not assigned to any special job.

One day Ena, a pretty young Slovak, who was chief doctor at the hospital, came by with the hospital Kapo, Orli, a graceful little brunette, and Rhode, a German physician. He listened to an account of my professional experience and said he was appointing me chief of the pharmacy soon to be set up in the hospital barrack. Thus my stay at Auschwitz began well, but for the time being I had to wait.

A short while later we received a large shipment of prisoners from Bedzin-Sosnowiec, who were said to have brought quantities of food, gold, and jewels with them. The shipment was immediately decimated by a selection at the railroad platform. Judith, a dentist from Sosnowiec who arrived on that shipment was assigned to the dentistry office, but she too had to wait for a job. I kept after Ena because I felt insecure without employment, a dangerous status when any selection was being made, until one day she told me bluntly, "Forget about the pharmacy. There is no vacancy there."

"But Dr. Rhode appointed me chief of the pharmacy."

"Well, someone else got the pharmacy, so you'll be a doctor."

"But I'm not a doctor, I'm a pharmacist."

"Can you take temperatures and dress a wound? That's enough. And don't be so finicky. There are women in the hospital who don't even know that much. A special infirmary for Jewish prisoners is being set up soon and you'll work there. We're short of doctors because the old ones are sent directly to the gas chambers, and the young ones don't have enough experience."

At last the infirmary was set up. Besides Judith, the dentist, and myself, the staff included Roza, a doctor; a Polish woman orderly; and Cyla, a pretty clerk whose husband was a rabbi from Bielsk. She owed her job to the same kind of pious Slovak women who held key posts at Birkenau as they had at Majdanek, and always did what they could for rabbis and their families.

When at last the infirmary was set up it consisted of an admissions room and a smaller room with two triple-decker bunks where we slept. Actually the infirmary was no more than a first-aid station and twice a day, after morning and evening roll calls, prisoners reported to us. They stood in line and one by one passed through the barbed-wire fence which surrounded the hospital area. We had some ointments, paper bandages, ersatz iodine, adhesive tape, and for medicaments, the inevitable aspirin. With them we had to deal with abscesses of all varieties, often in the most painful places, under the arms, in the crotch, on the neck, and so on. Old dressings were usually thrown into a pail and before long the room reeked from the revolting stink of pus, blood, and unwashed bodies. Vermin teemed under the old bandages, pus oozed from open sores which refused to heal, and paper bandages would not stay in place. Still patients were always greatly relieved when their dressings were changed. Serious cases such as those with high temperatures or those requiring surgery were sent to the hospital. I soon became expert at giving injections. German Barracks Elders and Kapos would come to me for intravenous injections of glucose and Neosalvarsan for syphilis, but they had to bring their own vials of those drugs, for we had nothing so grand in the way of medicines. For these extra services I was rewarded with a piece of bread, a bit of margarine, sugar, or even a sweater. As a result, my situation began to improve. We cooked our own food on a little stove and we had even organized white aprons, and the girls from the Canada detail brought us underwear. Eventually, we were exempted from roll calls and merely reported the number employed at the infirmary—five at first, six later—and that was all.

During the long autumn and winter evenings of 1943 and 1944, I talked for hours on end with Judith and we learned about each other's lives in the greatest detail, as only two prisoners can. Judith knew all about Michal, about our life together, and every one of Wlodek's "cute sayings." I, in turn, learned that she had studied dentistry in France, at Nancy, and spoke French, German, Hebrew, English, Italian, Yiddish, and Polish. An intelligent, reserved woman, she had, underneath her shyness and matter-of-factness, a warm, affectionate heart. I came to love her as if she were my own sister, and I was glad to have her there to help me bear the experience of Auschwitz. Originally she had come from a large family, but had suffered crippling losses—in Auschwitz she had lost a husband, two children, parents, and sisters—and was now alone. Watching her, I was once again amazed at human vitality, its powers of resistance to suffering and to the blows of fate.

I spent a year and a half at Auschwitz, and I was lucky, incredibly lucky. I lived through that time as if inside an ivory tower just on the edge of an inferno that still cries out for its Dante. How was I able to survive? Why didn't I have a nervous breakdown, at the very least? Why did my will to live remain unbroken? The answer is simple, perhaps too simple: I did not see; I did not hear; I did not want to see or hear or know. I wanted to live. When I got there, I was already a graduate of two great universities of human suffering—the Warsaw ghetto and Majdanek; I had already developed a heart of stone and nerves of steel, although that is at best a metaphor. I, who had formerly almost died of fright at the sight of a mouse, now slept at Auschwitz with enormous rats crawling back and forth over my face. I handled corpses without either fear or disgust. I trampled on human ashes but refused to permit myself to be aware of it. Not only my nerves, but my very senses were blunted, and I succeeded in creating in myself an induced amnesia: I simply did not dwell on the horrors I was living through.

At the same time I drove away the memories of my brothers, my sister, my sister-in-law Roza, the people I loved. I refused them admittance to my heart and mind so that I might not loose heart and mind. Like a snail, I curled up inside my shell and was cut off from the outside world. I never looked into the faces of the murderers and only once, by accident, did I see a procession of the doomed being led to a gas chamber. I refused to consider what my own end would be like. I knew only one thing: I had a son in Warsaw and I *must* stay alive. Perhaps that was all a form of insanity, perhaps it was my instinct of self-preservation but in any case, deafness and blindness were my armor. I went through a hundred selections and never once was afraid I would be chosen to die, not because I had no physical defects, took care of myself, and was plump by nature, but because the thought simply never occurred to me. When I was hungry—and for all my relatively privileged position, hunger often twisted my vitals—I was like an animal. I did not think, I did not remember, I forgot my husband and my child; and I thought only about one thing: bread.

But when hunger was allayed, the food stuck in my throat. Then I trembled for my child, wondered if he was ill, whether he cried out for me in his sleep, or would betray his origin when he ran a fever. It did not occur to me that he might be hungry, nor did I doubt for a moment that he was alive and that I would find him again. Nor did I doubt that Michal would survive the war. Everyone around me said I was stupid, and though I noticed their compassionate glances, I did not for a moment lose my faith. My personality was split: my brain knew what was happening, that we were all doomed; but my heart, or my animal instinct, remained confident and secure in the face of all the evidence. In a phrase, I silenced my reason.

Of course, all that only served to *facilitate* my survival, not to guarantee it: actually I survived Auschwitz because some merciful hand protected me. Beginning with that miraculous departure from Majdanek right up to my incredibly lucky return to Warsaw, one miracle after another kept me alive. And finally I had the luck to find faithful, devoted friends with whom I could share my life at Auschwitz.

For those reasons I am neither competent nor accurate in chronicling the monstrosity that was Auschwitz. I never saw the gas chamber because I didn't want to see it, but I did see smoke rising from the crematoria chimneys twenty-four hours a day and the scarlet glow over them at night, and day and night I smelled the acrid fumes of burning human flesh and bones. I did not see the little white house in a birchwood to which were driven crowds of people just off trains, which had brought them from every corner of Europe. There were days when the smoke covered the entire heavens like a thick shroud as if to make people forget there had ever been a sky, as if the murderers had no more to fear and those to be murdered could understand finally that there was no hope left anywhere.

I was not present at the selection in the hospital when several hundred French girls were taken away. When the horrible shouts of *"Lagersperre!"* rang out, and we heard the sound of trucks stopping in the hospital area, our hearts almost stopped beating and we huddled close to the walls of our barrack. We heard nothing. But when the engines started again and the trucks drove off, their headlights blazing in the dark, carrying these French women to their deaths, the sound of the *Marseillaise* rang out in the stillness of the night. I shall never forget that. The song grew, stronger and more powerful, filling every corner of the darkness and tearing at our hearts as we stood there frozen with fear and horror. It was a herald of some terrible day of wrath and it reached up into the perpetual scarlet glow that never faded from the night sky.

I did see Greek women "going to the gas." They had been brought to Auschwitz only weeks before, slender, black-eyed Salomes, homesick for their sunny land and huddled together against the sleet and cold of the northern October. They sang a sentimental song called *Mama*, whose melody made one weep. In a few weeks Auschwitz had withered those exotic flowers, their fiery eyes had become dull in sunken sockets, empty and dead. Emaciated, dirty, repulsive, those Greek women could barely drag themselves around. Once so shapely, they now had legs like sticks and their breasts hung like bags. Their complexions, made velvet smooth by the southern sun, were now covered with horrible abscesses, vermin bites, and the marks of scabies incessantly scratched. They stank of gangrene, dysentery, unwashed sweat, and wretchedness.

When they went to their deaths they sang the *Hatikvah*, that song of undying hope, the song of an old people, which has always carried the vision of Zion in its heart. Since then, every time I hear *Hatikvah* I always see them, the dregs of human misery, and I know that through mankind flows a stream of eternity greater and more powerful than individual deaths.

I cannot describe even a fraction of the horror that was Auschwitz, but what I did see was enough to make me lose forever the notion that man was created in the likeness of God.

Every day was like the next and then one evening, when a particularly large crowd stood outside waiting, a column of trucks drove up and out of nowhere. SS men, wardresses, and Barracks Elders appeared. A moment later the crowd in front of the infirmary was in the iron embrace of a "living chain." There was no selection, nobody bothered to inspect the young but disfigured bodies. Orders were barked, whips cracked, victims were loaded onto the trucks. The engines roared, the headlights flashed, and it was finished, the last screams of the women going to their deaths growing fainter in the darkness.

For a few days the infirmary was empty; the prisoners, afraid, stayed away. But with or without selections, the gas chamber threatened and eventually the infirmary was full again.

Auschwitz was a combination of Majdanek *and* the burning Warsaw ghetto. Perhaps the beatings were crueler at Majdanek, but then Auschwitz was several times larger, more "modern" and efficient. As in the last days of the ghetto the smoke and flame lit the skies and darkened them, but here we were no longer so sensitive to life-and-death matters as we had been in the Warsaw ghetto. We had lived our deaths in Warsaw. What survived of us now was only a cattle-car incarnation. They could destroy us, but they could no longer kill us: we were already dead.

One of my visitors at the infirmary was Aranka, an eighteen-year-old Slovak girl with unforgettable green eyes. She was a typical Auschwitz product, hard, pitiless, and alert. I treated her for a sore on the hand. She had been brought to the camp at sixteen, and from the railhead her father, mother, and younger sister had been sent straight to the gas chamber. Aranka was not afraid of beatings, but she couldn't bear hunger. Once when her Barrack Elder sneaked a lover into the barrack, Aranka smiled at him and he was bewitched by those fathomless green eyes. She gave herself to him right behind the partition in the barrack, on the floor, for a piece of bread, and the Barrack Elder caught them at it. She called Aranka a whore, took the piece of bread away, and beat the girl bloody. Later, that same Barrack Elder said it was a pity to let brutal males take advantage of such a pretty girl so Aranka became the woman's lover and thereby got herself appointed office clerk.

Another patient was Eva, from Kielce. She was well off, she told me, because her brother worked in the Sonderkommando; his job—driving the people into the gas chamber. He had everything and thought only of her, but she cried all the time for fear he too, would be liquidated because all such members of the Sonderkommando were sooner or later. They knew too much and had seen too much. One day she told me her brother had just visited her, terribly upset.

"You know, Eva," he said in a strange voice, "I saw Mother . . ."

"Mother?" Eva began to tremble and was afraid to ask any more.

"A shipment came from Plaszow. Straight to the gas chamber. I was there, loading the chamber. You know how I try not to look at them. Then, suddenly I heard a cry and sobs, 'My little boy!' I raised my eyes and my heart stopped. She hadn't changed. Meanwhile we were holding things up, the Kapo was screaming at me, and the SS men were coming toward us.

"'Mother, I'm doing my job now,' I told her. 'This is very responsible work, and they're very strict here. Go take a shower now and after work I'll come and get you. You'll stay with Eva. She's here, too. You'll be all right with us.'

"She looked at me with love in her eyes, you remember how she used to be. 'You've grown so tall and strong, my little boy,' she said, and stroked my hair. And then she went. . . ."

Early in 1944, Judith caught typhus. It was a time of cruel selections in the hospital area, so we decided to keep her in the infirmary. She had been sleeping in the lowest bunk, but we moved her up to the top bunk, mine, near the wall. When I knew a German was coming, I made the bed in such a way that it looked empty. Somehow we managed to get the work done without her, and when anyone asked for her, we said she'd gone to get something at the hospital.

I slept in her bunk, knowing full well that my turn would come in exactly two weeks. We had been able to move Judith, but the infected lice remained, and two weeks was the typhus incubation period. I was not wrong. Just as Judith passed the crisis of the disease, I began to have the typical typhus symptoms: high temperature, dizziness, shivering. The disease took a severer form with me: I raved and screamed in delirium, and dreamed incessantly that someone was stealing my food. I begged for an apple. Now I slept on the upper bunk, covered with a blanket, and the poor women trembled with fear that I would begin my raving when strangers were there. Ola, who had been working as a nurse in one of the hospital barracks, spent every free moment she had with me. Later on, she too got typhus, but she did not recover. So my oldest friend died, friend of my childhood long before I even knew Michal and married, and long my colleague and fellow worker. I gave her an Auschwitz funeral; that is, I wrapped her in a sheet and placed her on the pile of corpses behind our barrack to be taken to the crematorium.

No sooner had I finished my bout with typhus than the camp was deloused. For a day I lay on the cold stove that ran along the middle of the barrack and when I tried to get up that evening, I almost fainted. I had lumbago and the slightest movement was agonizing; to make things worse, there was very little food and I was ravenously hungry, with the appetite of the typhus convalescent twisting my insides. To add to that I received another blow. A new group of Polish women came to us and from them I learned the fate of the Lublin camps. I had been lucky to escape, but my brothers and their wives had been at Trawniki, and poor Izak Rubin along with so many others had been left at Majdanek. The ring of death drew tighter around me, but I refused to think about it.

More and more patients suffered from scabies. Allegedly, the Greek women had brought it into the camp, but now the scabies attacked all nationalities indiscriminately. We treated it with sulphur and Mitigal, of which we had only a very small supply. But our struggle against scabies was, under the sanitary conditions prevailing in the camp, hopeless. It became so great a problem that the notorious Dr. Joseph Mengele, the Nazi monster physician who conducted his experiments on human beings, began to take special interest in it. His previous idées fixes had been twins, then crossed eyes and other optical disorders, but now he added scabies. He began to call quite often and required reports to be submitted to him continually.

At that time Auschwitz had its great love affair. Every community has its legend, its myth; that of Auschwitz was a romance involving Mala, a girl who worked as a messenger, and her lover, a Warsaw Pole who also had a camp job. Though Mala had been deported from Belgium, she had been born in Poland. She was proficient in several languages, and universally admired in the camp for her intelligence and beauty. One day all Auschwitz was electrified by the news that Mala and her lover had escaped, he in an SS uniform and she in that of a wardress. They had had all the necessary documents and got by the guards easily. To all of us this was an impossible dream come true and the prisoners' pinched, starved faces lit up with smiles. Mala's fate became our main concern. They had escaped, we told ourselves; they were free and happy.

A few weeks later we learned that they had been caught, and were being kept in an underground dungeon and tortured to reveal the names of those who had helped them to escape. The man insisted that he alone was responsible, that he had persuaded Mala to run away with him, and had himself stolen the documents and the uniforms. We refused to believe that they had actually been captured, but alas, it was true. They had been caught in Cracow when he called at some office for papers. Mala was waiting for him outside on the stairs and when she saw the Germans leading him out, she went with him.

We were standing roll call when Mala was brought back to camp. She was to be publicly hanged as a warning to the other prisoners that no one could escape from Auschwitz, that the only way out was via the crematorium chimney. Mala stood in front of the SS men's barracks, pale and calm, and the hearts of the thousands of women who watched her pounded with hers. She had disappointed them when her audacious dream of happiness and freedom had collapsed, but she was not going to disappoint them now. No one knew how Mala got the razor blade; it was said that some charitable soul had slipped it to her earlier, when she was being questioned. Now she suddenly produced it and, before everyone, quickly slashed both wrists, severing the veins. An SS man ran up to seize the razor blade and she punched him in the face, screaming, "Get away from me, you dirty dog!"

The Oberkapo strode up to her and said, "You stupid Jewish whore, you thought you'd outsmart us, did you, that you could escape? You swine, is that how you show gratitude for our kindness?"

Mala had fallen to her knees, blood spurting from her wounds. Suddenly, she staggered to her feet and cried out in a terrible loud voice, "I know I'm dying, but it doesn't matter. What matters is that you are dying, too, and your gangster Reich with you. Your hours are numbered and pretty soon you'll be paying for your crimes!"

The SS men knocked her down and shot her. Then they dumped her into a handcart and several women were ordered to pull the cart around the camp so everyone could see it. Thousands of women stood there in the setting sun saying farewell to Mala. Later it was said that she was still alive when they threw her into the crematorium furnace.

Mala's death shocked the camp to the core. She had been our golden dream, a single ray of light in our dark lives. Prisoners who might momentarily be taken to the gas chamber, who lived in the shadow of the crematoria through which millions of human beings had gone up in smoke, wept bitterly when Mala was killed. One death moves the imagination more powerfully than millions; one death is a drama throbbing with emotion; a million, only dry-as-ashes statistics.

A short time later a shipment of Jewish women arrived from Majdanek, all of them sturdy and young, the pick of the camp. After the November massacres they stayed on to sort the clothing of the murdered. They were three hundred veterans of camp life, they had been through hell, and they knew what was in store for them. They had already seen too much and they knew they would be sent to the gas chamber, so they resolved to resist. But the Germans got wind of that and they were not sent straight from the train to the gas chamber. Instead, they were sent to the camp, were shaved and given showers, their names recorded in the files, and then assigned to a barrack. That night, while they were asleep, the trucks drove up, the SS men with submachine guns loaded the kicking, scratching women onto the trucks, and took them directly to the crematorium.

As the German Army retreated from Russia, camps were evacuated and prisoners sent to Auschwitz from all points of the compass. In May we began to receive shipments from Hungary, then the entire Lodz ghetto. Auschwitz was now in a fever of killing, a bacchanalia of murder; the Germans were in a hurry to kill as many of us as possible while the war was still on, while we were still under their heel. Night and day, load after load of people were driven directly to the birchwood. No one bothered with selections any longer. The four crematoria belched their acrid smoke, the two big ditches where the bodies of the gassed were burned over wooden pyres gave off its noxious stench, and the other prisoners watched horror-stricken. Darker smoke hung in low clouds over the open ditches and when the wind was right, it blew over the camp and put out the sun; it was truly darkness at noon and we were paralyzed with fear.

In this fashion unprecedented wealth came to Auschwitz. The men and women of the Canada, the *Werterfassung* of Auschwitz, worked overtime sorting the loot which deportees from every corner of Europe brought to Auschwitz with them. The Canada Kommando reached a peak of prosperity and SS men had food, clothing, pockets full of looted diamonds, gold, and other valuables, and some of it dribbled down to the lowest rungs of the camp hierarchy. The wealth of generations of Hungarian Jewry ended up at the railhead of Auschwitz and from there flowed in a tidal wave into the Reich.

The new arrivals had no idea that they were going to their deaths. Occasionally they put a question to an old inmate, which suggested their nervous foreboding, but it was the unwritten law of Auschwitz to conceal the truth, the only form compassion took in that benighted place. What good would it do to tell them? So the new arrivals walked along, calmly enough, passing the newly built sports field, on toward the wood where the little white house awaited them. Nor were the "permanent" residents of the camp ignored. One night in May all the Gypsies, whole tribes of them, went to the gas chamber. For two years they served to provide the Germans with subjects for "scientific study"; now the experiment was over, they were sent to their deaths.

Early in August, I learned that the entire camp of Radom had arrived, and I couldn't believe my luck: Michal, my Michal, would be right there with me. I'd be able to see him, speak to him, embrace him. I'd get him a soft job somewhere. I pulled every string I knew, and for three days at morning and evening roll calls in all male barracks, the order, "Michal Berg, step forward!" resounded. But no Michal Berg stepped forward and my joy turned to despair. The logic of Auschwitz was simple and inexorable: if a man was not in the camp, he had been taken to the gas chamber. Perhaps yesterday, while I was eating my soup or even humming a tune, no more than half a mile away, Michal. . . . I felt as if I were falling into a bottomless pit. But I was crushed by sorrow and despair for no more than a few hours because then someone from the central office came to tell me that the Radom shipment had only stopped at Auschwitz in transit, and then been sent on to Germany. But the women's camp of Radom remained.

That same night I was able to speak to some of the Radom women. One told me that Michal was alive, but that he looked seedy. "How he mourned for you. He thought you'd perished at Majdanek." I would have given anything just to see him then, for a moment, to assure him that I was still alive. Another of the Radom women told me that Michal had had mistresses by the score in Radom. "The dead have no right to be jealous. As far as Michal's concerned, I'm dead. Wasn't he told that I perished at Majdanek? Didn't he mourn me? If that helps him to survive, why not?" I answered her casually. But afterward I cried all night in my bunk.

Shortly thereafter, Mengele decided to carry out some of his scabies experiments, and we were told that our infirmary was being liquidated. A special scabies barrack would be set up in Barrack 25. We would still be part of the hospital though housed in one of the ordinary barracks outside the special hospital compound. This was a double blow. We would have to stand roll call and, more important, Barrack 25 had special connotations because it was the antechamber to the crematorium where prisoners who failed to pass the selections were collected. We had been afraid of Barrack 25 since we had come to Birkenau. When we heard the whistle and the field echoed with cries of *"Lagersperre"* terror gripped us. Every prisoner left her barrack and a moment later the order rang out: *"Jüdinnen, antreten! Zählappell."* (Jewesses, line up! Roll call!) The Jewish barracks lined up, the unfortunate women pinching their cheeks, hiding behind one another, trying to keep out of the front row. The Barracks Elders and orderlies cursed and beat them until finally an SS man appeared, accompanied by a wardress and the *Lagerkapo*. One after the other the women would be ordered to strip. Sores to the right; abscesses to the right; rashes to the right; flabby breasts to the right. Eyeglasses to the right. The chain formed by camp officials holding hands separated the rejected from the more fortunate inmates.

Half an hour later those selected to die would be marched slowly to Barrack 25. An hour before they had all been fighting for a piece of bread, for an assignment to a Kommando, for a thousand and one other trivial things living people are concerned with. Now it was all over. The Kapo would be very impatient: why did such carrion move so slowly? And she would urge them on with kicks and abuse.

Barrack 25 got no food. Prisoners sat there locked up for hours, sometimes for days, without food, without a swallow of water, without toilet facilities, dying before their deaths. For Auschwitz was governed by a strict rule: Berlin always had to confirm the gassing of those selected and, occasionally, confirmation was delayed. Berlin had plenty of other things to attend to. From that death barrack came screaming and lamentation, "Water, for God's sake, a little water." But no one responded. No one walked over to that barrack, no one ever gave the dying water. Helplessly, hands stretched out between the bars, imploring, but in vain. Barrack 25 was taboo.

When it was dark the trucks came for them, headlights flashing, engines roaring up, then silenced. When the engines started again there was the screaming, the last horrible cries of the women taken to the gas chamber.

It was in this barrack that Dr. Mengele decided to start his experiments. Bathtubs were set up and while the prisoners were bathing, sulphur in *statu nascendi* would come from the water with a horrible stench, but the results were nil. When one day the Aryans were transferred and Barrack 25 was reserved exclusively for Jewish women, we knew what that meant and we trembled lest we be taken with the patients. A few days later the trucks drove up and the infirmary staff was ordered to help load the patients. I ran and hid behind the barrack, seized by sudden weakness and thinking I would faint. Orli, the hospital Kapo, discovered me. "Do you think you're better than the rest of us? Do you think I enjoy loading trucks for the gas chamber? Get back to work!"

I walked slowly back to the front of the barrack, but it was all over. The trucks were about to leave.

What was the purpose of all this macabre comedy? All this nonsense about hospitals and treatment for women doomed to die. Why the cynical masquerade? Why didn't they just send us all to the gas chamber and get it over with?

After the scabies barrack was liquidated, Mengele came back to see Judith and me. Judith's German was better than mine and her answers apparently more satisfactory because a few days later I was transferred to the hospital while Judith was assigned to Field C, the Gypsies' former camp, now occupied by Hungarian Jewish women. Though formerly shipments from Hungary had been sent directly from the railhead to the gas chambers, now selections were made and part of each shipment was saved for the camp. Parting from Judith, after we had shared good and bad fortune for almost a year, was very painful to me.

When the Hungarian influx had ended, Auschwitz began to slow down. In October 1944, the gassing stopped and later, after a mutiny by the Sonderkommando, the crematoria were dismantled and the Germans began to burn documents and remove traces of their crimes.

The last big shipment consisted of people deported from Warsaw after the uprising. Embittered and unhappy, they said that there was no trace of the city left, and that if there was such an address as 52 Pius Street, it was now only rubble. If the inhabitants were still alive, they'd been deported. My son in a camp? I knew what that meant. But the news only grazed my surface, it didn't sink in; nothing could dent my inner armor of confidence.

Hunger stalked the camp. With the increasing breakdown of transportation, we no longer got our regular rations. Partial evacuation began to other camps in the heart of Germany: Gross Rosen, Flossenbürg, Buchenwald. On one of those shipments Judith left and she came to say good-by to me. She had heard she was going to Bergen-Belsen. We parted, as if forever, and at the last moment I was so sorry for her that I pressed my portion of bread into her hand.

I now became close friends with Sarenka, a pharmacist who worked inside the hospital-area pharmacy. Sarenka came from a small town in Poland and had been taken to Majdanek about the same time I had. Handsome, from an Orthodox Jewish family, and brought up by her grandparents rather than her parents, she was intelligent if bossy. While I was optimistic, she had no hope whatever. As a result, we often quarreled, for she was always making remarks like, "The hell we'll survive! No one is going to survive!" And I would reply spitefully, "All right. You won't survive, but *I will!* Let me alone!"

When the final evacuation began, we could have stayed behind, but all our patients were staying and we were afraid to remain with them until the critical moment. And so, on January 18, 1945, we set out from Auschwitz. It was a death march. My recently acquired ski boots proved completely unsuitable and after a few miles I had swollen feet and would have been left by the roadside after one of the SS men hit me in the back with a rifle butt, except for the fact that some fellow prisoners dragged me on. Sarenka had a big can of Ovomaltine which we mixed with snow. It was very tasty, but two days later I was sick with diarrhea that almost cost me my life. We got to Breslau, but were sent on because all the camps were jam-packed. We were taken into Ravensbrück for a week, then shipped to Neustadt-Glöwen, where we dug trenches. Everything was now a matter of physical endurance; the food was wretched; we slept on the floor; and we were tormented by lice. Only by gritting our teeth could we go on. The spring was unusually warm and that helped us hold out until May 2, when the SS men failed to appear at roll call. A few hours later someone announced triumphantly that the gate was open.

We walked out and along the highway. From the right a tank draped with an American flag was coming our way and behind it tall, slender boys in American uniforms. They were terribly embarrassed when unappetizing creatures who bore only a remote resemblance to women suddenly threw themselves at them, kissing and hugging them. Back in the camp wild enthusiasm broke out. But I, who had unflinchingly believed that the moment would come, now for the first time felt bewildered and lost.

Two days later we noticed the greatly increased traffic on the highway: the German population was fleeing to the West. I was reminded of the resettlement days of the ghetto: endless processions of women, children, old men, but only rarely men in the prime of life. They pushed handcarts loaded with furniture and carried knapsacks, suitcases, and heavy bundles.

The Americans were about to withdraw and hand Neustadt-Glöwen over to the Soviet troops, and when the Germans heard that, they stampeded west, toward Bergen-Belsen.

Soon Neustadt-Glöwen was occupied by the Russians. The Soviet soldiers reacted to victory much more emotionally and intensely than had the Americans. They had paid dearly for their victory and they celebrated with all the forthrightness and lack of restraint characteristic of Slavs. The camp teemed with amorous couples, but the majority of the liberated women, despite their sympathy for their liberators and admiration for the Red Army's heroism, were reluctant to express their gratitude with their bodies. The Russians were unable to understand that and the situation led to sharp, and occasionally tragic, conflicts. "Aren't you our girls?" the Russians would say, surprised by the reluctance. "We shed our blood for you. We liberated you . . . and you refuse us a mere trifle?"

Intoxicated by victory and often literally drunk, they felt they were entitled to anything and everything. Several times they took women by brute force, and I shall never forget the heart-rending screams and tears of a fifteen-year-old girl raped by a Soviet private in the barracks in front of hundreds of women. "No! No! I don't want to!" the girl raved. We heard those words for a long time afterward.

Four of us decided to leave the barracks and moved into a two-story house abandoned by its owners. We now had furniture and kitchen utensils, a pretty little garden, and most important of all, a radio which broadcast in all languages the words "unconditional surrender." At night we could see from our windows hundreds of Soviet soldiers walking around with bottles of vodka sticking out of their pockets and duffel bags. They played mouth organs and accordions, and were always ready to have "some fun" and "relax a little." We sat in our little house fully dressed, not daring to turn on the lights or make a sound. We put the youngest of our group, Nelli, to bed with a big white bandage around her head and on the door we tacked a sign that read, "TYPHUS: No Admittance." Besides barricading our bedroom doors, we barricaded the door that led to another part of the house occupied by four other girls we didn't know. Our precautions were not exaggerated. Every night there were orgies in the other part of the house and Russians would pound at our door. In the morning our neighbors would shower us with abuse: "What's the idea, you play the little saints while we put out our asses for you?"

One night the Soviet commandant of the town gave a party to celebrate the end of the war. It was attended by a number of army officers, including some female officers, and several women from our camp. The commandant, an elderly colonel with a friendly face, gave a toast and someone played Russian tunes on the piano. I went up to the colonel and asked him to help me get to Warsaw. He looked at me attentively and said, "All right, come to my office tomorrow morning." When I appeared at his office the next morning with Sarenka, he flew into a towering rage. "What's this? You brought a chaperone? God knows, you're old enough to come by yourself! You don't have to pretend you're a virgin!"

I burst into tears and through my sobs told him that I hadn't gone through all the agonies of the ghetto and the concentration camps to be treated like a whore. I had a husband, and had left my son with strangers in Warsaw, and I had to get back to them.

"Are you insane?" he shouted. "What are you talking about? There is no Warsaw. Your husband, your child, they're gone, dead. Try to forget all that. You're still young, you can find another man. Do you have to kill yourself? You're a grown woman, you might be able to understand that we've been in the front lines for weeks, fighting continually, facing death every day, and that a soldier needs a woman. So that's what your petty bourgeois gratitude comes down to, that's what we've been fighting for. . . ." He grew so incensed by his own words that soon he was yelling: "Get out of here, you moron! I won't help you! You're on your own!"

I *was* on my own, and the next morning I set out with Sarenka for Warsaw.

The roads of Europe were like swollen mountain torrents in spring, a Babel of people and languages, all former slaves or prisoners of the Third Reich. Where there were no vehicles, they went on foot; they ate and slept either at hastily organized repatriation centers or in abandoned German houses, and sometimes they simply and summarily drove Germans out of their houses and installed themselves in their bedrooms. I was one of that endless crowd, slowly making my way east, always east. Occasionally we got a lift on a peasant's cart or a military truck, but mostly we walked, mile after mile. That was easy for me: I had survived Majdanek, Auschwitz, and Ravensbrück; I was free and on my way home to find my son.

We had to wait a long time before we were allowed to cross the pontoon bridge over the Oder. There were mile-long traffic jams caused by military vehicles, artillery, endless columns of infantry. I lost count of the days and nights, but each one brought me closer to Warsaw. We slept in barns and other out-of-the-way spots, occasionally in refugee centers and private homes, but we never lacked food: every door was open to people coming back from prison camps.

Finally we reached Poznán, where I took a direct train to Warsaw. The closer I got to the city, the more uneasy I grew. At first sight of the ruins of Warsaw I didn't shed a single tear, but my heart constricted with horror and helpless despair. How would I find my boy in those ruins?

At the offices of the Jewish Committee in Praga, I pored over the lists of survivors, but I couldn't find a single name I knew. We were given a meal and spent the night on the staircase outside the offices. At daybreak I walked across the bridge into Warsaw and headed for 52 Pius Street. It was a long way, but I went as if on wings. When I reached the corner of Pius and Marszalkowska Streets my heart sank. The whole block was a pile of rubble. I walked down the middle of the street along a path already made through the debris and tried to figure out where Number 52 had been. There was a lantern dangling from the remains of a wall on which I could see the number 58. I turned back and slowly counted off 58, 56, 54, 52. There were little cards stuck up on the walls, exactly like those after the shelling of Warsaw in 1939, and I read them all carefully, but there was no Maginski. I stood for an hour or two in front of what had once been 52 Pius Street. My mind was empty; I did not think or feel. There was no 52 Pius Street. It was gone. Here Wlodek had played, his laughter had echoed. Here I was to come and find him. I had kept my word, but now there was nothing. Fourth floor, rear. There was no rear, no floors, nothing.

Someone advised me to try the police and the Red Cross, the Maginskis might be registered under another address. Early next morning, after a sleepless night, I stood in an endless queue in front of the Red Cross office. My turn did not come until noon. The girl at the desk rummaged in the files for a long time, then finally shook her head. They had nothing there. But she would take my name and address, and if they heard anything. . . .

At the police station—the police were now called "The People's Militia"— the whole thing took no more than a minute. "We're sorry, Citizen, but they're not on our lists."

My strength began to ebb. I was penniless, the tramping about had left me famished, and I had no place to sleep. Then, luckily, I ran into an old friend, Dr. Matys Berlowicz, who with his family had survived the war on the Aryan side. They took me into their small apartment, fed me, and gave me a few zlotys.

The next morning, like a lunatic, I returned to Pius Street. I sat on a stone in front of the ruins of the building and stared at it in silence. I walked back and forth in front of it, up and down the street, each time turning back at the corner: I could not go away. I touched the remaining walls of the house, I caressed the stones. Wandering over a pile of rubble, I suddenly saw an opening. I bent over double, crawled into it and found myself inside the former entrance, intact beneath the debris. When my eyes adjusted to the dimness, I saw a door and knocked at it. The door opened and I went in—under the debris, a room survived as it had always been—and a gray-haired woman with a kind face, lined with suffering, stood there.

"Are you looking for someone?" she asked.

"Yes. Did you live here before the uprising?"

"Yes. I was the janitor."

"I'm looking for the Maginskis."

"Ah yes, they are here. . . . I mean he is not with us, but she is with her sister at Grochow."

The janitor didn't know the sister's name or address, but I did not budge, waiting for some further clue. "Are you a relative of the Maginskis, or only a friend?"

"Neither, exactly. But maybe you'll know." I could hardly shape the words distinctly. "There was a little boy here. . . . I'm related to him."

"Wlodek! Why, of course, around here everybody knew Wlodek. . . . " There was a smile on her wrinkled face. "Yes, of course, you must be his mother," she said, looking me over shrewdly. "Yes, there's a lot of resemblance. No, I don't know what's become of him."

Grochow is a Warsaw suburb on the right bank of the Vistula. I went by streetcar to the local office of the People's Militia and asked for help. I said I was looking for a Mrs. Maginski, formerly of 52 Pius Street, now living with her sister somewhere in Grochow. . . . No, I didn't know her sister's address.

The young militiaman spread his arms helplessly, then his face lit up. "Maybe she's registered with us." He leafed through the register. "Well, this must be it. Maginski, Maria, née Laudyn, age 58. Her sister's name is Anna Jablkowski. Yes, of course, here's her address." He handed me a slip of paper.

It was only a few steps away. There, just around the corner. Once more I flew. A little house on the other side of the square. Ground floor, apartment one. Here, behind this door. . . . I was suddenly out of breath, my heart pounding violently. "Lena, you old veteran of Auschwitz," I told

myself, "courage." The door opened. In the doorway stood Maria Maginski, older, gray-haired, but the same. She made the sign of the cross, as if
she had seen a ghost, and gasped in an unnatural voice, "May God's name
be praised forever. *You are alive!*"

I went into the kitchen.

CHAPTER 8

The Marrano
and the Christian

This section was written by Mrs. Maria Maginski. The italicized paragraphs are
Wlodek's reminiscences recorded in 1945–46.

MY HUSBAND WROTE EDITORIALS for a popular daily paper in Warsaw and it was at the paper's offices that I was introduced to Mr. Michal
Berg, the publisher, and I was charmed by his personal culture and gracious-
ness. During that first conversation I learned that his wife had just given
birth to a son. It never occurred to me then that my life would one day be
so closely intertwined with the life of that child.

　　Then came 1939, and the years of terror, of bloody persecutions began. The first blow was Wawer. On December 26, 1939, a German soldier
was killed in a brawl at a small restaurant at Wawer, near Warsaw. In retaliation, the Nazi occupation authorities shot down a hundred men that same
night, men they dragged out of their homes and the cars of a commuter
train. People fled Wawer in panic, to which I was an eyewitness because I
was spending the holidays with my sister in Grochow, which is on the railroad line to Wawer. Crazed, desperate women milled around looking for
their husbands, sons, brothers—or for their bodies.

　　The enemy proceeded ruthlessly to annihilate our nation. Arrests,
shootings in the streets, raids on private homes initiated the German regime
of persecution, bestiality, and death. But as it spread over the country, it
inspired a spirit of resistance and conspiratorial struggle against the invader,
a spirit that grew daily.

　　Early in 1940, my husband and I joined the resistance movement.
Stefan monitored the foreign radio and wrote news summaries for the
underground press. Communiqués were mimeographed in our Pius Street
apartment, and my job was to distribute them.

　　One day rumor spread that the enemy was planning to cut off a section of the city and build a ghetto. Indeed, walls began to appear topped
with shards of broken glass and barbed wire. Before the ghetto was closed
off, my husband and I paid our first visit to Mr. and Mrs. Berg who were
then living on Orla Street. They seemed grateful for our call; any humane
treatment moved these people who had been so deeply humiliated.
My husband talked to Mr. Berg and his wife and I sat in the next room,
where their small son was playing. I looked at the boy and wondered

what dangers he would be exposed to in the months, perhaps the years, to come.

We had not yet appreciated the full range of the Germans' fiendish cruelty and it was impossible for us to believe that events would end so tragically for the ghetto inhabitants. I foresaw that there would be difficulties in obtaining food and I suggested to the Bergs that we supply them with necessities. They thanked us, but said they would manage somehow. My husband, less confident of the course of the future, suggested that the Bergs try to hide on the Aryan side, but they said that, regrettably, they had no such possibilities available. Like many other Jews they deluded themselves into believing that while life would be hard behind the ghetto walls, it would be possible to survive. When we said good-by, we all said we hoped we'd see each other again and that Hitler would soon be gone.

Life in Poland grew more and more difficult. Manhunts, arrests, deportations to Auschwitz multiplied. And the resistance movement grew, the Poles showing much ingenuity and unparalleled courage in the life-and-death struggle. In an effort to assure us of some kind of existence and a chance for an *Ausweis,* our friends in the resistance decided that my husband should become a factory night watchman. This had the great advantage that Stefan would be at work nights, [the time when] the Germans generally raided private homes and arrested people. Our apartment was by no means a safe hiding place because considerable underground activity went on there, but it did serve repeatedly and successfully to hide various persons in danger. Life, however, was filled with fear and anxiety.

One day my husband brought the news that the Germans were deporting the Jews from the ghetto. His face was ashen, and the shock almost deprived him of coherent speech. I wanted to know more, but at first he wouldn't talk; he couldn't bring himself to tell me the whole horrible truth about Belzec and Treblinka, about those small vehicles first used for gassing. He kept muttering that what he had heard must be a lie—yet it was true.

The Warsaw streets on the Aryan side no longer echoed with the scenes of Jews being driven to work by the German police. Instead, the Jews were being slaughtered en masse in death factories at Belzec and Treblinka. I was filled with a steadily increasing hatred, especially since the German acts of terror more and more involved people close to me.

Then it was 1943, and we learned definitely that the Germans had decided to liquidate the ghetto. I had news of the Bergs through one of Mr. Berg's former employees, Kazimierz Gonsiorowski, sad and scanty news, but the essential fact was that they were still alive, worked outside the ghetto boundaries in Leszno Street, and had asked to see us, hoping that we might be able to work out some way to avert inevitable destruction. I wanted very much to help them, but we had no money and my husband earned very little. We even shared our apartment with a friend in the underground army to obtain a little extra food.

One day Kazimierz Gonsiorowski took me to the Leszno Street house where Mr. Berg worked and I found both Bergs there. I was amazed at Mrs. Berg's composure, and faced by her poise and self-discipline, I was almost ashamed that I lived on the other, "better" side. My decision to help them grew firm, irrevocable. They told me that Mrs. Berg and her son had already been taken once to Umschlagplatz, where they say that people were loaded into freight cars to be shipped to the death camps, but Mr. Berg somehow managed to save them.

The little boy, Wlodek, was five years and three months old, and he ran around us happily, full of fun. Cheerful, handsome, the child looked well nourished, and did not yet show any signs of ill treatment. How much longer would his parents be able to save him? The Bergs wanted to find a place for the boy on the Aryan side, but they had very little money. Could I help?

I didn't know what to say. The child did not look especially Jewish and would undoubtedly be safer on the Aryan side, but it was not only a question of money. In my mind I ran through the possibilities. I had many friends, many were devoted to me, but most of them were up to their ears in underground work. My own apartment was too exposed. I considered each possibility and realized that neither I nor anyone else could guarantee the boy safety. The Gestapo could come clumping into any Warsaw apartment with rifle butts and grenades. Anyone who undertook to care for the child might at any moment be deported to a concentration camp and then what would happen to the small, defenseless boy? I knew that, whatever I decided, I would be taking the full responsibility on myself.

I promised to come back in a week with a concrete plan. First I talked to my husband. Stefan was a man with a deeply humane and sympathetic heart, but he pointed out all the difficulties we faced, saying that only luck could save the boy. The next day I set out to see where I could place the child. Among others, my friend Zofia Kasicka promised solemnly that she could place the boy with her sister in the little town of Warka. I knew the place well and thought the arrangement ideal. We planned to have the boy stay with me for a few days after leaving the ghetto, and then take him to stay with Zofia's sister.

A week later, as I had promised, I went back to see the Bergs and submitted my plan. Payments for feeding the child were surprisingly low, only the nominal cost of the food, and the Bergs immediately agreed.

Meantime, rumors began to circulate that the Germans had decided to liquidate the Jews very soon, and many Jews began to move from the ghetto to the Aryan side hoping to find safety with Gentile families. A friend in the underground army confirmed the rumors and my husband also heard it through other sources. I therefore paid a third visit to the Bergs, urging them to hurry. They tried to postpone the parting for a few more days on the excuse that they needed time to provide Wlodek with shoes and clothing. I understood how difficult it was for them to part with the boy, but I was adamant: tomorrow—or not at all. At last the Bergs consented, though they clung to one more "important" excuse: they wanted to get the boy a birth certificate. I rejected that, too, because I had already made arrangements for a birth certificate through the underground, and was, indeed, later given one in the name of Wlodzimierz (Wlodek) Jakubowski, with the boy's authentic birth date formally issued by the Catholic parish for a nominal 10-zloty fee.

I will never forget that day, April 6, 1943, when I walked out of the ghetto leading little Wlodek by the hand. His parents had been calm and composed, but I knew what turmoil was in their hearts. I can still hear Mrs. Berg's quiet assurance to the boy that she would come for him as soon as the war was over. Her instructions to Wlodek were simply to be good and always to do what Aunt Maria said.

The parents handed me a little gold chain and twenty gold dollars for the boy's board and other expenses—and the address of an aunt in Palestine just in case I should need it. I made a solemn vow that if I survived and the Bergs did not, the child would remain with me. I had received explicit authorization from them to raise the boy in my own faith and traditions. We decided not to take the boy's things along, but to get them later through Kazimierz. The boy, who heard us, asked permission to take with him a book he loved, and we took it. Mrs. Berg told me what his favorite foods were, among others rolls in hot milk. Then the last embrace, the last long look.

I took Wlodek by the hand and he put his in mine trustingly. In a few minutes we were on the Aryan side. We strolled slowly through the streets and when we came to the big toy store at the corner of Krolewska and Marszalkowska Streets, we went in. Wlodek was overwhelmed by the bustle, the novelty, and the variety of the toys kept him spellbound. He wanted to touch everything and couldn't make up his mind what he wanted. I was nervous, restless, upset, and the vision of the Bergs forced to so heart-rending a separation from their flesh and blood would not leave me. I pressed Wlodek to make up his mind. I was in a hurry to get home. Finally he picked out a little horse, then we got on the streetcar and reached home safely.

My husband and I had lived at 52 Pius Street for more than twenty-four years, since 1918, and we knew almost everybody in the apartment house. During the air raids of September 1939, the frequent meetings in the cellar shelter had changed superficial neighborliness into friendship. The most important person, of course, was the janitress, Mrs. Wladyslawa Roslaniec. A simple woman with a noble character, I had complete confidence in her. In 1937, her young son was sent to prison for Communist activity and she, eyes swollen with crying, told me she had no money to buy him food parcels. I had given her money, but never dreamed she felt she owed me a good turn. She and Wlodek soon became great friends.

Aside from my husband, the first people Wlodek came into contact with in his new world were Slawa Baranowska, a student and a daily visitor to our flat, and Wladyslaw Zakrzewski, with whom we were bound by long-standing friendship and our common underground activities. He later perished in a concentration camp. Slawa worked in the Reading Room of the Macierz Society on the ground floor of our building. An ingenious secret cache had been built into the Reading Room, which I and others took advantage of in our underground activities. The night I brought Wlodek home I was exhausted and grateful when Slawa offered to help me wash him and put him to bed. The next day Wlodek awoke cheerfully, came over to my couch, stretched out next to me and asked me to read aloud to him some verses from his favorite book.

For some time our life, though full of anxiety and tension, went its so-called normal way. A little past eight each morning my husband would come home from the factory and I would prepare breakfast. The first day we sat down at table Wlodek asked to be fed. I refused peremptorily, but finally gave in to his begging and coaxing. That was a mistake because subsequently at every meal Wlodek demanded to be fed and when I refused, he would scream. But I wanted to teach him independence. Later Wlodek and I would go out to do the day's marketing, which took until about 11 A.M. I tried to do all my errands at one time so that we did not have to go out again all day. When I couldn't take Wlodek with me, Slawa stayed with him. During the day many friends dropped by to see us, and Wlodek won their hearts with his unfailing charm. One of our friends also pointed out that a child with such pretty curls would attract attention, particularly because Polish boys of that age wore their hair short. She was right. It was essential to make the child as inconspicuous as possible. On our way to the barber I took Wlodek to a photographer to have his picture taken as a souvenir for his parents.

My husband, our friend Zakrzewski, and I concocted a story for the other tenants in the building: we were looking after the child because his parents had been arrested by the Germans. Wlodek was lively, handsome, and talkative, and attracted people's attention. Sometimes he asked questions which showed he had been brought up in a different environment. For instance, when the Whitsunday holidays approached, he saw people in the market carrying big bunches of sweet flag which they used to decorate their homes and he asked naively, "Auntie, what are those long onions?" The woman at the nearest stand gave him a sharp glance.

On the morning of the third day Wlodek woke up in tears, crying, "I want my Mommy." I tried to quiet him, Slawa and my husband both tried to cajole him, distract him with offers to go for a walk, buy toy soldiers, picture books, but nothing helped. The child went on sobbing. Evening came and I drew the weeping boy next to me on the couch. Exhausted by a whole day of crying he fell asleep and I, depressed, was assailed by black thoughts. What next?

The days went by, one, two, three, and still the child did not calm down. Then I had an idea. I told Wlodek, "I will go to the ghetto and tell your Mommy and Daddy that you want to go back. And I'll do all I can to make it possible for you to go back." That promise, which I did not intend to keep, worked. Wlodek quieted down and in the meantime, Kazimierz, like a good angel, arrived with a small bundle of the child's belongings. In a few days Kazimierz promised he would also bring shoes, clothing, and other things. Wlodek stopped crying, but kept asking insistently, "Auntie, when will you go to the ghetto to see Mommy?"

"Any day now," I promised, and I kept repeating that promise, hoping the boy would grow accustomed to his new surroundings. Finally, one day, I told him I had important news, but we had to wait until Uncle Stefan went to work and no one was around to disturb us, because it was a very big secret. The boy looked at me and nodded understandingly. When my husband left and we were alone, I said, "Wlodek, I saw your Mommy. She asked you not to cry and to wait here for her. She will come for you just as soon as the war is over, as she promised."

The child listened gravely.

"Where your mother is now, no little boy can be with her, because the Germans catch the parents of little boys like you and deport them."

He looked at me, bent his head with a serious air and in a low voice told me about his terrible experiences, about his little friend Marysia, two years old, who had been killed by the Germans, how he knew when and how to hide from the Germans. He assured me that Mommy and Daddy had such a fine hiding place that the Germans would never find it. "Well, all right," Wlodek concluded, with a sigh, "I'll wait." And after that talk the child did quiet down and seemed resigned to his fate. Meanwhile, something went wrong in Warka and the boy had to remain with us.

At first we did not imagine that Wlodek would be concerned with the world of adult ideas. But his quickness of mind, his phenomenal memory, and his intelligent questions amazed us all. We found out that he had got straight the names of various persons and what they did in life. Assiduously he had tucked away in his little head every name he heard. In order not to endanger these people we began to leave names and positions out of our conversation. Thus we changed Professor Pienkowski, Dean of the University of Warsaw to Director P., Mr. Stanislaw Garztecki to "the man with the top" (he had given Wlodek a top) and that of his wife to the "lady with the bird" (she sometimes wore a kind of bird on her hat). Mrs. Wilezynska, who had brought cakes for him, was called "Lady Sheepskin," and the violinist Stanislaw Jarzembski was "Mr. Jas." Mr. Jas knew how to play with Wlodek and the boy waited eagerly for his visits. Besides creating lots of fun the violinist always brought Wlodek some new toy. On paydays, my husband also took Wlodek to a toy store and the boy usually chose lead soldiers. And so peace seemed to have settled in the child's heart, though we adults continued to live torn by fear and anxiety.

On April 19, 1943, the ghetto uprising broke out. Red smoke hung thick over the northern part of Warsaw, and information that seeped through suggested that no one would emerge alive from that flaming inferno. Did Wlodek realize that that black smoke, the rattle of machine guns, and the boom of artillery meant his mother might never return for him? Let the boy dream his beautiful dream. . . . We avoided any discussion which even hinted that he would probably never see his parents again.

For safety's sake I reminded Wlodek nightly to say the Lord's Prayer, which he had been prudently taught before he came to us. He prayed with great confidence for the return of his parents, nor did he fail to ask repeatedly whether the war would soon be over. But he talked about his parents and the ghetto only when he was alone with me.

Wlodek was a sociable creature. Though all my friends lavished great affection on him, he missed the companionship of other children. I saw it on our daily walks. He would go up to completely strange children and try to run and play with them. A carpenter who lived near us had a daughter a little older than Wlodek and I asked her to come and play with him. He was always happy when she came. His imagination was fertile and he thought up many more games than did the seven-year-old girl.

When my husband sat and read the papers, Wlodek sat beside him and asked, "What is that letter, Uncle?" Soon he learned to put the letters together and could read the name of the paper. I remember once that among the legitimate papers was a copy of a communiqué issued by the underground under the title, *Iskra* (The Spark). Wlodek began to read, "I . . . S . . . K . . . R . . ." My heart missed a beat. How could I explain to a child that this too was a secret? The boy's mind and imagination were already overburdened with so many secrets that from then on I carefully hid all the underground press materials.

For all his intelligence, Wlodek was as mischievous as any child of his age. He liked to "fix" things. He made very realistic animals out of modeling clay. For his very own place I assigned him a corner in my husband's room, where there was a large original and attractive chest with Cracovian carvings. I kept my books there, and Wlodek set his lead soldiers up on it. Once, taking advantage of a moment when he was playing there, I lay down to rest, and was abruptly alerted by suspicious noises. I went into my husband's room, where Wlodek was, to find wood shavings from that beautiful Cracow chest flying through the air. Though the wood was dried out and very hard, Wlodek had somehow managed to whittle it. I told him that a big smart boy ought never to do naughty things like that. But many other objects fell victim to his passion for experiment. For instance, when I left my umbrella propped open to dry one day, Wlodek cut the material up to the very wires. When I scolded him because he had made me very unhappy and told him that as punishment I would not speak to him, he apologized and assured me he had not known it would make me unhappy. I always liked to grow flowers and plants and one day Wlodek cut all the leaves off the plants and flowers. "How could you do it?" I asked him. "You know how I love those flowers."

"Which do you love more, Auntie, the flowers or me?" he asked.

I realized then that the child wanted to be reassured about whether I really loved him. But I cautiously hid things like knives and scissors and disconnected the gas when I had to leave him alone for a while.

I often took Wlodek with me when I visited my sister in Grochow. From some white linen dish towels she made him a pair of pants to wear with a white shirt of his which had a navy-blue collar. With childlike earnestness Wlodek told me he had inherited the shirt from an older cousin.

In the evenings we usually went to the Reading Room to see Slawa. Because Slawa read poems and stories to him, and the Reading Room had space where Wlodek could race around to his heart's content, he loved to go there. Before he went to sleep, he liked to stretch out next to me on my couch. We would have long talks and he showered me with questions until he finally fell asleep.

Our walks often took us to Emilia Plater Street where the St. Paul and Peter Church was located. It was surrounded by shrubbery and spreading old trees, all that was left of an old church cemetery. Mothers, nurses, and housemaids brought children there to play and Wlodek, always anxious to play with other children, liked to go there. He even liked to play with children younger than he was. I kept a careful eye on him, always alert lest he betray himself. Later we would go into the church as did almost all the other women with children and soon Wlodek was acquainted with all the altars of the saints. He would select the altar we would pray at, one day St. Francis, the next the child Jesus. Yet, during the services, when the priest spoke from the pulpit, he would ask loudly, "Auntie, why is that man in the white shirt talking to us from that little old balcony?" I had to be careful that we were not overheard.

At dinner one day Wlodek took a fancy to one of the dishes and for a while tried in vain to define what it tasted like, until suddenly he said, "It tastes as good as . . . a real *chulent!*" Another time when a woman mentioned her relatives in America, Wlodek impressed her with the fact that he had an aunt in Palestine. . . .

Five months had gone by since Wlodek had left the ghetto. During that time I had had only one letter from his father, in July. I was convinced that both the Bergs were now dead.

One day at the end of September, while I was preparing dinner, there was a loud knocking at my door. Wlodek was playing in the room. When I opened the door, two Polish policemen and a civilian walked in. In a sharp voice they announced, in unison, "Inspection!" They shoved me aside, pushed into the room and surrounded the child, firing questions at him, "Where did you come from? How long have you been living here?" Wlodek stared helplessly and his eyes sought support from me. "Answer!"

roared one of the hoodlums. "Auntie will tell you," the boy managed to
say. I began my story, that the boy was my nephew, that his parents had
been arrested, but an evil grin contorted the hoodlums' faces. "We'll see.
Come here, boy, we want to take a look at you. . . ."

For a moment I couldn't speak. I realized that it was not a crazy nightmare, but that I must do something at once, take an attitude. "Leave that
child alone, please. Yes, the child is of Jewish origin. . . ."

*When Auntie left the house, I hid behind the bedroom door. She always left it
open. When she came back, she would make believe she was crying because I wasn't
there anymore. This time I ran and hid behind the door again and my heart beat
hard and loud. Auntie stood by the door in front of me. But they made her come
over to them and they all sat down at the table and talked. They said, "Close the
door." But when the door was closed they saw me. When they saw me, they grabbed
me and started to pull down my pants to see if I was a Jew. I began to scream and
kick and threw myself from side to side. One of them put a gun next to my head and
said to be quiet. Then Auntie told them to leave me alone, that I was a Jew. They
left me alone. I went up to the policeman and asked if I could see the gun. He took
it out again and showed it to me. "Please," I said to him, "put it back now. I don't
want to look at it any more."*

Some words one of the policemen said finally reached my consciousness. "You must have made a pretty penny for yourself, taking in that child.
I wonder just how much." My brain began to work. The men were searching
the house, their hands turning everything upside down. They gathered up
the household money from a drawer, went through my purse and found
a few pennies, and then kept snooping. They threw things around, then
trampled on them. No money! One day in 1940, I had hidden a few gold
coins inherited from a sister in some balls of darning yarn, which were in
a sewing box that stood on a small chest of drawers. One of the hoodlums
opened the box, but evidently thought it could not serve to hide anything
so important, and threw it aside. The twenty-dollar gold piece I had received
from the Bergs for Wlodek's upkeep I had put in a secret slot in my sewing
machine, which stood in the kitchen corner covered over with coats.

They found no money, but they found something else. From the
chest in the hall they took a big bundle of printed matter, *The Information
Bulletin* published by the Polish underground movement. And at that moment my husband walked in. They jumped on him and went through his
pockets. His wallet had only a few zlotys in it, but there were eighteen

copies of war communiqués based on forbidden foreign radio broadcasts. They looked at each other with peculiar expressions. One of the policemen pushed the communiqués and underground papers under the civilian's nose, but he only shrugged. "Those matters don't concern me. I'm interested only in Jewish matters. But one and the other together, well, it's a very ugly case."

I knew we were lost, all three of us, and with the courage of despair I began to threaten them. "I know you can destroy us," I said, "but you won't get away with it. You'll hear from us even beyond the grave. There are people who will investigate and who'll want to know how and why we were murdered. Even now, while you're standing here, sharp eyes are watching you. Those papers weren't printed by me or for me. I don't know what will become of us, but I don't envy you!"

During that summer Warsaw had been the scene of a number of heroic efforts by the Polish underground. Grenades had been thrown into the Café Club, where German officers met. An SS column had been showered with a hail of grenades, and the underground had taken severe measures against spies and blackmailers. Only a few days before I had been visited by several boys from the fighting units who had, on the underground's orders, carried out a death sentence against the police commissioner of our precinct. I was sure these hoodlums remembered the death of their chief.

They remembered all right. The civilian turned and said to me, "What now?"

I had nothing to lose so I kept talking. "Everybody must live. You won't find any money here, but I can get some for you so your time won't be wasted. How much?"

They quoted an astronomical figure. I laughed out loud and said that in that case they might as well go ahead and do what they wanted to do. I could never get hold of a sum like that. We began to haggle and two hours later they came down to 12,000 zlotys and I agreed, on condition that the money would be paid in two installments of 6,000 each.

Aunt Maria and Uncle Stefan came into the room, and the men said "We will give you five days to get him away from here. If we come back after that and see him here, we will put you and your husband and the child up against the wall and shoot all of you." They opened the closets, took out sheets and napkins and told Uncle to pack them in a suitcase and carry them downstairs for them. Auntie began to cry because she was afraid Uncle would not come back, but he did come back.

Mrs. Roslaniec had sized the situation up quickly. She had grabbed her broom and begun to sweep the street. She knew all our friends and thus could warn them not to go inside. The agreed-on signal was, "There will be no dinner today," but she had not succeeded in warning my husband.

After the blackmailers left, I was seized with fear and hopelessness, and I began to cry bitterly. In whose way was that little child? Who had denounced him and sent those scoundrels after us? That thought robbed me of my peace of mind. I realized I could no longer stay in that apartment, and that I couldn't let the child stay there any longer. They would come again, or send others who might even be worse, and how could I be sure I would be able to defend myself a second time?

Wlodek sat beside me and tried to comfort me, saying that if they had taken the sheets and would take the money, they wouldn't hurt us. I couldn't make sense of all the things that ran through my mind, I could only hear those hard-bitten words from a six-year-old child already so bitterly experienced.

Next day I sent my husband to the home of our very good friend, Mrs. Maria Bronikowski. He was to spend his days and take his meals there. Then I notified Mr. Zakrzewski not to visit the apartment because, in the underground slang, it was "burned out." I also asked him to supply me with a *Kennkarte* (an identity card) issued in another name. I decided to take Wlodek to visit my sister in Grochow; as soon as I got my documents, I planned to walk out of the apartment without informing anyone except Slawa and Mrs. Roslaniec where I was going. I would pack a few personal belongings in small bundles and ask them to take care of them in case any suspicious types tried to get into the apartment. It would not be difficult to get the packages because there was an exit into Poznanska Street through the Reading Room; I could use that instead of going out through Pius Street. Finally I decided to leave the apartment with only one package containing Wlodek's things. He packed his toys into a huge bundle and when I told him we couldn't take it, he burst into tears. "I can't leave my toys, Auntie. I had to leave everything before. You know where. I have too many pretty toys and I need them." To make the loss less painful I only took away the empty boxes and bottles.

My sister received us with great fear and apprehension. In a nearby house lived a plain-clothes policeman who tracked down fugitive Jews both for business and pleasure. Once we had settled down in Grochow, I began to look around for money to pay off my blackmailers. Well-wishers lent me as much as they could and in a day I had half the stipulated amount. I had many discussions with friends about whether I should pay at all, or consider the dubious deal to have fallen through. Tadeusz Garztecki, an old friend of my husband's, advised me to pay, but to make the installment smaller to gain time and to avoid whetting the appetites of those beasts for prolonging their blackmail indefinitely.

During this period a good friend, Mrs. Halina Pluzanski, let me sleep at her house. I stayed in touch with Slawa by telephone and she told me all was peaceful and quiet at the Pius Street apartment.

The day I was to meet the blackmailers drew near. Our meeting place was not in a secluded spot, but at the headquarters of our local police precinct. I took 4,000 zlotys with me as the first payment. One of the policemen was waiting for me at the door and greeted me as if I were an old friend. When I told him I had brought less than agreed on, he made a wry face, but I assured him I'd pay it all. I explained that I had to borrow the money from friends and was having difficulty. He told me that he himself had nothing against me, but so far as the civilian was concerned—he gave me a wink—I had to be very careful. The civilian was a very dangerous man. With unintended cynicism he called my attention to the beauty of the crucifix set up in the police station and I was struck by the discord; here was a man blackmailing me in front of the image of God, symbol of love, mercy, and goodness.

I promised to bring him more money in four days.

In the meantime, my sister Anka was after me constantly to take Wlodek away. She was afraid for him and for herself. The cordon of terror was closing in on us.

I spent a few days with Aunt Anka and I was naughty. I broke Adas's shovel. He is a little boy and his father is a policeman. I went back to Warsaw.

I kept searching for a safe place for Wlodek, but without success. Every home I could put a child in with full confidence already had a child or adult in hiding. And with a little boy it was harder because extra precautions were necessary. Stefan hoped for a while that we might be able to place him with Maria Wiewiorska, a close friend of ours and former secretary of Mr. Berg's paper, *Ostatnie Wiadomosci*, but she was already hiding little Elzbieta-Basia Lewin, whose mother was Maria's best friend, and who also had worked for the paper before she was married. Miss Jadwiga Czarniawska (Jackan) lived there, too, and moreover the house was a center for underground activities.

My second appointment with the police drew near. I now had the full sum but on Tadeusz Garztecki's advice I planned to delay the final "settlement of accounts" again. I took only 4,000 zlotys with me instead of the 8,000 due. The meeting was friendly. The policeman informed me that if he had known that in addition to harboring a Jewish child they would get involved in an underground activity, they would not have bothered us at all. What he said reassured me. I felt that the retaliatory measures taken by the underground had served their purpose; these vile creatures were really frightened. The policeman said that I could go right on living there with my husband and Wlodek in perfect safety, but I must realize that the civilian with them was an absolute scoundrel and a blackmailer. "You know, Gestapo."

I didn't trust the policeman. I was afraid to take Wlodek back to Pius Street. Anka kept after me, but I couldn't find a better place for the boy. The homes of underground members weren't safe.

They frequently served as small-arms depots because more and more often our people were deciding that they would fight it out to the last if they were raided. On the other hand, I couldn't resent it when people told me honestly that they were afraid because hiding a person of Jewish origin was punishable by death. My own experience had not been edifying and hardly gave me the right to encourage others. I was at the end of my rope when my friend, Halina Pluzanski, came to my aid. A cousin of hers was leaving Warsaw for two weeks and would like some trustworthy person to stay in her apartment and look after it. "Of course, she's a female full of fears," warned Mrs. Pluzanski, "so we can't tell her the truth or she'd refuse."

The apartment was in Nowiniarska Street and the owner had received it in exchange for evacuating her own flat in a quarter taken over by the Germans. I went there under the name of Mrs. Maria Michalski, a resident of Piaseczno. I was to state that I was a widow, guardian of a small grandchild whose parents were abroad. Victims of the war, like so many others, don't you know? . . . My doctor had told me I should have X-ray treatments, but commuting to and from Warsaw with the child would be just too much for me, and I had no one to leave him with.

The apartment was on the third floor of a huge building. As I climbed the stairs I went over my little speech, realizing how much depended on the impression I made. Wlodek and I would have a roof over our heads for two whole weeks! I pressed the bell and after a few moments heard the rattle of a key in the lock. Through the half-opened door two shrewd beady eyes looked me over. I said Mrs. Pluzanski had sent me and the woman asked me in. I saw immediately that she was one of those people who couldn't understand that anyone might think differently about anything from the way she did. My little speech worked, however, and she handed me the keys. Two weeks of peace during which I would have to find some more permanent solution. I was not required to report this two weeks' stay to the police, which was most convenient because I could hide all traces of where I had gone. Mrs. Roslaniec, our janitress, had, as was her duty, reported to the police immediately after Wlodek and I moved out of Pius Street.

I was afraid to move around freely in that strange apartment so that, instead of cooking, Wlodek and I ate in a restaurant. I also had another problem: I had to go out to make contacts with people and I had nobody to leave Wlodek with. I did succeed in getting some young girls from a group which had previously helped me distribute underground literature to act as sitters, but unfortunately they could not do so every day. The nicest of these girls was Magda Rusinek, a seventeen-year-old, who told Wlodek that good little spirits watched over him when Auntie was away, and who occasionally took him for a walk. But there were days when I had to leave Wlodek alone. I left him a basin of water and little paper boats, something to eat—a cup of milk, a piece of bread with butter or lard—and, of course, his chamber pot. Before I went out he always asked me to be sure to send the little spirits, and we would bargain about just how many. I said two would be enough, but Wlodek wanted four.

A week went by and I still had found no solution. At my third meeting at the station I handed over only 2,000 zlotys. My friend still insisted that he and his police associate got none of that money; the whole sum went to the civilian.

Auntie left me alone for a long time while she went to look for another place for me to stay. She left me bread and jam and water and tea. Nobody ever came there except Auntie. I had to stay in one room with the door locked and not go near the window. I had to be very quiet, and not jump or stamp my feet, because no one was supposed to know I was there. When I sneaked to the window anyway, and peeked out, I could see the German guard and Polish policemen. When the guard looked up, I hid so that he would not see me.

I heard big explosions. In the ghetto. The wall was very near.

I played with my abacus and I was very lonesome. One day when Auntie went out I walked around the room rubbing my finger against the walls. It broke in some places. I took paper, spit on it, and covered up the holes. I drew a bow and arrow on the wall with a blue crayon. One arrow was long as the whole wall and the bow was as little as my hand. When Auntie came back she said "Oh! The walls were just painted! Then she bought a loaf of white bread and instead of eating it, she used it to erase my drawings from the wall.

When Auntie went out she always promised to send the little spirits to watch over me and keep me company. I played with them and when Auntie came back she told me all the naughty things I had done. She said the little spirits had told her. I think that Auntie peeked through the keyhole from the other room.

In searching for a place to live I met the wife of Professor Henryk Beck, who had hidden in my apartment for five weeks. From him, she had heard of my troubles, and made an appointment for me with the Committee of Assistance for Jewish Children. I went there. They were willing to help, even to pay for the child's upkeep, but they couldn't find a place for Wlodek to live.

Our stay in Nowiniarska Street ended when the owner came back. I invited her to breakfast and she accepted gratefully. She lavished words of delight over Wlodek's beauty and charm, and kissed him on the head. I was grateful that his looks did not betray his origin. When I returned the keys to her, I thanked her for having made it possible to take my treatment. The situation was now desperate, and then, at the last minute, my young friends from the resistance came to the rescue.

In the evening Magda came, the girl who brought me from Grochow to the apartment on Nowiniarska Street. She took me to the house of a young couple who were going to be married. They lived with the girl's mother. An eleven-year-old boy, Woytus, came there to play with me. Once he made a gun for me, a real wooden rifle, because his father was a carpenter. The rifle had a real leather sling. Woytus brought it for me. He was very nice.

At night they made up a bed for me on two armchairs. The first night the chairs moved apart and I fell out on the floor. The girl's mother tied the legs of the chairs together with a rope so it wouldn't happen again. I spent three or four weeks there. I had a very good time. There was a deer's head with antlers on the wall. Auntie came sometimes and brought jam and other things for me. For them, too. Magda took care of everything.

Quite unexpectedly Mrs. Kurkowski, the wife of the public prosecutor, came to my aid. She knew a woman who, for money, would place boys of Jewish origin in a Catholic orphanage in Otwock. After long deliberation I decided that a Catholic orphanage might really be the safest refuge. When

I went to see the woman, she acted ashamed of what she was doing and explained that her husband was in an OFLAG (an officers' camp for war prisoners) and that she had to support a son and her daughter who had tuberculosis. The monthly payments were not too high for Wlodek, and the go-between asked for a lump sum of 2,000 zlotys for herself. I agreed. We arranged for her to take Wlodek to the orphanage, and a week later we would visit him together.

I went to see Mrs. Kurkowski again to ask if she was sure I could entrust Wlodek to this go-between, and she told me she had used the woman's services several times and that she had always behaved correctly.

After the ghetto was liquidated, many Jews went into hiding, and it was increasingly difficult to find a sanctuary. Heroism flourished, but at the same time the dregs of society were on the rampage and blackmail multiplied. No one knew when a Jew in hiding or a member of the underground was captured by the authorities whether it was by accident or through some foul informer. And there were also the *Volksdeutsche* (ethnic Germans), a plague deeply ingrown in the Polish nation. How was I to move in this human labyrinth? There were simply no locked doors behind which peace and quiet could be found, so finally I made up my mind to send Wlodek to the orphanage.

Fortunately, Wlodek took the separation calmly. He only asked when I would come for him. And Magda, would she come to see him?

One day a lady came, a friend of Auntie Maria's, who took me on the train to Otwock. We got out at the station and walked for about half an hour. We had bananas made of sugar frosting in a bag and stopped to eat them on the way. When we got there, my lady talked to another lady who was the superintendent and very fat. I played fire engines by myself. I rang and rang the bell . . . ding, ding, ding. The fat lady took me to some boys and they asked what my name was. The lady said Wlodeczek, and they began to laugh and make fun. Wlo-de-czek. Ha, ha, ha! The lady left.

I went to bed. About twenty boys slept in the room. The next morning we got up at 8. We dressed and washed in a basin. We had soup and bread for breakfast. Then we went out and played.

The building had only one floor and was built of wood. They called it Reymont House. The lady in charge of my group was Miss Olenka. She wore black stockings, a black sweater, had black hair and dark eyes.

Not far away German soldiers built a strawman and would run and stab him with their bayonets. They shot rifles and machine guns at a target. They marched, shouted, gave orders. Sometimes they borrowed shovels from us, but they were always polite. There were Russians there, too, prisoners. They walked without guards, but they did not run away. The boys called them cabbage heads.

My bed was right near the window and the first thing in the morning I always looked out. If the guard was a German, I said I was sick and stayed in bed all day. I was afraid the German might find out I was a Jew, or that one of the boys would tell him.

Once the German soldiers gave us candy as we came back from church. We went to church every Sunday. We said our prayers twice a day, in the morning and in the evening. We all kneeled down on the floor. When we sang, we stood up. Before we got out of bed, we said "Hail Mary" and other prayers. The same in the evening: "Our Father" first, then "Hail Mary" in bed.

My best friend was Stas Malinowski. He had white hair and blue eyes. Like most of the boys, he had no Mommy and no Daddy.

Now I was left alone and had no place to go. I telephoned Slawa. She told me everything was quiet in the Pius Street apartment house, but I was still afraid to return. Suppose they came back asking questions about Wlodek. I roamed the streets and spent nights at different places, one night at one friend's, the next night at another's. At the end of the week I went to the go-between, intending to visit Wlodek with her. She suggested I postpone my visit because two people coming to the orphanage might be conspicuous. I couldn't deny the logic of her argument. Since she was going there anyway, I asked her to take a parcel to Wlodek. She agreed. When I called on her the next day to hear the news of the boy, she told me everything was fine and that she had, of course, left the parcel with Wlodek. (It was a lie. She never left the parcel.)

We agreed that in a week we would both go together, but history repeated itself. This time her excuse was that there was a manhunt in Otwock. Again her logic was impeccable, but I made the trip myself the next day anyway. I found the child cheerful, even happy, but already showing traces of neglect. His delicate features were covered with scabs. The instructor explained that it was due to change of diet. I could understand that very well, for the orphanage was obviously very poor; the city paid only 3 zlotys per child for food. I asked her to let me bring some supplementary food for the child and I also offered to try to organize more food for the entire orphanage.

Mr. and Mrs. Kijewski, who owned the pharmacy where Mrs. Berg had worked, promised to send a food parcel every ten days. Their parcels were really wonderful, with sugar, butter, sausages, eggs, cookies, and white rolls. Mrs. Garztecki also became interested in the problems of the orphanage and, thanks to her propaganda, many anonymous food packages reached there. Every week I went to Otwock loaded down with parcels. I left Warsaw at seven in the morning and had to be back in Warsaw by noon. On those trips I often met Mrs. Jadwiga Jaracz, the wife of the famous Polish actor, Stefan Jaracz. She went to Otwock to visit her husband who, since his release from Auschwitz, had been in an Otwock sanitarium for incurable tuberculosis. Because she was a very discreet person she never asked why I made such frequent trips to Otwock. Occasionally I went to see Stefan Jaracz, and one day, he asked me point blank, "What is it that brings you to Otwock so regularly, Marysia, the desire to see me?"

I answered quite candidly. "I have a child here I have had to hide. He is in an orphanage and it is terribly poverty-stricken. I haven't spoken about it because I didn't want to worry you with my troubles, Stefan, since you have enough of your own."

He turned to his wife and said, "We must do something to help those poor children." Soon, thanks to the Jaraczes and their friends, more food began to flow into the orphanage. I checked frequently with the orphanage superintendent, Mrs. Klodecki, to make sure that Wlodek got everything I brought for him.

One day at Jaracz's request I took Wlodek to see him. Wlodek danced a Polish mountaineer's dance and sang several songs he had learned in the orphanage, and Stefan was deeply moved. When saying good-by he pressed some coins into the child's hand, for a chocolate bar.

One Sunday I took Wlodek to Warsaw. Among other things, I wanted to show him to the Kijewskis. I went to the drugstore like any other customer. Juliusz Kijewski was there and, delighted, Wlodek threw his arms around his neck. Behind a counter stood Mrs. Halina, who had been Mrs. Berg's friend for years, but she never betrayed the fact that she knew the child. Wlodek, too, held himself aloof. After a time, Wlodzimierz Kijewski walked in and we moved to the back of the store. Wlodzimierz asked the child how he was, and to a thoughtless inquiry about his parents, Wlodek replied resolutely and without faltering, "Mommy is in the country, sick, and Daddy is with her." That answer reassured me a good deal about the child's emotional state.

It was then the end of November 1943. Staying at a different place each night, with no home to call my own, I was exhausted. I was, after all, over fifty, and the years had not been easy. I talked to Slawa and Mrs. Roslaniec and they both assured me that there had been no suspicious loiterers around the apartment. Cautiously, at first, I began to make visits to my own home, but only during the day. I still looked for other places to spend the nights. Then, after a time, I decided to risk it, and I went back to my own flat to live. I kept up my regular trips to Otwock, taking parcels whenever I could, and as big as I could manage. Among them, I took Wlodek a pillow, a comforter, and some underwear.

My contact with Mrs. Beck resulted in my being asked to head an organization for the care of Jewish children who had found Aryan places to live. The idea was to create a center where their guardians could come to collect money for feeding and caring for the children. I accepted Mrs. Beck's proposal and offered my apartment for the purpose. I drove out of my mind all thoughts of renewed blackmail because, I told myself, the blackmailers' principal lever, the boy, was no longer present.

Christmas was approaching and I received many toys for the children at the orphanage. I was also given some money to buy Wlodek a pair of winter shoes. Mrs. Jaracz brought a large quantity of bacon and noodles, and we set out to take the gifts to Otwock. The children greeted us happily. Wlodek looked well and as always inquired about his friends: How was Uncle? How was Magda? Slawa? And so on? Narrowing his eyes, he asked significantly, "Will it be over soon?" On the advice of the wise and prudent Mrs. Beck we had also bought gifts for the staff: a set of smart underwear and a pair of stockings for the instructor, stockings for the cook. That poor overworked woman said, "I don't need anything. I have been working in this orphanage since the end of the first war. I love these children. What would I do in this world if I didn't care for them?" We also thanked Mrs. Klodecki, the superintendent, for her Christian and humanitarian handling of the children. The children themselves put on a little Christmas show for us, singing carols, dancing and reciting poems, and Wlodek was the leader of the children's dramatic group.

From the moment I accepted the task of helping the Jewish children, the house was always full of people—people applying for help, for advice, for money. I also called on many individuals to deliver their payments. We were plagued by cold; there was no electricity and no coal. And, of course, I was keeping house and cooking meals again for my husband, Slawa, and Mr. Zakrzewski.

Easter approached and Wlodek took an active part in all the preparations. With the teacher he pasted together a stained-glass window representing "The Resurrection of Christ," and was delighted by the various Easter activities.

The Germans continued to devastate the country. So-called "rasp-berry" lists were posted with the names of people sentenced to public exe-cution. During Holy Week a group of people was executed in Zelazna Street, among them an old friend of my husband's, Wladyslaw Waroczewski. A young girl who belonged to the resistance group I had worked with was executed in Pawiak Prison. She was Ewa Pohoska, daughter of a former vice mayor of Warsaw, who had been shot at Palmiry. The country seethed. Warsaw was preparing for an uprising. At the end of July, anticipating the approach of the insurrection, I took the train to Otwock with a parcel from Mrs. Kijewski. The organization had sent me money a few days ahead of time and I wanted to make all the payments, including the one for Wlodek.

I found Wlodek in good health and spirits. We went for a walk in the woods and I was relieved by the thought that he would not be in Warsaw when the uprising broke out. In view of the new danger and the possibility that I might lose my life, I sent to a friend who lived in Cracow province all the information I had about Wlodek, including the address of Mr. Berg's sister in Palestine.

On August 1, 1944, the uprising exploded in Warsaw. The story is well known and I need not describe it again. At the outbreak of the uprising my husband was in another quarter of the city and we lost track of each other for long months. Day after day the hellish death and destruction continued until our hopeless resistance ended. The Germans ordered the entire population to quit the city. Through rubble-strewn streets, past the charred skeletons of buildings, amid the smell of rotting flesh and death, the people of Warsaw took leave of their city. Everyone, the able-bodied, the sick, wounded, and feeble, packed as many of their belongings as they could carry and left. During that terrible time I wandered through the streets of the city, exhausted and becoming ill.

On October 7, 1944, my sister and I left the ruined city on foot. The first day of that wearisome journey took us to Ursus. After a night there, we were loaded into freight cars. Then followed thirty-six hours in the car jam-packed with people, all standing because there was no room to sit. No one knew where the Germans were taking us, but the camps were apparently too crowded so we got only as far as Charsznica, near Cracow. After that or-deal I could not leave the train under my own power, I had to be carried out.

One day Miss Krysia took us to where there were swings, and we swung on them. The man who owned them asked for money. Miss Krysia said, "We have no money but we will pray for you," and the man said all right. That night and next morning we prayed for him. We often prayed for Auntie Maria because she brought us so many good things — cakes, white bread, candy — and gave them to everybody. One day we had noodles in milk. Everybody liked them very much and we wanted more. Miss Olenka told us to pray for the milkman. We prayed, but there was no more milk.

I saw some cooked potato peels on the porch. They were put there for the rabbits. I was very hungry and began to look through the peels. I picked out the biggest ones and I found one tiny whole potato. I didn't wait, I ate it right there. Usually we put potatoes in the ashes and waited until they were baked. But lots of times other boys ate mine before I came back. Once I collected twelve small potatoes and when I came back to see if they were done, not a single one was left. I was very hungry and I felt bad.

Once they brought some great big potatoes to the orphanage. The boys told me, "If you go get us some, we'll give you a share when they're cooked." I crawled under the wagon and picked up a lot of potatoes and beets. I took them to Lutek, who had a brother named Rys, and he promised to make soup out of them. He kept his word. He even apologized because he said the soup was too salty. They put my big potato into the fire and baked it. When they took it out, another boy shouted that it was his. I didn't argue. I grabbed it and ate it quickly. It was still raw inside, but I didn't care.

Mostly we ate potato soup or oatmeal. I liked the potato soup because you didn't have to spit out the oat husks. It was watery soup and we didn't get much bread.

Mr. Genek who fixed things at the orphanage went with some of the big boys to fight for Warsaw. Miss Olenka told us. And then we began to be hungry all the time.

Auntie Maria didn't come and bring us packages any more. Because of the uprising in Warsaw nobody could get out of the city. I was very hungry. Once I started running to the privy and the sister wouldn't give me any bread at all. She said I'd have pains in my belly if I ate black bread and would never get rid of the loose bowels. But I lied. I told her I had no pain, that my bowels were all right. I begged her for a teeny piece of bread. Then I couldn't sleep all night and had to run up and back to the privy outside, barefoot in the ice and snow, but I didn't get sicker.

Once when I was very hungry I asked a boy for some bread, but he said no. I promised to give him my pajamas if he gave me his bread. He said all right, but I gave him only the bottoms first for two slices of bread. A few days later I gave him the tops for two more pieces.

One day someone said, "Wlodek, get up. Wlodek, Heniek, Andrzej, Wojtek, Dziudzik, get dressed." About ten boys climbed into the truck. Five big boys and five of us. Miss Krysia and Miss Marysia came with us. The priest also rode in the same truck. It rained, but we sat under a canvas and didn't get wet. We sang and had a good time.

When we got out we saw a big farm with cows and horses, a stable and a building. A Mother Superior came out of the house, an old lady in a long skirt with a black scarf. "I am very pleased to have such nice boys to keep me company," she said, and smiled. The place was called Skórzec. It was near the city of Siedlce. A lot of sisters lived in the building and a few little girls with them. We had dinner, bread, soup, meat, and potatoes. There was nothing on the bread, but it tasted as if it had lard on it, it was so good. We ran outside and looked at everything. There were three horses, two work horses and a colt, too young to work. There was a man who took care of them. The sisters took care of the cows and the pigs and chickens.

There were many sisters. They were good, but they called me "little Jew." Probably Miss Krysia told them. Once I went up to a sister and she asked me, "When are you going to bed?" I answered, "I have to say my prayers." And she whispered to me, "Have you already said your Jewish prayers?" I told her that I didn't know what she meant. I didn't know any Jewish prayers.

The boys tried to make me say I was a Jew. "Admit you're a Jew and we'll give you something." But I would never admit it because then they would have teased me. They called me names anyhow: calf, cow, traitor, dirty Jew. . . .

We all lived in one big room. We got up at eight, washed, said our prayers, ate breakfast, played for a little while, then did our lessons. A lady who came from Otwock before us was the teacher. We played with the horses and cows. We went to pick mushrooms. Every Sunday a priest came to the little chapel on the farm. Later my best friend Stas Malinowski came with the rest of my group. Miss Olenka brought them.

When Miss Krysia was doing the laundry, I went into the washroom too, because I liked her. I asked her if I could take off my shoes. She said, "No, not till your feet get well." I had sores on my feet and pus in them. Once I asked the boys to pray for me, so my feet would get better, but they said they wouldn't pray for a Jew. I was unhappy and I walked away.

One evening, Miss Olenka had talked to me. She asked me in a low voice if I was Jewish. I said no, of course. She said I could trust her, she wouldn't tell anyone. I told her, as a secret, that I was Jewish. She told me that I should be converted by being baptized. She took me to see a priest and I told him how much I wanted to be baptized. He promised to do it, but before he could, I had been sent with nine other boys to Skórzec.

Miss Olenka came to Skórzec with us. She told me I would have to give up all Jewish things. And my Mother, if she came for me after the war. If I died I was afraid for my soul, so one night I arranged with her to baptize me herself. After everyone was asleep, she came in. I couldn't sleep because I was so excited. She brought a pitcher of holy water. Then she cut off a little piece of my hair. She told me it was to be sure that the holy water touched my scalp. If anyone asked, she told me to say the rats had chewed my hair during the night. So I was baptized.

At Skórzec we played a game called "suffering for Jesus." We tied ourselves up, knees against our chests, our arms clasped around our knees and hands tied in front. Then we put a long pole, usually a broomstick, under our knees and over our arms. When we were tied up that way, very tight, we were uncomfortable. That way we did penance for Jesus. The sisters encouraged us and praised the boy who suffered most. I had to suffer more because I was a Jew, one of the people who crucified Jesus. I tried to suffer harder and longer than the others. The sisters rewarded me and made me an altar boy at Mass in the farm chapel.

One day a big truck arrived to take us back to Otwock. I began to cry because I liked it there very much and I was afraid my Mommy and Daddy would find me in Otwock. Then they wouldn't let me pray. Miss Krysia told me that Jews were very bad. They drank the blood of Catholics on their holidays. They kill a young boy or girl, suck out their blood and put it in jars. Then they add it to the dough when they make their matzos. Miss Krysia talked to me about Auntie Maria. She said if Auntie Maria tried to take me back to my Mommy, I should run away to the woods. I prayed that my parents would not come back for me. I believed in Jesus very much. I loved Him and prayed to Him.

We got back to Otwock late that night. The orphanage was in another building. We were told to go to sleep right away.

One day when Miss Helena was coming back from church she saw some strange soldiers. They were Russians. They ordered us to move out, the whole town of Otwock had to move away. We walked to Srodborow. When a Russian officer drove by in an automobile, we stopped him and begged him to get a ride for us. We waited with him for a long time until two big horses and wagons came along. The officer stopped them and told them to take us to Ostrow. There were about forty of us. We climbed into the wagons, but they wouldn't drive us all the way into Ostrow. We had to walk the rest of the way. It was night, but there was a moon and it was light enough to see. We had nothing to eat and we were hungry. When we got to the place, we threw down our bundles and fell asleep on them.

It was a small barn and we slept there for a week, on the floor, with our coats over us. Across the road was a big field with broken tanks and cars. They told us there were lots of grenades and mines there, but that's where we played.

There were Polish soldiers near us. They gave us food from their kitchen. They brought bread and soup in big kettles. One day they gave us borsht and potatoes for lunch and dinner, and I filled up both times. Then I had to go to the outhouse, but someone was there. I waited and waited until I couldn't hold it any more, and I did it in my pants. When the boys came out of the outhouse, they called Miss Olenka. She washed me and my clothes. The other boys didn't make fun of me, because it happened to them too, even the biggest boys.

One morning we got up and Miss Olenka said, "Brush your clothes." We all started to go someplace and we saw a Polish flag. We saluted and went back to Otwock. But this time it wasn't so bad because the Polish soldiers took us in trucks. In Otwock one boy was sent to the other of our two buildings. He reported the Russians were still there.

I was very sick. In December I had the first news of my husband. At least I knew then that Stefan was alive. He had a bad case of typhoid fever and I myself lay in bed, worn-out, helpless. Thanks to the kindness of my hosts, I had a bed. It was a blessing to lie in a bed and not on the floor. That was my situation on January 14, 1945, when I looked out of the window and saw German soldiers on the run.

Soon the Red Army entered Charsznica.

Everyone wanted to go back to Warsaw right away, but that was difficult. Railroad tracks had been torn up and there was a shortage of locomotives and cars. The depot was besieged by people trying to get home and you had to fight your way into the overcrowded cars. I was in no condition for such a struggle.

Easter fell on April 1, and my roommate and I—she was a painter and the mother of a two-year-old child—thought that fewer people might be traveling on a holiday. But at the station we found thousands of others who had had the same idea. The place was mobbed. We were definitely not up to such an ordeal. In the confusion we got to the stationmaster's office and told him we had a small child. He showed some humane feelings and with his help we managed to squeeze into a car the next morning. We made the twenty-four-hour trip standing up and finally reached Warsaw. Or rather the suburb of Szczesliwiec. From there we could either walk several kilometers, or hire a horse and wagon. The price was exorbitant, but we pooled our money and hired a carriage.

I went straight back to Pius Street. I didn't expect to find anything standing, but the doorway was still there; inside I found the janitress's little cubbyhole and in it, Mrs. Roslaniec! She greeted me with joy, friendly as ever, and told me the Germans had set the house on fire on January 7, just ten days before the Soviet Army entered Warsaw. When she saw I had no place to go, she suggested I stay with her, and that night Mrs. Roslaniec and I slept together in the same bed.

Refreshed by a good night's sleep, I started looking for my husband the next morning. I found him in a strange family's home, in pitiable shape. Stefan had lost a great deal of weight and his clothes were in tatters. We stared at each other, feeling lost and helpless. But life had to go on. We had to create a new life for ourselves. First we decided to find out if my sister's apartment in Grochow had survived. If it had, then we would at least have a roof over our heads. Next morning, I went to Grochow. It was a long trip and I was still weak. I had trouble walking and the grimmest visions raced in my brain. I was sure that the building could not be standing. But the building was there! I went into Anka's apartment and wandered through the rooms as if in a dream, staring at the table, the couch, the chairs. I was so relieved and so weary that I finally collapsed on the couch.

My husband joined me on Sunday. Slowly I was getting my strength back and by Monday I felt strong enough to take the early train for Otwock to look for Wlodek. As I approached the orphanage I was struck by the silence. My heart sank. Where were the children? The first person I spoke to was reassuring. She told me the children had been taken elsewhere and the superintendent, who was still there, would tell me all about what had happened. The superintendent did. She explained that the children had been sent to the country because it was easier to feed them there. Wlodek, she said, was well and had stayed well throughout. I could, of course, go to see him immediately, but it was too far to walk and too expensive to hire a carriage. The children would be coming back in a few days, and she suggested that I wait. I went back to Grochow in a much better frame of mind.

We were living miserably, impoverished, and I tried to figure out a way to get some money. In the meantime, what could we do with Wlodek? How could we bring him up? I discarded the outlandish idea that his parents might still be alive. To make sure, I went to the office of the Jewish Committee at Targowa Street. No, they had no record of the Bergs. I had no one to talk the problem over with. All my friends were as poor as I was, so I made another trip to the Jewish Committee. The chairman received me and told me they were willing to extend all possible help on condition the child be placed in a Jewish orphanage. He told me that the Jewish orphanage was well supplied with food and had excellent living conditions. I was faced with another, grave decision. Every day of delay meant another day of hunger for Wlodek in the Catholic orphanage. On the other hand I was reluctant to uproot him suddenly from where he had been for some time. Would I, in trying to satisfy Wlodek's physical needs, ruin his peace of mind? I was bound by the promise I'd made to his parents that if they didn't survive the war, my home would be his home, and I would try to take their place. I felt the responsibility deeply. I explained my dilemma frankly to the chairman and asked him for some emergency help until I could clarify my own thinking. I explained that I had no money at the moment to buy food for the child and I had no place for him to sleep.

The chairman was very firm. They'd help if they took charge of the child. They would not help if the child remained with a Gentile family. The chairman spread his hands, as if to say, "I cannot help it." I realized that I'd never get any crumbs from that rich table and went back to the temporary haven at my sister's. I talked it over with my husband and we both decided that if help could be had only on such unenlightened terms, we would simply have to forget about the Jewish Committee.

When I went back to Otwock I took a tiny package with me, a little bread, a bit of sugar, some fat. The children were still not back, but I was told that they'd be there in a few more days.

Worn out as I was, plagued by ailing health and constant depression, I had the feeling that the ground I stood on was slipping out from under my feet. Then, one day, there was a knock at the door. When I opened it, there stood Wlodek's mother. . . .

It has been a source of great joy to me to know that this family survived the bloodbath unleashed by Hitler and his henchmen. I am happy to have had the chance to add my one small brick to the wall of protest the world threw up against the Nazi murderers. I succeeded in keeping Wlodek alive.

CHAPTER 9

THE REMNANT
THAT WAS SAVED

The end of the story as Lena and Wlodek saw it.

AT DAYBREAK THE NEXT DAY we took the train for Otwock. I still had enough of the money Berlowicz had given me to buy tickets with. When Maria and I walked up the street, there was a big villa, typical of the country houses around Otwock. It had a wooden fence around it, a few small frame buildings, and some pine trees on the grounds. The superintendent recognized Maria and greeted her warmly. "This is Wlodek's mother," Maria introduced us. It took them a long time to find Wlodek.

Miss Olenka called me and said, "Hide in the bushes, Wlodek. Some Jewess has come for you." I had a couple of potatoes under my jacket, which I had taken from the nearby Red Army ditch that was always full of potatoes. I ran to the bushes right away, but I began to wonder. Who had come for me? Had they brought something to eat? So I sneaked out to where I could look, and I saw Auntie Maria with some other lady. I walked over to them with the other boys.

When Wlodek finally came, I didn't recognize him. They all stood there, in dreadful rags, barefoot, with close-cropped heads.

They all looked alike, every face pinched with hunger; I couldn't have picked my own child from among them. Not until he ran up to Maria and threw his arms around her did I see the two hollows at his temples, the marks made by the forceps when he was brought into the world.

"Do you know who this lady is?" Maria asked him.

"I think I know. Let me guess," he replied. He looked me over apprehensively. His feet were covered with monstrous sores. My experienced eyes immediately diagnosed scabies. Could this little starveling, this ragged creature, frightened to death and looking like a hunted animal, could this be the pampered little boy I had longed for night after terrible night in Auschwitz? My poor baby! How he must have suffered to be in such a pitiful state. Even Maria had not expected anything like that, and she burst into sobs.

I did not say anything, I did not cry. After a little, I went closer to him and stroked his head lightly. He did not move away. When the other boys went away, he took a couple of potatoes out from under his jacket. "Come with me, my little boy," I said, "I'll buy you something to eat. Do you know where I can get food around here?"

"Of course." He was more animated now and I recognized his voice. "There's a grocery store just around the corner."

I bought him a big roll. We sat on the empty porch and he began to eat it, biting off big pieces and swallowing them without chewing. I could hardly hold back my tears.

"That was good," he said when he had finished. He looked at me more closely.

I bought him some ice cream. "Do you recognize me now?" I asked him gently.

"Yes, I do. But Mama had curly hair, now it's straight."

So he had preserved some image of me through those years. I edged closer to him.

"Wlodek, would you like to come with me and stay with me forever?"

"No, I want to stay with the boys," he said, his eyes glistening with tears. Then something occurred to him. "Mama, if I come with you, will I ever be hungry again?"

"I swear to you that never, never as long as you live, will you ever be hungry again."

He huddled closer to me and squeezed me. "Well, then, I suppose I'll come."

I asked Maria to tell the superintendent at once. She got busy, and was going to have his things brought from the laundry. But I didn't want his things; I didn't want to wait. I took him as he was and would not let go of his hand.

The train was crowded and we lost Maria. Only after the train started did I burst into tears, whether from my own happiness, because of the pitiful little creature who was my son, or my own sudden exhaustion. I realized that I had no place to sleep, no money, and no one in the world except this boy to whom I had just solemnly promised that he would never go hungry again. Wlodek was excited, too. He couldn't stop talking for a minute, and soon all our fellow passengers knew that his mother had come back from a camp, that his father had not come back, and that he had just been taken from the orphanage. He looked so miserable that one passenger, with tears in his eyes, thrust a banknote into Wlodek's hand. I came to my senses just in time. Not that, not while I was alive.

I decided to go back to the Berlowiczes, and on my way, ran into Sarenka. When she saw us, she drew back as if frightened, as if she had seen a ghost. She held her head in her hands, and stared goggle-eyed. "You found him!" she cried out. And then she told me that never for a moment had she believed that my son would be alive, nor had any one of the others. They had looked on my faith as harmless madness, to be humored because it helped me to survive.

The Berlowiczes received us warmly, and we spent the night on an armchair. Wlodek could not sleep. Because he was so excited or had eaten too much, he had diarrhea. The next day the Berlowiczes showed great energy. They found me a tiny, dirty room on Zabkowska Street, but to me it seemed like a palace. And Dr. Berlowicz also got me a job. I was to organize a pharmacy for the Jewish Committee with the medicines it had received from America, from Palestine, and from the Polish government. I had a place to sleep, the Jewish Committee would give me breakfast and dinner, food for Wlodek, and a little money as well. My life took on meaning and purpose once more.

It didn't take long to get rid of Wlodek's scabies; cleanliness, better food, and some medical treatment worked wonders. But I had more trouble with his mind, which had become warped. He was a regular guttersnipe who talked the language of the streets. And he had also been infected with rabid anti-Semitism; he hated everything Jewish. I shed bitter tears over this child of mine. I knew it would take all the love and devotion I had to get him straightened out. The greatest tact would be necessary if he was to grow up without serious emotional difficulties. I had no particular theories on the score; I simply trusted my feelings.

The day after we moved into the little place on Zabkowska Street, where under the name of Jakubowska, I occupied one room and an elderly Gentile woman the other, Wlodek said prayers from morning to night, on his knees. I pretended that it didn't bother me, but even my neighbor was surprised by such excessive religious zeal. "Wlodek," she remarked to him, "not even priests pray that much. Just say an 'Our Father,' that's quite enough."

To wipe out the memory of the past few years, I sang the lullabies I used to sing him when he was a child and I was happy when he joined in. "I want you to remember these lullabies," I said to him. "When you grow up and have children of your own, you'll sing them the same songs your mother sang to you."

"I won't have children," he replied, quite serious. "I want to be a priest. But if you want to have grandchildren, try to have a little girl. And do it quickly, before Daddy comes back, so he'll have a surprise."

He would ask me in the middle of the day, "May I pray to the Lord Jesus?" I never said no.

One day when I came home from work—I had to leave Wlodek alone during the day—he handed me a letter he had written, which was addressed to "Miss Olenka." "Please put a stamp on it and put it in the mailbox," he said. "But you mustn't read it. It's secret."

The letter read: "Dear Miss Olenka, I am well, Mother is very good to me, and I am never hungry. Mother even bought me a red radish once. And what we talked about—it's all right for now." He wrote several such letters. Later, he told me that "what we talked about" referred to his prayers. He had agreed with Miss Olenka that he would run away and go back to her if his mother did not let him pray.

I was not too upset by Wlodek's Catholicism. My own Jewishness was rooted in tradition rather than religion, and I was ready, if that was necessary, to pay for Wlodek's rescue with his conversion to Christianity. The world needs true Christians as it needs true Jews. But after the ordeal we had lived through, simply for being Jewish, I could not endure the hatred my child had been taught. His was no true Christianity based on love of his fellow man; instead, his mind had been poisoned by a medieval distortion of Christianity, a fanatic version of Catholicism impregnated with hatred for his own people. I was deeply hurt by his anti-Semitic songs and chatter. When he repeated them out of childish spite, they made me wince. "All Jews are thieves and swindlers," he would say, with firm conviction. "They killed the Lord Jesus and now they kill Christian children to mix their blood in the matzos." Sometimes he hummed a song which made fun of Jewish speech and habits, and explained, "You see, Mommy, that's how Jews pray."

One day I had had it. "Look here, Wlodek," I said, "we've got to talk about this once and for all. You're Catholic, I'm Jewish. You may pray to God the way you want to and as often as you want to. I won't tease you about it. But don't you dare to make fun of my religion, or the way I say my prayers."

"But you never pray!"

"I don't have to kneel two hours a day and put my hands together in order to pray. I pray in my mind and God can hear and understand me. I could make fun of you, too, because you have to kneel, and press your hands together, and pray for hours on end. But I don't. And I don't want you to do it either. Then we can be friends."

That stopped him for good.

He often asked me to take him to church, and I would walk with him as far as the door and tell him, "Go in, say your prayers. I'll wait outside."

"Please come in with me."

"No. I'm Jewish. I won't go in, but I promise not to budge from this spot until you come out."

He never went in alone; he was afraid to. For many years he was to be pursued by the fear that he would suddenly find himself deserted by everyone.

Every day at 6 A.M. a woman would come by with milk and I always ran to get some for Wlodek. Once I bought him an egg, hard-boiled it, and sliced an onion into it so he would get the vitamins. When he saw the onion, he burst into tears and bitterly reproached me: "Why did you have to spoil a nice egg like that? Onions stink. Only Jews eat onions." But he couldn't resist the temptation and so he ate the Jewish dish with great relish. "You know," he said, "it's not so bad after all . . ."

He could be very cruel, with all the cruelty of children. One time he told me that I was not his real mother because otherwise I wouldn't forbid him to do anything he wanted to do.

"Now, what makes you say that?" I asked. "Don't you see that I know all kinds of things about you and I sing your old lullabies for you?"

"That's nothing. You were in camp with my real mother. She told you all about me. And you promised her you'd take care of me. But you're not my real mother."

Though I wept about such things, they grew rarer and he became increasingly attached to me. Once he cuddled up to me and said pensively, as if talking to himself, "All Jews can't be bad. You're Jewish and you're not bad at all . . ."

Wlodek had not been sick for two years, but now his whole organism seemed to be making up for all that time. The moment his scabies disappeared, he had stomach troubles, then bronchitis. Though I had a job, I didn't earn enough to buy him shoes and he went around barefoot. I still wore my heavy ski boots and he had nothing. One day it was raining when I took him to the doctor, and that was when a cold became bronchitis. The doctor, a woman, examined him and filled out the usual form. "Name? Address?" When she asked about his father, I said, "His father has not come back yet."

"What do you mean? Have you heard from him?"

"No. I have not heard from him, but he has not yet come back."

The doctor looked at me strangely, but asked no further questions. As for me, I had not the slightest doubt he would come back. My Michal would not disappoint me; he'd be back. I waited for him impassively, just as I had waited for the moment of reunion with Wlodek. Hundreds of people came to the Committee, pored over the records, hoping against hope. Then they turned away, sagging, apathetic, hopeless. I kept very much to myself, putting people off with, "Wait until my husband returns." People around me thought my experiences had unbalanced me, that I was a victim of a kind of madness. My unflinching faith shocked many. How could one be so self-centered in an epoch of universal disaster, and refuse even in one's innermost thoughts to let go of something one had possessed? But I believed in Michal. When people tried to bring the subject up, I would reply, "Until someone comes and tells me that he saw Michal die with his own eyes, Michal is alive as far as I am concerned, and I shall wait for him."

Early in July a stranger who came to the Committee offices suddenly threw himself into my arms and began to kiss me. It was Melcer. "Send someone to the city gates to tell your husband you're alive. He is convinced that you're dead. If he sees you suddenly like this, he'll drop dead on the spot." But I sent no one. And I was not a bit surprised when Michal appeared in the doorway, in an old German uniform, emaciated and white as chalk. I felt strong and calm. I pushed him gently away from me and said over and over again, "Now, now, calm down," but everything in me sang. The dingy Committee offices were suddenly bathed in light. I had my husband back, I had my son. Life had the promise of new happiness. We were not only liberated, we were saved.

Strangers crowded around us. Everyone wept. They wept not only because they had witnessed an incomprehensible miracle, an improbable joy. Their tears were also a terrible lament. They wept for the millions who would never come back, who for all ages will remind us. . . .

POLITICAL BOUNDARIES
as of September 1, 1939

Afterword

After the events described in this book, my father, with the help of a childhood friend who was a member of the new government, quickly made arrangements for our family to immigrate to the United States. We lived in New York City where my father established a printing business. My mother committed herself to trying to make our home as normal as possible, and I enjoyed the benefits of New York City's fine schools. I was able to sublimate most of the horrors of my earlier childhood because of the warmth of the relatives we found here and, above all, because of my parents' nurturing devotion. This free and wonderful country to which my father had brought us provided the atmosphere in which I could grow up without fear and in which I could participate in all the experiences necessary for the development of a whole person. I returned to the religion of my family and my wife and I have brought up our three children Jewish, with the silent prayer that they will some day not have to pay the price that I, and so many other even less fortunate children, paid for their Jewishness.

It was more difficult for my father. For thirty years he was tormented by bitter memories and horrifying dreams; he was unable to forget the years that we had spent in the ghettos, the orphanages, and the concentration camps. He needed to tell the story in the name of all those who had suffered with him, and of those who had perished. He experienced a partial catharsis with the original publication of this book in 1965. From its title the entire era of the Holocaust has taken its name.

In 1978 my father retired from his printing business and dedicated the rest of his life to combating the apathy and enormous ignorance in America about the Holocaust. With seed money from lifelong friends, he established Holocaust Publications, a non-profit organization dedicated to publishing books about those painful years when Europe was the captive of Nazi tyranny, and the Jews its principal victims. That was a time, we have recently learned, when even greedy "neutrals" were skewing the odds against the tortured victims.

Within a period of five years, during which I was privileged to help him, we managed to publish or reprint fifty-six titles relating to the Holocaust: stories that had never been told, or that had been permitted to go out of print. Alexander Donat died in June 1983.

Since then, Holocaust museums have been established in many cities, university presses have continued the Holocaust publishing program he started, colleges offer courses on the Holocaust. Finally, educators, historians, and legislators have come to realize that to ignore the horror of those years may mean being condemned to repeat them. Much of this awakening and continued interest can be credited to Alexander Donat and Holocaust Publications.

I have recently photographed my mother, Lena, with one of my two granddaughters (her great-granddaughters). In this photo my mother's arm prominently displays her Auschwitz-acquired tattoo, number 49397. I wanted this picture for these children, so that when they grow up they will have no doubt about the Holocaust and their direct relationship with it. Perhaps this is our family's greatest triumph over Hitler; we thrive, and we shall remember.

My father's name was originally Mojzesz (Moses) Grynberg, but at an early age his nickname within the family became Saszek (Polish equivalent of the Russian "Sasha"), hence he took Alexander as his first name early on and used it in all but official government papers.

Originally his father's family name was Prurzanski. As the second son in his family, however, he would have been drafted into the tsar's army for twenty years. He was therefore sent to live with some relatives named Grynberg and was represented as their only son. According to then prevailing tsarist laws, he received the deferment that was offered to only sons, expected ultimately to be the sole supporters of their families.

Alexander (Saszek) Grynberg married Lonia Liberman whose father's name was Szmul (Samuel) and whose mother's maiden name was Sara Draiman. Lonia became Leona when we came to the United States, just as Wlodek (Wlodzimierz) became Willy to our American relatives and ultimately, William.

The real names of the older Christian couple who were bravely willing to take me in when I was smuggled out of the ghetto were Maria and Stefan Magenheim.

It is understandable why the editors at the original publisher, Holt, Rinehart and Winston, in 1965 did not want to confuse the reader with a

German-sounding name for a Polish family, and hence changed Magenheim to Maginski; but I do not understand the transition to Michael Berg and to Lena from the original names. The editors may have thought that these sounded more "Jewish" or perhaps they believed that these would be easier to remember. I truly don't know. If such was indeed the case, why did they not execute similar editorial license with my original first name, which was so typically Slavic?

The names of remaining characters, to the best of my knowledge, are historically correct.

William (Wlodek) Donat
October 1999

INDEX

Franto, Lieutenant, 165, 172
French Jewish girls
    at Auschwitz, 264
Frydrych, Zygmunt (Zalmen), 109,
    118
fumigation, 10–11

G
Gamels, 176
Ganzweich, Abraham (leader of
    "The Thirteen"), 24, 32–34,
    45
Garztecki, Mrs.
    interest in Otwock orphanage,
    297
Garztecki, Tadeusz, 291
Geipel, Hauptsturmführer
    Property Control Office and, 61,
    64, 66
Germasinski, 166
ghetto, Warsaw
    beginning of revolt, 91–92
    construction of, 22
    destruction, 119, 168
    establishment of, 22–23
    institutions and organization,
    26–31
    internal resettlement decrees
    (August 10–15, 1942), 63
    life after "cauldron" episode,
    80–82
    liquidation, 119–36
    manhunt and roundups, 43–44,
    53–57, 78
    map (summer 1942), 29
    map (1943), 125
    resettlement decree of July 22,
    1942, 47–48
    resistance issues in, 85–88

sections, 27–28
Gliksberg, Dr., 76
Globocnik, Odilo (SS police chief),
    48, 100
Goldman (Radom printshop
    foreman), 189, 192
Goldsobel, Jozef, 82
Gonsiorowski, Kazimierz, 107, 117,
    187, 280–81, 284
Gran, Vera, 37
Greek Jewish girls
    at Auschwitz, 264
grief
    of inmates, 229
Gross, Dr. Emanuel, 222–23, 236,
    242
Grossman (Hessenthal-Schwäbisch
    Hall inmate), 231
Grynberg, Mojzesz (Moses), 316
    See also Berg, Michal
Gypsies
    at Auschwitz, 270

H
Hagen, Dr. Wilhelm, 10, 40
Haller, Dr. (chief of Hessenthal
    air-base hospital), 236–37
Haus, Mietek (author's brother-in-
    law), 59, 67
Heller, Zelig, 34
Hergl, Anton, 13, 83
Hess, Rudolf
    trip to England, 39
Hessenthal airfield, 224
    Allied bombing of, 232
    hospital, 226–27
Hessenthal-Schwäbisch Hall, 223
    conditions at beginning of 1945,
    230